The Chinese Have *a* Word *for* It

The Complete Guide to Chinese Thought and Culture

Boyé Lafayette De Mente

PASSPORT BOOKS

NTC/Contemporary Publishing Group

Library of Congress Cataloging-in-Publication Data

De Mente, Boyé.
    [NTC's dictionary of China's cultural code words]
    The Chinese have a word for it ; the complete guide to Chinese thought and culture
/ Boyé Lafayette De Mente.
       p.   cm.
    Originally published: NTC's dictionary of China's cultural code words. Lincolnwood,
Ill. : NTC Pub. Group, 1996.
    ISBN 0-658-01078-6
    1. China—Social life and customs—Terminology.   2. Chinese language—Terms
and phrases.   I. Title.
DS721.D39   2000
951'.0014—dc21

00-37455

Other Books by Boyé Lafayette De Mente
The Japanese Have a Word for It
Japanese Etiquette & Ethics in Business
How to Do Business with the Japanese
Japanese Secrets of Graceful Living
Japanese Business Dictionary
Reading Your Way Around Japan
Everything Japanese—An Encyclopedic Reader on Things Japanese
Japanese Influence on America
Discover Cultural Japan
Japanese in Plain English
Korean Etiquette & Ethics in Business
Lover's Guide to Japan
Business Guide to Japan—Opening Doors and Closing Deals!
Survival Japanese
Japan Made Easy
NTC's Dictionary of Korea's Business and Cultural Code Words

Cover design by Monica Baziuk
Cover illustration copyright © Christie's Images/The Bridgeman Art Library

Originally published as *NTC's Dictionary of China's Cultural Code Words*
This edition first published in 2000 by Passport Books
A division of NTC/Contemporary Publishing Group, Inc.
4255 West Touhy Avenue, Lincolnwood (Chicago), Illinois 60712-1975 U.S.A.
Copyright © 1996 by Boyé Lafayette De Mente
Printed in the United States of America
International Standard Book Number: 0-658-01078-6
        05   20 19 18 17 16 15 14 13 12 11 10 9 8 7

CONTENTS

Contents

Contents

Contents

Contents

Contents

PREFACE

All languages are reflections of the emotional, spiritual, and intellectual character of the people who created them.

The older, more structured, and more exclusive a society and its language, the more words it has that have deep cultural implications.

China is therefore a quintessential example of a country in which "cultural code words" play a vital role in the lives of its people.

Many of China's key code words are derived from the sayings and writings of its greatest philosophers and contain wisdom and guidelines that are both universal and eternal. Others are new and come and go with the times.

Knowledge of China's code words is especially important to foreign visitors, businesspeople, and others involved with China because the cultural nuances of the terms are often misunderstood and misused—or ignored altogether—by foreigners. And just as often, the Chinese presume that it is their cultural imperatives, as defined by these words, that will be followed in any relationship.

The problem of dealing with China's culture-bound words is far more sensitive and complicated than is generally assumed. Being only a little off in the interpretation or use of a term can be enough to prevent a relationship from beginning—or destroy one that already exists.

This presents an extraordinary challenge to those who approach China without the benefit of professional training or personal experience in any of the languages or the culture of the country. One of the first steps in overcoming this challenge is, of course, to become familiar with as many of China's code words as possible and to learn something about when and how they are used.

Most of the words in this book are in the Beijing or Mandarin dialect of Chinese—known as *Putonghua* or *ordinary language*—which was made the "official" language of China by the Chinese Communist Party in 1949 and has been taught in schools throughout the country since the 1950s.

All of the terms and expressions appearing in this book also exist in the other major Chinese languages (Cantonese, Shanghaiese, Fukienese, Hokkien, Hakka and Chin Chow). And although the words are written with the same ideograms or "characters" in each of these languages and have the same meanings, they are pronounced differently.

Words that appear in their Cantonese or other versions (because they are better known in those languages) are labeled as such.

Boyé Lafayette De Mente
Beijing, China

GUIDE TO KEY CULTURAL THEMES

For the reader's convenience, I have cross listed entries under themes that are central to Chinese culture. All entries that touch upon the theme of "politics," for example, are listed numerically. The reader can therefore explore a theme more thoroughly by reading the related entries.

Business Morality and Practices/Economics 3, 7, 10, 28, 30, 46, 54, 63, 65, 70, 75, 93, 94, 102, 104, 116, 118, 119, 120, 121, 129, 137, 149, 167, 178, 181, 193, 207, 210, 219, 229, 233, 235, 239, 244, 258, 299.

Culture and Customs 4, 5, 13, 14, 15, 17, 18, 19, 22, 25, 26, 31, 32, 33, 38, 39, 40, 42, 45, 50, 52, 62, 66, 79, 81, 83, 91, 123, 124, 125, 126, 131, 135, 143, 150, 159, 160, 169, 197, 202, 237, 249, 255, 260, 268, 269, 279, 280, 285, 289.

Ethics, Morality, and Education 12, 21, 41, 58, 69, 130, 132, 141, 146, 151, 154, 156, 157, 171, 180, 199, 200, 201, 204, 212, 220, 221, 242, 259, 267, 273, 286, 290, 291.

Etiquette and Role-playing 27, 73, 82, 111, 127, 144, 145, 147, 152, 158, 164, 165, 166, 168, 170, 174, 196, 214, 216, 218, 231, 250, 253, 274, 304.

Family and Family Business 49, 103, 109, 110, 115, 198, 230, 236, 241, 246, 247.

Foreign Element, Chinese Language, Aesthetics, and Creativity 86, 87, 97, 98, 101, 108, 142, 153, 161, 162, 175, 184, 186, 191, 203, 217, 220, 234, 252, 263, 272, 288, 293, 300.

Hospitality, Eating, Drinking, and Sleeping 23, 43, 59, 90, 128, 182, 192, 195, 243, 262.

Men, Women, and Sex 1, 2, 6, 44, 61, 84, 99, 106, 211, 224, 225, 240, 254, 256.

Philosophical Beliefs; Mental and Physical Health 8, 16, 20, 24, 29, 34, 37, 47, 48, 53, 56, 57, 67, 68, 74, 76, 88, 96, 105, 112, 113, 117, 122, 133, 134, 136, 148, 179, 185, 187, 188, 189, 190, 208, 209, 213, 222, 223, 232, 245, 264, 265, 266, 270, 275, 276, 277, 278, 282, 283, 287, 292, 298, 305.

爱

Ai

(Aye)

"Loving Chinese Style"

Romantic love between men and women has been rare in the history of China. In a society based on absolute hierarchical relationships, the survival of the family name, suppression of individuality, the primacy of the family-group, and arranged marriages, there was virtually no concept of romance in the Western sense.

From a young age, boys and girls were more or less raised separately. Young men and women did not date, and any feelings of love they might develop for a member of the opposite sex were seldom consummated.

In higher class families in particular the separation of males and females into different worlds made it virtually impossible for men and women to learn how to relate to each other on the basis of mutual respect or anything approaching equality and helped to perpetuate the concept that females were inferior to males.

Personal feelings, in every aspect of the society, were sublimated to the interests of the family, the clan, the village, and the nation at large. Romantic love, with all of its uncertainties and unpredictabilities, was the exact opposite of the Chinese commitment to order, harmony, and predictability.

But this is not to suggest that the Chinese did not want and need *ai* (aye) or love, or that there was no love in their lives. The Chinese were very much aware of and appreciative of the emotion of love. They chose to control it and to channel it in directions that would contribute to the stability and survival of their society.

Not surprisingly, the Chinese took a philosophical approach to defining and dealing with the emotion described as *ai*. Many of the great sages of early China saw love as a spiritual manifestation, as the ideal bond uniting mankind and the cosmos—a concept that included the "love thy neighbor as thyself" morality advocated by Christianity.

This idealized concept of love extended to one's personal character and behavior. A person truly motivated by love would have a good heart, be well-behaved, and live a graceful life in tune with one's self, one's neighbors, and the cosmos.

But in the reality of the Chinese political and economic environment, love in this broad sense of selfless giving was an impossible dream. Even the most virtuous of emperors failed to live up to this philosophical ideal.

Because love in the sense of a private, personalized thing, applying primarily to members of the opposite sex was forbidden to the Chinese, they focused their love-emotion on their children, their ancestors, their arts and crafts, and the spirit world.

Romantic love as a human right is therefore a relatively new phenomenon in China. In a broad sense it dates only from the latter years of the 1970s when the Communist Party, recognizing that it was in danger of self-destructing, began allowing people the freedom to make some decisions for themselves.

Although the Communist government of China passed a law prohibiting arranged marriages in 1950, they still occur, particularly in remote rural areas. But dating and love matches are now commonplace, as is divorce.

With the flowering of romantic love in crowded China one of the greatest challenges facing urban couples is finding places where they have enough privacy to engage in intimacies. Two places most often used are city parks and theaters that feature semi–private two-seated booths, which, appropriately, are offered as "love places" or "corners of love."

Since romantic love is not compatible with Confucianism or most of the other foundations of traditional Chinese life, however, the effect that it is having on China is revolutionary.

2

安

An

(Ahn)

"Heaven on Earth"

Scientists tell us that the cosmos began with the mother of all "big bangs"— an explosion that created all of the stars and star matter of the heavens, setting in motion actions of such violence, such destruction and creation, that it is more like a dream than reality.

Scientists also tell us that in all of the chaos of the heavens there is an order, a scheme to everything, and that the most random actions are a part of this great order.

The Chinese were among the first to grasp the essential nature of the cosmos, to see the order in its seemingly unending cycle of destruction and creation, and they went much further than most in applying this knowledge to the making of their own world.

One of the pillars of the original Chinese concept of universal order in their world was the supremacy and dominance of the masculine sex. Men were the keepers of the keys to heaven, and everything flowed from that basic concept.

In the Chinese world, men were the positive, forceful matter of the universe on high, and women were the negative, receptive matter below. In this masculine context of things, the only way that *an* (ahn) or "tranquility/ stability" could be achieved between men and women on earth was for women to be subordinated to men.

This cosmic view of earth-bound tranquility between the sexes is dramatically illustrated in the ideogram used to denote the concept. It consists of a character meaning *woman* under an ideogram representing the roof of a house. In other words, tranquility is a woman in a man's house.

An, with its underlying connotations of universal tranquility and male dominance over female, is a key part of several other important words, including *safety*, *anxiety*, and *peace* of mind.

To maintain friendly relationships with Chinese, in business or personal matters, it is essential that *an* be given its due. But the degree of harmony that traditionally existed between the sexes in China is a thing of the past. Women no longer automatically view men as superior or as their masters, and cross-sexual disharmony is growing at an exponential rate.

Among the unplanned benefits to China that one might attribute to Communism (1949–) and the Cultural Revolution (1966–1976) was partial emancipation of Chinese women. So much of traditional China was obliterated during those decades of destruction that there was no going back to the absolute male chauvinism of the past.

In China today, just as in other countries around the world, women are slowly but surely proving that they are generally more rational, more adaptable, and often more talented than men and are gradually achieving the respect and control of their own lives that has been denied them since the beginning of Chinese civilization.

With the extraordinary resilience and diligence bred into Chinese women for millennia combined with equally deep yearnings for self-realization, there is no telling how far Chinese women may go in the future.

3

帮

Bao

(Bah-oh)

"Bartering 'Social' Credits"

Life in China is based on a set of rules that are very different from the typical American and European experience. These cultural differences go to the very heart of the Chinese way of thinking and doing things, and are an ongoing challenge to Westerners dealing with the Chinese.

Westerners are generally conditioned to base their personal and business relationships on impersonal rules that apply to everyone—friends and acquaintances as well as strangers. These rules, in turn, are founded on the principles of frankness, fairness and a sense of equality that pervades our most fundamental concept of the world at large. In principle, we can approach anyone, anytime and expect to be treated fairly and courteously.

Chinese, on the other hand, are acculturated to deal with people on the basis of social debts built up through a variety of personal relationships in the past—with family members, relatives, teachers, friends, business associates, and employers. In accepting help, of whatever kind, from various people the Chinese build up a reservoir of debt that they owe to these people. By the same token, they also build up a bank of "receivables" from people they help along the way.

Paying and collecting these social debts serves as the primary means of interpersonal relationships in China, from purely social to business and political affairs, and is controlled by the concept of *bao* (bah-oh), which might be translated as "social reciprocity."

Fulfilling the obligations of *bao* is one of the most important ways the Chinese maintain and nurture their "face." Failure to properly discharge social debts that are owed is regarded as one of the most dishonorable things a Chinese can do. People who ignore *bao* are regarded as uncivilized.

While more and more Chinese who are involved with outsiders socially, economically and politically, make some attempt to break away from the rigid bonds of *bao* in order to accommodate new relationships that are not based on social obligations, virtually all Chinese automatically make a strenuous effort to very quickly establish the kind of obligatory social debts they are used to because that is the only way they know how to react.

Newcomers to the world of China will find that their way is much smoother if they give building "social credit accounts" the highest possible priority. In fact, speaking broadly, it is often impossible to operate effectively in China, in virtually any capacity, without such "social credit," so there is no other acceptable choice.

Anyone proposing to go to China on business or for any professional purpose should begin to lay the groundwork for establishing "social credit" prior to arriving there by getting as many introductions as possible, and taking along a grab bag of gifts and favors.

And, of course, these introductions should include as many foreign residents of China as possible because they represent a trove of insights and contacts that help newcomers begin the process of establishing their own networks.

Those who have no mainland China contacts to begin with would be well advised to make their approach to China through Hong Kong, spending whatever time is necessary there to obtain the all-important introductions.

4

报仇

Baochou

(Bah-oh-choe-ou)

"The Need for Revenge"

Chinese history is gory with stories of Imperial usurpers, victorious warlords, generals, criminal chieftains and others wiping out entire families, including uncles, aunts, and cousins, as a way of ending family lines and future threats.

The same "final solution" has also traditionally been used by those in power to eliminate intellectual dissidents and military leaders who failed in revolutionary attempts.

Part of this propensity for killing one's enemies came under the heading of *baochou* (bah-oh-choe-ou) or "revenge," the need for which was built into Chinese culture.

The Chinese were never restrained by any religious beliefs in the sanctity of life or in the concept of forgiving one's enemies and thereby avoiding sin and gaining favor in the eyes of some deity.

Quite the contrary, they felt under deep obligation to extract their own revenge because there was no God in Chinese heaven who would eventually do it for them, and no body of law on earth that could be depended upon to protect and preserve them.

They were ruled by personal, hierarchical relationships rather than by laws based on equality and human rights. It was left up to individuals to keep these relationships in order.

Without equitable laws to guide, restrain and protect them, the Chinese had to depend upon their personal connections and their reputations or "face" to survive and function within their society.

Because this system was based on personal rather then objective factors, the Chinese developed extreme sensitivity to slights, insults and actions they perceived as threatening to their "face."

Every blemish that they suffered or believed that they had suffered had to be wiped clean. If they were not in a position to revenge themselves overtly, they felt compelled to do it behind the scenes, no matter how long it took.

Baochou thus became a characteristic trait of Chinese behavior, and survived from tribal times down through the ages. Much of the mass slaughter that occurred during the 20-year war between the Nationalists and Communists resulted from this revenge factor.

Chinese Communist Party leaders have routinely taken revenge against critics as well as against competitors within the Party, either imprisoning them or exterminating them.

It is not likely that this trait will be fully exorcised from the psyche of most Chinese until they have lived for two or three generations in a society in which human rights are protected by law, and behavior is based on rational, universal standards of fairness rather than political power and personal idiosyncrasies. Fortunately, the growing number of Chinese who are exposed to Western educations and cultures, and become involved in foreign trade, are leading the way in putting this tribal trait behind them.

保甲

Bao Jia

(Bah-oh Jee-ah)

"Your Brother's Keeper"

The initial success of communism in China should not have been a surprise to those who knew the country well. From the time of the Shang Dynasty (1550–1030 B.C.), China's government was centralized down to the smallest detail and the people lived in tightly organized family, village, city and regional units.

All of the rituals of work, religious activities and civic responsibility were minutely prescribed and deviations were not allowed. Independent thought and behavior were taboo. Government representatives were everywhere, and maintained a close watch on everyone.

Upper class families (the equivalent of the Communist elite) were bonded together through clans and lineage organizations, lived in walled and guarded compounds, and were rabid believers in the feudalistic doctrines that were the basis of their power.

One of the most draconian methods of social control used by early China's authoritarian governments was a community mutual responsibility system known as the *bao jia* (bah-oh jee-ah), or "household groupings."

Beginning with the Sung Dynasty in A.D. 960, all households in China were required to belong to a *jia* or group of one hundred families. Ten *jia* were grouped together to constitute a *bao*—or one thousand families.

Jia and *bao* were supervised by head men chosen from among their own members on a rotating basis. The head men were responsible for making sure that every member of each family was properly registered (gender, age, relationship and occupation), for ensuring that the members paid their taxes, and for seeing that they obeyed all of the other customs and laws of the land.

If any member of a *jia* misbehaved or failed to carry out his or her responsibilities, the head man as well as the other members of the group were held responsible. In China, every man was truly his brother's keeper. (And, as a result of this system of enforcing order and obedience, the job of head man was not that popular.)

American and European traders, diplomats and others who began showing up in China in the 18th century and ran afoul of the law were shocked to discover the collective nature of Chinese justice. Because they were not members of any *bao jia*, however, Chinese authorities first let them get by with paying fines for felonies, including murder.

But before the end of the century, the Chinese began asserting their right to judge and execute foreigners guilty of serious crimes, often using the threat of collective punishment to force ship captains and consulates to surrender fugitives.

The *bao jia* system of mutual responsibility naturally played a vital role in programming the Chinese to be especially circumspect in their own personal behavior and to exercise extraordinary pressure on members of their own families and *jia* to scrupulously obey all laws.

China's Communist government continued the system of organizing the country into family and work-unit groups, with only slight changes in the focus and labels. Mutual responsibility remained a key factor in the nature and intent of the groups.

During the madness of the so-called Cultural Revolution, which began in 1966 and lasted for nearly ten years, whole families were punished for the alleged sins of individual members.

Collective punishment is no longer applied in a blanket fashion in China but it is still a significant factor in the thinking and behavior of both the authorities and the public at large.

Families of individuals accused of "political crimes" invariably suffer through discrimination of one kind or another, including the loss of educational, employment and other opportunities.

6

包间

Bao Qi Lai
(Bah-oh Chee Lie)

"Booking Mistresses"

Virtually all better Chinese restaurants, in China as well as in such East Asian and Southeast Asian cities as Bangkok, Seoul, Singapore, Taipei and Tokyo, have one or more separate rooms for groups that want to dine in some privacy.

Many restaurants, particularly in Taipei and Hong Kong, feature private rooms and cater especially to businessmen and others who are interested in *more* than just private areas for dining.

Some of these latter restaurants include attractive young women on their "menus" to act as hostesses and companions for male diners. These restaurants often have adjoining apartment-type accommodations available by the hour.

In its original meaning, the Cantonese term *bao qi lai* (bah-oh chee lie) refers to booking a private room in a restaurant. But in cash-flush Hong Kong of the 1980s and 1990s it took on an added dimension, and came to also mean "booking" up-and-coming movie and TV starlets on short-term "mistress contracts."

It became common for businessmen, usually those suddenly made rich by successful manufacturing and exporting operations, to offer beautiful young starlets anywhere from one to several million dollars to become their exclusive mistresses for three months to longer periods.

The word in the film industry is that the present minimum rate for a "new face" on a three-month *bao qi lai* contract is one million dollars. Well-known stars who opt for such contracts are said to receive several million dollars for similar periods.

In addition to cash payments, Hong Kong's contract mistresses also receive luxurious gifts that include gold, diamonds, furs and cars. It is said that some of the more popular starlet mistresses become quite wealthy within a few years by fulfilling several successive contracts.

While film starlets may have become the most sought-after mistresses among Hong Kong's business tycoons, the majority of the city's mistresses come from the huge pool of women who work in the night-time entertainment trade as club and cabaret hostesses.

Many of these Suzy Wong–types can be "rented" by the hour or night. Others are generally available for longer term liaisons on an exclusive or near-exclusive basis, and play a role similar to that once performed by second wives and concubines.

A famous story reported in *Fortune* magazine and the business press in Asia relates how a billionaire paid off his mistress with a blank check, which challenged her to avoid greed because she did not know how much was in the account after the wife ordered the affair to be ended.

Mistress-keeping by foreign male residents of Taipei and Hong Kong is common but few if any of these arrangements are on a *bao qi lai* contracted fee basis. (The Mandarin equivalent of this term is *bao jian*. Hong Kong in Mandarin is *Xiang Guang*.)

備

Bei

(Bay-ee)

"Keeping Your Powder Dry"

One of the primary reasons why China has survived over the millennia has been the meticulous control exercised by its huge cadre of bureaucrats who were trained to maintain the status quo at whatever the human cost, and were the elite of the country by virtue of their unassailable, absolute power.

The effectiveness of China's bureaucratic power was based on controlling the minds as well as the behavior of the people through enforcing long-established customs and a body of taboos and guidelines that covered practically every aspect of human behavior. Virtually nothing was left to the free will of the people.

This concern for and control of thought and behavior down to minute details was one of the key points made by the great military strategist Sun Tzu. The first of his thirty-six stratagems in his classic book, *The Art of War*, was *bei* (bay-ee) or "foresight," under which he subsumed the gathering and synthesizing of knowledge and planning.

Sun Tzu taught the not-so-always-obvious philosophy that one should always assume that an enemy will eventually attack if you give him an opportunity, so the best strategy is to always be prepared to withstand and counter any invasion.

This stratagem has now been co-opted—some would say corrupted—by China's business community, including government bureaucrats who mix politics with operating commercial enterprises.

In Sun Tzu's original discourse, he said the successful ruler should follow a number of fundamental factors in pursuing war: make sure that the people will follow him without reservations or fear; take seasonal and other environmental conditions into consideration; make sure that local conditions in getting to and confronting the enemy are understood and accounted for; ensure that the general is up to the challenge of command by having the right combination of wisdom, sincerity, benevolence, courage and strictness; and make sure that the troops are well-organized, well-trained and well-supplied.

When these axioms are translated into business terms they cover (a) setting the corporate mission; (b) analyzing all of the factors that will or may impact on the mission; (c) establishing specific policies and objectives; (d) developing strategies that take the fullest possible advantage of personnel, technology and such external conditions as the weather, politics, economics, and so on; (e) implementing the strategies; and (f) monitoring and evaluating the results.

Sun Tzu's main point in this stratagem, the unending pursuit of knowledge (about one's products and services and their relation to the marketplace), combined with careful attention to both internal and external factors, are usually the precise areas where businesspeople falter, particularly when they are attempting to enter a foreign market.

While skills in cross-cultural human relations cannot be obtained from books or other secondary sources—that requires personal experience—having advance knowledge of the attitudes, behavior and expectations of the people concerned dramatically shortens the learning curve.

And again taking a cue from Sun Tzu, it is often the most trivial appearing cultural factor that trips up the novice in China.

8

比

Bi

(Bee)

"Unity the Chinese Way"

A quick, superficial glance might suggest that China is a paragon of cultural and social unity—a huge country, over five thousand years old, with the benefit of a long line of distinguished philosophers who delved into the depths of human nature and came up with guidelines for every activity, every possible eventuality in human affairs.

But somewhere between the philosopher's well and the reality of Chinese history, much of the wisdom that was gained was either relegated to a tiny elite minority of academics, or subverted to serve the interests of emperors, kings and bureaucrats.

The rulers of China, past and present, understood the importance of order and *bi* (bee) or "unity," but their way of maintaining these key social factors was to use brute force rather than work cooperatively with the populace.

China's philosophers, themselves essentially victims of the prevailing political powers, could not prevent the common people from being cooped up and silenced for century after century; a situation that resulted again and again in the gradual buildup of friction and frustration that could only be alleviated by outbreaks of violence.

In this setting much of the *bi* that existed in China was artificial. It existed only because the people were forced to live and work in closely supervised unity, with virtually no freedom of choice.

Of course, there was unity in China resulting from race, common philosophies, common experiences and a need for defense against outside threats. But this unity too was subverted because it was held together by constant pressure rather than the free will of the people.

In present-day China the lack of unity in virtually every nook and cranny of society is shocking, and represents a threat both to the people of China and the world at large. Having had no historical experience in coming together on their own accord, peacefully settling their own differences, and forging natural bonds of *bi*, the Chinese are not good at doing it.

Some three thousand years ago the *Book of Changes* noted that true, natural unity was essential not only for the proper functioning of societies but for individuals as well. But it is only now that the Chinese people themselves are finally, little by little, gaining the freedom necessary to learn and adhere to the lessons first taught so many centuries ago.

There is also a warning in the *Book of Changes* about the loss of unity that applies to people everywhere. Unity, like everything else in life, flows in cycles. What goes up must come down. Unity must therefore be continuously nourished and recreated to stay in harmony with the times and not deteriorate into chaos.

9

变

Bian

(Bee-enn)

"Stay Loose and Win"

"Bending with the bamboo" has long been a Chinese concept for the kind of behavior that is essential for survival and success in any area of life, from dealing with nature and the bureaucracy to operating commercial enterprises.

This belief has philosophical foundations in the Chinese acceptance of fate as a major factor in their lives. From earliest times, the Chinese viewed the world as in a constant state of interaction between positive and negative forces. The best of all worlds was a balance between these two forces, but achieving that ranged from difficult to impossible.

Chinese have always been at the mercy of the weather and their governments, with no choice but to endure the idiosyncrasies and rages of both, taking what they could get when they could get it.

There have, of course, been many occasions during the long history of China that the people reached a breaking point and rebelled against local warlords and bureaucrats and even against the Imperial throne itself. But in every case, the succeeding powers soon lost any virtue they may have had in the beginning, and began anew the cycle of repression and abuse.

Sun Tzu, China's most famous military theorist, made the concept of flexibility—of sudden change—one of the pillars of his strategies for winning wars. He taught that in order to win at war the general must be ready to change his tactics and goals at a moment's notice.

Sun Tzu incorporated this concept into the term *bian* (bee-enn), which includes the idea of both anticipating and adapting to changing circumstances as they occur. In his book, the commander who was not prepared to modify his tactics as the situation changed was unlikely to be victorious.

This meant that the general had to have up-to-the-minute intelligence, know his own strengths and weakness thoroughly, and know *when* and *how* to take advantage of the circumstances.

All Chinese businessmen are steeped in this stratagem of war, and some are skilled at putting it to good use in their negotiations and ongoing relationships—particularly when dealing with foreign counterparts because foreigners more easily fit the definition of enemy.

This situation can be a fatal weakness for foreign businessmen who arrive in China charged with the responsibility of hammering out a contract with an enemy when they are limited in their flexibility, and cannot counter moves made by their opponents.

Foreign businesses dealing with China are also often handicapped by their own ethics of right and wrong, as well as by the standards and policies of their companies and governments. The challenge in such cases is to go into such situations totally informed about your would-be ally, state your objectives and standards, and hang tough for as long as it takes.

10

标语

Biaoyu

(Bee-ah-oh-yuu)

"Life in Slogan Land"

During the heyday of the Communist regime in China (1949–1976), virtually the whole country was wired into a public address system that blared out announcements, exhortations, warnings and Party-line music from early morning until the end of day.

About the only way one could escape from this incessant barrage of information and Party propaganda was to get off somewhere in an unpopulated area. But only the very old or very infirm had any chance of doing that because every able-bodied man and woman in the country had an assigned task and one or more people monitoring their behavior.

In addition to this mass use of sound waves to reach and endoctrinate the people, the Communist Party pocked the country with millions of signs carrying similar messages. No matter which way you turned, which way you looked, the hand of the Party was before you.

A great deal of this broadcast time and poster space was devoted to *biaoyu* (bee-ah-oh-yuu) or "slogans"—a traditional Chinese as well as Communist method of capturing people's attention and influencing their attitudes and behavior.

Some authorities say that most of Mao Zedung's extraordinary success in defeating the Nationalists and conquering China came from his understanding of the importance of words in inciting people, and his skill in mastering the art of propaganda. Mao's China literally ran on "Red" slogans. There was a *biaoyu* for every dogma in the Communist line, for every goal on the Communist agenda. Every significant event was marked by a spate of slogans—on banners, broadsheets, newspapers, buildings and walls.

Every policy change—and these occurred with frightening frequency—called for earlier slogans and signs to be discarded and replaced by new ones—keeping an enormous army of slogan-writers and sign-makers busy. "Good Thought" slogans were permanent.

Among the national campaign slogans that were typical of this period: To Rebel Is Justified; Oppose the Vendors of Spiritual Pollution (democracy, capitalism, etc.); Resist America and Aid Korea; Suppress Counterrevolutionaries; Never Forget the Class Struggle; Down with Imperialist Running Dogs; East Is Red; Reform First, Production Second; The Four Modernizations; New Socialist, Communist Man; Anti-Lin Biao, Anti-Confucius.

Mao's passing in 1976 and the opening of China to Western trade and investment from 1978 on saw a dramatic drop in the number of political slogans originated by the Chinese Communist Party, and a spurt in slogans created by students and others calling for more democracy, more freedom, and culminating in the Tiananmen Square massacre in June 1989.

By the mid-1990s, the preponderance of political *biaoyu* had given away to advertising slogans hawking everything from Coca-Cola to bras. One of the most famous of the post-Mao slogans—"To Be Rich Is Glorious"—which is often attributed to Deng Xiaoping (who became premier after Mao) apparently grew out of a comment made by the daughter of one of the veterans of the famed Long March. She is said to have said: "What's wrong with making money? I'd like to be a millionaire!"

With *biaoyu* now primarily used for commercial rather than political purposes, this venerable custom is finally being used to inform and benefit the people of China rather than misinform and control them.

See **Zi Bao, Minzhu Qiang**.

剥

Bo

(Bow)

"When Things Fall Apart"

The Chinese learned a long time ago that evil people in power are eventually destroyed by their own evil, but rather than attempt to hasten the demise of evil doers by any kind of action, they were taught to be submissive and wait until time brought them down.

This concept is subsumed in the ideogram *bo* (bow), which means *to come apart* or *deterioration*—in reference to the cyclical appearance of troubled times during which incompetent people gain power and make the situation, whatever it may be, worse.

These times include political affairs on either a national or local level as well as business and personal affairs.

Bo also incorporates the concept of inferior people somehow coming into power, in government or in private enterprises, and themselves bringing on periods of deterioration. This generally happens when the same generation of "good" people have been in power too long, lose touch with the times, relax their guard and become soft and vulnerable.

Despite the fact that China's sages preached that only men of virtue should be entrusted with power, and that once those in power lost their virtue they should no longer be supported, the same sages taught that the "heavens" would bring the evil doers down and that people should be patient and allow nature to take its course.

Of course, this philosophy helped to prolong the reign of one evil regime after the other and contributed immeasurably to the suffering inflicted upon the Chinese over the centuries.

Present-day Chinese are still acutely sensitive to the cycles that come and go, particularly in political affairs, because they have been subjected to them numerous times in the last century. But, they are no longer as passive or submissive in their acceptance of *bo* cycles.

The excesses of the Nationalist forces under Chiang Kai-shek during the 1930s and 1940s and of the Communists under Mao Zedong from 1949 until 1976, combined with democratic precepts that had seeped into China from the West, finally broke the spell of the ancient sages.

The Chinese people are no longer "respectful" of the cycles of nature or the evil men that are spawned by *bo*. They are no longer willing to "seek wisdom" in accepting things that are unacceptable. They are no longer content to withdraw into themselves and wait for better times.

This does not mean that Chinese businesspeople, bureaucrats and politicians are no longer cautious and conservative. Most of them are. But the majority of them are also aggressively combatting the evils of *bo* and bringing about fundamental changes in the way the Chinese think and do things.

From now on the cyclical *bo* that strike China may not have to reach rock bottom before the time of rebuilding begins.

12

不带头

Budaitou

(Buu-die-toe-ou)

"Waiting and Watching"

Confucius taught that things done in haste are seldom done right—a message that was probably just reaffirming what the Chinese had already learned in the several thousand years of history that predated the great sage.

In any event, the concept of fast-thinking and fast-acting seems to have been totally at odds with Chinese civilization, which, until recent times, unfolded in a slow, stately manner that was more in tune with the seasons and life cycles than any man-made sense of urgency.

But this was all to change with the appearance of Mao Zedung and the Chinese Communist Party in the 20th century. Mao not only broke with the pattern of thought and behavior that had characterized the Chinese for millennia—the bad as well as the good—he set out to destroy, in a few frenzied years, everything that made up the heart and soul of Chinese culture.

Mao and his henchmen planned and implemented a series of mass campaigns of genocide, wholesale imprisonment, deprivation, punishment, fear and brain-washing, that succeeded in destroying virtually all of the land- and business-owning classes in China and wreaking irreparable havoc on the nation's intellectuals. But Mao fatally exaggerated the appeal and efficacy of

Soviet-style communism, and just as mistakenly underestimated the resilience of Chinese traditionalism.

His nightmarish attempts to change the essence of Chinese culture by eliminating all that was traditional, while simultaneously dealing a death blow to the emerging forces of capitalism, were only partly successful.

He did succeed in dramatically reducing such practices as ancestor worship and chauvinism, but his efforts to communize China backfired and resulted in the CCP having to reverse its policies and promote capitalism and a free-market economy in order to save itself.

One of the traditional Chinese patterns of behavior that re-emerged following the Communist onslaught was *budaitou* (buu-die-toe-ou), a phrase that literally means *don't be the first one,* and refers to a cautious "watching-and-waiting" approach, then taking advantage of circumstances when they are in your favor. This phrase also contains the concept of imitating or copying those who are successful rather than exposing yourself by taking the lead.

Generally speaking, *budaitou* is still today typical of all Chinese behavior, and is especially conspicuous in their international political and business affairs.

Budaitou behavior impacts on everyone on a personal as well as business level. Foreign businesspeople, particularly Americans, often find it frustrating because it stretches out and otherwise complicates negotiations and operations.

One of the obvious reasons for this caution is that Chinese government policies and regulations are typically vague, with the result that everyone is always operating in something of a fog.

13

不担心

Budan Xin

(Boo-dahn Sheen)

"Sincerity Plus Understanding"

Chinese businesspeople having to make a trip will go several hundred kilometers out of their way and take a mode of transportation that is conspicuously uncomfortable in order to avoid dealing with people they do not know—in public transportation ticket offices or elsewhere—along the way.

Businesspeople wanting to buy a product from another company or government agency that they do not already have personal relations with will approach the potential supplier directly only as a last resort. Instead they will spend considerable time and money attempting to find a personal contact they can use to make the initial approach.

These are just some of the surface signs of things that make life in China different. When one penetrates below the surface, these differences become much more complex and important.

Understanding and dealing with Chinese government agencies and commercial enterprises takes on an entirely new light when viewed from the Chinese perspective. Almost nothing follows the straightforward, expedient lines of thought or steps that the logical and law-oriented Westerner expects.

The Chinese are naturally much more attuned to these differences than their foreign counterparts, and are generally experienced in explaining them in terms that eventually make sense to the perplexed, irritated and doubtful foreigner.

In the West, the rationale for understanding and accepting situations invariably comes down to logic, even though it may have to be bent a bit.

Not so in China. There is a subtle but vital difference for the basis of Chinese understanding and accepting things. This difference is expressed in the term *budan xin* (boo-dahn sheen), which means something like *sincerity plus understanding*.

In this case, *sincerity* refers to conforming completely to the standards and expectations of the customs and traditions of the Chinese way—all of the personal obligations; all of the social connections that make up the foundation of Chinese behavior.

The "sincere" person is the one who can be depended upon to do what is right regardless of the circumstances—and, of course, what is "right" in this sense means what is right in the Chinese context of things.

When the other half of *budan xin*, *understanding* is added to this equation the expectation is that whoever has been called upon to demonstrate *budan xin* will accept whatever the situation is because he or she *understands* it from the viewpoint of sincerity in the Chinese context—meaning that the person concerned will be sympathetic to the Chinese position, and favor it.

Both government officials and businesspeople frequently call on their foreign counterparts to display *budan xin* in their negotiations and relationships. What they are doing, of course, is asking the foreign side to think and behave the way the Chinese do, and accept their position.

The best recourse for the foreign side is to remain firm in calling for a relationship that is fair and beneficial to both parties—reciprocal sincerity instead of slanted sincerity.

不方便的

Bufangbiande

(Boo-fahng-be-enn-duh)

"How to Say No in Chinese"

There are a number of Chinese customs and cultural practices that are universal in their appeal, and cross cultural barriers with the greatest of ease.

These include the Chinese custom of making family and banquet-style meals into social encounters that educate the young, provide adults with quality time with each other, and bind people together—something that is sorely missing in many Western families.

There are also enormous benefits to be derived from the Chinese custom of ritual politeness because it forces people to stay aware of the feelings of others and to conduct themselves on a higher plane of existence.

It is a well-established fact that familiarity more often than not breeds contempt, particularly among close friends and spouses. Confucius observed ages ago that this common human failing can be avoided simply by maintaining a degree of formal politeness in all of our personal relationships.

Ancestor worship is not something that would appeal to many Westerners (and it is dying out among the Chinese as well), but it has contributed to a number of cultural practices, such as respect for parents and the aged in general, that are worth retaining and should be emulated by other people as well.

One Chinese cultural trait that is not likely to go over outside of the Confucian sphere of Asia, however, is the practice of not giving a direct response, of speaking in vague, fragmentary terms that leave the objective-minded Westerner confused and frustrated.

Part of the cultural conditioning of the Chinese is to avoid any response or comment that might be upsetting, in the interest of the other party's feelings and in maintaining harmony.

One of the key terms coming under the heading of harmony-keeping words is *bufangbiande* (boo-fahng-be-enn-duh), which means *inconvenient*.

When the Chinese want to say that something cannot be done or they can't do something, or they don't want to do something, for whatever reason, they will often say it is *bufangbiande* and let it go at that.

To the Chinese this answer is sufficient, and to insist that they explain why, which foreigners typically do, is a serious breech of etiquette.

In the Chinese context of things, the "why" insofar as *most* of their actions are concerned is a part of an ephemeral world that is not to be addressed directly, but is to be understood by intuition—by cultural telepathy.

Of course, foreigners in China can also use *bufangbiande*, and they generally have many opportunities to do so because it is especially common for the Chinese to ask them to do things that are unreasonable and out of the question.

The main thing to keep in mind is that when you use this term you don't have to explain it. Generally the Chinese do not want to hear a complicated explanation, whether it is valid or not.

(*Bufangbiande* is the equivalent of the Japanese word *muzukashii* which means "difficult." When the Japanese say something is "difficult" it means they are not interested; they can't or won't help you; what you want is impossible; etc.)

When uninitiated foreigners hear either of these two words their tendency is to push even harder, saying such things as "I understand that it is inconvenient/difficult, but that's to be expected, and it's worth it," and so on.

Unfortunately, the harder one pushes with either the Chinese or Japanese the less chance there is for them to change their response.

Another institutionalized way of saying no is *yanjiu yanjiu* (yahn-jew yahn-jew), *I'll/we'll study the matter*. Another version of *it's inconvenient*: *butai fangbian* (boo-tie fahng-be-enn), meaning *it's not too convenient*.

See **Kaolu Kaolu**.

15

不女

Bu Hao

(Boo How)

"Avoiding Social Obligations"

This term literally means *no good* or *not good,* but it is also used as an institutionalized ritual to reject praise or compliments and thereby avoid adding to one's social obligations.

See **Nali, Nali.**

16

不合逻辑的

Buhe Luoji De

(Boo-hay Loo-oh-jee Duh)

"The Power of Fuzzy Logic"

There are three distinct categories of "logic" in China: traditional Chinese logic, Chinese Communist logic and Western logic.

Until the 1980s creativity in thinking and behavior for the average Chinese was practically taboo. One of the primary policies of successive governments during the long history of China was to maintain the status quo—to discourage and prevent changes that would make it possible for common people to make decisions on their own, become well-to-do, or gain political influence.

For generation after generation, the Chinese, on virtually every level of society, were conditioned to do things exactly the way they had always been done; to never question anything that was established by law or custom.

In this environment, the natural curiosity of the Chinese was suppressed to the point that it not only became politically and socially dangerous, it literally became un-Chinese.

People did not have to ask questions about most routine things because they were common cultural knowledge. Asking questions about things that did not directly concern them came to be considered a threat to the state.

This cultural conditioning now impacts on China's foreign relations in a number of ways and areas. Westerners have been taught to ask questions until they understand every bit and piece of a subject. Chinese have been conditioned to think and behave in terms of *buhe luoji de* (boo-hay loo-oh-jee duh), which I translate as "fuzzy logic;" keep quiet and learn things by slow osmosis; to not get involved in all of the background facts of plans and decisions. They do not automatically begin considering a wide range of possibilities when presented with something new.

As a result of their cultural conditioning, typical Chinese businesspeople often appear unimaginative, with little or no creative ability, by foreign standards. It is therefore often necessary for foreign partners to spend considerable time teaching their Chinese counterparts about the basics of many aspects of promotion and marketing.

One of the first mistakes that Westerners make in dealing with the Chinese is to take too much for granted; to presume that their counterparts understand, agree with, and will act on the things they say. This common failing is indirectly responsible for most of the problems that befall the inexperienced newcomer in China.

Another mistake that foreigners typically make in their dealings with non-Westernized Chinese is underestimating their intelligence and knowledge because they do not speak English or any other foreign language well, and because they often demonstrate cultural traits that seem irrational or childish.

It is very important to keep in mind that unless the individual Chinese has been educated abroad or has had substantial cross-cultural experience in China or elsewhere, his or her stock of knowledge and perceptions are totally different. Even several years of study and experience abroad is not enough to convert many Chinese over to the Western way of thinking and acting. They quickly come to understand Western thought and practices, but their values and motivations are more likely to remain Chinese.

On both a professional and personal level, non-Westernized Chinese are generally so ethnocentric in their views that they find it difficult to believe that non-Chinese can do such simple "Chinese things" as eat with chopsticks, and they often ask questions that make them appear simple-minded.

But the Chinese way of "fuzzy" or ethnocentric thinking should not be regarded as a deficiency or handicap that makes it possible for people to take advantage of them. Their successes in the various sciences are proof of their ability to think and behave logically when they are free to do so.

In many ways, the most difficult form of Chinese logic for foreigners to understand and deal with is the third category, Chinese Communist Party (CCP) logic.

CCP logic is based on agreeing with and abiding by all of the policies and goals of individual Party leaders and the Party as a whole—policies and goals that are often irrational and inhuman, and change with the circumstances.

Chinese-American author Bette Bao Lord says the Chinese go through life constantly switching between two "masks," a social mask and a CCP mask, each of which requires a different kind of logic, depending on the situations they encounter.

Lord says there is a carefully scripted role for each mask and that both roles are charades that must be acted out with great skill and unquestionable sincerity to avoid unmerciful punishment.

Within these two broad categories of behavior there are sub-categories that determine the logic to be used and the behavior. These include a "family mask," kinship mask," "old friend mask," "co-worker mask," "mask to be worn when dealing with superiors," and so on.

Each person has to wear the right mask at the right time and follow the prescribed logic and behavior or risk serious problems. During the first four decades of the Communist regime, not wearing the politically correct "mask" of the moment could be fatal. Lord says the demands of this system invariably led to paranoia.

CCP logic is dissipating at a fairly rapid rate and will hopefully be gone within one or two decades, but China's traditional logic is not likely to disappear for at least several generations.

不行

Buxing

(Boo-sheng)

"You Have to Be Kidding"

Over the centuries the Chinese developed a deeply embedded custom of giving the shortest possible answers to questions, and never going into detail or trying to explain any situation they were questioned about. Their reason for behaving that way was to avoid complicating their lives and/or getting into trouble with government officials.

One of the results of this situation was that in China the saying "a picture is worth a thousand words" was often transformed into something like "a single word speaks volumes"—and if you couldn't fill in the ninety-nine percent that was unspoken that was your problem.

This syndrome is still characteristic of the average Chinese, even in situations where there is no danger, and when a clear, comprehensive answer would be very much to their benefit.

One of the most common of these abbreviated, all-purpose responses is *buxing* (boo-sheng), which literally means *no go* and is used in the sense of *it/that is impossible.*

You can begin to get some idea of how inadequate and frustrating this response can be by imagining any number of situations in which that is the only response that you get to a suggestion, question or proposition.

Some common examples: *buxing* is often used to turn down business propositions that involve so much red tape they are not considered worth the trouble. The same goes if a quoted price is regarded as too high, or if a request for a quotation would require special effort.

Buxing is frequently used when people feel incapable of doing something because of personal inadequacies that they are unwilling to admit to. The expression is also used when the people concerned are afraid that doing something, whatever it might be, would displease a superior who would take some action against them.

Generally speaking, *buxing* is used as an out when people do not want to do something for any reason; including such personal and selfish reasons as not wanting to get up out of a chair to check on something.

Contending with the *buxing* syndrome is one of the cultural challenges facing foreigners in China. There is no single solution to the problem, but whatever the situation, patience and tact are essential.

Getting angry and showing emotion to Chinese generally results in making the situation worse. They take this as a sign of uncivilized, uncultured behavior, providing more than enough justification for not helping you, for persisting in their persecution of you, or whatever.

One gimmick that helps break down the *buxing* barrier is to humble yourself, make it sound like a life-or-death situation. This kind of behavior may go against the cultural grain of most Westerners, but it often is the only positive choice.

There are numerous anecdotal stories of foreigners who succeeded in overcoming the *buxing* barrier by, in fact, feigning a life-and-death situation. One of the more popular ruses: threatening to have a heart attack in their taxi or office. This would greatly complicate their lives, and gives them the necessary incentive to do whatever it is you are asking for.

18

不在

Buzai
(Boo-zie)

"Nobody Here But Us Chickens"

The Great Wall of China is the largest man-made artifact on earth, and is the most famous attraction in China. If the Chinese had never accomplished anything else of note they would still have gone down in history as the builders of the Great Wall.

But what is generally not known is that there are dozens of other "great walls" in China—not physical walls made of stone and mortar, but linguistic walls that provide more of a barrier to getting "inside" China than the Great Wall itself.

One of these great linguistic barriers is the term *buzai* (boo-zie), which literally means *not here*, but is used as a multi-purpose code word in a variety of situations that can leave the uninitiated foreigner mumbling darkly about the pedigree of the Chinese concerned.

In its simplest form, *buzai* is used in a straightforward manner to mean that the person you want to see or meet or speak to on the phone is not there. Period. End of conversation. If you pursue the matter beyond this point, the meaning changes to apply to any number of circumstances—all of which are left to your imagination.

Another common meaning of *buzai* is that the person you are asking about is there but doesn't want to meet you or talk to you for whatever reason. In this case, the person you are asking may be the person you are looking for.

A third possible meaning of *buzai* is that the person you are inquiring about is there but is not prepared to see you—again for reasons that are generally not explained.

A fourth possible meaning of this versatile phrase is that the person you are asking has never heard of the person you are inquiring about;

inferring, but not saying, that you are in the wrong place, have dialed the wrong number, or that the person does not exist.

Buzai may also mean that the person you are looking for does exist but is no longer in that location, having moved or been transferred somewhere else. If you pursue the point you may or may not be given the person's new location.

If this multi-purpose use of *buzai* were just an initial reaction that could readily be surmounted by follow-up questions it would be a hindrance but not a serious barrier. It frequently becomes a "great wall," however, because the Chinese do not like to be bothered by further questioning, or pinned down on detailed things.

If you are attempting to determine the presence or location of someone by phone, it may require a great deal of fast-thinking diplomacy to prevent the party on the other end of the line from hanging up before you have a chance to inquire further.

Similar diplomacy is usually necessary if you are making the inquiry in person.

19

不知道

Buzhidao
(Boo-chih-dah-oh)

"I Haven't Got a Clue"

Over and above the traditional patterns of behavior that make interacting with the Chinese an interesting and often frustrating experience for out-siders, the fallout from communism and socialism have further muddied the cultural waters, adding immeasurably to the challenge.

Confronting Chinese behavior today it is often impossible to tell where the traditional culture stops and dregs of communism and socialism begin— in many cases because there is really no difference. All three systems were based on suppressing the natural instincts of curiosity, ambition, self-interest, and personal responsibility.

The similarities between Chinese traditionalism and Communist ideology is no doubt one of the reasons why communism, in its first decades, was as successful as it was in China.

One of the areas of Chinese behavior that has its roots in the traditional culture and reinforced by communism was the "escape from responsibility" syndrome, a key part of which is expressed in the term *buzhidao* (boo-chih-dah-oh), literally *not know*, with strong overtones of *I don't care*, and *don't bother me*.

Buzhidao is one of the most frequently heard expressions in China today. The term itself, in its present usage, dates back for centuries, but it is now used far more often than what it was in the past because more demands are being put on people by changes in the political, economic and social systems.

There are a dozen or more situations which often elicit the *buzhidao* response which, in a Western context, would result in a number of different answers.

One of the more common usages of *buzhidao* occurs in the latter part of the afternoon when a person, most often a government official, does not want to get involved in anything that might delay his or her leaving the office.

Another occasion that regularly results in a *buzhidao* response is when you ask someone to do something and they don't have the authority to do it and are not interested in trying to get the necessary permission.

Even more common is when you ask someone to do something or about something that is not one of the specific functions of their department. More often than not they will respond with *buzhidao* rather than make any attempt to accommodate you.

Generally speaking, you may get a *buzhidao* response any time the party addressed really doesn't know, feels that it is inappropriate for them or for you, or simply doesn't want to be bothered.

Unless you happen to be someone with enough demonstrable influence to intimidate people who respond in this manner, and are willing to make a fuss, there is very little if anything that can be done. Most Chinese accept this kind of treatment as one of the many things that cannot be helped.

20

才智

Caizhi

(T'sie-chih)

"China's 'Amoral' Wisdom"

In any consideration of its intellectual heritage, China certainly compares with, if not overshadows, any other nation in the world, past or present.

For practically every accomplishment of early Greeks, Romans, Indians, Arabs or more contemporary people, there is a Chinese equivalent, and in numerous such comparisons the Chinese win without any argument whatsoever.

But there was a fundamental difference in the Chinese approach to understanding the world at large, and in the way they ended up relating to it.

Whereas Western and other philosophers were primarily concerned with the nature and role of man, the Chinese took a much broader view and attempted to understand and deal with the whole physical cosmos. To the Chinese, man was only a minor character, not that different from any other animate form in the universe.

Western philosophers and religious leaders put man at the center of the universe, and some imbued him with a divine spirit. The Chinese put man much closer to where he actually belongs—somewhere out on the edge of the universe, but they did believe that he had a spirit that survived death.

A key principle in Western philosophy and religion, particularly in Judaism, Christianity and Islam, was an absolute division between the concepts of right and wrong, good and bad. God himself (in whatever form he was envisioned by these groups) established the guidelines of good and evil and set the standards for human behavior.

There was no such god in Chinese heaven. All things, all acts, had a positive or negative character but neither was seen as inherently right or wrong, good or bad, because both were essential for existence and both were circumstantial.

There were, of course, standards of behavior in China. In many respects these standards were much higher than those practiced by other people, but the morality underlying these standards was not based on the sanctity of human life, or equality, or fairness, or any other "god-given" principle.

Morality in China was based on maintaining harmonious relationships between the ruler and those ruled, and between inferiors and superiors. People were conditioned not to question the rights of officials to make decisions affecting them.

Any law, any force, necessary to protect and preserve this hierarchical social system was "right." Anything that disturbed this harmony was "wrong."

In Western terms, Chinese wisdom did not distinguish between absolute principles of right and wrong, and in that sense was *caizhi* (t'sie-chik) or amoral. The only absolute established by Chinese morality was the right of those in power to stay there, and to take whatever measures were necessary to achieve that goal.

Broadly speaking, the only "sin" in China was failure to follow the precise guidelines of filial piety or to obey the dictates of the government.

Also generally speaking, the foundation of present-day Chinese behavior, particularly the behavior of government officials, is essentially *caizhi*, determined more by circumstances and policies than by principles.

诚

Cheng
(Chung)

"Judging Your Sincerity"

Rudyard Kipling's line that "the East is East and the West is West, and never the twain shall meet" was a perceptive and provocative comment on the fundamental differences in the way Eastern and Western people think and behave.

The East and West *are* meeting and talking today, but Kipling's dictum still holds true. They are not yet meeting on common ground because the cultural differences and motivations are so profound and so pervasive.

All of these differences are, of course, the result of what we experience in our respective cultural environments, beginning, some say, before we are born.

Just one of the areas of difference between Chinese and most Westerners is delineated in the term *cheng* (chung), which is generally translated into English as *sincerity*.

As is often the case, the word *cheng* means a lot more to most Chinese than sincerity does to most Westerners. The reason for this is quite simple. Sincerity plays a far more profound role in Chinese life because they are so fundamentally dependent upon personal relationships.

Sincerity, in its fullest Chinese sense, is also deeply embedded in the philosophical framework of Chinese culture. The Chinese believe that without sincerity one cannot achieve perfection of one's own character or influence others to strive for mutually beneficial goals.

The classic work on Confucianism, *Chung Yung*, proclaims that achieving sincerity, in words as well as deeds, should be the ultimate goal of all men because it is the *Way to Heaven*.

For Westerners to succeed in any dealings with China today it is first of all necessary that they "prove" their sincerity—a challenge that is always an uphill battle because what the Chinese interpret as sincerity is not always the same as the Western interpretation.

Today's Chinese, particularly government officials, tend to use sincerity toward them and toward China as meaning behavior that directly benefits them regardless of whether the Western side views it as fair or equitable.

There is no quick, easy answer to the problem of satisfying Chinese expectations of sincerity. About the only meaningful way to handle unreasonable demands where business is concerned is to emphasize the long-term benefits and the limitations imposed by your own government and company, and stay on the moral high road.

It also helps to bring up the cultural differences in Chinese *cheng* and Western sincerity, letting your Chinese counterparts know that you are aware of the differences and want to work with them to overcome the problems they cause.

The Chinese sometimes refer to clever but insincere people as having *kou mi fu jian* or *honey tongue and gall heart*.

———————◆ 22 ◆———————

诚

Cheng
(Chung)

"Personal Loyalty First"

Generally speaking, the Chinese are inherently incapable of trusting people they don't know and do not have close personal ties with. And since the Chinese have been conditioned to put their trust only in individuals—not in institutions, including governments—it is especially difficult for the Chinese to deal effectively with large foreign corporations and foreign governments.

Dealing effectively with the United States on a government or commercial level is particularly difficult for the Chinese because American diplomats, politicians and corporate executives come and go like the weather.

In the Chinese context, it takes three or four years of regular face-to-face socializing and exchanging of hospitality to get to know people well enough to trust them and do business with them, which means they never reach that point with many Americans in business or the government.

Because many international business relationships begin without the traditional process of a lengthy courtship and period of establishing personal bonds, the Chinese side automatically attempts to build in as many extra safeguards as possible, and is still likely to remain suspicious and ill-at-ease in the partnership.

American and other foreign businesspeople who go into shotgun-style "weddings" with private Chinese companies as well as state-owned enterprises should keep this deeply ingrained cultural syndrome in mind, and thereafter make a point of developing the kind of personal bonds that are necessary to consummate the relationships.

There is nothing mysterious or subtle about the process of establishing *cheng* (chung) or personal bonds with Chinese, but it requires more time, care and investment than what is customary among Westerners.

Meeting and sharing a drink, meal or recreation time once a year, or even less often, is generally enough to maintain a business bond among Americans and Europeans. But this does not fully satisfy the Chinese.

Chinese prefer relationships that are kept warm by frequent meetings over food and drink, with three or four times a year stretching the outside limits. They especially appreciate *cheng* relationships that are kept hot by weekly, bi-weekly or monthly meetings.

When actual face-to-face get-togethers are impossible or impractical because of distance, time and cost, foreign businesspeople should make a custom of keeping in regular touch with their Chinese partners by phone or fax, by sending them small gifts such as liquor or a scroll of calligraphy on special occasions, or providing them with special-interest magazine articles or books, and so on.

It is especially effective to include their wives and children in such remembrances.

23

吃

Chi
(Chuh)

"Eating Is Heaven"

The Chinese are probably more food-conscious than any other people. Their vocabulary relating to foods is especially rich. A polite traditional greeting is not "How are you?" but "Have you eaten?"

In fact, it has been observed that while Westerners are obsessed with sex, the Chinese are obsessed with *chi* (chuh) or *eating*.

Food is a very geo-psychological thing, and people tend to be timid about styles of cooking that are not their own. But *Zhong can* or "Chinese food" appears to be an outstanding exception.

Having been developed and refined by a unique culture over a period of some five thousand years, Chinese cuisine is more than just basic nourishment. It is meant to feast the eyes, to please the palate, to "repose benignly on the stomach," and to ensure optimum health.

Family and banquet meals in China have even broader dimensions. They serve as therapeutic roundtables at which people slough off the burdens of the day and re-energize their spirits.

To fully savor Chinese cuisine requires a certain degree of learning and aesthetic appreciation. It is not an automatic thing that comes with the food.

Both hosts and guests must recognize and respond to choices well made; to dishes of exceptional quality; and to the ambience of the occasion.

While the Chinese have traditionally eaten almost anything that grows, from snakes to birds' nests, they are masters at transforming the most questionable ingredients into gourmet delicacies.

Furthermore, the Chinese have traditionally been guided in their preparation and eating of food by the ancient *yin-yang* principle, which holds that everything in the universe is either positive or negative, hot or cold, wet or dry, etc., and that the foods that people eat must be a harmonious balance of these cosmic forces if they are to stay physically, emotionally and spiritually healthy.

Within this thesis, every food has its own specific *yin* or *yang* character, and must be consumed in combinations and quantities that are balanced. *Yin* foods are thin, bland, cooling and low in calories. *Yang* foods are rich, spicy, warming and high in calories. Boiling foods makes them *yin*; frying them makes them *yang*.

In the Chinese lexicon, there are five food tastes—spicy, bitter, sour, salty and sweet—and each of these tastes is intimately linked with the five primary elements traditionally believed to make up the cosmos—metal, wood, water, fire and earth.

Further, the Chinese believe that each individual is constitutionally *yin* or *yang*, or a combination of the two. These three types of people are described as "positive," "negative" and "nervous"—the latter being those who are a mixture of *yin* and *yang*.

According to Chinese theory, this *yin-yang* factor in people must also be taken into consideration in their eating habits because the effects of various foods differ with the personalities and physical make-up of the individuals.

The Chinese believe that peppery foods clean the lungs; that bitter foods relieve gastroenteritis; that sour foods refresh and strengthen the liver; that salty foods strengthen the kidneys and bones; and that sweet foods invigorate the spleen.

They also believe that abalone calms the nerves and clears the eyes; that almonds form a protective lining on the stomach walls thereby reducing the effects of alcohol; that bamboo shoots and burdock speed up metabolism and stimulate bowel activity; that cayenne pepper speeds up blood circulation and the functioning of the internal organs; that chestnuts are an excellent energizer; that dried orange peels stimulate digestion; and that clams have a tranquilizing, restful effect.

Other foods with reputedly specific effects on the body that have long been famous among the Chinese include ginseng, which helps regulate the functions of the glands; seaweed, which reduces inflammation; lotus root, which has a significant sedative effect that greatly benefits insomniacs and contributes to elasticity of the blood vessels; and garlic, which is said to stimulate the internal organs, warm up the body and aid in the absorption of nutrients.

There are dozens of cuisine styles in China, with the four main ones being Peking/Mandarin (North), Shanghai (East), Cantonese (South), and Szechuan (West). Each of these regional styles has at least one hundred distinctive dishes. Some Cantonese style restaurants in Hong Kong have over three hundred items on their menus.

In a country that has been overpopulated for centuries and where food has always been scarce, it is no wonder that one of the best-known proverbs is "For the people, food is heaven."

Chinese pragmatism about both food and sex is the subject of a famous saying, *Dong Shi, Xi Su*—literally, *Eat in the East and Sleep in the West*. A long time ago in the state of Qi the parents of a girl received simultaneous wedding proposals from two families with sons. The son of the family living to the east was short and ugly but his parents were very rich. The son of the family living to the west was tall and handsome, but his parents were very poor.

The parents of the girl asked her to decide which son she wanted to marry by raising her left hand if she preferred the boy from the east and her right hand if she preferred the boy from the west.

Finally, blushing, the girl raised both hands. When asked why, she replied: "I would like to eat with the east family and sleep with the west family!"

Points of dining etiquette: It is customary for Chinese dinner guests to arrive well ahead of the set time as a matter of courtesy, and to avoid the possibility of being late.

In smaller groups, it is customary for the host to begin the meal by serving guests from the common dishes, so guests are expected to wait until the host serves them; or when there are larger groups, until the host invites them to help themselves.

After the first serving, guests are expected to serve themselves. Some hosts insist on doing the initial serving each time a new dish is brought out.

崇

Chong
(Chung)

"Revering the Dead"

Legend has it that all *Han* Chinese, the main racial group of the huge population, are descended from one hundred families, and one still hears and reads about references to "The Old Hundred Names of China."

According to the legend, these one hundred original Chinese families settled along the banks of the Yellow River some five or more thousands of years ago. Recent archaeological finds indicate that ancestors of present-day Chinese lived in the region long before that timeframe. "Peking Man," also discovered in this area, dates from 300,000 to 500,000 years ago.

In any event, by about five thousand years ago the Chinese had developed a fairly sophisticated method of writing, and one of the things they were meticulous about was keeping detailed records of their families, generation after generation.

It was the records of the one hundred families that eventually led to those ancestral families being referred to, with a great deal of *chong* (chung), or "reverence," as "The Old Hundred Names."

The reason for this dedication to keeping family records was that worshipping one's ancestors had become a key element in Chinese culture long before the beginning of their recorded history. The gradual development of a writing system made it easier to keep track of those who had gone before, and therefore became a vital part of the custom of revering ancestors.

Chong itself is written with radicals meaning *ancestor* (figuratively a *person* under one's roof), and *mountain* (because ancestors were traditionally buried on mountainsides so their spirits could watch over those still living).

Ancestor reverence is still a part of the lives of most Chinese, but it is under attack by many who see it as a handicap, as compelling the Chinese to look backward instead of forward. The family name and the family record are still of vital importance to the Chinese, however, and are still regarded with a great deal of *chong*.

Outsiders dealing with the Chinese should be aware of this special respect for family names, and take care not to commit cultural errors in their use or treatment of people's names. To avoid such faux pas it is essential to get the name right the first time, particularly since there are various spellings of the same name.

The problem of keeping names and people straight in China becomes more compelling when you consider that there are only a few thousand surnames in the country of more than one billion people, and that approximately ten percent of the population is named Zhang (Chang)—one of the original one hundred clan names. Other common names include Chen, Liu, Wang and Li.

Chong for past traditions remains a defining element in the character of the Chinese, including those who have become coated in a patina of modernization.

25

Chou
(Choe-ou)

"Beware of Criticizing"

Most life in pre-"democratic" China followed a precise form and order that had been scripted and perfected over a period of some four thousand years. Propriety or "etiquette" was the essence of Chinese society. Harmony—intellectually, emotionally, spiritually and physically—was the overriding principle of Chinese civilization.

The best way to imagine the degree to which Chinese life was programmed is to view the whole of China as a great stage, with the role of each individual written out in detail. This script of life covered all beliefs, attitudes and actions, including manner of speaking, which was determined by the relationship between the individuals concerned.

The goal of this careful staging was social and political stability—a factor that took precedence over virtually every other consideration, including human feelings.

There was a life script for female children, male children, wives, husbands, parents, grandparents, and so on. Each had to learn specific roles that were as demanding as any stage play.

Failure to learn one's role or deviations from the script were taken seriously and almost always resulted in some kind of punishment. Failure to bow properly or using the wrong speech to a superior, for example, could result in a beating or even death.

One of the strongest taboos in the authoritarian Chinese system was criticizing the government, government leaders, public officials, parents, or anyone who was in a superior position in the vertically structured society.

This cultural principle was a key factor in the maintenance of surface harmony, but it was also a major factor in perpetuating mediocrity and the status quo throughout society, and thus had a significantly negative impact on the social, economic and political development of the country.

When China's Communist Party took over the country in 1949 it not only continued the taboo against criticizing the government and its leaders, it made the penalties even more harsh, executing dozens of thousands of people and sentencing several million to hard-labor "reform" prisons.

While the CCP still today treats any criticism of the government as a traitorous act, and routinely imprisons people for speaking out against the government, criticism per se is no longer taboo.

Government leaders and officials themselves now regularly criticize other public officials, businesspeople, students, teachers, parents or anyone else whom they feel does not live up to their socialist standards.

But ordinary citizens are not free to dissent with the government, and personally criticizing individuals, whether they are government bureaucrats, businesspeople, professors, service personnel in stores or taxi drivers, is still mostly taboo and dangerous.

Both government-sponsored and independent news media now freely criticize any segment of society they believe behaves in an unacceptable manner. One of the words they often use is *chou* (choe-ou), which means *smelly* or *stinky,* and refers to things that stink (are not right) and to people who are incompetent and therefore inefficient in what they do.

Again, this term is almost never used directly to anyone because such direct criticism is still considered uncivilized and insulting, and generally results in the individual concerned taking some kind of revenge.

Foreigners in China should be especially wary about criticizing anyone personally, particularly government workers and officials. Where employees are concerned, any criticism should be done in private in a very diplomatic way, as a suggestion rather than a put-down.

愁

Chou
(Choe-ou)

"Indulging in Melancholy"

I would not describe the Chinese as a moody people. They have their moods, of course, but there is something in Chinese culture that makes the Chinese an optimistic and light-hearted people, no matter how poor or deprived they may be by other standards.

The Chinese have a great sense of humor. They are compulsive pun-makers and love jokes. Their enjoyment of humorous entertainment is legendary. They also have a deep-seated sense of the seasons that is reflected in their psychology and customs, and adds a special dimension to life in China.

All human beings are, of course, affected by the circadian cycle of the spinning earth, and those who live in temperate zones away from the equator are also subject to deeply ingrained mood swings from the changing seasons, particularly the approach of spring and the coming of fall.

It is universal folk wisdom that the approach of spring, with its signs of renewal and new life, has an uplifting effect on people. The first leaves, flowers and blossoms of spring have always been celebrated for the emotional and spiritual balm they bring.

But it seems to me that the Chinese reaction to fall is more pronounced and more revealing than their reaction to any of the other seasons.

The key "fall" word in the Chinese lexicon is *chou* (choe-ou), which is the equivalent of *melancholy* but is made much more poignant by its graphic representation. The ideogram for *chou* is made up of the symbols for heart, burning fire and a stalk of ripe grain.

The image the ideogram portrays is that of the melancholy that results from the ancient practice of burning the stalks in fields after the grain has been harvested. The once beautiful green fields are reduced to blackened ash and rubble, reminding everyone that life is short and ends with all things being returned to the earth.

Because the Chinese have a special affinity for the cultural nuances of fall, the Fall Festival is one of the two major celebrations of the year (the other one being New Year's), during which people remind themselves of where they came from and their inevitable fate.

There is a poignancy about the celebrations of fall but it is not an unhappy time. Rather, it is a time to take stock of one's life and make a special point of enjoying its pleasures because they are ephemeral.

Visitors in China can get into the spirit of fall activities, and impress their Chinese friends and associates, by acquainting themselves with some of the famous "fall" poetry that has been written over the ages, and by displaying wall scrolls that celebrate the season.

27

出风头

Chu Feng Tou
(Chuu Fung Toe-ou)

"The Show-offs"

Virtually everything in China's long history, from the prevailing philosophical beliefs, social structure and etiquette, to its authoritarian political system, conditioned the people to maintain a low profile and avoid attracting attention to themselves from any source.

Part of this conditioning was to maintain a modest front in dress and behavior as a fundamental concept of the prevailing Confucian morality. At the same time, it was particularly important not to dress or behave above one's social class because that was prohibited by law and resulted in severe punishment for anyone who broke the taboo.

This facade of conservatism included the outward appearance of homes. Even the well-to-do, rather than blatantly flaunt their affluence and create envy and ill-will, built their homes with modest exteriors, concealed them behind walls, and kept the signs of luxury out of sight.

But much of this enforced modesty is now a thing of the past, thanks to the efforts of the Chinese Communist Party and the spread of capitalism and democratic ideals in China.

The CCP, inadvertently, began the process of breaking the low-profile beliefs and habits of the Chinese by making an all-out attempt to destroy every aspect of traditional Chinese culture during the first three decades of its regime.

The introduction of a significant degree of American style independence and individualism from the 1980s on brought a totally new look to China—a look that was pioneered by successful young business entrepreneurs and entertainment stars who used their new wealth to publicly indulge themselves.

One of the new cultural code phrases that came into vogue during the 1990s was *chu feng tou* (chuu fung toe-ou), which literally means something like *display one's charms*—in other words, to deliberately seek the limelight.

When this term was first introduced it was used with a decidedly negative connotation to criticize people who dared to stick out from the crowd. But as more and more "people became celebrities" the appellation began losing some of its sting.

Now it is more apt to be used out of envy rather than as a moral condemnation of such behavior, and will not doubt serve as an inducement to encourage other members of China's growing well-to-do class to come out of the "closet."

Commercial advertising via television as well as print media are now far more influential in determining Chinese mores than either the heritage of Confucianism or the political goals of the People's Republic of China.

In one way or another, the desire to *chu feng tou* will no doubt infect all mainland Chinese, and in the process help them achieve the personal identity and individualism that has been denied them since the beginning of their history.

28

単位

Danwei
(Dahn-way-e)

"Big Brother"

Traditional Chinese beliefs and behavior were primarily forged in agricultural communities made up of precise groupings, beginning with the family and expanding outward to include the courtyard or *hutong*, its immediate neighborhood, village brigades and entire villages.

Each community was bound together by networks of individuals with equally precise hierarchical positions and mutual responsibilities. Relations within the networks were personal and intimate. What one did or did not do reflected on everyone else. Responsibility was collective. The whole group could be, and frequently was, punished for the misdeeds of a single member.

In towns and cities where economic activity consisted mostly of manufacturing, the retail trades, service industries and craft work, the primary groupings were families, street associations and places of employment, which were known as *danwei* (dahn-way-e) or *work units*.

Life from birth to death followed carefully prescribed patterns based on social rank, sex, age and occupation. Individual thought and behavior, especially for those in the lower orders of society, were severely limited.

With the coming of the Communist dynasty in 1949, the *danwei*, which included village brigades, factories, schools, hospitals, government ministries and agencies, in fact, all companies and organizations in the country, assumed more and more responsibility and control of the lives of their members.

During the heyday of the Communist period, from the 1950s to the mid-1980s, the *danwei* became responsible for *all* of the activities, welfare and behavior of the employees and their families. The *danwei* decided what kind of work employees did, where they worked and how much they were paid.

Danwei were also responsible for providing housing and all health care, controlled all travel, operated company stores for their employees, controlled rationing coupons, designated how many children employees could have, and acted as judge and jury when members broke any of the *danwei* regulations or ran afoul of the cadre in charge of the work units.

One of the most invidious methods of control used by the *danwei* was food stamps. Members of each unit were issued stamps that could only be used in their own commissaries. They could not buy food anywhere else, and therefore could not "quit" their unit and move away.

Another control method, which had been used historically, was personal files kept on every member in every unit. Still today, extensive details about each person's family, birth, education and activities, real and alleged, are kept in company and organizational personnel files, which are not accessible to the individuals concerned.

Like members of military units, no individual can change jobs without his or her dossier being released by the original workplace and sent to the new one. If the personnel director or anyone else with authority in the *danwei* does not want a person to leave all they have to do is refuse to forward his or her file. For Chinese students hoping to travel abroad, the approval of the *danwei* requires bribes and political favors, particularly after the Tiananmen Square massacre in 1989.

During the first decades of the People's Republic of China all *danwei* were administered more or less like political states, exercising the prerogatives of independent dictatorships. Larger work units acted as hosts and guarantors for foreign visitors. All foreign businesspeople who visited China or took up residence there could do so only under the sponsorship of a *danwei*.

Thereafter, all of the activities of the individual businessperson, from licenses and foreign exchange to negotiations and contracts with other Chinese companies or government agencies, were done under the auspices of the host work unit.

The role of the *danwei* became so pervasive in the lives of the Chinese, and often foreign residents as well, that people were required to identify themselves as members of specific work units rather than individuals. A person who was not a member of a work unit was a non-person, unable to get a travel permit, to obtain housing, to get food rations or health care, to register children (so they could go to school and receive other government entitlements), or to do any of the myriad things that required official approval.

Foreigners who were unlucky enough or unwise enough not to become associated with one of the larger, more powerful *danwei* were often severely handicapped in what they were able to do in China.

Of equal importance to foreigners was getting on and remaining on the good side of the individual *danwei* cadre who were assigned to be in charge of them, take care of them, and be responsible for their actions.

Internal changes in China have mitigated the presence and power of the *danwei* to some extent. People now have substantially more personal control over some aspects of their lives. But work units continue to exist and to play a central and often draconian role in Chinese society.

(The *danwei* was a Chinese Communist concept that was applied only in mainland China. There was nothing like it in Hong Kong or Taiwan. It is assumed, however, that after China takes over Hong Kong it will be introduced, at least on a limited scale, into the former British colony.)

29

道

Dao
(Tah-oh)

"Taking the High Road"

In this day and age of environmental concerns and growing awareness of the interdependence of everything in nature, it is humbling to consider that the West and other areas of the world only recently picked up on a concept that has been an integral part of Chinese philosophy for more than twenty centuries.

Lao Tzu, also known as Ze Dao (the Great Master), born in the year 604 B.C., is generally credited with being the first Chinese sage to create a philosophy based on the scientific theory of the oneness of nature.

Daoism, the oldest of the three main religions of China, is a nature-based philosophy that begins with the duality of all things in the universe and a natural order that tends to keep the dual forces in harmonious balance.

It teaches that this harmonious balance is the essence of beauty, and that the only way mankind can achieve fulfillment and its highest potential is by staying in harmony with nature—going with the flow rather than against it.

Lao Tzu based his philosophy on the concept that the cosmos itself began as One (the time before the Big Bang!); that everything that now exists sprang from this One, and thus has a common origin. He added that although everything in nature is made up of the same kind of energy, each thing has a unique combination of energy atoms, and must be true to its own nature.

The Great Master based his teachings on this "law" or "truth" of the universe, advising rulers and subjects alike to conduct themselves in conformity with the inter-relatedness of nature. By following the *Dao* (tah-oh) or *The Way of Truth*, Lao Tzu said, the government and the governed could exist in harmony.

But the universal laws that Lao Tzu perceived were too esoteric, too advanced, to be translated into practical guidelines for life in 5th century B.C. China, and his teachings were soon overshadowed by those of one of his own pupils, Confucius, who had a much more pragmatic and expedient message for the rulers of the day.

Confucius believed that peace and prosperity would best be served by an all-powerful but benevolent ruler who earned the respect and loyalty of his subjects, and by people who obeyed the ruler because of his virtue. This was a lot more acceptable to China's early rulers than Lao Tzu's message of interdependent equality.

In the centuries that followed, students of the original teachings of Lao Tzu split them into a number of schools, including one that incorporated magic as an important element in achieving the "Way," and another one which held that copious indulgence in sex was the right path to follow to achieve harmony with the cosmos.

The supreme deity in Daoism is the Jade Emperor, and there are numerous lesser deities, including the God of Wealth (*Fu*), the God of Happiness (*Lu*), and the God of Good Luck (*Shou*).

Despite the mystical aspects added to Daoism over the centuries, the inherent truth of Lao Tzu's philosophy was too powerful to be destroyed and forgotten. It continued to exist alongside of Confucianism and Buddhism, and to color the thinking of the Chinese down to the present time.

In fact, Lao Tzu's writings are said to have been quoted more often than any source in the history of man, except perhaps the Christian bible.

What Lao Tzu discovered by inductive reasoning, Western scientists are now demonstrating scientifically—from the Big Bang and the common atomic energy base of all things, to the importance of maintaining harmony with the physical and spiritual universe.

Hopefully, one of the areas in which China can eventually interface in a positive role with the rest of the world is through merging the philosophy of Lao Tzu's *Dao* with the technology and practical experience of the West.

One of Lao's most famous sayings: "Gods and spirits are not needed when man follows *Dao*, The Way."

Daoism also teaches the principle of *wu-wei* or *active not-doing*, which, in modern-day political terms, is expressed as *positive non-interference*. This refers to creating a positive environment in which desirable things are more likely to happen, but not becoming directly or publicly involved in making them happen.

This philosophy, in part at least, helps explain the Chinese penchant for doing things behind the scenes, often in secret.

------------------------------ 30 ------------------------------

韬光养晦

Daoguang Yanghui

(Tah-oh-gwahng Yahng-whee)

"Keeping Your Claws Sheathed"

Tigers were abundant in the wilds of early China, and have played a major role in Chinese culture, art and mythology. One story that readily comes to mind features the great sage Confucius as one of the main actors.

In this story, Confucius and some of his disciples are passing through the mountains in a remote part of the country when they come upon a woman weeping.

Confucius has one of his attendants ask the woman why she is crying. She tells the attendant that her husband has just been killed by a tiger, and that the same fate befell her father and her grandfather.

On hearing this, Confucius asks the woman why she continues to live in such a remote and dangerous place. The woman replies that because it is remote and infested with man-eating tigers she does not have to worry about the government interfering with her life.

Confucius nods his head in understanding, and remarks to his disciples that an oppressive government is even more fearful than man-eating tigers.

There are several versions of the man-eating tiger story. In another slightly different version the gray-haired mother has just lost her third and last son to a tiger.

Among the attributes of tigers that the Chinese especially admired were their calm, placid manner when at rest, their patience in hunting, and the fact that they kept their claws sheathed until they went for the kill.

Chinese philosophers, intellectuals, military strategists and others who concerned themselves with success in business, politics, war and the martial arts held the tiger up as a worthy model for men to emulate.

The Chinese were great pupils, and a *daoguang yanghui* (tah-oh-gwahng yahng-whee) or *sheathed claw* approach became a central theme in all areas of their lives.

Historically, the Chinese who have been the most dangerous have generally been those who kept their claws sheathed and were soft, kind and gentle toward their families and friends, but showed no mercy to enemies.

Today, Chinese businesspeople, politicians and diplomats who radiate calmness, quiet confidence, wisdom and a benign spirit, but are capable of striking with lightning speed and overcoming or destroying their opponents, are living up to the image of the tiger.

This dual personality is difficult for most Westerners to deal with since we expect aggressive and truly ruthless people to look and act the part at all times.

And, of course, this is not to suggest that all Chinese are ruthless or that it is necessary to be cautious of all Chinese who are quiet, gentle and kind—which most are!

The point is that many Chinese—usually in government—are, in fact, "tigers" behind their traditional facade of civility, and that it is important to be able to distinguish between tigers and lambs.

31

大腕　　　大款

Da Wan, Da Kuan
(Dah Wahn, Dah Kwahn)

"The New Fat Cats"

For centuries ordinary Chinese had been conditioned to believe that attempts to amass wealth were immoral. Then along came the Communist Party in 1949 with its savage efforts to erase all vestiges of capitalism from China and reduce the population to the same economic level.

In the 1980s China's supreme leader Deng Xiaoping, perhaps unintentionally, officially recognized the failure of communism in China when he approved of the idea that to get rich is glorious. But this announcement was not welcomed with open arms by everyone.

This sudden flip-flop by the Communist Party of China was just too much for many Chinese to stomach—sometimes because of genuine intellectual objections to this new advocacy of materialism, and other times because they were so disadvantaged they knew there was no way they could compete with others in a race to get rich.

These feelings of anti-materialism and anti-capitalism were exacerbated by the behavior of entrepreneurs who became affluent almost overnight and flaunted their new wealth with an abandonment never before witnessed in China. In rural and suburban areas, for example, *nouveau riche* families added second-story bedrooms to their houses. In a few celebrated cases, indignant neighbors pulled the ostentatious buildings down, brick by brick.

In a gesture of disapproval, critics of the newly rich, particularly those with access to news media, labeled them *da wan, da kuan* (dah wahn, dah kwahn), literally *big arm, big fat*, in a richly suggestive reference to their sudden affluence.

Somewhat surprising, perhaps, this appellation continues to be used more often in reference to newly rich artists or writers than to business entrepreneurs, possibly because writers and artists are not perceived as working as hard as businesspeople, and therefore are less deserving of their wealth.

Of course, this syndrome is not by any means unique to China, but it is likely to be more virulent and pose more of a social problem in China because the lack of opportunity for most of China's billion-plus people, combined with the lingering influence of their Confucian and Communist heritage, will generate a higher level of hostility toward the rich.

Where foreign tourists and resident foreign businesspeople are concerned, it is still common for ordinary Chinese as well as many company executives and government officials to perceive them as *da wan, da kuan* "fat cats" who not only can afford to pay more than the local market price for any goods or services, but are morally obligated to do so.

Because of this attitude the Chinese government and many private commercial enterprises maintain a two-level pricing system—one for Chinese, and the other one for foreigners.

Pretending to be anything less than affluent in China can be a two-edged sword, however. People who dress well and are obviously affluent are generally treated much better, especially by government officials and run-of-the-mill bureaucrats, than people who look low class and impoverished.

32

大戏

Daxi

(Dah-she)

"Culture in Action"

Traditional Chinese culture survived for several millennia because it was carried forward by the language, by the arts and crafts—in fact, by the total social system of structured hierarchical relationships, etiquette and morality.

One of the most conspicuous—and enjoyable—of the many mediums that helped to preserve the culture and pass it along from one generation to the next was *daxi* (dah-she) or "Chinese opera."

Until co-opted by the Chinese Communist Party in the 1950s and 1960s, *daxi*, which dates back for several thousand years, was not avant-garde theater. Its focus was on the past. Its story lines were based on folk tales, legends and past heroes.

Throughout the long history of *daxi* there have been a variety of schools. Today, there are three traditional schools, along with the "opera as propaganda" form that was created by the CCP in the 1950s.

In traditional Chinese *daxi* actors and actresses play the parts of emperors, empresses, generals and other military figures, scholars, beautiful heroines, ladies, common people and so on, dressing in costumes and styles of the Qing and Ming dynasties.

The colors of the costumes generally signify the rank and characters being portrayed. Yellow apparel signifies royalty; red indicates someone who is loyal to the emperor, maidens wear pink, military men wear dark red. (In Chinese culture, red is symbolic of joy, fire and summer and wards off evil spirits; white stands for purity; blue relates to heaven; black to darkness; green to life and spring; purple to the emperor; etc.)

The headgear worn by the players is also indicative of their social rank and profession—and since there are over 100 different categories of headgear, being able to identify all of them is a major accomplishment.

There are presently three predominate schools in *daxi*—*nan xi* and *bei xi*, which have been popular since the 12th century, and *ping xi*, which dates from the 1800s.

Nan xi plays are very elaborate, with lots of drums, flutes and singing. *Bei xi* plays also feature drums, flutes and singing but are heavy on martial arts. A common theme of *ping xi* plays are stories and legends taken from the period of the Three Kingdoms—one form emphasizing family life and the other lots of martial arts action.

During the heyday of the Chinese Communist Party, when all of the entertainment arts were required to advance the aims of the Party, *daxi* became vehicles for Red Chinese propaganda, extolling the virtues and power of the People's Liberation Army, the peasants and the working class. Tiang Xing, Mao's wife, was an actress and strong proponent of *daxi*.

Communist-inspired *daxi* were marked by military uniforms, red flags, guns and loud martial music.

Traditional *daxi* give visitors a bird's eye view of some of the pageantry of old China, and still today provide lessons in Chinese culture.

33

大爷

Da Ye

(Dah Yay)

"Big Daddies"

For the more than four thousand years of China's Imperial history, about the only way to wealth and power was through political office or banditry on a massive scale (as practiced by warlords who held sway over their own fiefs throughout most of the dynasties).

Ordinary people, particularly farmers who made up the bulk of the population, were generally locked into self-limiting occupations by birth and had few if any options for bettering themselves. Most were condemned to a subsistence-level existence for generation after generation.

During China's short and disastrous "republican" period from 1912 to 1949, it was again politicos, warlords and a few merchants who were the only elite. When the Communists took over China in 1949 they eliminated warlords and well-to-do families alike, leaving only the higher echelons of Party officials in command of financial resources.

For the first three or so decades of the Communist regime, ordinary people were even worse off than they had been before. Millions lost what little property they had. Other millions were sent to prison farms and prison factories, and more millions died by execution and starvation.

By 1976 the potency of the Communist Party had begun to wane and its orgy of destruction was replaced by attempts to return some rationality to the government and rebuild the country. In a sudden about-face, the Communist Party relaxed its death-grip on the people and began promoting the introduction of free-market principles and allowing people a measure of personal freedom.

Over the next decade something remarkable happened. Huge numbers of Chinese, overcoming the terrible suffering inflicted upon them by the CCP, turned themselves into successful farmers, businessmen and businesswomen.

Freed for the first time in their lives to develop their own potential, dozens of thousands of people mastered a variety of technical, managerial and marketing skills and began marketing themselves in a development totally new to China.

This new breed of Chinese was quickly labeled *da ye* (dah yay), which is something like *big daddy*, in reference to people who are self-sufficient, oftentimes conspicuously affluent, and spread their money around in a flamboyant manner, particularly on food, clothing and women.

The term also includes the connotation of *mastery* and *independence* in reference to the fact that this new type of Chinese are no longer dependent upon job placement by government agencies or any other connection for them to not only survive but to succeed in joining the ranks of China's newly affluent.

There is every reason to believe that the *da ye* syndrome will expand like wildfire as the Chinese gain more and more freedom to develop and exercise their talents for entrepreneurship.

34

大有

Da Yu

(Tah Yuu)

"Avoiding a Swelled Head"

The worst dangers facing early mankind may have been animals competing for the same food and same space. But the more mankind advanced, the more this changed. Sometime long before the beginning of recorded history, humans had become their own worst enemies.

Recognizing that the more power a person has the more dangerous he or she is likely to become, China's earliest philosophers spent a great deal of their time contemplating this dilemma and striving to come up with guidelines to alleviate it.

The problem of how individuals dealt with power was so important that it was one of the topics covered in the collection of sixty-four hexagrams handed down from prehistoric times as *I Ching* or *Book of Changes*, which was more or less the rule book for Chinese life.

In this collection the subject of power was treated under the heading *da yu* (tah yuu), now translated as *sovereignty*, and literally meaning *having an abundance of things*.

The connotation of *da yu* is that the accumulation of things (land, money, material goods) brings power and authority—*sovereignty*—over others.

King Wen, founder of the Chou Dynasty in 1150 B.C. and his son, the Duke of Chou, recognized the moral and philosophical facets of this problem and wrote about it in their commentaries on the sixty-four hexagrams.

In his additions to the *Book of Changes*, Wen incorporated his own metaphysical, philosophical and psychological insights, and applied the hexagrams to everyday social, political and economic matters.

Wen also revised the order of the sixty-four hexagrams, making how individuals dealt with power number fourteen because of its importance in the scheme of human affairs.

Some six centuries later, Lao Tzu and Confucius, two of China's most influential sages, added their thoughts to this perennial problem, as did other contemporary as well as later famous philosophers of old.

Present-day Chinese are just as concerned about *da yu* as their ancestors were three millennia ago, and the guidelines written then are still the ideal for those who are successful in business or politics and have authority over people.

These guidelines, which are certainly not always followed, call for people in positions of power to be unselfish, kind, generous, humble, openminded, flexible and dignified. If you follow these guidelines, the sages promise, people will not be jealous of your power but will be drawn to you and will offer you their loyalty and support, thereby guaranteeing that you can maintain your power and accomplish worthwhile things.

The sages wisely warn that the successful management of *da yu* requires that it be kept personal, that it will fail if it becomes institutionalized into bureaucracies.

Obviously, this is another area of social conduct in which the power holders of China have consistently ignored the wise advice of their philosophers.

But the wisdom of *da yu* remains valid not only for Chinese but for others as well, and can be particularly important to foreign managers working in China.

大跃进

Da Yue Jin

(Dah Yuu-eh Jeen)

"Mao's 'Dragon Dream'"

Mao Zedung, who became the primary founder of the People's Republic of China because he recognized that any real success that communism might have in China would have to be built on the backs of peasants, had his own version of the famous "Dragon Dream"—a dream that has been the Holy Grail of millions of Chinese since the end of the Ming Dynasty in 1644.

Mao's dream was to once again make China into a great and glorious nation, but one that was totally different from the Confucian-oriented, maledominated and socially and economically divided country of the past.

To succeed in this goal, Mao was willing to virtually destroy what he referred to as "Old China"—meaning all of the beliefs, values, attitudes, customs and practices that had distinguished the Chinese for thousands of years.

He was also willing to see millions of people die in the process of creating a new, Communist state—at first based on the concepts of Karl Marx and Frederick Engels and the experience of the Soviet Union, and then on his own interpretation of Communist-inspired socialism. (In his later years, when an interviewer made some comment about how many lives communism had destroyed, he remarked, "People are like grass. They spring up and are mowed down!" By some estimates, Mao caused the death of more people than any other person in world history.)

By May 1956 Mao was so frustrated by the re-appearance of bureaucratism and traditional conservatism that he resolved to shake the CCP to its roots. His way of doing so was to inaugurate the so-called Hundred Flowers Movement, which was an invitation for the intellectuals of the country to offer constructive criticism to the CCP.

Mao got more than he asked for. The country's intellectuals began verbally tearing the Party apart. One year later, to quell the criticism and the unrest that it was causing, Mao launched a nationwide "Anti-Rightist Campaign."

All workplaces were given a quota of "Rightists" to turn in to the Public Security Bureau. Any company or organization that failed to turn in enough names to meet its quota was presumed to be hiding "enemies of the people," and its leaders were subject to punishment.

Some half a million of the people who had dared to criticize the CCP were arrested and sentenced to various kinds of "thought reform" prisons. Dozens of thousands of them died from torture and abuse. Many were executed.

In 1958, nine years after taking over China and establishing the People's Republic, Mao initiated a program labeled *Da Yue Jin* (dah yuu-eh jeen) or *Great Leap Forward* that was intended to convert China into a pure socialist state by purging the country of all private ownership and effort, and collectivizing both agriculture and industry in one huge step.

Mao's plan was based on radicalizing the nation's peasants and workers, imbuing them with the kind of revolutionary zeal that had brought the Communist Party to power, and harnessing the enormous power of these millions in a totally planned economy that would bring agriculture and industry together as the "two legs of China."

By this time, 92 percent of all peasants in China had already been incorporated into nearly one and a half million cooperatives, of which some 800,000 were "higher stage" cooperatives, with 200 to 700 members in each one. Only a few of these peasants had managed to keep small plots of land for their private use. The rest had lost all control over their lives.

Mao's dream was to merge all of these co-ops into communes, with cadre officials controlling all of the social, political and economic activities of each group. Each commune started out with 5,000 households, but this number was soon reduced to 1,600 because the larger groups were simply impossible to manage.

These smaller communes were divided into production brigades, production teams and production groups. At first, all members were paid the same in money or kind, or according to their needs, but this did not work, and some communes were soon switched to payment based on work done.

It was as if the whole country had been enrolled in one giant civilian service corps. The brigades were assigned to specific work projects that ranged from raising grain, mining and irrigation canals and dams, to widening streets and building a remarkable maze of underground shelters beneath Beijing and other cities.

In this process, hundreds of thousands of people were moved to remote regions of the country to open up new farm lands and to work in new factories. Huge amounts of the grain raised by farm communes was shipped to the Soviet Union to pay for machinery.

Mao's goal was to turn China into a major producer of coal, grain and steel virtually overnight (he referred to them in military terms as "General Coal," "General Grain" and "General Steel").

As part of this remarkable effort, Mao ordered every village in the country to build a large furnace to smelt iron ore and iron implements, and make steel. The idea occurred to him one day when he was in his swimming pool. The whole country was set to collecting every piece of metal that could be found, resulting in families turning in their metal kitchen utensils and even the knobs off their doors.

Millions of farmers left their fields and began constructing smelters out of mud, plaster and brick. Within a year more than one million smelters had been built. But in the end the steel that was produced by the smelters was such low grade that none of it could be used.

Another Great Leap Forward program ordered by Mao was a campaign to kill all of the sparrows in the country (because they ate so much grain). Virtually all other activity in the country stopped, and for three days and nights millions of Chinese were in the fields, in streets and on top of buildings beating drums, gongs and metal lids; ringing bells, blowing horns, waving pieces of cloth and shouting to prevent the birds from landing.

By the end of the third day and night, millions of sparrows dropped to the ground, dead from exhaustion. In Beijing, where sparrow flesh was considered a delicacy, millions of the dead birds were gathered up and eaten.

For a brief period it looked like the Great Leap Forward was working. But the image was false because the information provided by the communes was grossly misleading. Then a disastrous series of floods and draughts struck the country for three years in a row—1959, 1960 and 1961.

Production in all areas fell drastically—as much as 70 percent in some categories. Between 1959 and 1962 over twenty million people, half of them children, died of starvation *in just one province*.

Mao's dream of glory had become a nightmare. The Great Leap Forward knocked China to its knees and forced it to crawl for the next several years.

The turmoil caused by the famine and the *Da Yue Jin* was such that Mao and his cohorts had hundreds of thousands more people arrested and confined in prison farms and factories to avoid the possibility that the CCP might be toppled from power, and to get the country back on the Mao-road to Socialism.

One of these prison farms, Qinghe, had 100,000 inmates, according to journalist Hongda "Harry" Wu, who was confined there during the latter part of this period. Wu said that during that period, rations for prisoners at the prison farm consisted of two corn buns a day, and inmates were reduced to eating insects, rodents, snakes, tree bark, roots and grass. He added that the living space allotted to each inmate in the farm's dormitories was only 60 centimeters wide.

Among the desperate measures that Mao and the CCP took to recover from the disaster of the Great Leap Forward was to initiate a Socialist Education Campaign that was referred to as *Si Qing* or *Four Cleanups*—in this case an attempt to make the system work by promoting collectivism, patriotism and socialism; eliminating capitalism, feudalism and extravagance; promoting the building of socialism and love for the collectives; and promoting "democracy" and frugality within the communes.

(None of these programs worked, and in 1985, nine years after Mao's death, the communes were abolished altogether.)

See **Wenhua Da Ge Ming**.

大壮

Da Zhuang
(Dah Chuu-ahng)

"Using Power Wisely"

Chinese wisdom takes into account the obvious fact that power in the hands of people who are unworthy invariably leads to misuse of the power and trouble of one kind or another. And just as obviously, the greater the power the greater the potential for both abuse and trouble.

Because of this unfortunate fact of life, China's early philosophers recognized the danger of *da zhuang* (dah chuu-ahng) or *great power,* and created a series of guidelines to help people who have such power deal with it in a moral and productive manner.

It goes without saying that very few of China's powerful men, in early or recent times, met the test of the philosophers. But the conduct prescribed to counter the evil portent of power represents the ideal character portrayed in Chinese culture, and still sets the standards by which business and political leaders are measured.

In the concept of *da zhuang* the power itself is viewed as having been sent by heaven, and therefore is inherently good. Furthermore, the strength to use this power is also heaven-sent. The presence and use of such power is therefore something that is in harmony with the cosmos.

But how *da zhuang* is used is in the hands of earthly people, and therein lies the danger.

China's wise men thus observe that the first challenge for those with power should not be what they are going to do with it, but *how* they are going to use it and what they must do to make sure that they use it correctly—that is, in harmony with society and the universe at large.

Naturally, the philosopher's answer to this challenge is for those with power to make sure that their values, motives, goals and timing are above reproach and in concert with the needs and interests of others.

The second most important criterion established for people with power by China's sages is to avoid doing new and untried things, particularly during periods of turmoil, and to stick with conservative, well-proven actions.

Sages also warn people who have *da zhuang* to keep in mind that power in their hands does not necessarily equate with virtue, and that it should be viewed as a test and as an opportunity to strengthen their character.

Another of the sage insights that goes with *da zhuang* is the fact that it works best when it is used quietly and surreptitiously and no one knows who is yielding the power.

This latter factor is something that most foreign businesspeople dealing with China are especially familiar with, since it is often difficult to discern who really exercises power in Chinese companies. It seems that the more powerful a Chinese becomes the more likely he or she is to operate behind the scenes.

德

De

(Tuh)

"The Power of Virtue"

One of the most profound concepts ever postulated for human behavior is that virtue brings with it a spirituality that is all-powerful, and that virtue is the ultimate force in shaping the behavior of people; not laws or other kinds of restraints.

This concept lies at the heart of Daoism, the school of thought originated in the latter part of the 5th century B.C. by the great sage, Lao Tzu—and also arrived at nearly six hundred years later by Jesus of Nazareth.

Lao Tzu taught that *de* (tuh) or *virtue* is an inherent characteristic of human beings; that when we are born we are absolutely virtuous and that it is only in the process of growing up that most people lose this built-in quality.

Christianity, on the other hand, teaches that all human beings are born without virtue, having lost it because of the original sin of Adam and Eve, and that the only way to return to the path of true virtue is through belief/faith in the teachings of Jesus.

This fundamental difference of judgment in the nature of humanity is one of the many reasons why Christianity has not been more successful in China.

Lao Tzu proclaimed that the only legitimacy for a ruler was virtue; that only the truly virtuous were capable of resisting the corrupting influence of power and could therefore conduct the affairs of state on behalf of and in the interest of the people. There have been few, if any, truly virtuous male or female rulers in China or elsewhere since the time of Lao Tzu. But this does not prove that he was wrong; only that true virtue is very rare among people who have the ambition, courage, energy, and skills—or luck—necessary to become rulers or high government officials.

During the Ming Dynasty (A.D. 1368–1644) an especially diligent high-ranking member of the Court came up with a new way of encouraging bureaucrats to be virtuous, to eschew lining their own pockets and enriching their relatives and friends, that would surely make an impression on present-day government officials in Tokyo, Washington and elsewhere.

This official first had miscreant bureaucrats executed. Then he had their bodies stuffed and placed in their offices...to remind their replacements of the fate that awaited them if they abused their positions.

Another facet of Lao Tzu's teachings was that *de* is its own reward, and will of itself attract good fortune to people who follow its path—something that has yet to be proven on any significant scale, anywhere.

But among common people in China today there is still a deep, fundamental belief in the value and benefit of virtue, despite so much evidence to the contrary. Of course, this belief exists in the context of China's overall culture, not as a universal principle that applies to everyone at all times in exactly the same way.

Furthermore, there is Chinese virtue, and there is other virtue. The ongoing challenge facing Chinese and non-Chinese today is to find common grounds of virtue on which they can establish and maintain positive, constructive relationships despite their cultural differences.

One of the most interesting and important aspects of the Chinese/Daoist concept of virtue is that when the Chinese do, in fact, perceive individuals, in business or politics, as truly virtuous, they will honor them, be loyal to them, cooperate with them, and voluntarily do their utmost to carry out their wishes.

This behavior is fundamental and universal enough that it crosses racial and cultural lines. The Chinese respect and readily cooperate with foreigners whom they perceive as virtuous and having goodwill toward them.

Deng

(Doong)

"By the Numbers"

Long-time foreign residents in China frequently comment on the fact that there is a specific "Chinese way" of doing everything from the most mundane actions of eating and housework to behavior at formal banquets.

This Chinese way has been in existence for well over two thousand years, and is no doubt one of the primary reasons why Chinese civilization has survived so long—and why Chinese who have never lived in China continue to follow many of the cultural customs of their ancestors.

The heart of the Chinese way is bound up in the concept of order and harmony in the cosmos—the idea that everything has its place, its role, its way, and that to be right with the universe human beings as well must follow this same cosmic imperative.

One of the key foundations of the Chinese way is expressed by the term *deng* (doong), or *order*—everything and everybody in their place, behaving in the right manner.

The Chinese have been virtually obsessed with *deng* for most of their history. As early as 2000 B.C., their whole social system was based on a precise form and order that took precedence over everything else. Also by this time they had already begun classifying everything natural and supernatural, arranging both the visible and invisible world in precise, ranked categories.

In Chinese society interpersonal relationships between males and females, husbands and wives, parents and children, inferiors and superiors, friends and the like, along with all of the systems of child-nurturing, education, work and politics, were precisely detailed in a hierarchical order.

This collective conditioning in thinking and doing things in the Chinese way became an integral part of the glue that bonded the Chinese as a people, and still today marks them as members of one of the world's most pervasive and powerful cultures.

One of the primary strengths of the Chinese obsession with *deng* is that it has made it possible for them to survive in a crowded land that has historically been beset by natural and man-made disasters that would have destroyed a less focused and determined people.

But in keeping with the well-known Chinese acceptance of the duality of nature, the way of *deng* has also had its down-side. Among other things, rote conditioning in the Chinese way made it practically impossible for the Chinese to be flexible and innovative. In Chinese universities, students were taught *what* to think, not *how* to think, severely limiting their potential as innovators for the future.

Locked into a predetermined style and process of doing everything, they became unable to react in a positive, rational manner to new and strange situations and events. Encounters that were outside of the realm of Chinese experience thus led to friction, misunderstandings, chaos and violence.

China's encounter with the advanced industrialized nations over the past three centuries was a greater threat to the survival of Chinese civilization than any other event in the country's long history, and the Chinese are still reeling from the shock.

But the cohesiveness of Chinese culture is so great, and the magnitude of Chinese society is so enormous, that once again they are well on the road to absorbing and Chineseizing this foreign influence, just as they did to the Mongols and Manchus in centuries past.

The big difference today is that China no longer has either the luxury of isolation behind its Great Wall or the centuries of time to absorb the cultures of not one but many powerful outside groups. This presents China with the challenge of dealing with vast numbers of people on a basis that is totally beyond its experience.

In this now endless encounter, both the *yin* and the *yang* of the Chinese tradition of *deng* will be put to the extreme test.

One of the more conspicuous manifestations of the Chinese obsession with order and precise labeling that continues to add a distinctive flavor to life is the custom of naming and numbering virtually all social, economic and political programs and campaigns.

Some of the more interesting ones: *The Four Modernizations* (agriculture, industry, national defense, science and technology); *The Five Pests* (rats, flies, mosquitoes, sparrows, Rightists); *The Four Beauties* (beautiful language, beautiful manners, beautiful heart, beautiful environment); *The Old Fours*—that Mao Zedung ordered the Red Guards to destroy during the Cultural Revolution of 1966–1976 (old ideas, old culture, old customs, old habits); *The Three Highs* (a high salary, an advanced education, and height of over five and a half feet) or what a man needs to get a wife.

Experts say that the influence of the ideograms or characters with which the Chinese write their language is one of the contributing factors in their penchant for formalizing ideas and slogans into absolute concrete numbered terms.

These same experts add that the Chinese language makes it difficult for people to think in abstract terms; that they cannot deal effectively with "if" and "what if" thinking.

This factor accounts for some of the "solid wall" problems foreign businesspeople run into in their dealings with Chinese, particularly bureaucrats.

39

登记

Deng-Ji
(Doong-Jee)

"Signing in at the Door"

The foreign traders, missionaries and others who descended upon China soon after the Industrial Revolution in Europe were not a new experience for the Chinese. Numerous times during the long dynastic history of the country waves of outsiders had sought out the Middle Kingdom for one purpose or another.

The conquest of China by the Communist armies of Mao Zedung, Zhou Enlai, Zhu De, Peng Dehuai, Lin Biao, Deng Xiaoping and other Communist leaders in 1949 was not the first time that China had been captured and subjected to mass destruction and an attempt to convert the people to an alien ideology.

The public executions practiced by the Communists on a massive scale, the public security measures and collective punishment system imposed by the Communists that turned friend against friend and children against parents, were also not new barbarisms invented by the Communists. All had been experienced by the Chinese before, over and over again.

When the Communist regime implemented measures to control communication and relations between the Chinese and foreigners, particularly those resident in the country, it was not something that was new to the Chinese.

The strict sexual puritanism preached by the Communist Party was no more than a continuation of traditional Confucianism.

Thus when the new Communist regime established the *deng-ji* (doong-jee) or *sign in* system to monitor meetings between Chinese and resident foreigners, it was a major inconvenience and represented a serious danger, but it was the kind of thing the Chinese had always lived with.

Prior to the death of PRC founder Mao Zedung, the Communist Party was ruled by paranoia. The slightest hint of resistance or unacceptable conduct was viewed as a major threat to the country and dealt with severely.

Such innocuous things as wearing a piece of Western clothing, especially blue jeans, high heels, or lipstick, or being seen with an English language magazine or book was regarded as a traitorous act calling for arrest, brain-washing and imprisonment at hard labor.

Under the *deng-ji* ruling, gate- and doorkeeper guards were assigned to all hotels, apartment buildings and other locations housing foreigners. All Chinese visiting these locations were required to identify themselves, explain the purpose of their visit, and sign a registration form which thereafter became a permanent part of their personal record maintained by the dreaded Public Security Bureau.

Visiting a foreigner's home or office or being seen in the company of a foreigner in public resulted in instant suspicion, followed by surveillance, and often arrest.

The *deng-ji* system is still used by a variety of universities, hotels, commercial companies, state-run enterprises and offices in China but now it is little more than a standard security measure.

40

Dong Yi Xia
(Doong Ee She-ah)

"Just a Moment, Please"

At any one time a very large percentage of the one billion-plus people of China are standing in line, waiting for something. At a wild guess, the number of services and other facilities in the country are probably able to serve less than ten percent of the needs of the population at the same time.

Competition for existing services, from trains and planes to bathrooms, is intense and sets the tone for much of life in the crowded country. Even the

Great Wall is unable to accommodate all of the visitors who descend upon it, and virtually every day, rain or shine, there are long lines of people waiting to get on the wall and other lines waiting to get off.

Because of this crowding, another of the cultural "code terms" that one hears from a few to a dozen times a day, and must be properly translated to fit the peculiar Chinese setting, is *deng yi xia* (doong ee she-ah), or *just a moment.*

Of course, *deng yi xia* never really means *just a moment,* and in that respect is the same as the English version. In China the big difference is that you hear it more often, you wait more and for longer periods of time, and there is less certainty that you are going to get what you are waiting for. For this reason you often hear a variant on this phrase, *deng yi deng,* or *wait and wait.*

One of the complicating factors for foreigners who stand in line for something in China is that they often want something that is not absolutely routine, which upsets whatever process is going on.

Generally, store clerks or office staff cannot or will not do anything that is out of the ordinary, and automatically come out with *deng yi xia,* following which they may go ask someone else about your question or request. This may result in a discussion or a deadend, during which you remain waiting.

In other cases when the staff cannot take care of you immediately they will ask you to wait while they continue taking care of those who are behind you. This happens when they don't understand what you are talking about, as well as when there is no one else handy for them to consult with.

None of these things are unique to China. But they are generally much more time-consuming and can be much more frustrating because usually no one explains the reason for the delay or can give you any idea of how long the delay will last.

An obvious ploy that many Chinese and experienced foreigners alike use to avoid spending so much time waiting in lines is engaging other people to stand in line for them.

But this generally works well only when the matter at hand is something simple and routine, like buying train tickets (which itself can be a shock to visitors because on some train lines you must buy a separate ticket for each leg of the journey—you can't buy a through ticket even though you are not getting off at any of the interim stops).

Where foreigners are concerned, the language barrier may be part or all of the problem. One way of helping to reduce or eliminate this obstacle is to have someone write out in Chinese exactly what it is you are after, so you can hand it to the staff member when your turn comes.

41

德育

De Yu

(Duh Yuu)

"Moral Education"

While it appears that all societies began with spiritual and secular leadership combined in one person as both chief and chief priest, most societies eventually split these areas into their earthly and heavenly segments. Morality (the Church) went one way, and politics (rulers) went another.

In China, however, this split never occurred because the spiritual side of Chinese life was never separated from their secular life. There was no all-powerful, single god to attract and hold the allegiance of the people.

Instead, there were numerous gods and spirits in an amorphous mass that permeated everything around them—the heavens, oceans, mountains and rivers; the houses they lived in; the food they ate.

Rather than basing their morality on individual responsibility to all-powerful gods, as Westerners did, the Chinese created moral mandates that were far more pragmatic and secular than those of the Christian West.

Christian morality was spiritually oriented and was designed to control the behavior of individuals by the threat of eternal punishment in Hell and the promise of eternal bliss in Heaven, and was embodied in the Church and its religious leaders.

Chinese morality, on the other hand, was designed specifically to maintain social order and guarantee continuity of the existing political system, and was embodied in the lifestyle itself—in the social structure and in all personal relationships within the society.

In pre-modern China, failure to live a "moral" life brought swift and often fatal punishment right then and there—no waiting for some future punishment in Hell.

Because there was no separation between secular life and spiritual life in China, morality was the central theme of all family-based socialization and institutionalized education in China down to the beginning of the Communist regime in 1949.

And, of course, the morality taught in China down through the ages was strictly *Chinese* morality, which gave precedence to the state, the community and the family, instead of the individual. Groupism was moral; individualism was immoral.

In pre-modern China, loyalty and subservience to superiors was morally the right thing to do. People did not have rights that were guaranteed by law or by tradition. They had responsibilities and certain privileges that the state could withdraw at any time. This millennia-long conditioning in groupism and obedience to authority—in so many words, China's traditional morality—was a primary factor in the early successes of communism in China.

Now it is growing repudiation of both Confucian-oriented and communist morality that is helping to transform China, economically, socially and politically.

Still, *de yu* (duh yuu) or *moral education* remains a paramount factor in the education of all Chinese. Only now, it is education that more and more is recognizing the individuality of people and the existence of inalienable human rights.

One of the greatest challenges facing present-day China is continuing to rationalize its *de yu* along with its economy—and in doing so, its emphasis on moral education could well become a role model for other nations, East and West, to follow.

地方保护主义

Difang Baohuzhuyi

(Dee-fahng Bah-oh-huu-chuu-ee)

"The 'Good Old Boys'"

It seems that neither communism nor capitalism can change some things in China, particularly things having to do with regional attitudes and behavior.

Despite the seemingly awesome power of China's Imperial Court down through the ages, the farther away people were from the various dynastic capitals, the more autonomous their beliefs and practices.

Beijing, far to the north and a journey of many days and weeks away from the southern and western portions of China, was only a name to most Chinese during the last thousand-plus years of the long Imperial period.

During this great expanse of time, the central government did not attempt to homogenize the people of China. Even the main core of Han Chinese who lived in distant regions were left more or less alone, speaking their own languages or dialects and carrying on as they had for ages.

The main role of the mandarin magistrates assigned to each district in China was to see that taxes were paid, that community projects were carried out and that peace and stability prevailed.

Because of both geographic and ethnic reasons, all of the well-defined regions of China developed distinctive living styles and strong feelings of loyalty to their own areas.

These feelings of localism, made even more significant by the traditional practice of ancestor worship and subsequent attachment to the place where one's ancestors were buried, led to what the Chinese call *difang baohuzhuyi* (dee-fahng bah-oh-huu-chuu-ee), translated as *local protectionism*.

Difang baohuzhuyi is so strong in many areas of China that local authorities virtually ignore national laws, and favor the interests of local residents and businesses over national interests regardless of the situation.

In legal disputes brought against local people or businesses by outsiders, for example, local courts will delay cases indefinitely or simply refuse to hear them. When they do hear such cases, they invariably favor the local party.

Obviously such behavior is not unique to China, but when foreigners are involved it is especially important that *difang baohuzhuyi* be taken into consideration—preferably before any problems arise.

Because these regions have their own way of doing business that may or may not conform to national laws or practices that are common in other areas, it is essential that foreign businesspeople be aware of any differences going in. Instances where local authorities and courts do not know the national laws are common.

If problems do develop, the foreign side often cannot depend upon either the principles of fairness or impartiality, or what they believe to be the laws of the land. When such disputes do arise it is wise for the foreign side to bring in a mediator or attorney from a higher regional level; from Beijing if possible.

43

点心
Dim Sum (Dian Xin)
(Deem Sum)

"Cute Little Hearts"

The Chinese have learned over the centuries that food comes before morality; that one does whatever is necessary to obtain enough food to survive, and that anything that has any nutritional value and is not poisonous—or can be rendered safe—can be turned into food.

This philosophy has resulted in the Chinese developing one of the world's most varied and extensive cuisines, and becoming masters at producing attractive, tasty dishes out of things that other people would die rather than eat.

All of the larger regions of China have their own styles of cooking and their own preferences for ingredients, but none are as widespread or as well-known around the world as the cuisine of Canton (Guangdong).

One of the most interesting, colorful and satisfying of Cantonese meals is one made up entirely of *dim sum* (deem sum) or *little hearts,* which are miniature fixings of several dozen dishes that range from tiny "custard pies" to meat or vegetable-stuffed buns that have been steam-cooked.

Other common *dim sum* ingredients are crab, shrimp, lotus kernels, bean and nut paste, and chicken.

In larger *dim sum* restaurants employees push wheeled carts bearing a variety of *dim sum* dishes around among the tables, letting diners choose what they want. Each of the servings is on its own dish or in its own little basket, and at the end of a meal, the diner is charged by the number of saucers or baskets he or she has accumulated.

Many people in Hong Kong, Guangzhou and other cities in the province who eat breakfast out also prefer *dim sum*, making *little hearts* restaurants lively and noisy places for all three meals.

A point of special interest to Americans and Europeans in particular is why affluent Chinese can indulge themselves in eating huge meals of food that is obviously rich in calories, and never get fat.

My Chinese friends say it is the tea they drink with their meals. Classier Chinese restaurants may serve jasmine tea, but the "house tea" of run-of-the-mill restaurants and generally also served at home, is oolong (Cantonese), a brown tea that most southern Chinese drink in copious amounts with each meal.

Oolong tea, say the Chinese, bonds with the fat in the foods they eat, and carries the would-be calories out of the body as liquid waste. (Versions of oolong tea have been sold in the U.S. for years under the brand name "Slim Tea.")

A final note: People who like fried bean curd, known as *mapo dofu,* might reflect on what the name really means the next time they are enjoying it: *soya bean cheese of the pock-marked old woman.*

44

第三者

Di San Zhe

(Dee Sahn Chay)

"Introducing Third Parties"

Using go-betweens to help establish relationships and to settle differences in China is an honored tradition that goes back thousands of years.

One of the most important roles of go-betweens over the generations was helping to arrange marriages. Now there is a new twist in the use of bringing in outsiders to resolve marital issues—this time involving the dissolution of marriages.

There is no emotional attachment between many Chinese couples because their marriages were arranged, they were forced by their job assignments to live apart for many years, or any of the other usual reasons why couples cannot get along.

This factor, combined with the new political environment that allows people to reject the traditional Confucian concepts of the sacredness of the family, has resulted in a growing number of couples splitting up.

A significant percentage of divorces in China occur because of *di san zhe* (dee sahn chay) or *third parties*—referring to the men and women who become involved with people who are already married.

Some people seeking divorce "play the third-party card" on purpose to convince their spouses to agree to the split, using the argument that since there is a *di san zhe,* whom they love and want to marry, divorce is the only acceptable solution to the situation.

Chinese sociologists and family research groups say that many young Chinese women who married men of their choice and do not want to get divorced are nevertheless unhappy because of the chauvinistic attitudes of their husbands.

These women complain that their husbands not only expect them to work full time but to also take care of all the home chores. And some say their husbands believe it is their right to beat them if they disobey or displease their husbands.

China's sociologists say this problem cannot be resolved until a younger generation of Chinese males are endoctrinated in the concept of human rights, including sexual equality.

In the meantime, Chinese women in particular will no doubt remain more susceptible than usual to "third-party" relationships as they seek to better their lot.

Not surprisingly, Chinese women who are most apt to divorce selfish and abusive husbands are those who have been directly exposed to Western influence, through education, work experience or both.

45

对不起

Dui Bu Qi
(Doy Buu Chee)

"Sorry About That!"

Most Westerners who are newly arrived in China find the general absence of the concept of privacy, private time, private space or personal belongings, very upsetting; particularly so in the case of sensitive business matters.

Another area of "modern" Chinese behavior that foreigners—and Chinese—find upsetting is the way many people commonly use the term *dui bu qi* (doy buu chee), which means *excuse me,* or *I'm sorry.*

Rather than using *dui bu qi* only in its traditional sense of expressing contriteness, it is now often used as a callous cover for a wide range of self-ish, unfair and sometimes rude conduct that makes a farce of the Chinese reputation for politeness.

As China's traditional restraints on aggressive behavior weaken, a growing number of people are flouting tradition for their own personal convenience with what now amounts to a hollow use of *dui bu qi*.

Among the more conspicuous occasions when *dui bu qi* is used to ostensibly "apologize" for selfish, thoughtless and sometimes unethical behavior is breaking into queues, and showing up at a person's door unexpectedly at inopportune times.

More and more Chinese now complain loudly and vociferously when these incidents take place in public settings and involve strangers. As the traditional cultural conditioning in social harmony continues to weaken, such behavior will no doubt lead to an increase in physical violence.

Chinese say this breach in the traditional standards of etiquette is an aftermath of the Cultural Revolution and other Communist programs that were designed to obliterate everything having to do with "old" China, including ordinary politeness.

They say that during the Cultural Revolution in particular the youth of China were encouraged—and often forced—to be cynical, callous and rude toward adults.

Millions of high school and university students who became members of the notorious Red Guards during the early years of this tumultuous period degenerated to the level of savages in both manners and actions, harassing, torturing and sometimes killing men and women with calculated cruelty.

Most of the survivors of this rampage, both perpetrators and victims, were so numbed by the degree of violence and inhumanity of the Cultural Revolution that they blocked it from their minds as soon as it was over.

But the damage to the Chinese spirit was enormous, and as memories of the pain subsided, people began to come out of their shells and talk about the damage, and what could be done to return a sense of empathy and responsibility to society.

By the early 1990s there was a growing movement to rekindle the kindness and goodwill that was so much a part of the traditional Chinese character by once again emphasizing morality and etiquette in the home and in the educational system.

46

妒嫉

Duji
(Doo-jee)

"Dealing with Envy"

Early Chinese sages recognized that *duji* (doo-jee) or *envy* was one of the strongest and most dangerous of all human characteristics. They also noted that it appeared to be inherent in humans (as it was in other animal species— a product, no doubt, of competition for food and sex).

In any event, the wise men of China eventually came up with a social philosophy designed to keep *duji* at bay in the interest of social and political stability.

But two and a half millennia of Confucianism did not eradicate envy from China. It merely kept it in the closet and resulted in people becoming extraordinarily discreet in displaying it.

Now that the philosophical, social and political sanctions have been lifted, envy, like the long suppressed sexuality of the Chinese, has come to the fore with an often uncontrollable force.

Duji is now said to play a major role in the generally poor communication and cooperation between sections and departments in commercial firms, government agencies and ministries, and between ministries, agencies and companies.

The reason for this inter-departmental and company/agency envy is no longer directly related to food or sex, but it still derives from a sense of competition that precludes willing cooperation between non-group members in virtually any Chinese setting.

This sense of competition is a product of the Confucian-oriented social system that divided society into inclusive groups, beginning with the family, and emphasized groupism to the point that outsiders were automatically regarded as competitors or enemies, not to be trusted, not to be dealt with.

The psychological distance between departments in a company or government agency is so strong that members generally will not contact each other, exchange information, or cooperate in any way, until they have been introduced by a third party and developed a personal relationship.

When the individual a person needs or wants to do some kind of business with is in a totally different agency or company, an intermediary is even more important, and instances when nothing is done until a suitable contact is found are very common.

One of the reasons why foreign companies and individual foreigners so often run into uncooperative people and people who go out of their way to cause problems is basic envy—envy that is magnified by political as well as cultural feelings.

It is difficult for some Chinese to accept the idea that foreigners, whom they often regard as undeserving, can have so much while they have so little.

About the only way to neutralize this kind of *duji* is to dress modestly (not poorly, but conservatively) and speak and behave in a humble manner.

47

Fa

(Faah)

"Looking Into a Mirror"

It was not until competition from Japan, Korea and the other Confucian tigers of Southeast Asia had already scuttled several segments of American industry, and were threatening the viability of virtually every other industrial category in the country, that U.S. businesspeople in the 1970s and '80s began to take stock of their own corporate cultures.

American managers were aware that they had policies and ways of doing things before the threat from Asia captured their attention. But they did not fully comprehend the nature, the strengths, or the weaknesses of their own management systems. It had simply never occurred to them to take a rational, holistic look at themselves, their markets—or the new breed of Asian competitors they faced.

Some 2,500 years ago China's famed military strategist Sun Tzu made a big to-do about the axiomatic truism that an army or any other organization is only as strong as its weakest link—a fact of life that was as well known in the West as it was in the East.

But this simple bit of wisdom has traditionally been downplayed or ignored by most military, political and business leaders, and still today gets the attention it deserves only when doom looms on the horizon.

Japan, Korea and the other tigers of Asia owe much of their economic prowess to their ability to understand the nature of their own organizations and make the most of them—a concept and practice that Sun Tzu labeled *fa* (faah), which means something like *doctrine* on the surface, but also incorporates the idea of *law* in the sense of being guidelines for behavior.

In Sun Tzu's usage, *fa* refers to analyzing all of the internal factors of an organization in order to make sure each part—equipment, supplies, transportation, personnel, etc.—is up to par, and then devising strategies to utilize the organization effectively.

China is still handicapped in its attempts to adapt the insights of Sun Tzu to the commercial challenges and opportunities of today because of centuries of oppressive, negative conditioning of its people, and by ongoing restrictive policies of the government.

But the wisdom, motivation and energy are there, progress is being made, and there is every reason to believe that these so far mostly unused assets will help return China to its former position as the mother of all tigers.

Americans and others who have not yet recognized the importance of *fa* or learned how to use it to bring out the best in their efforts may end up as their predecessors did—making regular pilgrimages to Beijing to pay homage and seek favors from the new Middle Kingdom.

法律

Falu
(Fah-luu)

"Virtue Versus Law"

Confucius, the great rule-maker himself, did not believe in rule by law. In one of his most famous statements he said: "Attempting to rule people by laws that require them to act the same leads to resentment and disobedience of the laws and to feel no shame. If people are ruled by virtue and guided by ritual they will have a sense of shame and behave themselves."

During the long Imperial dynasties, most of China's *falu* (fah-luu) or "laws" were not codified, and were open to interpretation by local magistrates and mandarins as they saw things according to their understanding of Confucianism and historical precedents. Justice was made even more arbitrary because these magistrates were detective, judge and jury all rolled into one.

Absolute laws, with their clearcut black and white divisions between what is right and what is wrong, what is acceptable and what is not acceptable, were incompatible with the personalized nature of relationships, obligations and duties in Chinese society.

The Chinese were not protected by law. Their only protection was in conforming to the roles prescribed for their social class, sex, age and position.

The Chinese social system called for absolute role-playing within a rigid hierarchy; first within the family, then within the community and finally within the nation. The sanctions used to enforce conformity to the prescribed role were despotic in nature. The more any misbehavior was seen as a threat to the system, the more severe the punishment for deviating from the set norm.

Historical records show that the punishment for something as mundane as striking a superior, especially a parent or senior member of a family, was often like something out of the most degenerate kind of horror movie.

Punishment, deliberately designed to strike fear in the hearts of others, was carried out in public and didn't stop with the individual directly concerned. A common practice was to have the accused skinned alive. In extreme cases, the closest kin were also killed by skinning, the next closest kin beheaded, the third circle of relatives hanged, and the forth circle beaten with bamboo staves and exiled.

In some cases, close neighbors were also executed or beaten and exiled.

Penal law in Imperial China generally applied only to peasants, however. Torture was routinely used to obtain confessions. Torture methods included hanging by the hands and then whipping with strips of bamboo, and squeezing in wooden screw presses.

It was more or less assumed that higher class people need not be subject to penal law because it was believed that they would naturally behave well, obeying all of the etiquette and rituals of the Chinese way without the threat of punishment hanging over their heads.

Men who had passed the lowest level of civil service examinations held regularly by government authorities were also exempt from being physically tortured if arrested on any charge. They also did not have to contribute their labor to public projects.

Punishment in dynastic China was invariably harsh, but conviction did not always mean execution or imprisonment. Those adjudged guilty could buy their freedom with gifts or money, with the value determined by the nature of the charge or crime. In cases where freedom could not be bought, a regular flow of gifts to guards, jailors and sometimes magistrates as well would buy more lenient treatment.

Law and order in the last decades of Imperial China and the early decades of Communist China primarily meant killing the leaders of the opposition and imprisoning their followers. Authorities used spies to identify those who were against them, promised their victims leniency, then executed them.

While constantly reassuring the people they had nothing to fear, the government ruled by fear. The Communist regime, in particular, was a textbook case of George Orwell's *1984,* with its thought-control and brainwashing techniques that included both mental and physical torture.

From 1949 until 1980 the government of China primarily ruled by directives, not formal civil or criminal codes, resulting in officials becoming arrogant and dictatorial. Whatever top officials said, or were said to have said, often became new directives that were arbitrarily enforced in some instances and ignored in others.

In this setting, the only way innocent people could get justice was through bribery. Confessions were regarded as necessary to convict suspects, and those arrested were routinely tortured until they confessed.

As has traditionally been the case in China, local officials still today frequently ignore national laws, or are not aware of them in the first place. This harks back to the days when the Imperial Court and its agencies routinely kept some laws secret on the theory that the people would be more circumspect in their behavior if they were not aware of laws they might be breaking.

Foreigners resident in China and visiting there must be especially cautious in their comments and behavior because laws, real and imagined, are often used by unscrupulous officials to gain commercial advantages, and to punish people who refuse to cooperate with them.

Any comment or action that can be construed as critical of the state can be declared a crime, and the "guilty" person can be punished—severely, when the government wants to use the occasion as a warning.

One ploy regularly used to squelch critics of the government or the Party is to charge them with being enemies of the people, or, "counter-revolutionaries"—a charge that no one beats.

Some Chinese say that the government has repeatedly been guilty of entrapping people by announcing that it was all right to criticize the Communist Party and the government, and then arresting and imprisoning those who revealed themselves as dissidents.

Because the tradition of using laws to protect people is still young and weak in China it is important for people, and especially for businesspeople, both Chinese and foreign, to have strong political connections—i.e. godfathers—who can be called in to act on their behalf when they run into obstacles or are falsely accused of something.

Some foreigners with substantial experience in China say that establishing and nurturing relationships with godfather figures—usually powerful officials—should be the first step for anyone wanting to do business there.

Just one example of the *falu* pitfalls that can trip one up in China: a great deal of the information that is considered, and handled, as public in Western countries is treated as a state secret in China, and penalties for asking about it or revealing it can be harsh.

There are two kinds of crime in China: wrongdoing and political "crimes." And in the Chinese system, an accused person is considered guilty until proven innocent. At this writing, the accused are not allowed to have legal assistance until one to three days before trial, and in some courts attorneys are not allowed to enter a not guilty plea on behalf of defendants. These courts generally limit the role of attorneys to pleading for leniency, and there is no right of appeal.

Chinese law forbids people from exercising any freedom or right that infringes on the interests "of the state, of society, and of the collective"—and it is left up to courts and Communist Party officials to decide what contravenes this law.

Another key factor in law enforcement in China are the various methods of social control, including personal identification cards, personal records kept on people by their schools and work organizations, and the surveillance systems in residential neighborhoods and work places, which make it very difficult for anyone being sought by the law to hide out for any length of time.

At the beginning of the Great Proletariat Cultural Revolution (1966–1976) all law schools were closed, their libraries destroyed, and faculty members and students were sentenced to hard labor on farms, in construction camps and factories. In 1979 the Ministry of Justice was re-established, law schools were reopened, and some of the surviving faculty members were returned to their former positions.

But lawyers and judges are viewed as representatives of the government, not the accused, and are expected to uphold the so-called Four Cardinal Principles of the Communist Party (adhering to socialism, the dictatorship of the Party, the leadership of the Party, and the thought of Marx, Lenin and Mao).

China's legal system is basically an arm of the Communist Party and is used by the CCP to maintain its power and to pursue its goals. Judges, and in a somewhat lesser sense lawyers as well, are expected to protect the government from the people.

Especially during anti-crime campaigns and campaigns against political enemies, the laws are routinely ignored by the courts. Rounding up and sentencing hundreds of thousands of people to prison is known in Mao jargon as "mass-line" justice.

The people's attitude toward the law is expressed in a well-known saying, *You fa buyi, zhi fa bu yan, wei fa bu jiu! (We have law but no obedience; we have violations of law but no investigations!)*

Because of these factors, the Chinese have traditionally preferred mediation to settle disputes, and there are mediation committees throughout the country. It is estimated that well over half of all civil cases filed in China are resolved through mediation.

Given the cultural background of China, in combination with Communist ideology, it is unlikely that law in China will ever be anything more than a distant cousin of Western law.

番

Fan
(Fahn)

"The Family Clan"

Family-related clans were a basic social organization in China long before the beginning of recorded history, and continue to have importance today.

As the population grew and society became more complex, the primary role of the clans expanded from protecting family members from outside threats to enhancing social, educational, economic and political prospects of the extended family—all things for which they could not depend upon the government.

Clans that became successful and wealthy, usually as government officials and landowners, made up the elite of the country and generally were able to perpetuate themselves as the permanent well-to-do class.

It was these family clans that provided the artisans, poets and philosophers for which China has long been famous, and it was the richer families in this group that created the style of refined, elegant living for which upper-class Chinese have been equally renowned.

Throughout China's history, including during the recent Communist-led revolution that resulted in the People's Republic of China (PRC) being established in 1949, lineage organizations played significant roles in towns and villages, providing various kinds of support for community members and dominating the politics of the areas.

Fan (fahn) refers to the traditional five-generation family group that was the historical heart of China's lineage organizations, some of which persist today in mainland China as well as among overseas Chinese. (In the Chinatown communities of New York, San Francisco, Vancouver and other magnets for Chinese immigrants, clan "associations" help members with finances, social issues, legal and other advice.) This is the basic Chinese clan, in which all members are known to each other and form an identifiable network.

China's family clans suffered grievously from the various policies and programs of the Chinese Communist Party from 1949 until well up into the 1980s, especially its forced labor programs that broke individual families up by shipping husbands and wives to widely separated areas, putting children into permanent care centers, and imprisoning millions of men and women who were considered "enemies of the people"—meaning almost everybody in the middle class and above.

As part of its campaign to force people to totally break with old customs and traditions, the CCP also ordered the hundreds of thousands of clan or lineage associations in the country to disband, then banned them altogether.

How extended and how active present-day *fan* are in networking for social and professional purposes depends upon the individual group—its location, its background and its overall economic situation. Many of the lineage groups have re-established ties to varying degrees, but in most cases there are no longer five generations in the groups.

The PRC's policy of limiting families to one child, inaugurated in the 1970s, will have an equally profound effect on the long-term survival of the country's famous clans.

━━━━━━━━━━━━━━━━━〈 50 〉━━━━━━━━━━━━━━━━━

发烧友

Fashaoyou

(Fah-shah-oh-yuu)

"Hot Friends"

When Mao Zedung and his Communist Party took power in 1949 and introduced programs designed to gradually break down the traditional attitudes, values and behavior of the Chinese, the long-dead Confucius must have begun turning in his grave.

During the 1966–1976 Cultural Revolution, when Mao attempted to totally eliminate all aspects of traditionalism from Chinese culture by brute force, Confucius's slow turn surely became a fast spin.

But by the early 1980s, most of the young urban people of China were out of the Confucian bottle and adopting new patterns of social behavior that would bring more changes to China in one decade than had previously occurred in a thousand years.

In addition to dating and pre-marital sex, millions of young Chinese came under the influence of popular commercial music, television shows and films—something that no doubt caused the spirit of Confucius to disintegrate altogether and whirl off into space at warp speed.

Young Chinese first became fans of pop musicians and film stars from Hong Kong, Taiwan and Japan. This gave rise to home-grown stars and to *fashaoyou* (fah-shah-oh-yuu) or *rabid fans,* the likes of which had never before been seen in China.

Very much like their counterparts in the United States, Japan and elsewhere, this new breed of Chinese fans became obsessed with their favorite stars, spending a significant percentage of their income and free time in pursuing this very un–Chinese-like interest.

During the first years of this extraordinary phenomenon China's official news media routinely castigated the behavior of the *fashaoyou,* and warned that such "spiritual pollution" was unacceptable in the People's Republic of China.

But once the genie was out of the bottle it expanded like air, and there was no putting it back in. Now, instead of music in China being used to instill a very conservative morality and etiquette as Confucius intended, it has become a medium for spreading social diversity and extreme kinds of behavior that contribute to chaos rather than harmony.

The appearance of *fashaoyou* in China is one of the most conspicuous signs of change in Chinese culture, and despite the negative influence of protest and rebel music, it may do more to spread democracy in the country than more formal and official attempts.

In June 1989 one of the key figures involved in the Tiananmen Square occupation was Hou De Jian, a rock star who was among the first Chinese "cult" figures.

51

非官方

Feiguanfang

(Fay-e-gwahn-fahng)

"No-Man's-Land"

All political ideologists have their own jargon and put their own spin on the meaning of ordinary words. But few have ever gone as far as the Communists in their efforts to befuddle and seduce friends and enemies alike.

And among the Communists none were more imaginative or more prolific than the Chinese Communists in creating new combinations of words, and giving old words and phrases new meanings.

The Chinese Communist practice of changing the meaning and use of words and phrases was not just a ploy to confuse people. Because it was a way of thinking and behaving that the average person could not understand or cope with, they used it as a sinister and malicious tool to deliberately entrap people.

Fortunately, the failure of communism in China has greatly diminished the use of "Communist-speak," but enough remains that it continues to be a serious problem, particular for those who encounter this kind of intellectual manipulation for the first time.

One of the facets of ongoing Chinese Communist Party (CCP) thinking that is especially difficult for Westerners to understand, and is often the source of friction, is contained in the word *feiguanfang* (fay-e-gwahn-fahng), which means *unofficial.*

In the CCP context, *feiguanfang* refers to any idea or concept that is not approved by the government, and therefore by definition is regarded as *buzhengtong* or *unorthodox,* which has the further connotation of being *deviant* and thus taboo.

This uniquely Chinese version of these concepts makes it difficult or impossible to have free and open discussions or debates about ideas or programs that have not received the CCP stamp of approval.

Suggesting to a Chinese contact that you are interested in an "unofficial" relationship means a lot more than a relationship that would not be publicly acknowledged or legally binding. Generally speaking, it means you are proposing something that is anti-government and could have serious repercussions.

This problem is compounded by the custom of the CCP to make vague pronouncements and pass vague laws, and to systematically deny positions and/or policies when they first come to the attention of the public.

Part of the democratic movement in China is to change the political environment to the point that *feiguanfang* ideas, no matter what the subject, are not considered deviant or punishable behavior, and are legitimate topics for discussion.

Until this concept is firmly established and backed up by both law and tradition, it will no doubt continue to be dangerous to speak out too publicly and boldly about ideas that the CCP can construe as a threat to its image and power.

52

飞书

Fei Shu

(Fay-ee Shuu)

"China's 'Flying Books'"

Book publishing has been an important industry in China for more than 2,000 years. China's first history book, written by hand by a man named Sima Qian around 100 B.C., covered a period of 3,000 years, and consisted of more than half a million Chinese characters.

Publishing with moveable type was invented in China around A.D. 1000, and within a century there were numerous private libraries.

Probably the largest book the world has ever seen was published in China in the early 1700s. This was the *Gu Jin Tu Shu Ji Cheng* or *Complete Collection of Illustrations and Writings from the Earliest to Current Times.* The book had 800,000 pages, and covered history, geography, literature, natural sciences and politics.

Another huge publishing project undertaken a short time later was a 36,000-volume anthology of the classics, philosophical works, literature and histories published up to that time.

Unfortunately, most of the books published in pre-modern China were in a classical language that ordinary people could not read, were considered inappropriate reading material for non-scholars, or were severely controlled or banned for other reasons, ranging from sexual content to matters that were considered dangerous to national security.

Just like the Imperial dynasties, a significant part of the Chinese Communist Party's early attempts to control thinking was based on controlling and limiting what could be published.

This censorship program resulted in a revival of the traditional Chinese custom of people surreptitiously hand-copying articles, short stories and novels that were prohibited, and secretly circulating them hand-to-hand.

Hand-copied books, or *shou-chao ben,* were especially popular during the 10-year Cultural Revolution (1966–1976), when everything except hard-line orthodox Communist-Socialist literature was totally banned.

The most popular of the *shou-chao ben* included detective stories, spy novels, books on magic, books with pornographic themes and stories about beautiful women who used their sexuality to get ahead—all subjects that were supposed to be outside the range of interest of true believers.

Other subject matter included criticism of the government and its leaders, personal stories, poetry and religious beliefs.

Producing a hand-copied publication in China during this period was a serious and dangerous undertaking. Copiers had to steal the paper from their own work unit or from some other office or company, and do the copying in secret. According to stories that abound, most of the copying was done at night by flashlight beneath bed covers.

Copying larger works was a laborious undertaking, resulting in longer books being divided up among several people.

Finished copies were bound with string and then passed from one person to another, sometimes within small, closed groups and sometimes to larger groups. When books were circulated only among smaller groups they normally were returned to the copier or chief copier after a period of time.

Some *shou-chao ben* were so popular, however, that they took off and became *fei shu* (fay-ee shuu) or *flying books* that never made it back to their original source. Some *flying books* are known to have traveled the length and breadth of China.

Perry Link, one of the editors of *Unofficial China—Popular Culture and Thought in the People's Republic* (Westview), recounts that author Zhang Yang, recopied his original story, "The Second Hand-Shake," seven times. Zhang, Link adds, was finally arrested as a counterrevolutionary and sent to prison where he contracted tuberculosis and pleurisy and nearly died.

Hand-copied books included original work, titles published before the revolution, translations of foreign books, and condensations of existing materials.

After the end of the Cultural Revolution and the partial opening of China to Western trade in 1978, the appearance of tape recorders provided a much simpler, faster and safer process for publishing banned material. But tape recorders remained relatively rare for many years, and *shou-chao ben* continued to flourish.

Perry Link notes that when Zhang's "The Second Hand-Shake" was finally printed by an underground press in 1979 it sold 3.3 million copies within a few months and was later turned into a radio drama and cartoon strip, and was produced as a movie and a stage play.

The heyday of China's *flying books* has passed, but the dissemination of information in China is still controlled to the extent that people must depend upon unofficial "people" channels for much of the news about what is really going on in the country.

See **Xiaodao Xiaoxi.**

53

Feng
(Fung)

"Your Cup Runs Over"

One of the human weaknesses recognized by China's great *I Ching* or *Book of Changes* is the propensity for people to let success go to their heads, to forget how they achieved success in the first place, especially who helped them, and to become unable to cope with any diminishing of their exalted status.

I Ching points out that people who allow material wealth and power to take possession of them invariably become proud; lose touch with their family, friends and associates; and become isolated—forfeiting those very things that in the end are the only ones that really count.

Coping with success, say the ancient sages of China, includes understanding and accepting the fact that achieving any pinnacle of achievement, expressed in the term *feng* (fung), meaning *zenith* or *abundance,* also contains within it the seeds of decline, since there is always a limit to the heights that one can reach and the length of time one can stay at the top.

Feng denotes the highest peak of success and power, in whatever field, and infers that the point is something like a sexual climax. Trying to sustain this highest possible state of sensual pleasure inevitably results in failure.

The *Book of Changes* acknowledges that the clever person may temporarily lengthen the period of *feng* by expanding his or her perspective and activities, but warns that this can lead to aberrations in behavior, sensory overload and loss of the ability to enjoy the normal pleasures of life—much like a sadist who can no longer be satisfied by normal sex.

A superior person, continues the *Book of Changes,* will not be concerned about the decline that follows *feng,* and will not take a chance on losing his or her balance by trying to transcend its natural limits. Rather he or she will utilize the growth period to build a solid foundation of love and respect among his or her family, friends and co-workers so that when the inevitable decline in strength and skills begins he or she will not be left alone.

Further, *I Ching* adds, the brief period of *feng* itself should be used as a time for achieving inner awareness; to come to terms with your own true nature and relationship to the cosmos so that the rest of your life may be lived in serenity, regardless of your material wealth or political power.

Some of the additional common sense advice offered by the creators of *I Ching* to help people achieve as well as live with success includes seeking the company of people who have similar interests and goals; soliciting the opinions and counsel of others; remaining truthful and sincere, and being patient.

As always, the philosophy behind the concept of *feng* is that all things are cyclical, and that people must learn to live with the ups and downs of life, remaining true to themselves. The Chinese are usually adept at dealing with *feng* because their social world is generally limited to their family group.

风水

Feng Shui
(Fung Shuu-ee)

"The Dragon's Breath"

Early Chinese believed there was a spiritual as well as a magnetic connection between everything in nature, and for nature to work "right" there had to be harmony between these energy forces.

In this concept, all physical things—hills, mountains, valleys, bodies of water, manmade structures and so on—influenced the ebb and flow as well as the positive or negative effect of the earth's magnetic force fields and their spiritual components.

This belief first led the Chinese to develop guidelines for the location of propitious burial sites for the dead to make sure their spirits were in harmony with nature. As time passed, they began using the same guidelines to select the sites and orientation of buildings and other structures, and plotting the layouts of their fields.

Eventually, this science of geomancy came to be known as *feng shui* (fung shuu-ee) or *wind-water* because of the relevance of these two things to agriculture.

Belief in the power of *feng shui* to play a positive or negative role in the affairs of people is still strong in China, including very international and cosmopolitan Hong Kong, as well as in Vancouver, where practically no building of any consequence has been built in recent years without the guidance of a geomancer.

The imposing 47-story Hong Kong and Shanghai Bank building in Hong Kong is one of the more impressive examples of the ongoing power of *feng shui*. After the architects had completed their drawings for the building, a geomancer was called in to review the plans. He recommended a number of dramatic changes in the design that were duly made, resulting in a very conspicuous improvement in the appearance as well as the user-friendliness of the building.

There are numerous examples in Hong Kong and elsewhere in China of buildings having been constructed without reference to their *feng shui* correctness, and the owner-tenants thereafter having nothing but bad luck in their business. Finally, after calling in a geomancer and following his instructions in reorienting the door (always a key point) and/or making other changes, they thereafter enjoyed significant success.

According to Chinese beliefs, the *feng shui* correctness of a building affects not only the actions of the people who use the building but their physical and mental health as well—a concept that Westerners finally began to pick up on in the 1980s.

In fact, more and more Western architects and builders are beginning to publicly agree that there is something to *feng shui*. During a visit to Hong Kong, Michael Sudarskis, secretary-general of the International Urban Development Association, said, "*Feng shui* is based on very sound cultural principles—accommodating man and nature by balancing natural and manmade environments."

Sudarskis added, "The Chinese have a cultural instinct for how to organize space in living communities. As far as we know, the world's first 'masterplanned' community was in China."

In Chinese terms, the first challenge to the *feng shui* expert is to determine which way the *qi* (chee) or *cosmic breath of the dragon* flows—which is determined by the rise and fall of the land and anything else that would alter its direction of movement. Hills are regarded as the bodies of dragons—and one place you *don't* want to build is on the eye of the dragon.

The purpose of *feng shui* is to court favorable influences and defend against bad influences by making sure that the wind and water are channeled in the right direction.

Each room in a building and the building itself also has *qi* and it is therefore important to make sure that all doors face in the direction that prevents the entry of "bad breath," invites the entry of "good breath," and then keeps it from flowing out.

The *qi* of a room determines where and how the furniture should be arranged.

To determine the flow of *qi,* geomancers use a compass that locates the magnetic north in conjunction with sixty-four lines and thirty inner circles drawn on a circular wooden or copper plate. The more buildings or other obstacles there are in the area being measured for *qi,* the larger the compass needs to be. Chinese geomancers note that since the whole cosmos is in a constant state of flux (also something Western science has picked up on), the orientation of *qi* is not fixed. It experiences a minor change every twenty years and a major change every sixty years.

Not surprisingly, there are some *feng shui* experts who are unscrupulous, and will use their knowledge of the power of the dragon's breath to bring bad luck to people—if they are paid a sufficient fee.

Most Western people have experienced the breath of the dragon without being aware of what it was. The next time you are in the lobby of a building or in front of a building and everything about it—the landscaping, the direction the building faces, the architecture, everything—just "feels" right and good, you are basking in the breath of the dragon.

(If you are interested in a detailed discussion of *feng shui* as it relates to business, I recommend *Feng Shui for Business,* by Sinologist Evelyn Lip, Times Books International, Singapore, Kuala Lumpur.)

55

Fenpei
(Fun-pay-ee)

"The Assignment System"

Shortly after the Chinese Communist Party achieved power in 1949 the new government prohibited all private enterprise and grouped the entire nation into rural cooperatives and communes, and urban *danwei* or *work units* (business enterprises, government ministries and agencies, etc.).

One of the key aspects of this program was the *fenpei* (fun-pay-ee) or *assignment system*, under which the CCP controlled all job-placement, food, housing and other key essentials. Local officials were responsible for assigning jobs and housing, and passing out food coupons to families according to their perceived needs.

Eventually, job-placement was confined to college graduates. Those who did not go beyond elementary school and high school were responsible for finding their own jobs.

Under the *fenpei* system, companies and organizations that wanted to hire new employees submitted employee requisitions to the political cadre assigned to them. These requisitions were then forwarded upward to the national level where officials consolidated them, prepared "quotas" based on the total number of requisitions, then sent them back down to regional and local "neighborhood committees" for implementation.

These neighborhood committees made the actual job assignments—and more often than not who got what job was determined by personal connections and the bestowing of gifts on committee members.

In universities, job assignments were made by Party officials assigned to each of the university departments (as opposed to neighborhood committees). These Party officials were free to dole the available jobs out as they saw fit, and typically they did so in ways designed to benefit themselves.

Another key factor in the *fenpei* system was that political reliability took precedence over professional qualifications. In fact, those in professions relating to foreign expertise or foreign technology were routinely discriminated against because having such knowledge made them suspect.

Maintaining good personal relations, on every level of the system, also took precedence over ability and productivity.

Said one Chinese critic of the system, "Rationality and professionalism often play absolutely no role in the staffing of companies or offices, or in their management. It is an elaborate game of looking out for one's self, family, friends and connections, and staying out of trouble with the Party."

Because the number of more desirable jobs was always far below the demand, the *fenpei* system resulted in rampant intrigue and intense jealousy that further hampered the effectiveness of the organizations and work units.

The majority of China's intellectuals saw the *fenpei* system was one of the greatest detriments to the rapid modernization of the country, but they generally dared not criticize it for fear of losing their own jobs, being blacklisted, and ending up in a hard-labor prison factory or on a prison farm.

By the early 1990s the job-assignment system had begun to show cracks. State-run enterprises continued to pile up enormous losses each year, both because of over-employment and because the enterprises had little control over the qualifications of the people assigned to them.

In 1994 Chinese Communist Party leaders began taking steps toward establishing a free labor market, giving employers the right to fire unneeded and incompetent workers, and giving workers the right to change jobs on their own.

The job-assignment system has not disappeared from China, and probably will not in the foreseeable future. But it is gradually being rationalized to function more like Western style employment agencies and executive headhunters.

Food distribution is no longer a government monopoly under the *fenpei* system, but housing is still controlled and allocated through a government housing authority.

56

佛教

Fojiao

(Foe-jee-ah-oh)

"The Appeal of Buddhism"

Fojiao (foe-jee-ah-oh) or Buddhism came from India to China very late in the history of the country—some time around 100 B.C.—well over five hundred years after the founders of Confucianism and Daoism. And it was another five hundred years or so before it had become fully Chineseized and seeped into the culture.

In its Chinese incarnation, Buddhism taught that people should strive to achieve nirvana by eliminating all ego and all selfish desires and becoming one with the cosmos—a process described as enlightenment, or the ability to recognize the fundamental reality in all things and merge one's self with that reality.

Not content with sitting under a tree and waiting for enlightenment to just happen (as it did to the founder of the religion), later adherents developed a number of meditative techniques to institutionalize the process.

One of these approaches, developed by an Indian monk named Bodhidharma and brought to China around A.D. 500, was labeled *Chan (Zen* in Japanese) Buddhism. *Chan* is a Sanskrit word meaning *meditation*. (Bodhidharma is famous for having meditated for nine years facing a wall— during which he is said to have become so sensitive to his surroundings that he could hear ants communicating with each other.)

While Buddhism started out in India as a very human philosophy of sub-limating one's ego and selfish desires, thereby becoming saint-like, in China it gradually absorbed some of the tenets of Daoism, Confucianism and animism that permeated Chinese culture, becoming more spiritual and mystical.

Because the Chinese had practically no control over their Confucian-oriented external lives, the egoless, selfless inner world of Buddhism was an intellectual as well as a spiritual refuge that was especially appealing to them. And because it was more specific and structured than Daoism, it was more fulfilling to their emotional and spiritual needs.

Chinese Buddhism taught that the soul is eternal and is reincarnated in a cycle of life and death until it accumulates enough merit in successive life-times to achieve nirvana, putting an end to the cycle.

Part of this belief includes a Purgatory (*Diyu*) where people go after death and are judged by their character and deeds in life. In Purgatory each person must go through 10 "courts," the first of which is the Mirror of Retribution, in which all of one's earthly actions are reflected.

The first "court" determines the degree of punishment for each soul. From there the soul goes from one court or level to the next until it is cleansed and ready for reincarnation. Before it is reborn, however, the soul sips a special kind of tea that erases all memory of its past life so that it starts out fresh.

Buddhists revere Sakyamuni (Gautama) Buddha himself, and a variety of famous disciples, including kings and the famous Five Hundred Saints (dis-ciples who achieved nirvana and became buddhas) with supernatural powers.

In addition to its spiritual influence, *fojiao* also had a profound practical effect on Chinese architecture, painting, printing, and literature, becoming the genesis for new forms and new styles that were to permeate the culture and give it the distinctive look that has since been associated with China and things Chinese.

Fojiao thus became a lifestyle rather than a religious belief. It was not a matter of consciously expressing a belief in Buddhism or "joining" the Buddhist church. The beliefs and rituals that were central to Buddhism were an integral, indivisible part of Chinese culture, just as were Confucianism and Daoism.

Buddhism was thus absorbed naturally, along with all of the other beliefs and customs making up the spiritual as well as the secular world of the Chinese.

Confucianism and Daoism provided the Chinese with their ethics and morality. Animism and Buddhism provided them with their spiritual connection to the cosmos.

Unlike Christianity and Islam, Buddhism was not an exclusive God-driven, aggressive cult, and therefore did not create friction, engender violence, or compel the Chinese to engage in proselytizing wars or missions to convert others to Buddhism.

57

Fu

(Fuu)

"It's About Time"

One of the most consistent themes in Chinese philosophy and guidelines for daily behavior is the importance of understanding one's own nature and being true to it. This view holds that many of the things that occur in one's life that are believed to be random are in fact the result of forces that the individual sets in motion.

The complementary aspect of this viewpoint is that the only way you can get the maximum amount of joy out of life is to accept some of the more negative events that occur as something you can't do anything about—as part of your fate—learn from them, and try to do better the next time.

And there is always a next time in the Chinese scheme of things—at least until you pass on to the spirit world—because a key part of the Chinese cosmology is that everything, including human life, occurs in cycles.

Because life is a series of cycles, there must necessarily be a series of beginnings and endings, each of which is an important time for improving the quality of one's life.

Chinese cosmology gives the most emphasis to *fu* (fuu), or *returning*, meaning to return from an old cycle to begin a new one—which incorporates the concept that each cycle is a complete journey within itself.

Among the challenges people face in staying in harmony with these cycles is to recognize when an old one is ending and a new one beginning.

Both are important but if you do not recognize that a cycle is ending, many or most of the decisions that you make are likely to be wrong.

According to Chinese beliefs, the time of the ending of an old cycle and the beginning of a new one is when you should take stock of your values, attitudes and behavior, and change them if you are unhappy in your relationships and work.

Because of the coming and going of cycles, *fu* is generally looked upon as having a positive nature—as offering you another opportunity to get your life in order. But it often happens that the positive aspects of *fu* cannot be rushed. If there is any resistance from any quarter about the changes you resolve to make, *fu* will be served best if you are patient and let things evolve on their own.

The *Book of Changes* notes that the cycles in human life range from emotional relationships with others, financial problems, and employment problems to illnesses; with each having its own nature and calling for its own response. Whatever the cycle, there is a reason which the individual concerned must decipher.

People who are unable to read the messages revealed in the cycles of their lives are often doomed to relive the bad ones.

Belief in *fu* is one of the things that has provided the Chinese with the fortitude to recover from one disaster after the other.

58

Fu

(Fuu)

"Shades of Chinese Truth"

Early Westerners who visited China for commercial or religious purposes frequently reported, some with a great deal of vehement frustration, that the Chinese were among the world's greatest liars—that they lied about big and small things, that they lied when it was obvious that they were telling an untruth, and that they lied even when there was no advantage, real or imagined, in lying.

These outsiders, and many visitors since, were encountering a kind of cultural behavior with which they had had no experience, and which was totally irrational by their standards.

Of course, this is not to suggest that Westerners, including those involved in cultural encounters with China, do not lie or have never lied. What we are describing is a circumstance, common to Confucian-oriented cultures, that is so far from the experience of most Westerners that it shocks them.

The ideogram that the Chinese use to write *fu* (fuu) or *truth* gives some indication of the nature of the concept in the world of China. The character depicts a bird sitting on its eggs or its young, concealing them from view. This very clearly states that it is up to the viewer to discern what the truth is by his or her knowledge or by intuition.

The kind of knowledge inferred by this pictogram relates not only to factors pertaining to the matter at hand, but also to the great stock of cultural knowledge to which all Chinese are privy. In other words, the viewer is expected to know enough that he or she can provide his or her own answer and not need to ask questions in the first place.

The intuitive factor in this situation relates to what I call cultural telepathy. The person seeking the truth is expected to be so tuned into the circumstances, cultural and otherwise, that the truth comes to him or her out of the cultural ether (which, of course, leaves virtually all foreigners out since this ether is "Chinese").

In other words, down deep the Chinese do not believe they are obligated to provide people with any kind of information, or to reveal to others things that are hidden. It is simply not their responsibility; that belongs to someone or some office higher up—if to anyone. And so they profess not to know.

This deeply embedded circumstantial treatment of the truth no doubt evolved over the centuries during which it was exceedingly dangerous for the Chinese to get involved in anything outside of their immediate, personal sphere, and even more dangerous to provide information that might be in error or displeasing, or regarded by someone in power as confidential.

Throughout most of the history of China virtually every piece of information or statistic, from the weather to population figures or the incidence of diseases or crimes, was regarded by the government as a state secret which was not to be revealed to foreigners.

The draconian role of this official position was made worse because deciding on what was a secret was often left up to local authorities, who had virtually unlimited authority to arrest and punish people.

This ancient custom of trying to prevent foreigners from learning about China has not yet disappeared, and the truth still tends to be circumstantial, so much so that it is often necessary to use trusted Chinese go-betweens to get at the real *fu*. See **Tifa**.

59

福

Fu
(fuu)

"Dreaming of Happiness"

There is a famous Chinese saying that *shiwu* or *food* is heaven to a peasant, a stark reminder that throughout most of China's history the spector of starvation was a constant companion to the majority of the people.

So compelling was the threat of hunger that the Chinese used the symbols of a cultivated field and a mouth integrated with heaven, representing a full stomach, to mean *fu* (fuu), or *happiness*.

Today the ideogram for happiness is one of the most popular "good luck charms" in the country, and is familiar to patrons of Chinese restaurants around the world.

The role that food plays in Chinese life is one of the most conspicuous and important aspects of their culture, and one that can be fully enjoyed by outsiders as well after only a few minutes of orientation.

A Chinese meal served and eaten Chinese style is a tableau of the culture in action, graphically depicting the hierarchical order within the family or the group, the etiquette that controls their behavior, and the substance of their relationships.

The typical Chinese meal eaten in a restaurant—and the Chinese love to eat out—is an even more dramatic representation of Chinese culture. Evening meals in particular are typically banquet style, a thanksgiving for the food and a celebration of family ties and the bonds of friendship.

Unlike some Western cultures that require people to eat quietly and quickly, when a typical Chinese family or group eats out it is a noisy, lengthy affair, brimming with the hubbub of humor and ribaldry.

To the Chinese, the banquet table is more than just a convenient meeting place for a meal. It is the place where they confirm their cultural identity and just as important if not more so, enjoy *fu* and their Chineseness to the fullest.

It is around the informal banquet table that the Chinese let their formal hair down, nurture the bonds of old relationships, and make new ones. The informal banquet table is thus a doorway—the only easily accessible doorway—to the inner circle of Chinese life.

Outsiders wanting to establish close relationships with Chinese, for whatever purpose, must eventually enter this "doorway to happiness."

Demonstrating awareness of Chinese style banquet etiquette and its importance in establishing personal relationships is a key step in doing business with the Chinese.

It therefore behooves foreigners who want to do business in China to study up on not only the etiquette of Chinese dining but also on the *yin-yang* principles that determine the order in which the Chinese eat the various dishes that make up a meal.

Chinese take a great deal of pride in their knowledge of food, and are especially impressed when others share their enthusiasm.

福利

Fuli

(Fuu-lee)

"Cradle to Grave Welfare"

When the Chinese Communist Party took over the country in 1949 one of its avowed goals was to guarantee that everyone who could and needed to work would have a job—a policy that was referred to as "the iron rice bowl."

This vision was part of the overall CCP concept of destroying all of the class and occupation lines in China, and turning the entire population into one huge family that ate from the same wok.

In the rural areas all adults, men and women, were first assigned to cooperatives, and then these work groups were consolidated into huge communes. In urban areas, men and women were assigned to state-run enterprises and agencies.

At first, people were mostly "paid" in kind, receiving whatever amount of goods and services the local Communist cadre presumed was sufficient for their survival. Later, slightly larger amounts of money was added to the payment received by urban workers. (The discrepancy between the average pay of a city worker and that of a farm laborer accounts for a great deal of the tension between urban and rural populations today.)

The goal of the government was to provide every individual with *fuli* (fuu-lee) or *cradle-to-grave welfare*. In theory, no one would ever be out of a job or go without food or have to do without the vital services necessary to sustain a viable livelihood.

Following the establishment of the People's Republic of China, two generations of Chinese were raised on the concept of *fuli*. It made no difference what they did, or how well or how badly they did it, their share of the national wok was guaranteed—in theory.

But as history has proven time and again, communism and socialism do not work on a scale any larger than a few dozen families, much less in a nation populated by over one billion people.

In the case of China the inherent defects in the *fuli* concept were exacerbated enormously by the irrational economic programs introduced by CCP Chairman Mao Zedung, particularly his attempt to convert millions of peasants into steel makers in a matter of months in his so-called Great Leap Forward.

The scale of the subsequent failure of government-sponsored *fuli* in China was in direct proportion to the size of the population. In rural areas that were the most adversely affected by the Great Leap Forward, millions died; other millions suffered grievously.

But despite the fact that the CCP failed to deliver on the promise of *fuli*, or "happiness and fulfillment," millions of Chinese, particularly urban workers, nevertheless came to believe in and depend upon the doctrine.

It was not until the introduction of limited free-market principles into China in the late 1970s and 1980s that a few million lucky Chinese got a chance to compare the CCP's *fuli* welfare system with anything else.

As economic freedom spreads in China, the day should come when the Chinese can provide their own *fuli*.

61

妇女问题

Funu Wenti
(Fuu-nuu Wun-tee)

"The Woman Problem"

Mao Zedung, of all people, recognized that China would never be able to throw off the shackles of the past, especially the limitations imposed by Confucianism, until it resolved its *funu wenti* (fuu-nuu wun-tee) or *woman problem*.

From the beginning of Chinese civilization until 1950, women in China were generally treated as the property of men, and were used and abused according to male needs and whims. Records of women who escaped this domination are rare—but they do include a few instances of female bandit leaders, warlords and generals.

The plight of China's millions of pre-modern peasant women was likened to that of "frogs in wells." Most of them lived and died without ever having gone more than a few kilometers from their birthplace, and their only journey away from home was often to a nearby village to get married.

As early as the Ming Dynasty (1368–1644), a number of China's better known male writers began advocating education for women and other changes in their social status—pointing out that China could not become a modern nation as long as women were held in virtual bondage, and that emancipating women would greatly enhance the quality of life throughout Chinese society.

But this first public recognition of the plight of women in China had no positive results. Generations later several noted writers in the following Qing Dynasty (1644–1912) picked up on the same theme. Between 1895 and 1910 a number of revolutionary-minded women were among the Chinese who flocked to Japan to study. Some of these young women gained national but short-lived prominence upon their return to China.

Other young Chinese women formed alliances to support each other in unbinding their feet and seeking education. The heroes of these young women were Joan of Arc, Florence Nightingale and other noted Western women, since they had no Chinese female role models.

Still, as late as 1909 there were only 13,000 girls throughout China enrolled in schools. And as late as the 1920s many girls were still being forced to bind their feet, so powerful was this ancient custom. Westerners visiting China in the 1960s reported seeing women with bound feet working in the fields, precariously balancing themselves on the stubs of their heels. Arranged marriages were also still the norm.

Oddly enough, it was Mao, the great Communist revolutionary himself, who became the first champion of women in China with the power to do something about his beliefs.

Long before the Communists took power in China, Mao had identified himself as a dedicated feminist, railing against treating women as property, keeping them in servitude, and forcing them to marry against their will.

In 1950, the year following the Communist takeover of China, Mao backed the "Marriage Law of 1950," which prohibited arranged marriages, concubinage, foot-binding and child marriages; limited doweries that could be paid for brides, and made divorce easier.

About the only portion of this law that was strictly obeyed, however, was the prohibition against foot-binding, which had not been widely practiced since the last years of the Qing Dynasty (1644–1912). But the law marked the beginning of emancipation for Chinese women.

Continuing discrimination against women, particularly in the home, resulted in a revision of the marriage law in 1981. The new law stated that women were to be treated as equals in the home, that husbands as well as wives were responsible for taking care of aged parents, and that a breakdown in relations between husbands and wives was sufficient grounds for divorce.

But this new law has not resolved China's *funu wenti* or *woman problem*. Cultural beliefs and customs that go back for some five thousand years are not easy to erase. Chinese women still shoulder most of the burden of housekeeping, child-raising and caring for aged parents, and virtually all of them work outside the home as well.

As in most societies around the world, discrimination against women in China is also still common in schools and in workplaces. There are fewer opportunities for women, they are paid less, and are routinely subjected to various forms of sexual harassment.

Also as in other countries, Chinese women will surely have to emancipate themselves by more aggressively resisting discrimination and fighting for their rights—and in this battle they have an advantage.

Most foreigners who are intimately familiar with China say that Chinese women are stronger willed, often more intelligent, and generally more flexible and ambitious than Chinese men, and that given the smallest opportunity to better their situation they will seize it with extraordinary tenacity.

62

复杂

Fuza

(Fuu-zah)

"Don't Complicate My Life!"

In China what you see, or think you see, might be described as "virtual reality" rather than reality itself, because what you see is often not what you get.

Throughout Chinese history there has been an often invisible but very real wall separating life into two dimensions—one that took place out in public, so to speak, and another that took place in private, behind the public facade.

This division was not a matter of modesty or personal privacy. It was the manifestation of a split-level morality that condoned one set of ethics for "public" or "official" use, and a second set for the real world.

China's segmented public/private morality was spawned and kept alive by its authoritarian, bureaucratic government, which denied the existence of human rights and created a system in which both officials and the people had to resort to subterfuges of all kinds to survive.

One of the results of this system was that people were forced to become skilled at avoiding responsibility, which also led them to be wary of taking on any kind of new obligation, no matter how minor or innocuous it might appear to be.

Among the many ploys commonly used to avoid getting involved in new situations was the use of the term *fuza* (fuu-zah) as a put-off or turn-down.

Fuza literally means *complicated*. When used in response to a proposition or request for some action, the inference is "Because whatever it is you are talking about is complicated, it can't be done or I can't do it."

Fuza is still one of the most commonly used phrases in China, and as such amounts to a significant barrier in getting things done. Its use is often a totally transparent excuse for not making any effort at all to serve a guest or potential customer, and is the kind of thing that drives some foreigners up the wall. Government employees are probably the biggest users of *fuza*, but it is also commonly used by workers in service companies—most often, it seems, by people charged with responding to questions and problems of people who walk in from the street.

Fuza is also a common response given to questions, propositions or whatever instead of a straight "no" when there is legitimate reason for a negative reaction. This is especially frustrating to foreigners who want to know "why" the response is negative.

Another of the most frustrating uses of *fuza* is when someone asks to see the person in charge. In this case, it means he or she is out or has told the staff to tell you he or she is out; the staff doesn't approve of you; the staff believes/knows that if the person in charge sees you it will add to their work or their problems, and so on.

It often seems that if there is one overriding rule in China, notwithstanding the reputation the Chinese have for harmonious relationships, it is to make everything as complicated as possible.

This is another one of the many cultural paradoxes that are common in China, and that foreigners have to learn to live with.

63

负责人员

Fuze Ren Yuan

(Fuu-tsuh Rune Yuu-enn)

"Finding the Right Person"

In the typical Chinese company or organizational environment, responsibilities of individuals are as precisely delineated as their seniority and their place in the overall social hierarchy.

This sometimes obsessive attention to categorizing and ranking people and things is part of the fundamental fabric of Chinese culture—everybody and everything has its place, its use, and in the case of people, their exact roles and responsibilities.

Because of this culturally conditioned compulsion to structure everything and everybody, the Chinese, over the centuries, developed standardized ways of thinking and doing things. There is a precise way—and this is often a uniquely Chinese way—of doing virtually everything, whether lounging in a park, folding a towel, or eating food.

While the formal structure of Chinese society provides for an extraordinary degree of order and predictability—which are essential to survival in a densely populated community—the system also has a serious downside.

When the person in a government office or company or any other unit who is in charge of the function you need is busy or absent, generally speaking no one else will or can help you. This greatly extends the amount of time it takes to accomplish things in China, and in the case of foreigners who are not used to the system, adds to the frustration level.

The system is also used as a ploy by people who are present but want to avoid doing things for one reason or another—and is a favorite technique of government bureaucrats. Using this gambit, they can delay projects or other activities for indefinite lengths of time, often killing them altogether.

When deliberate absenteeism is suspected, about the only possibly effective recourse is to go through a connection in the same organization who is in a position senior to the offender, and get him or her to come to your aid. An outsider who has clout with that particular company or organization can also be helpful in such situations.

If you do not have any influence you can bring to bear on the individual or unit concerned, you are at a serious disadvantage and may not be able to do anything until you develop such a connection.

Another aspect of the structuring within Chinese society is the practice of putting a specific individual in charge of the various pieces of equipment in offices, factories, and so on—a responsibility that most of the individuals take quite seriously because there are strict sanctions if something happens to the equipment.

It is generally necessary to get permission from the *fuze ren yuan* (fuu-tsuh rune yuu-enn) or "responsible person" before any particular piece of equipment can be used.

This is another situation where the security and responsible use of equipment is greatly enhanced, but at the same time it also frequently presents a problem. When the *fuze ren yuan* is not available, generally no one else will or can authorize the use of "his" or "her" equipment.

Getting on the bad side of a *fuze ren yuan* can be worse than not being able to find them. If for some reason a "responsible person" gets down on someone, that individual is likely to find that the fax, copying machine or reference manual that he or she wants to use is busy or not working.

This means that it is essential for everyone in an office or with access to an office to have good connections with the reigning *fuze ren yuan*.

See **Guanxi**.

64

干部

Ganbu

(Gahn-buu)

"The Party People"

China's formidable national bureaucracy is said to date from 221 B.C. when the country was unified under the Imperial system. During the Sui Dynasty (A.D. 581–618) it became the practice to select all government officials on the basis of extremely rigorous national civil service examinations that matched them against the best in the country.

During the first centuries these examinations were held annually in the capital. But as the population and the bureaucracy grew, regional exams were also instituted.

Once would-be scholar-bureaucrats had passed the required examinations, they were appointed government officials, judges and tax collectors all-in-one, and were served by a cadre of petty officers who acted as administrators and enforcement agents (police in modern-day terms).

Over the centuries, officials in charge of larger districts and more influential posts eventually began running them more or less as their own fiefs, virtually usurping Imperial power. As time passed and the bureaucratic system was extended to the far reaches of the empire, many of the emperors and their highest ministers were little more than figureheads.

Over the ages the bureaucrats supported the Imperial system no matter how corrupt or inept it was because it was the source of their legitimacy and they would do nothing to jeopardize their elite positions.

In the way of bureaucracies everywhere, Chinese officials created numerous overlapping regulations, resulting in the need for massive amounts of documentation and more bureaucrats, a legacy that has been passed on full-blown to present-day China.

Ganbu (gahn-buu), the term now used for *cadre* or *bureaucrat*, originally referred to people who did not do manual labor, and had the authority to tell others what to do. Eventually, and in an ironic twist of pragmatism that has often characterized Chinese behavior despite their lack of freedom, it came to mean government workers in general, and, in more recent times, especially those in the lower ranks.

Now, *ganbu* is also used in reference to white-collar workers and to managers or leaders in general.

The national examinations for government service were eliminated in 1905, shortly before the end of the Qing (Ching) Dynasty in the fall of 1911. In the 1980s a number of government agencies began holding their own civil service exams because of a significant drop in the quality of government employees.

However, the status of Chinese officials today remains lower than it has probably ever been in history, and with good reason. A significant percentage of all officials on practically every level routinely use their offices for their own personal benefit—in ways and to degrees that would have been beyond the imagination of their mandarin predecessors.

Contemporary native critics of China's Confucian-oriented *ganbu* culture say that as a whole the Chinese do not know how to handle authority on a rational, equitable basis because of their conditioning in authoritarianism. Some compare it to giving power to children. They inevitably end up abusing it.

More unscrupulous *ganbu* officials, particularly those in outlying provinces, are frequently denounced for using their control of enforcement agencies to falsely accuse people of wrongdoing, arrest them and then demand bribes as the condition for release.

It is now common for government authorities to publicly admit that corrupt officials use their power to embezzle, blackmail, demand bribes—even as small as cigarettes, alcohol or candies—and pursue private interests.

Even more so now than in the past, the bureaucratic system of China breeds corruption. There is virtually no possibility that the problem can be significantly improved, much less eliminated, until the system itself is dramatically changed.

At the same time, most of China's bureaucrats continue to take it for granted that they can and should control the lives of people down to the smallest detail.

Ganbu is now synonymous with white-collar worker, government employee, or leader in any category of employment.

See **Kaoshi**.

65

干劲

Ganjin

(Gahn-jeen)

"The New Can-Do Breed"

China has always had its burglars, bandits, and warlords—singular groups of people who had the courage to defy the authorities, and the wit and skills to survive on their own.

These social outcasts and maverick generals were, in fact, about the only classes of people in pre-modern China who acted on their own and took personal responsibility for their behavior, no matter how reprehensible they might have been.

For generations on end the mass of ordinary Chinese functioned as cogs in cells, following precise forms of behavior that had been created ages ago. With limited exceptions, the society of China did not tolerate personal initiative or innovation by its members.

About the only use of human imagination in pre-modern China was by poets, philosophers and a few inventors, whose activities did not directly threaten the authorities or alter the livelihood of the people at large.

In many respects, the traditional environment of China was something like that of a huge colony of bees in which the survival and welfare of the queen bee and her attendants took precedence over everything else.

Despite enormous changes in Chinese society since the downfall of the Qing (Ching) Dynasty in 1911–1912 and the beginning of the end of the Communist regime in the 1970s, enough of the beehive nature of Chinese society remains today that it is readily visible.

But there is no longer just one hive, and members are no longer absolutely bound to the same colony.

By the mid-1990s there was a totally new sound in the air of China; a buzzing sound of frenetic activity by people who were free for the first time in the history of the country to use their imaginations, talents and energy to create something on their own, for themselves.

This new breed of Chinese is often described as having *ganjin* (gahn-jeen), which means *strength, energy*—in the sense of having both the ability and courage to do something well enough that one can earn a living at it, and in a growing number of instances become rich.

The concept of large numbers of individuals having the courage and the technical or managerial ability to survive as independent entrepreneurs or by hiring themselves out as skilled professionals is so new to China that the word *ganjin* was created to describe them.

Given the several million examples of the courage and ability of overseas Chinese to survive and prosper in mostly hostile environments, the appearance of dozens of millions of *ganjin* Chinese in China proper conjures up visions of a resurgent Middle Kingdom that is awesome to behold.

In any event, the more Chinese there are with *ganjin* the greater their influence will be in unshackling China from the feudalism and authoritarianism of the past.

66

高考

Gao Kao
(Gah-oh Kah-oh)

"The Great Divide"

Most of China's young people still live in rural areas, and most of them attend school for only nine years—from the age of six through fourteen. Those who continue their education beyond this point take municipal or regional examinations for entry into three-year high schools. Exam results generally determine what kind of high school they enter—college preparatory, secondary professional, or vocational.

Students wishing to enter college must take and pass the very difficult *gao kao* (gah-oh kah-oh) examinations, which last for three days. These tests in effect separate the young people of China into two profoundly distinctive categories. Those who fail to pass the *gao kao* tests are more or less permanently locked into what might be characterized as the blue collar class, while those who pass the tests are virtually guaranteed white collar status.

Like virtually everything else in China, the political aspect of education is often more important than the academic element. Schools are charged with the responsibility of teaching students discipline, morality, culture, a devotion to diligence and hard work, physical fitness, and politically correct thinking.

All schools and departments within schools have full-time Communist Party "secretaries," *danwei shuji* (dahn-way shuh-jee), who are responsible for seeing that the Party line is taught. The authority of Party secretaries generally takes precedence over that of academic administrators.

Each school class in China also has one or more political agents (*tuan wei*) who review all study materials (to make sure they are politically correct) and monitor the behavior of both students and teachers. Any "wrong thinking" or misconduct is reported to higher political authorities for disciplinary action.

This system of thought control is endlessly frustrating to the majority of the young people of China. In addition to a dehumanizing effect on their character and personality, it diminishes their ambition to study and to take responsibility for their own lives. Those who are more susceptible to the government Party line become the ones who help keep the system alive.

Naturally enough, those who are the most dedicated to following the Party line are the ones who generally go on to become officials in the various government bureaus, and are the ones with whom both other Chinese and foreign residents and visitors must deal in conducting personal and business affairs.

Chinese critics of the politicization of education say that China will not be able to achieve anywhere near its economic potential until the system of Party secretaries and political agents in schools is abolished. For it is only then, they add, that the qualifying process provided by the *gao kao* will be the most effective in benefitting China.

It is possible, however, that educational emphasis on morality, discipline, culture and hard work, regardless of the source of the motivation, will turn out to be the best for China.

67

革

Ge

(Koe)

"Keeping Your Balance"

China's philosophers and scientists were among the first people to recognize that change is the only constant in the universe, that nothing stays the same. Yet for more than three thousand years the Chinese people were subjected to a succession of governments that were based on keeping things as nearly the same as possible.

One Imperial dynasty after the other sought to preempt any kind of conflict, which might lead to change, through a hierarchical system of rigid political, economic and social control that managed to keep the country in a kind of time warp for century after century.

But because the suppression of all conflict in human affairs is virtually impossible, particularly in social systems where most human rights are denied, *ge* (koe), or *changing*, remained an ever-present threat to China's dynasties, bringing each of them down in turn.

China's sages also recognized that most people fear change because they do not know how it will affect their future and they suspect the worst. And those who are in power fear change even more because they do not want to lose their privileged positions.

In present-day China, *ge*, which is another word for *revolution*, has the upper hand because for the first time in the history of the country most of it is bubbling up from the bottom in a way and at a time when the government is no longer powerful enough to prevent it from spreading.

Most of the advice given by Chinese philosophers on how to contend with *ge* is directed toward the individual, not governments, because in their day and time that would have been treason and resulted in the death penalty.

In the famous *I Ching* or *Book of Changes* itself *ge* is forty-ninth in the key elements pertaining to human affairs, obviously in recognition of the difficulty of dealing with change.

However, *ge* recognizes that change is absolutely essential to avoid stagnation and degeneration—something that is especially inevitable in the case of governments, commercial enterprises and other types of organizations—and provides guidelines for contending with this need.

Ge guidelines begin with carefully analyzing the situation to confirm that changes are needed. Or, if they are already going on, to see that they are going in the right direction, are carefully regulated, and are gradual enough that negative and destructive consequences can be avoided.

In conjunction with such regulated changes, the sages further advise that old things and old ways that are no longer compatible or productive should be discarded.

Also as always, the sages warn that those who take the lead in bringing about dramatic changes must first see to their own character and motives, make sure they have the interests of others at heart, and are not acting out of illusions or delusions that will result in more harm than good.

Some of the guidelines of *ge*, particularly those having to do with making sure that changes are controlled and gradual, have been readily visible in most of the changes the Chinese government has ordered since the takeover by the Communists in 1949.

But the guidelines that call for unselfishness and high moral standards have been just as conspicuously missing from many of the government's actions—often with disasterous results.

Foreigners involved with China must quickly become experts at dealing with *ge*, not only in terms of laws but also in day-to-day practices, because very little stays the same for very long.

68

Gen

(Guhn)

"Eyes on the Road"

Most people automatically presume that it is possible to "still the mind"—not think about anything; have no specific conscious thoughts—for minutes if not hours. But a noted Japanese Zen priest once astounded his novice disciples by stating that the longest he had ever been able to keep his mind blank was one second.

Other evidence that has been accumulated over the centuries indicates that most of the time even the most disciplined mind is a kaleidoscope of jumbled thoughts that continue even when we are asleep.

Zen priests of Japan, who adapted the practice of religious meditation from China, developed techniques for focusing on a single object or single sound for extended periods of time as a way of strengthening control over the mind and making it possible to concentrate more effectively on subjects and challenges.

These techniques were used by Japan's samurai warriors to improve their skills with the sword, as well as by master garden designers to give them deeper insights into the metaphysical content of their designs.

While the practice of Zen meditation originated in China, there was another older, more common, practice known as *gen* (guhn) or *meditation (keeping still)*, that had broader applications.

Gen basically means stilling the mind to the point that you can focus objectively on your innermost desires and needs as well as on your surroundings and immediate situation. It is primarily a technique for narrowing the focus of one's thoughts down to the essence of what is uppermost in importance at the time.

The ongoing objective of *gen* is to achieve and maintain inner peace and become "centered" in all of one's thoughts. This entails calming the mind and conquering the ego so that your thoughts and subsequent actions are pure and unrestrained.

Chinese sages point out that most of the personal difficulties encountered by people are caused by prejudices and ego which embroil them in one irrational situation after the other, and prevent them from coming to terms with reality.

They advise that these unsettling forces can be eliminated through cleansing the mind with *gen*, which not only renews and invigorates the mind but also refreshes the body as well, thereby putting the whole being in harmony with the cosmos.

The Chinese recognize that stilling the mind (which generally also means ridding it of destructive thoughts) is a difficult thing to do, and that in the first stage of this process achieving a degree of objectivity is usually the best that one can expect.

At this low-end level, the sages continue, attempts to apply objectivity to fast-moving events can fail, and the best one can hope for is to maintain composure while continuing to pursue the power that eventually comes from being centered.

Additional efforts, however, lead to transcending the ego, self-mastery, and the ability to influence people well beyond the immediate circle of your family, friends and co-workers.

The concept of *gen* is built into Chinese culture. Everybody uses it to varying degrees; mostly without having to consciously will the action. Outsiders involved with China can enhance their relationships with the Chinese—and improve their mental and physical health at the same time—by participating in *gen* exercises.

69

个人主义

Gerenzhuyi

(Guh-rune-chuu-ee)

"Immoral Individualism"

Confucius once said that people the world over are pretty much the same, and that it is only their learning that makes them different. The great sage was obviously emphasizing what human beings have in common as a way of dismissing both racial and cultural prejudices.

But this intellectual wisdom does not diminish the power or importance of the learned differences that do, in fact, dramatically distinguish races, cultures and societies—even communities within societies.

All Han Chinese are basically the products of the same culture and share many fundamental beliefs and customs. But China is not a single, homogenous society. It is made up of hundreds of regional and district societies in which the people are different enough that they can readily tell each other apart and regard each other with long-standing prejudices that are powerful enough to influence the country socially, economically and politically.

One of the facets of Chinese culture that has traditionally made the Chinese even more different from Americans and most other Westerners is their concept of self—of how they distinguish themselves from others and how this concept influences their attitudes and behavior.

Most of this cultural factor can be explained in terms of individualism— or in the case of Chinese society, the lack of individualism, because individualism was traditionally taboo in China.

The Chinese word for individualism, *gerenzhuyi* (guh-rune-chuu-ee), itself graphically illustrates the traditional response of the Chinese to the

111

concept. Literally, *gerenzhuyi* means *one-person doctrine*, which in Chinese terms refers to "selfish" and "immoral" behavior.

While encouraging and rewarding individualism has been the primary theme of Western child-raising and education for centuries, it was just the opposite in China. The heart and soul of Chinese society was based on group consciousness and group behavior. Individualism was a sin against society, and was severely punished.

Despite dramatic changes in China in the past century, it is still normal for most Chinese to be repelled by overt displays of individualism, and generally to regard such behavior as disrupting and unprincipled.

Westerners, whose individualistic behavior and expectations are just as subconsciously programmed, should be especially sensitive to this cultural difference in all of their dealings with China.

While there are a growing number of individual-minded Chinese, they must still live within a group-oriented society.

个体户

Getihu
(Guh-tee-huu)

"Grand New Tradition"

Communist Party attempts from 1949 to 1976 to totally homogenize all Chinese by eliminating differences between farmers, manual laborers and white collar workers cost millions of lives, caused indescribable suffering to hundreds of millions, and failed miserably.

Finally admitting this failure in 1978, the CCP authorized farmers to engage in "side occupations" to increase food production, and began allowing residents of towns and cities to operate private businesses.

These new businesses were designated *getihu* (guh-tee-huu), which literally means *individual households*, but is more appropriately translated as *urban private entrepreneurs*. *Getihu* were officially limited to members of a family and up to seven non-family employees.

Supreme leader Deng Xiaoping, a strong proponent of *getihu,* put the final touch on this new approach to economic revival by announcing in the early 1980s that it was not only permissible but "glorious" for individual Chinese to become rich—an announcement that was one of the most momentous occasions in modern Chinese history.

This new government policy broke with over four thousand years of tradition and set the stage for a new kind of revolution—a revolution by the people for the people, that had the blessings of the supreme power in the land.

By unleashing the pent-up ambitions and frustrations of millions of talented people, Deng was unwittingly placing the final straw on the back of China's old social and political systems, guaranteeing that their days were numbered.

The new government-backed policy not only encouraged families and individuals to become *getihu*, it also took the brakes off of private entrepreneurship within the government itself. Thousands of government offices and agencies across the country that had not already gone into commercial business quickly entered the fray.

These moves were so successful—there were over 14 million *getihu* employing over 26 million people by 1988—that the government created a new category of private business called *siren qiye* or *private enterprises*, which were authorized to have more than eight non-family employees. The upper limit for employees depended on the kind of business and the personal decision of local government officials.

Both *getihu* and *siren qiye* enterprises have since continued to boom and now account for a significant percentage of the total economic output of the country.

But the transformation of China into a *getihu* paradise is far from complete, and is causing problems and pains for which there is no practical remedy and which will simply have to dissipate on their own over the next two or three generations.

Getting a license to become a *getihu* is not that easy. Would-be entrepreneurs must not have a job, quit whatever job they may have, or take an indefinite leave and continue to pay benefit dues to their former employer to maintain their benefits and seniority in case they fail as private entrepreneurs and have to return to salaried employment.

Applicants for *getihu* licenses must also take either a written test or give a practical demonstration of their skill involved in the trade they want to enter—a requirement that resulted in the appearance of numerous training schools in a variety of skills.

Not surprisingly, the largest percentage of *getihu* is made up of people who could not get a regular salaried position after leaving school, former political prisoners (who number in the millions), and people who were "sent down" to work in rural areas and have returned to cities. There is also a growing number who are quitting their regular jobs to take a chance on their own.

Hundreds of thousands of "Forced Job Placement" workers transformed themselves into *getihu* entrepreneurs when they were released from labor camps—mostly because there were no jobs available, or companies wouldn't hire them because of their prison records.

The problems of the *getihu* are many but the most frustrating is probably ongoing hassling by government cadre assigned to oversee their activities. These officials are empowered to tax the entrepreneurs, to fine them for alleged wrongdoing, and to collect a variety of administrative fees—all of which lend themselves to being abused.

In addition, *getihu* must pay protection money to Public Security Bureau officials and make regular donations to schools, parks, care of the elderly, and so on. They must also depend on state enterprises for most of their supplies, which means they are vulnerable to being squeezed by bureaucrats who use their positions to extract bribes of one kind or another.

Some entrepreneurs try to register as collectives or cooperatives in order to reduce the amount of taxes they have to pay, reduce their vulnerability to being gouged by unscrupulous bureaucrats, and the possibility that they will be raided by government agents seeking speculators and contraband goods.

Throughout their long history the Chinese were conditioned to believe that making money for the sake of getting rich and living high on the dragon was immoral. Today, many of the millions of Chinese who are unable to go into business for themselves, and are consumed by jealousy and resentment, still feel that way.

These people regularly rile against entrepreneurs, accusing them of being unscrupulous, greedy, and *un-Chinese*. Some of this reaction derives from the ancient cultural beliefs. Part of it is a hold-over from Marxist-Leninist propaganda that was pumped into the population for more than half a century.

Much of the criticism heaped upon China's entrepreneurial businessmen and businesswomen is deserved. The "bitter sea" of China continues to breed corruption and immorality, and the ranks of this new class of people is rife with those who do whatever it takes for them to succeed.

Some of the strongest resentment is aimed at government officials who take advantage of their positions and authority to engage in private enterprises. Individuals who join the Communist Party in order to use Party connections within the government to further their commercial ambitions are accused of suffering from the "red eye disease."

The entrepreneurial turmoil that is now convulsing China will probably never make even the majority of the people rich, but it will surely add to their freedom of choice and standard of living.

The concept of private entrepreneurship contradicts both Confucianism and Communism, and is therefore having a revolutionary impact on Chinese traditionalism as well as on the Communist-Socialist philosophy espoused by the government.

Getihu and *siren qiye* are rapidly undermining virtually everything the Chinese Communist Party holds dear, and whether or not the CCP allows them to continue will determine the future of China and impact the rest of the world as well.

71

共产党

Gongchan Dang
(Goong-chahn Dahng)

"Rise and Fall of the CCP"

Although the communization of the government of China did not occur until 1949, the process began with the success of the Bolshevik Revolution in Russia in 1917.

When the Communists took power in Russia in 1917, Dr. Sun Yat-Sen, the famous Chinese revolutionary who had helped bring down the Qing Dynasty and install nominal constitutional government in China in 1912, sent a congratulatory note to Lenin.

Dr. Sun and a small number of Chinese intellectuals saw the overthrow of the Russian Czar and the crushing of the elite class that had ruled the peasantry of Russia with an iron hand for centuries as analogous to social conditions in China.

These intellectuals began talking and writing about the lessons China could learn from the new Soviet Union. Marxist study groups were formed. Articles advocating Marxism for China began appearing in widely read publications.

The new Soviet government announced that one of its primary goals was to help free China from the yoke of foreign domination, and that it was unilaterally cancelling all of the unequal treaties that had been forced on China by the Czarist government.

More and more young Chinese students, intellectuals and revolutionaries who had helped topple the Qing Dynasty began joining the Marxist study groups. One of these young intellectuals was Mao Zedung who was too poor to attend university, and worked as a clerk in a Beijing library. He had previously worked as a laundryman and later was to become a teacher.

An older intellectual, Li Dazhao, became the leading proponent of remolding Marxism to fit the needs of China, which was rife with corruption, and suffering from a devastating cycle of famines and depredations by warlords and foreign powers.

Students at Beijing University began spreading Li's message to the countryside. In March 1919, Lenin established the Third International of the Communist Party (the Comintern) to foster social revolutions in other countries. He had already sent Comintern agents to Beijing to begin the groundwork for setting up a Chinese Communist Party.

On May 4, 1919, some 3,000 Chinese students gathered in Tiananmen Square and, displaying five resolutions they had created calling for the repudiation of unequal treaties with foreign powers and other reforms, marched on the foreign-legation quarter. This incident, in which British troops fired on the students, killing several of them, became famous as the "May Fourth Movement."

From this point on, the Communist movement in China grew. Some students went to Moscow to learn more about the Russian experience. Others, including Zhou Enlai, who had been a leader of the May Fourth Movement, and Deng Xiaoping, went to Paris to learn about the French Revolution.

The first meeting of the *Gongchan Dang* (goong-chahn dahng), the Chinese Communist Party (CCP), was held in Shanghai in July 1921. Mao Zedung, the young teacher who had established a Communist cell in Hunan and become known as a writer, editor and leader of labor groups, was invited to attend the new party's first plenary meeting and was appointed a member of the Central Committee.

Mao was 24 when he published his first essay in 1917, and thereafter became a prolific writer. His first article, "A Study of Physical Education," was published in the popular journal *New Youth*. In the article Mao exhorted the Chinese to change from being "passive, grave and calm," to being "rude, aggressive and savage"—a portent of what was to come.

The following year, 1922, the party still had only around 200 members, but their ranks were joined by some of the new Communist recruits who had been in Paris. Soviet agents continued to play a leading role in the growth of the fledgling party.

In the meantime, Dr. Sun Yat-sen had restored his National People's Party (*Guo Min Dang*), which he had disbanded in 1919, to coordinate his fight against the other forces contending for power in China. One of the rising stars in the *Guo Min Dang* was Chiang Kai-shek, a young military officer.

The *Guo Min Dang* and the new Communist Party, with the urging of the notorious Soviet agent Borodin, joined forces in their efforts to control the government. Sun Yat-sen died in 1925, leaving much of the country in the hands of warlords.

Nationalist armies under Chiang Kai-shek and the Communists finally joined forces in an attempt to defeat the larger warlords and unify the country.

But the alliance between the Nationalists and Communists was short-lived because both groups were determined to become the supreme power in the land. Strikes, riots and rebellions plagued the country. Revolutionary groups began attacking foreign legations and foreign holdings. The Japanese continued pressing for advantages and encroaching on Chinese interests from Manchuria.

Chiang Kai-shek used force to extort money from wealthy businessmen to maintain his armies. There was fighting and disorder all over the country.

In the meantime, Mao Zedung was having his own problems. In 1927 he was kicked off the CCP Central Committee because of the failure of his troops in battle, but he was apparently too busy in the field to even learn about the committee's action.

As the struggles of the Nationalists, Communists and warlords continued, Mao was pushed further into the hinterlands and began more and more to depend on the peasants in the areas where his military forces were paramount. It was this experience that led him to develop his own ideas of how to win over the peasants and use them to achieve his goals.

Among other things he prohibited arranged marriages, stopped the selling and buying of brides, made it simple for couples to get divorced, and encouraged women to be active outside the home.

Between 1927 and 1934 Mao and other Communist generals consolidated their positions in rural areas of southern and western China. Chiang Kai-shek, with the aid of the United States, continued his war against the Communists and warlords, as well as against the Japanese, whose encroachment on China turned into an armed invasion on January 29, 1932, when they launched a land, air and sea attack on Shanghai.

Little by little the fighting with Japan grew into a major conflict (full-scale war with Japan broke out in July 1937). Meanwhile, Chiang Kai-shek also continued his campaign to destroy the Communist leaders and their armies. To avoid being trapped by the Nationalist forces, Mao, Zhou Enlai, Lin

Biao and other Communist generals led their forces from Jiangxi to Shaanxi Province on what was to go down in history as the "Long March."

This huge column of some 80,000 men and a number of women left Jiangxi on October 16, 1934 and reached Shaanxi on October 25, 1935, after having spent 370 days trekking almost 6,000 miles over some of the roughest terrain imaginable, including wild rivers and high, snow-covered mountains. Fewer than 10,000 of the original group survived the march.

The war with Japan worsened, and it seemed as if the whole of China would be captured by the marauding Japanese. This resulted in a new uneasy alliance between the Communists and Chiang Kai-shek to fight the common enemy.

Even before Japan was defeated by the U.S. and World War II ended in 1945, Chiang Kai-shek once again set about attempting to destroy the Communists' Red Armies. But Chiang's own ruthlessness and corrupt administration had soured the vast majority of the peasantry, opening the door for Mao to mold a huge Red Army that soon became unstoppable. Civil war raged for the next four years, bringing death to additional millions.

Each time the CCP forces captured a town or city they set up a network of "street committees" made up of residents to be responsible for the public services in their districts and to maintain obedience and security.

In 1942 the CCP inaugurated a combination brain-washing/re-education program called the "Yan'an Rectification Campaign" to achieve Party consensus by using group pressure and intense intimidation to force CCP members to criticize their own attitudes and behavior until they reached the point that they all thought alike. Later, the CCP was to make brain-washing one of the central activities of its regime.

The CCP forces also took stern measures to eliminate child labor and other abuses attributed to landlordism and capitalism. In contrast to the behavior of the Communist troops, the Nationalist forces under Chiang Kai-shek were notorious for their brutal treatment of the people.

When the Nationalists recaptured areas that had been under Communist rule they systematically shot one member of each family that had participated in land reform (accepted land from deposed landlords). In some instances, the Nationalists buried village leaders and their families alive.

When the Red Army surrounded Shanghai, the last Nationalist stronghold, the Nationalists rounded up every person in the city who was even remotely suspected of being a Communist sympathizer, herded them into the streets and shot them all.

By the summer of 1949 Chiang Kai-shek admitted defeat and fled with the remnants of his armies to Taiwan. The People's Republic of China was proclaimed by Mao Zedung on a reviewing stand on top of the Gate of Heavenly Peace overlooking Tiananmen Square on October 1, 1949.

After taking over the country, Mao and his Communist colleagues unleashed a series of their own murderous campaigns to solidify their control and to complete the communization of China. These campaigns consisted of exterminating people who were identified as having been Nationalists or having Nationalist sympathies, and brain-washing those that were left in an effort to make them ardent supporters of the CCP.

These 1950–1951 campaigns included mass rallies designed to turn the people against "counterrevolutionaries" and bind them to the CCP. Hundreds of thousands of "committees" were formed in villages, towns and cities across the country to identify and report business owners, landlords, intellectuals, "bandits, criminals, spies" and anyone else who did not fit the peasant mold favored by the Communists.

In one brief period in Guangdong (Canton), 28,332 people who had been identified as class enemies by local "committees" were executed. One of the most frightening examples of the inhuman pragmatism with which the CCP pursued its goals was forcing people to pay for the bullets used to execute their own family members.

During the same campaign, the CCP disarmed the populace of China, gathering up more than half a million weapons in Guangdong alone.

Other measures taken to ensure absolute control of the population included the formation of five-person "mutual guarantee groups" in which each person was responsible for the attitude and behavior of the others. All persons over the age of 15 were required to obtain residence identification cards from the police and carry them at all times.

The avowed aim of the CCP was to destroy all of the loyalty that had traditionally held Chinese families together and bound individuals to their friends, and to intellectually and emotionally mold the entire country into one huge Communist family.

Mao's subsequent attempts to communize the entire country in the same way that he had organized and controlled peasants in rural regions under his command eventually ended in failure. The country was simply too large, the challenge too complex, and the Communist Party principles inadequate for the task.

The advancements that the CCP did bring to China were built on the bodies of hundreds of thousands of people executed, and millions imprisoned. As early as 1958 the inability of the CCP to fulfill its promise was already obvious. By 1966 the Party was beginning to self-destruct. A *Party* remains today but it is no longer a *Communist* Party.

See **Gongchanzhuyi, Lao Jiao.**

72

共产主义

Gongchanzhuyi

(Goong-chahn-chuu-ee)

"The Cult of Communism"

Chinese communism, like *gongchanzhuyi* (goong-chahn-chuu-ee) or *communism* everywhere, eventually became more of a religious cult rather than a social philosophy. All members of the Party had to accept the beliefs of its leaders, regardless of what those beliefs were, and to obey Party leaders without question, or face expulsion or elimination.

Shortly after the Chinese Communist Party took over China in 1949 the Western concept of "human rights" was classified as anti-Communist and any mention of the idea was prohibited.

Subsequent actions to put more of a humanistic face on the Communist regime were primarily window dressing. Generally speaking, the Chinese constitution and the laws pertaining to the rights of the people and limiting the actions of the government were a sop to the rest of the world and to the Chinese people.

It was the publicly expressed policy of the CCP to ignore both the constitution and any of the country's laws any time it saw fit to do so—a policy that continues in effect today. The only rationale government leaders need to do this is to take a position that whoever or whatever they dislike and want to squelch is a threat to the state—an "enemy of the people."

The Chinese version of communism was primarily an embodiment of the thoughts of Mao Zedung, and in early 1960 when it seemed like he might be losing control of both the Party and the country, his long-time friend and fellow Long-March veteran Lin Biao, then the minister of defense, and his fourth wife, ex-actress Jiang Qing, began a sophisticated program to turn Mao into a cult figure and make his philosophy the only creed allowed in the country.

Lin made a collection of the more quote-worthy aphorisms from Mao's hundreds of articles and speeches and published them in 1963 in a little red book entitled *Quotations from Chairman Mao*.

Promoted nationwide by the CCP and the People's Liberation Army (300 million copies were given away), the Little Red Book (*Shao Hongse Shu*) quickly became the "bible" of the faithful, and was used as a totem representing the heart and soul of Chinese communism, all incorporated in the image of Mao.

The Little Red Book was translated into dozens of languages and sold millions of copies around the world. No one alive during the remainder of the 1960s and the early 1970s who had access to TV news could possibly forget the image of a million or more people, massed in Tiananmen Square, holding their copies of the Little Red Book aloft as one, and screaming their allegiance to Mao. The spirit of Hitler must have been writhing in envy at this spectacle.

But just as Mao was mortal and soon died, the cult that Lin and Jiang had worked so hard to build around him was nothing more than a hologram that disappeared with his passing. Instead of being remembered as one of China's and the world's greatest leaders, Mao was soon to be revealed as a villain without par; a monster, made mad by his dreams.

Deng Xiaoping, one of the last of the heroes of the Long March, assumed the mantle of "emperor" of China shortly after the demise of Mao. He defined his view of Chinese communism in terms of Four Cardinal Principles: "Stay on the Socialist road; Maintain the dictatorship of the proletariat; Maintain the leadership of the Communist Party; Uphold the thought of Marx, Lenin and Mao."

But as in all things in China, how these four principles were interpreted depended on the individuals involved and the political and economic circumstances at that time. Up to the two or three years preceding Mao Zedung's death in 1976 it was primarily "Maoist communism" that held sway in China.

Mao's goals had been to destroy all of the old cultural concepts and customs of China, including both the structure and consciousness of social classes, replace them with pure Socialist-Communist beliefs, and create a new classless society of egoless, totally cooperative human beings who would labor in happy union for the benefit of all.

Mao was willing to kill, imprison, brain-wash and enslave as many millions of people as necessary to achieve his goals—but in the end it didn't work because there was a limit to how long he could live and how susceptible people are to being stripped of their humanity, dignity and spirit and still be productive members of a viable society.

Commenting on how many people had been sacrificed to his dream, Mao boasted that he had killed more people than any other Chinese leader, including the most notorious ancient emperors.

While most of the survivors of Mao's holocaust now look upon him as an amoral monster, he may go down in history as the greatest of China's revolutionaries. Ross Terrill, the noted scholar and author of *Mao: A Biography*, compares Mao with the most famous Tang, Han and Ming emperors, and points out that his impact on China was at least as great as that of Confucius—and that it occurred during his lifetime, in less than 50 years.

There was no time during the heyday of Mao and the CCP that more than 10 percent of the Chinese believed in and willingly followed the philosophy and policies of Mao or the CCP. But like a black plague, communism had to run its course and die of its own genetic defects.

Deng Xiaoping, himself twice made a victim of Mao madness, was to become a new kind of "Communist"—determined that the CCP would maintain exclusive power, but also determined to use whatever economic system was needed to transform China into a world power. Deng's fall and return to power on two occasions must have reminded him of the famous saying, *Si hui fu ran—Dying ashes burn again*. Or maybe *Dong shan zai*, the *East Mountain rises again*.

Foreign businesspeople and visitors in China must keep in mind that the government and the judicial system are still instruments of the so-called Chinese Communist Party, and that the first priority of high-level Party members is to maintain control—exactly the same priorities that motivated the Imperial dynasties of China for more than four thousand years.

The built-in survival instinct of Communist Party leaders is more powerful than any ideology, which means that the CCP, whatever it has evolved into, will likely remain in control of China for the foreseeable future.

73

恭维

Gongwei

(Goong-way-e)

"The Flattery Factor"

Survival and success in Chinese society have traditionally depended so much on maintaining good relations with other people that this factor alone had a fundamental impact not only on the overall etiquette system but also on the Chinese language—in terms of vocabulary as well as how the words are used.

There are numerous words in Chinese that are designed and used to show respect and deference, to acknowledge social inferiority and demonstrate social superiority, to recognize sex and age differences, to account for extended-family relationships, to seek favors, and so on.

And although there have been marked changes in interpersonal relationships among Chinese, particularly among the younger generations in large cities and especially among those who have become "Westernized" to some extent, most of the traditional customs and rules for surviving and succeeding still apply.

Another vital factor in interpersonal relationships in China is the role and importance of "face"—keeping one's own reputation spotless, avoiding actions that might harm someone else's face, and doing things that "give face" to others.

Protecting and giving face involves the careful and timely use of the "right" language, and is an integral part of the overall Chinese etiquette system.

The importance of interpersonal relationships in China, combined with the extreme sensitivity that such relational morality causes, resulted in the Chinese becoming habitual users of *gongwei* (goong-way-e) or *flattery*.

Gongwei has traditionally been an art form to the Chinese. They use it regularly as a part of their efforts to keep all relations harmonious. How much of the constant *gongwei* is sincere, and whether or not it is deserved, is up to the recipients to decide.

But the Chinese are acutely aware that accepting compliments obligates them to the other party, and they generally make a point of denying that they are deserving of them (See **Nali, Nali**).

The Chinese learned very early in their dealings with the West that Westerners are not as resistant to flattery as they are, and are far more susceptible to being influenced by it.

From that time on the Chinese have systematically used *gongwei* to soften and manipulate foreigners for whatever purpose they have in mind— a syndrome that has played a key role in China's political and trade relations with the world, particularly the United States.

Americans, particularly high-level government officials and politicians, appear to be especially susceptible to the kind of flattery and red-carpet treatment that the Chinese, on every level and in business as well as politics, specialize in.

At a minimum, Americans need to learn to use *Nali, Nali*!

垢

Gou

(Gouh)

"Avoiding Temptation"

It is a well-established truism that the more power government officials have the greater the temptation to misuse it, and when all power rests in the hands of government officials and bureaucrats, the situation is dangerous indeed.

Historically in China, high-level government officials had life-and-death power over those below them. Even the lowest level government functionaries had extraordinary powers, and often arbitrarily assumed additional powers.

Because of this system, government officials and bureaucrats legally lorded it over people below them, traditionally using and often abusing ordinary people to the extent that their lives were made hellish.

Here too, China's teachers took a universal view of *gou* (gouh), or *temptation*, considering it from the viewpoint of the role it plays in the lives of everyone. They noted that *gou* by itself is neither good nor bad but represents a dynamic force that can become destructive or constructive, depending on how one reacts to it.

In the Chinese context, the truly superior person will withstand the negative attractions of temptation, use the dynamic power of the situation to improve his or her own character, and become even stronger in resisting *gou* in the future.

To effectively resist *gou*, said the old masters of China, it is essential that one speak up at the first hint of temptation, and that failing to do so may allow it to unobtrusively penetrate one's defenses and do its dirty work.

They add the obvious that many temptations appear to be minor when first encountered and may be regarded as indulgences that will not do any harm. It is human, they admit, for individuals who have worked unusually hard and sacrificed years of their lives to feel that they deserve something extra.

But minor indulgences have a way of becoming major flaws in one's character and behavior, the masters continue, and should be resisted as valiantly as the greatest temptations—and here again, these regular encounters should be used to temper one's own character.

Today's China is rampant with *gou*, and there appears to be less and less ability or desire to resist it—a heritage of the four hundred–plus centuries during which the people were forced to live within a split-level morality that denied them the right to make their own choices about temptation.

Foreign businesspeople and diplomats dealing with China are constantly being confronted by people, particularly lower level bureaucrats, who have embraced *gou* as a way of life.

These people often offer business relationships that appear to be very attractive—and sometimes there appears to be no other choice. But such relationships invariably contain seeds of danger and should be approached and managed with caution.

Deals that come together easily in China, especially when they are based on personal advantages to individuals, can just as easily come apart. Foreigners involved in business relationships that began this way should strive continuously to put them on a more solid foundation.

蠱

Gu
(Guu)

"Shoring Up Your Defenses"

There are many stories in Chinese literature that emphasize the importance of education and persevering to reach goals once you start out to achieve them. One that comes to mind is appropriate to the lesson to be learned from *gu* (guu), which figuratively means *shoring up one's defenses.*

A young man, newly married, left his bride to go to a distant place to learn a trade. But after about a year he missed his new wife so much that he gave up his studies and returned home.

Rather than welcome him with open arms, however, the young wife, who was obviously much wiser than her husband, lectured him on his short-sighted behavior, telling him his weakness jeopardized the future of the family.

Properly chastised, the young man retraced his steps back to the distant place and labored away for something like fifteen years before mastering his trade and rejoining his wife.

Among the many guidelines for character-building and behavior that have been handed down in China for more than three thousand years are those that have to do with recognizing the "decay" that is natural in both things and in one's own standards of behavior, and applying *gu* or "repair" in timely fashion.

These guidelines note that some decay in situations—personal relationships, business, politics or whatever—is the result of outside influences. But they go on to say that a significant percentage of such degeneration is caused by individuals ignoring or discounting things that should have been noticed and repaired before they did serious damage.

Gu is not regarded as a negative factor, however. According to the teachings of the masters, things damaged by neglect are readily susceptible to being repaired by the individuals responsible, because the damage was done by their own shortsightedness or carelessness.

To begin with, "guilty" parties are admonished to very carefully consider the circumstances that led to lapses in their behavior. Once they see clearly why they failed to do the necessary ongoing repair they must first change their attitudes, then they can set about aggressively correcting their mistakes.

The guidelines go on to say that applying *gu* to serious problems may not be easy and may take a long time, especially if the problems developed over a long time-frame and the decay is deeply imbedded in the circumstances. But, the wise men promise, perseverance will pay off and will reflect well on both your character and reputation.

This piece of Chinese wisdom emphasizes the never-ending importance of paying attention to the smallest details in one's affairs, personal and business, avoiding decay if at all possible, and going about repairing any damage with energy and zeal, but being sensitive to the feelings of others in the process.

The Chinese frequently criticize Westerners for trying to do things too fast, and for ignoring the need for constant *gu* in their personal and business relationships.

In the case of foreign business managers in China, a key part of the process of *gu* is frequent visits to the workplace, spending time with individual employees, asking them about their families, sharing tea, etc.

权

Guan

(Goo-enn)

"Becoming Wise"

Foreigners involved with China often tell stories that illustrate how complicated and time-consuming dealing with Chinese businesspeople and bureaucrats can be. One such story concerned a contract that required the approval of over one hundred separate agencies and individuals and took almost a year to accomplish.

This was something of an extreme case, but was nevertheless indicative of the extent to which red tape has been one of China's leading growth industries since the development of a bureaucratic form of government over two thousand years ago.

But rampant bureaucracy is not the only reason why things typically move at a slower pace in China. In general terms, the pace of life in China traditionally hinged on the seasons, which could not be hurried. Life was not measured in hours, days or weeks, but in years and in long, leisurely stages.

The etiquette system taught by Confucius and China's other social philosophers stressed a stylized form of behavior that made hurried actions virtually taboo. Hasty actions were not only ill-mannered, they were equated with lack of education and adequate preparation for whatever task was at hand.

In parallel with this perspective of the well-mannered life, educated Chinese were also imbued with the importance of *guan* (goo-enn), or *contemplating*, in their search for understanding and dealing with the world about them.

In its Chinese context, *guan* is a way of linking one's self with the cosmos, with the cycles that are inherent in all life, and coming to understand the nature of life, including the affairs of man.

The ultimate goal in *guan* is to become one with the cosmic laws that control the universe, thereby making it possible for people to instinctively act in harmony with the cosmos. Once you are able to act in complete harmony with nature you have enormous power over yourself and your immediate environment.

Chinese philosophers say that once an individual has come to understand the nature of life through *guan*, he or she will also be able to exercise considerable control over current business and political affairs, and determine to a considerable extent what is going to happen in the future.

Guan cannot be hurried, the sages add. The strength that derives from contemplation takes time to develop. You must experience life fully, observe and listen carefully, and weigh all opinions before you can see and understand the heart of each matter—a state that obviously cannot be achieved by the very young.

This understanding, continue the sages, will bring great strength of character and will, and attract people to you, allowing you to become a successful leader in business, politics or any other endeavor.

One of the secrets of *guan* is to see every situation as part of a cosmic whole; not as something that pertains only to yourself or any other individual alone. This, the sages add, will allow you to transcend your own ego and achieve the ultimate in influence over others.

As always in Chinese philosophy, a prerequisite for the successful use of *guan* is self-knowledge. Generally speaking, the Chinese see Westerners as weak in both holistic thinking and self-knowledge.

官倒

Guan Dao
(Goo-enn Dah-oh)

"Official Profiteering"

When one of the Chou Dynasty emperors made private enterprise and profit-making taboo more than 2,000 years ago, he unwittingly set the stage for the development of a society in which economic morality was eventually reduced to its lowest common denominator. In the struggle for survival, and especially the accumulation of any assets above the survival level, the end justified the means.

The bureaucratic system devised during the Han Dynasty (206 B.C.–A.D. 220), which gave enormous powers to the mandarins and other officials administering the country, made bribery and other forms of corruption an integral part of the government.

Bribes, often in the form of gifts in kind, became an everyday part of dealing with officials from the highest levels in the Imperial Court down to neighborhood policemen.

Among the lowest level of bureaucrats a significant part of their income was made up of gifts. Higher level officials in especially key positions often amassed large fortunes from bribes, kickbacks and commissions.

Thus the custom of *guan dao* (goo-enn dah-oh) or *official profiteering* has been well-established in China since ancient times. Only the methods of profiteering have changed.

One of the most common forms of profiteering today is for officials to siphon off significant amounts of money from funds allocated for public works by state-run enterprises.

Another common practice is for officials to buy merchandise at special government procurement prices, and then turn around and sell it in the commercial market at inflated retail prices.

Still another gambit routinely used by bureaucrats to fill their pockets is to charge fees for the services they are mandated to provide. A variation of this approach is to let it be known that kickbacks or commissions are expected for the licenses and other services they are supposed to provide without charge.

One of the most innovative official scams that became common in the 1990s was for bureaucrats connected with the construction industry to demand housing units in new apartment buildings as their payoff for the financing.

The most flagrant aspect of this scam was for the new apartments to be padlocked and kept unoccupied until the children of the officials concerned grew up, got married and moved in.

It is often difficult to distinguish between the universal custom of gift giving and *guan dao*. Where foreign businesspeople are concerned, this is an especially sensitive area because normal Chinese expectations are often greater than what the foreign side thinks is reasonable and fair.

In situations that are especially touchy, and the foreign side really wants or must have the license, the cooperation of the official, or whatever, one of the better ways to approach the problem is to bring in a third party to negotiate a "settlement."

78

官商

Guan Shang

(Goo-enn Shahng)

"Mixing Oil and Water"

The apparent Westernization of Beijing and other areas of China is mostly symbolic. Beneath the facade of Western dress, Western manners, highrise buildings, Coca-Cola and McDonald's hamburgers lies a hybrid social, economic and political system that is made of unequal parts of traditionalism, communism, socialism and capitalism.

The Frenchman who coined the phrase, "The more things change the more they stay the same" could have been talking about China. Despite all of the changes that have created a New China since the first "Great Opening" in 1978, the fabric of Chinese culture remains virtually intact, and all of the abuses that have been a part of life in China since the first dragon emperor ascended the throne continue to flourish.

There are bandits in the hills. Thieves roam the market places, and now ride the trains, and bureaucrats are still trying to run the lives of the people. One of the biggest worries of the leaders in Beijing is their weakening control over the more prosperous provinces, and the threat this represents to the Communist dynasty.

Corruption, in places high and low, remains characteristic of China's whole social and economic system, and is now fed by fires of ambition and greed that are much greater than anything seen in the past.

But there *is* one thing in today's China that is new, and is bringing about fundamental changes in the economic, political and social systems. This new ingredient in the great *wok* of China is the emergence of *guan shang* (goo-een shahng) or *bureaucrat-business*.

In the 1980s China's leaders opened a Pandora's box by authorizing government ministries, agencies and departments, including the military, to engage in commercial business. Hundreds of thousands of bureaucrats gleefully joined the frenzy unleashed by supreme leader Deng Xiaoping when he gave the general population of the country permission to get rich.

This new wrinkle in the Communist mandarins' recipe for economic growth in China may not be as economically disastrous as Mao Zedung's Great Leap Forward, but by vastly expanding the role of the bureaucracy in business it greatly reduced the competitive power of private enterprise and set the stage for a new kind of socialism.

Not surprisingly, the new class of business bureaucrats immediately began taking advantage of their privileged official positions. Just one of hundreds of thousands of examples: a provincial tax bureau set up a "private" tax consulting firm next door, and let it be known that people who wanted to make sure their tax returns were in order would use the new tax service.

Beset by *jing-shang-re* or *business fever*, China's new class of business bureaucrats are not about to voluntarily allow private enterprises to compete with them on advantageous or even equal terms. They naturally use their official power to protect and enhance their own turf, bringing a new dimension to political corruption.

Among other things, these so-called semi-legitimate businesses use their special privileges and connections to make unearned income through collecting fees for services they are supposed to provide to private enterprises without charge. They also take advantage of the government's dual-track pricing system to purchase raw materials and other goods and services at prices well below those paid by private businesses.

China's private business sector complains vociferously about *guan shang*, which is growing and becoming stronger, but to no avail. The system is vintage Chinese, and like other practices in China that have become institutionalized will probably have to go through its own dynastic rise and fall.

Perhaps even more significant than allowing government entities to engage in profit-making enterprises, was extending this approval to the People's Liberation Army. By the mid-1900s the PLA was operating a business empire whose known profits surpassed that of the entire military budget.

PLA-controlled businesses now run the gamut, from manufacturing munitions, refrigerators, air-conditioners, trucks, motorcycles, and knitwear to plush stuffed toys. PLA companies own and operate their own office buildings, guest houses, hotels and nightclubs.

Military-run businesses are so numerous, and the control so Byzantine, that government officials admit they have no idea how large or how profitable the PLA's business empire has become—a phenomenon that suggests all kinds of future scenarios, including the possibility that the PLA's generals may become too busy managing their profit-making enterprises to get involved in making war.

79

关系

Guanxi

(Gwahn-she)

"The Chinese Life-Line"

Of all the influences and elements that went into the forging of traditional Chinese attitudes and behavior, none played a more critical role than lack of personal freedom.

From the inception of the first Chinese kingdom some five thousand years ago, the people of China were subjected to the will, the grandiose dreams and whims of absolute rulers who treated them more or less as slaves of the state. The laws of the land were essentially designed to protect and preserve the ruling powers; not to franchise the people. The primary purpose of local authorities was to carry out the policies of the national government, not to serve the interests of local residents.

People were saddled from birth with an all-encompassing web of obligations and responsibilities. Peasants, who made up the bulk of the already huge population, had practically no personal choices open to them. Virtually their whole existence was fixed at birth. They were not free to move from one village or district to another. They could not travel without an officially acceptable reason and formal written permission. Their marriages were arranged; their occupations were generally inherited from their parents.

Since people had to have permission for virtually everything they did outside of their ordinary routine, either from their parents, from village elders, from workplaces, or from government officials—and often from all of them— developing and maintaining cooperative relationships, called *guanxi* (gwahn-she), usually translated into English as *connections*, with key individuals in all of these categories, or knowing someone else who had the necessary relationship that they could call on for help, became the way of life.

Guanxi, which cannot be precisely translated in one English word (its full meaning is something like *relationships based on mutual dependence*, with the active element being *feelings* and *emotion*) are more important in present-day China than they were during the long course of the country's feudal past because life is now far more complicated.

Individuals, in both rural and urban areas, must deal regularly with a variety of public officials, agencies, associations, and commercial operations for personal as well as business reasons. If they do not have their own *guanxi* within these organizations or cannot call on people who do, their chances of getting whatever it is they need or want are greatly diminished and often zero.

The whole of China, socially, economically and politically, runs on personal connections, on *guanxi*. People therefore spend a great deal of time, energy, creativity and money on developing and nurturing connections.

Chinese critics of the *guanxi* system say that what should take no more than a five-minute discussion typically takes five hours or even five days in China, because nothing is straightforward and simple. Every little nuance of personal interest or the possibility of personal interest must be covered. "Our lives," they say, "consist of talk, talk, talk."

Foreigners doing business with China invariably find that they cannot function efficiently without *guanxi*, and building these relationships is one of the first and most critical things they should do. These connections should include a wide variety of people who are in positions that can be useful to them—from hotel staff and restaurant managers to Chinese businesspeople; and of course, government officials in the ministries and agencies concerned with their areas of business.

The need or desire for *guanxi* works both ways. Foreigners are also regularly targeted by Chinese seeking to gain favors or advantages that only a foreigner can provide. And, of course, these relationships are usually reciprocal—with mutual connections exchanging favors.

But a word of warning is in order. Many Chinese establish relationships with foreigners, giving them gifts and doing various favors for them, for the specific purpose of using them, sometimes for acceptable enough reasons, but other times for underhanded reasons that may cause serious problems for the foreigners.

There is a special term for people who use the *guanxi* system for illegal, immoral or generally unworthy purposes. They are called *guanxi dawang* or connection masters. It is usually possible to identify *guanxi dawang* from their behavior, and it is best to diplomatically distance yourself from such people.

Most experienced foreign residents in China attempt to stay *even* with anyone who gives them gifts, treats them to meals and drinks and does other kinds of favors for them, to avoid the buildup of undesirable obligations.

If they do not stay even, they may be considered insensitive, ungrateful and selfish, or put in a position of not being able to turn down requests for favors that go beyond the bounds of ordinary friendship and mutual help.

There is constant jockeying for advantage in *guanxi* relationships, and people are often better known for their connections than for their personal attributes.

Another complicating factor is that practically nothing is simple when it comes to exchanging favors. All interactions, including minor ones, are treated as matters of considerable importance.

Newcomers to China should keep in mind that maintaining an acceptable balance with personal relationships is a subtle and sometimes mysterious challenge. It is best to seek general guidelines as early as possible from bilingual, bi-cultural Chinese and foreigners whom you know well enough that they will be candid with you.

Despite dramatic changes in the overall social mores of China since capitalism began replacing communism, the need for *guanxi* continues to be of vital importance in Chinese life—a baleful hangover from the authoritarian regimes that reigned supreme during China's long age of Imperial dynasties.

80

官儿

Guarner (Chuuarguan)
(Gwah-nur)

"The New Mandarins"

China's dynastic *guarner* (gwah-nur) or *mandarins*—government officials who administered the laws of the land on a regional and district level—were not wise men/father figures who had made good, were respected by the population, and with whom the people could establish strong, life-long ties.

They were always outsiders who were assigned to different districts every three or four years, like military commanders of an occupying force. They were not assigned to their home districts, and were moved frequently, as a means of reducing the corruption that inevitably followed personal ties.

The mandarins lived in large, multi-roomed homes in walled compounds, with numerous servants, and armed guards at the gates. Many of China's cities and towns were also walled, with huge guarded gates that were closed at night.

Mandarins were not there to protect the people or intercede with the government on their behalf, but to see that they stayed peaceful and orderly, performed their public duties and paid their taxes.

There were exceptions, of course. Over the centuries many of the mandarins were capable, enlightened individuals who devoted their lives to earnestly and sincerely trying to improve both the social and economic infrastructure of their districts.

But the overwhelming majority of the country's famous scholar-administrators were primarily concerned with protecting their own reputations and positions, which meant emphasizing traditional attitudes and practices—not innovative and disruptive changes.

In law enforcement, mandarins were the investigator, prosecutor, jury and judge. The accused were considered guilty until proven innocent.

During the heyday of the Communist regime in China (1949–1976) the role of the traditional mandarin was usurped by Communist cadre manning national, regional, district and local offices. These individuals had, or assumed, enormous authority that virtually gave them the power of life or death over anyone in their jurisdictions.

For most of this period of Communist ascendancy, the primary role of China's new "Red" mandarins was not to maintain stability and peace, but to destroy all of the old patterns of thought and behavior. A major part of this process was based on the extermination of large numbers of people, both to get rid of them and to serve as a warning to others.

Another key facet of this "out with the old" and "in with the new" revolution was a subhuman program to literally turn all Chinese into non-thinking socialist drones.

The results of this revolutionary effort were exactly the opposite of what the CCP wanted and expected. Instead of turning the mass of rural and urban Chinese into perfect Communist workers, it destroyed what little standing the Communist Party had, and made it clear to everyone that this new breed of mandarin was far worse than the *guarner* of the past.

See **Falu**.

81

归妹

Guei Mei

(Gway-ee May-ee)

"Keeping a Low Profile"

Among the most significant of China's cultural code words are those that have to do with avoiding trouble, patiently biding your time and hoping that circumstances will change in your favor—something that for the overwhelming majority of Chinese has been nothing more than a dream since the founding of the first dynasty.

This unfavorable element in Chinese history was recognized by its early wise men, and a whole philosophy was created for bending with the social, political and economic winds as a means of survival.

One of the key compounds in this philosophy is *guei mei* (gway-ee may-ee), which means *subordinate*, and is the fifty-fourth hexagram in the famed *I Ching* or *Book of Changes*.

Guei mei recognizes that there are times when no amount of knowledge, experience or special skills is enough to surmount the various obstacles people face and allow them to achieve significant success. The concept is also ready-made for people who lack the attributes for individual success in the first place.

The *guei mei* hexagram is designed to cover those situations when an individual has practically no control over his or her situation, cannot change things, and can survive only by keeping a low profile, working hard but doing nothing to attract undue attention and waiting until the circumstances change. (As Deng Xiaoping did when he was ousted from the ruling elite during the 1966–1976 Cultural Revolution.)

When in this subordinate mode the person is advised to remain perfectly passive, avoid mistakes if at all possible, quickly correct any unavoidable errors, stay calm and polite, not attempt to force anything, and not do anything more than he or she is supposed to do.

Once again, say the wise men, the time people spend in *guei mei* situations is best used to reflect on their own character, attempt to raise the level of their self-awareness and thereby achieve a clearer view of the forces aligned against them.

Guei mei suggests that most people are not destined for success on their own and can succeed only in positions subordinate to others. If this is done diligently, however, and you overcome your own feelings of pride and vanity, the sages contend, you can be assured of security and recognition for your efforts.

There is also a warning inherent in the *guei mei* concept that people who just go through the motions of being a subordinate, without serious intent to do well in that position, put their security in jeopardy.

The *guei mei* syndrome is very conspicuous in China, where millions of people used to and still deliberately "bury" themselves in subordinate positions—or are "buried" there by their superiors—and remain there for most or all of their lives, content with staying out of trouble by not questioning or rattling the system.

To a great extent it was the *guei mei* factor, built into the Chinese character by millennia of behavioral conditioning, that made it possible for millions of Chinese to survive the brutal brain-washing campaigns carried out by the Communist Party during the early decades of the People's Republic of China.

82

Gui
(Gwee)

"Fighting for Honor"

It often seems that the less political freedom people have the more concerned they are about their own personal reputation and the more likely they are to have a strict code of honor.

One explanation of this perverse-sounding attitude is that since people without freedom have little or no personal choice in what they do and how they do it, they are prone to emphasize the personal attitudes and behavior that no outside power can deny them.

When lack of personal freedom is combined with a social system based on hierarchical groupism, as it has been in China since ancient times, the importance of both reputation and personal honor is intensified, often to the point of becoming an obsession. When a person's survival and livelihood are based on maintaining harmonious relations with groups of people and with government officials who have arbitrary powers, and the individual cannot alter this relationship or leave it and join other groups, loss of reputation can be disastrous.

For people to maintain a sense of self-respect in this kind of system it is essential that they have a strong personal sense of honor, of *gui* (gwee) as it is called in Chinese, in order to maintain emotional, intellectual and spiritual balance.

It was apparently taken for granted in early China that only people who distinguished themselves from the crowd, particularly those who became financially successful, were worthy of *gui*. The ideogram used to express the concept still refers to money.

And although China's earliest philosophers recognized that common men were innately as deserving of respect as the wealthy and powerful, and incorporated this concept into their teachings, it did not result in any change in the attitudes of the elite or in the social position or prerogatives of common people.

While common Chinese were imbued with a sense of personal honor and "face" through the philosophical foundations of their culture, they were permitted to publicly exercise this sense only in the context of serving the interests of an authoritarian government.

The result of this contradictory environment was that the Chinese became practically obsessed with maintaining their reputations and saw themselves as people of exceptional honor. But their concept of honor did not become universal. It was primarily limited to their own group and to serving their own personal interests.

For the most part, honor and reputation in today's China are still subjective, still applied on a circumstantial basis, and often conflict with Western rationalism. In any situation involving a point of honor it is therefore important that the term be culturally defined.

The fact that *gui* also expresses the concept of *expensive* may suggest that it is not a common commodity, but it is nevertheless important to all Chinese, regardless of their social or financial level, and care must be taken not to impugn it.

In this respect, *gui* is very close to the Chinese concern with "face." Loss of "face" generally equates with loss of honor, although the latter is deeper and broader in scope and harder to overcome.

83

国粹

Guo Cui

(Gwoh T'sue-ee)

"The Essence of China"

There are many reasons why China is the world's oldest surviving nation, including its relative isolation over the millennia, its huge size and large population, its early development of a comprehensive writing system, its early mastery of a unique system of governmental bureaucracy, and the early development of technology that made agriculture more efficient and large cities possible.

But there was more to early China than what these physical manifestations suggest. There was a heart, a spirit, that grew out of philosophical beliefs that had accumulated since the appearance of the Chinese race—beliefs that were continuously refined and expanded to provide comprehensive concepts of both society and the cosmos, along with specific guidelines for every contingency.

Despite the fact that the most important of these philosophical beliefs, particularly those pertaining to society and government, were seriously flawed, they were nevertheless strong enough to sustain the people and the nation in the face of both natural and man-made disasters of biblical proportions.

In addition to imbuing the Chinese with remarkable staying and recovery powers, Chinese culture also infused the people with a unique outlook on themselves, their surroundings, and the world at large.

This unique outlook and the lifestyle that developed from it created a *guo cui* (gwoh t'sue-ee) or *national essence*, that distinguished the Chinese and their civilization from all other people.

The arts and crafts for which the Chinese have long been famous are products of this national essence. Traditional Chinese novels, poetry and plays are also manifestations of *guo cui*, as is Chinese etiquette and its underlying psychology.

But China's national essence has been under attack from within and without for the last four hundred years. The impact of alien religions, philosophies, politics, and economic systems is in the early stages of transforming China's *guo cui* into some kind of amalgamation of Confucian traditionalism, communism, socialism and capitalism.

There are strong indications that the potency of Confucian traditionalism and communism has been spent, and that the end result of the transformation now underway will be some combination of socialism and capitalism.

But what is not so clear is how much of the aesthetic, metaphysical and spiritual aspects of China's national essence will survive its political and economic transformation.

Much of this will no doubt depend upon whether or not the Chinese government and the business community realize what will be lost if they allow the *guo cui* to disappear from the nation's arts, crafts, fashions, consumer products in general, and from the best of the traditional Chinese lifestyle.

It goes without saying that the outsider cannot truly understand or appreciate the Chinese without being intimately familiar with what remains of their still powerful *guo cui*.

84

裹脚

Guo-Jiao

(Gwoh-Jee-ah-oh)

"Power of the Shackled Id"

Nothing is more indicative of the power, and often the perversity, of Chinese culture than the custom of *guo-jiao* (gwoh-jee-ah-oh) or binding the feet of young girls to prevent them from growing. This intensely painful procedure, started when girls were five or six years old, resulted in their feet being turned into misshapen stubs and prevented their legs from developing properly because they could not walk normally on their feet.

Such was the cult-like hold of the *guo-jiao* custom that it spread from the upper and middle classes down to the peasant level. Girls in many of the more pretentious farm families, who could get by without the field labor of female members of the family, also were victimized by the practice.

Among the more affluent classes that followed the custom of footbinding, girls who had normal feet were not acceptable as candidates for marriage—a factor that guaranteed the perpetuation of the practice.

The irrational custom of foot-binding grew out of a combination of sexual deprivation and sexual perversion that was allowed to go to an extreme.

Like the Christian church, early Chinese society attempted to control human sexuality by forcing it into the very narrow, limited channel of procreation.

In Christian-dominated countries attempts to limit and control sexuality resulted in a wide variety of violence that is still characteristic of such societies. In China, on the other hand, the Confucian-dominated social system made external violence by ordinary people virtually unthinkable.

One of the ways this sexual repression manifested itself in China was in the appearance of sexual fetishes that became widespread among the upper classes.

Two of the most prominent of these fetishes involved women's feet and the cloth slippers that girls and women wore.

This foot and slipper fetish, originally practiced by wealthy men dedicated to satiating their most basic desires, became focused on smallness—the smaller the feet or slippers the greater their sexual turn-on.

It was already customary for powerful men to have sexual access to young girls (members of the emperors' harems were as young as eight years old) who naturally had small feet, and this obviously contributed to these fetishes.

In Chinese literature it is copiously recorded that many rich men carried the shoe fetish to the extreme of taking along trunks of tiny slippers to view and fondle while they were away from home on trips. Young women and girls with small feet were much in demand by these men.

Ultimately, this rich-man preference for women and girls with small feet resulted in families binding the feet of their female children in order to keep their feet small and make the girls more attractive as brides.

The practice of foot-binding became more and more serious and sophisticated. Foot-binding and helping young girls get through the excruciatingly painful ordeal became a profession.

Finally, foot-binding passed the point of being just a perverted fashion followed by families trying to make their daughters more eligible for marrying well. It became socially obligatory for all upperclass girls and even spread into the peasantry.

Tiny feet, no more than three or so inches long, became a primary standard of feminine beauty and sexual attractiveness. A common euphemism for *guo jiao* was *lily feet*.

It was not until well into modern times that a few Chinese began to publicly criticize the custom of foot-binding as barbaric, shameful and wasteful. In 1820 a Chinese novelist described the age-old custom of foot-binding as squeezing blood and flesh into a pulp, with little remaining of the feet but dry skin and bones.

In the late 1800s the Qing Court issued an edict prohibiting foot-binding, but the custom was so deeply entrenched in society that it was continued by many families until well up into the 1920s.

In the 1980s Western visitors reported seeing women with bound feet in cities and in fields, using crutches and canes to support themselves or precariously balancing themselves on what remained of their heels.*

85

国民党

Guo Min Dang
(Gwoh Meen Dahng)

"National People's Party"

Probably the three best-known Chinese names since the downfall of the Qing dynasty at the end of 1911 are those of Dr. Sun Yat-sen, Chiang Kai-shek and Mao Zedung.

Dr. Sun, as head of the Revolutionary Alliance, played a key role in the fall of China's last Imperial government. When the Qing government agreed to resign in the fall of 1911, Dr. Sun changed the name of the Revolutionary Alliance to *Kuo Min Tang* (KMT), or *National People's Party*, which is now romanized in Mandarin as *Guo Min Dang* (gwoh meen dahng).

Dr. Sun's attempts to form a stable, effective government under the banner of the *Guo Min Dang* failed. From 1912 until the victory of the Chinese Communist Party in 1949, China was rent by back-to-back wars that cost the lives of millions. The first war was between Nationalist armies and hold-out Qing forces. The second war was between the Nationalists and powerful warlords, and among contending warlords themselves.

The third war was between the Nationalists and Communists, which was interrupted by a full-fledged invasion by Japan in 1937, and resumed immediately when Japan was defeated and World War II ended.

Chiang Kai-shek appeared on the scene in the early 1920s as a field officer in the *Guo Min Dang's* Southern Army. He first became famous for helping Dr. Sun Yat-sen escape from Canton (now Guangdong) in the summer of 1922.

*In condemning the practice of foot-binding, one should not forget the irrationality of wearing shoes that have stiletto heels that are four or five inches high and are too small.

142

Chiang had spent several months in Moscow studying at a war college, and because of his new prominence was appointed first commandant of the newly opened Whampoa Military Academy.

Chiang used the first graduates of the school to form his own personal army and over the next few years, with Soviet aid, Chiang rose to become the paramount military figure in China, gradually defeating the more prominent warlords in a series of battles.

By this time, the Chinese Communist Party (CCP) had become a military threat. The CCP, with financial help and guidance from Soviet agents, was founded in Shanghai in 1922. At first the Communists cooperated with the Nationalists in defeating the more powerful warlords. When this had been accomplished, the Nationalists and Communists went back to fighting each other for control of the country.

Also by this time, Chiang Kai-shek had become commander in chief of all *Guo Min Dang* forces, and generally conducted himself as the military dictator of China.

In the meantime, Mao Zedung, who began as a fringe member of the Communist Party had risen in the ranks of the Party's military leaders. In 1934, Mao and other soon-to-be leaders of the Party (Zhou Enlai, Lin Biao, Deng Xiaoping), led the Communist forces on the famous Long March from central China to the far west—a 6,000-mile odyssey that took over one year—to avoid annihilation by Chiang's *Guo Min Dang* armies.

In addition to fighting the Chinese Communists, Chiang's forces were increasingly engaged in battles with the Imperial Japanese Army. In the summer of 1937 the Japanese invaded China in full force, quickly conquering all of eastern China, and forcing Chiang to also retreat westward—in his case a thousand miles up the Yangzi River to Chungking (Chongqing).

For the next seven years China suffered as never before—victimized by the Nationalists, the Communists and the Japanese alike. The Japanese forces were rapacious and destructive beyond belief. The Nationalists were even more corrupt and often as brutal to the civilian population of China as the Japanese.

The Communists, on the other hand, attempted to institute land reform and social reforms in the areas they controlled, and during the long years of the war perfected the strategy and tactics they would eventually use to defeat the *Guo Min Dang* armies and take over the country.

When World War II ended, it took Mao Zedung and his armies four more years to completely rout the Nationalists. Military historians say Chiang's forces simply "disintegrated" because of lack of motivation and morale and the utter corruption that marked Chiang's leadership.

Chiang saw defeat coming (despite the massive aid he received from the United States), and as early as 1947 sent a Nationalist army to take control of Taiwan, which had been regained from Japan in 1945. Chiang's forces arrested and executed thousands of Taiwan's most prominent citizens, particularly intellectuals and political leaders.

By early 1949, Chiang had over 300,000 troops in Taiwan. In the fall of that year, he, his family, his personal entourage, and well over a million additional officers, soldiers and their families, fled to the island. Chiang also had several hundred tons of China's most valuable works of art crated up and shipped to Taiwan.

Having "conquered" Taiwan, the *Guo Min Dang* proceeded to establish a "Free China" government, and to maintain that it was the true, legitimate government of China. This facade continued, with U.S. help, until 1979, when the United States formally recognized the government of the People's Republic of China as the sole government of China.

By this time, both Mao Zedung and Chiang Kai-shek were dead. The *Guo Min Dang* had evolved into a more democratic institution, and Taiwan, because its manufacturers and exporters had access to the American market, had become one of the economic successes of the century.

Despite the good intentions of Dr. Sun Yat-sen, the *Guo Min Dang*, or National People's Party, like so many other so-called *people's institutions* in China, was quickly subverted into anything but a party of or for the people.

To most Chinese today, the term reeks with the blood and cries of millions of innocent people.

86

鬼佬

Gweilo

(Gway-ee-low)

"The Foreigner Syndrome"

There is an old story in China that reveals a great deal about traditional Chinese attitudes toward other people. This is the story of the "Master Baker"—or Master People Maker (God!) in Western terms.

As this story has it, the Master Baker burned the first batch of dough he tried to cook, and produced black people. He undercooked the second batch, and produced pale-faced Caucasians. Finally, on the third attempt he got it right and produced the Chinese.

Ever since, the Chinese have looked upon themselves as the "chosen ones," and viewed all other people with a jaundiced eye.

For more than four millennia the Chinese image of other people was similarly prejudiced by the fact that its borders were continuously being breached by relatively uncivilized tribes given to mayhem and destruction.

When the first Caucasians appeared in China they were automatically included in the category of outside barbarians who had not had and never could have the full benefits of Chinese culture. Over the centuries, the behavior of many Caucasians in China and around its borders did nothing to convince the Chinese that they had been wrong in judging all foreigners as barbarians.

Among the colorful terms the Cantonese Chinese came up with in reference to foreigners was *gweilo* (gway-ee-low), a Cantonese term that means *foreign devil* or *foreign ghost*. The North China equivalent of this term was *yang gui zi* or *ocean ghosts*.

Another common slang term used to denote foreigners (generally Caucasian foreigners) is *da bidze*, which means *big nose*, and is pretty much self-explanatory.

Obviously, all of these terms were derogatory, reflecting the overall Chinese feelings of superiority to outsiders—superiority not only in a material sense but in a philosophical and spiritual sense as well.

Times have changed. *Gweilo* is still commonly used in the Cantonese region of China and elsewhere, since it has been spread around the world by Cantonese immigrants. But the connotation has gradually softened to where it is now used more or less in the sense of *foreigner*, much like *gringo* in Mexico and *haole* in Hawaii. (I've always gotten a huge charge out of the fact that *haole* actually means *white pig*.)

Foreigners themselves have helped to change the image of *gweilo* by using it in reference to themselves and other non-Chinese, originally because it was one of the first Chinese words that foreigners learned, and they appreciated the humor involved. Now it is also used simply because it is a convenient way of distinguishing between Chinese and non-Chinese.

It is certainly a lot more expressive than the regular Mandarin Chinese term for foreigner: *waiguoren* (wie-gwoh-wren), which literally means *foreign country person*.

87

汉语

Hanyu

(Hahn-yuu)

"China's Secret Code"

The real Great Wall of China is not and never was the massive rampart built to protect the country from the militant tribes of the north. The Chinese have traditionally been walled off from the rest of the world by their languages and awesome writing system.

There are ten major *Hanyu* (Hahn-yuu) or *Chinese languages* in the family of Chinese languages—including Mandarin (or *Putongua*, which the government has designated as the national language), Cantonese, Shanghaiese, Fujianese, Fukienese, Hokkien, Hakka, Chin Chow and Amoy; along with dozens of regional dialects and minority languages.

Not only have the Chinese languages prevented outsiders from actually getting *inside* China, they have also served to keep the Chinese isolated behind their linguistic walls, to preserve their culture and to transmit it from one generation to the next in what historically amounted to a secret code.

As late as the mid-1700s foreigners were prohibited from studying *Hanyu*, and it was a felony offense for a Chinese to teach any of the Chinese languages to a foreigner. Any foreigner who ignored this taboo, even unknowingly, and was found out, was subject to severe punishment.

The first great challenge the Chinese themselves must face and overcome just to be literate, much less succeed to even a modest degree in business or any other profession, is learning how to read and write their own language. This alone is such a formidable undertaking that it requires extraordinary diligence and perseverance over a period of many years—a factor that has a profound influence on the overall character and personality of the Chinese.

In addition to conditioning the Chinese to be persistent and extremely meticulous, to approach everything in a precise order and to expect everything to have precise structure, training in writing the thousands of ideograms making up the writing system greatly enhances the manual dexterity of the Chinese.

All of this combined conditioning contributes enormously to making the Chinese especially suited mentally and physically to perform detailed manufacturing applications.

In fact, a great deal of the work ethic for which the Chinese, especially overseas Chinese, are famous surely derives from the demands of their *wen zi* or *written characters*.

Traditionally, the textbooks studied for the national civil service exams, which more or less divided all Chinese into "haves" and "have nots," were written in classical Chinese which was so grammatically and structurally different from everyday Chinese that people couldn't read the books without first being trained in the classical language.

One of the reforms promoted by revolution-minded writers in the last decades of the Qing Dynasty (1644–1912) was replacing this very difficult classical style of writing with ordinary Chinese.

Grammatically, the family of Chinese languages is similar to English— subject, verb, object. But there are no other similarities. There are no verb tenses, conjugations, declensions or inflections. Genders are used only in writing. However, Chinese is a tonal language. One word can have four different meanings, depending on the tone. Cantonese has nine tones, Mandarin only four.

Another factor that makes the learning of Chinese a formidable task is the existence of a *formal* as well as a common language. Formal Chinese is very much like a dialect in its own right, and requires extraordinary additional effort to learn and to use properly.

Most Chinese family names have only one character, which makes it easier for non-Chinese speakers to distinguish between them and the first name. Chinese usually have two-character first names, which are sometimes run together as one word when written, as in Xiaoping, or separated by a hyphen, as in Kai-shek—reportedly to help foreigners avoid mistaking them for the family name.

There is a growing trend for Chinese couples to use only one-character given names for their children, so the one-character name always being the family name is not a hard and fast rule. In short, Chinese last names are a "closed" family tradition that has been passed down for generations. They are so well-established that no Chinese confuses them with ordinary words. The most common family names are Zhang, Wang, Lee, Zhao and Liu.

The ideograms used to write Chinese words are written without any "word" spaces between them. For some foolish reason, it has become the practice to also run the Romanized spelling of many words together as if they were single words. For example, *Chinese language* is normally written as *Hanyu*, instead of *Han yu*. The English language in Putongua is *Ying yu*.

But having to contend with 10 languages, dozens of dialects and an ideographic script that kept most of the country's millions illiterate until the middle of the 20th century was not the worst of China's linguistic problems.

Even more serious was the presence of "two" languages in one—the common language spoken in ordinary conversation and a "formal" or "official" language, *wen yan*, used by scholars and the government bureaucracy.

The formal language was made up of classic vocabulary and ideograms that ordinary people, not educated in the classics, could not understand when it was spoken or read it when it was written.

As late as the 1930s only a tiny fraction of the people of China could read the hundreds of newspapers and magazines being published at that time. Mao Zedung, who was to become the founding father of the People's Republic of China, was one of the first to write and publish in *bai hua* or *plain speech* in a magazine he founded and edited (*The Xiang River Review*) in the late 1920s.

When Mao and his Communist Party took over China in 1949 they made *bai hua* or *plain speech* the official "language" of the country, but they ended up replacing the traditional *wen yan* or classical speech with *Communist-speak*, which, again, became a language within the language.

See **Tifa**.

88

和

He

(Hoe)

"The Cost of Harmony"

Looking back at the length of China's cultural history in light of the suffering the people have endured over the ages, one might be tempted to feel that the culture was too powerful, too encompassing, and that it lasted much too long.

While it was the strength of Chinese culture that resulted in it surviving for more than five thousand years, the very things that made it so strong were generally the ones that also made it anti-human, that stifled the individuality and independence of its people, and that kept most of them at the lowest possible subsistence level.

It could be argued that if the political culture had been less potent and more susceptible to change, the practical nature of the Chinese people would have led to the evolvement of a materially advanced society that could have totally changed the history of the world.

If, for example, the Chinese people had been free to take the fullest possible advantage of all the technology they invented, from the compass to gun powder and rockets, they could well have been the dominant power in the world. And, of course, with freedom and economic incentives, they surely would have invented far more.

But the restraints imposed upon the Chinese by their culture of ancestor worship and their overall philosophy of social authoritarianism kept the country locked in a virtually motionless time-warp until the beginning of the 19th century.

One of the facets of Chinese culture that played a key role in its stagnation was attempts by the government to make absolute *he* (hoe) or *harmony* the foundation of all behavior.

In its Chinese context, the principle of *he* was not just earth-bound etiquette. It incorporated the spirituality of the heavens and the cosmic order of the universe, and was therefore much more than just a commitment to formalized behavior.

Living according to the precepts of Chinese-style *he* included absolute obedience to government authorities and doing nothing to disturb the peace or upset the hierarchical order of things. It meant sublimating one's own feelings and interests on behalf of the family and others. It meant knowing your place and keeping it, and fulfilling all of your obligations without question.

Present-day Chinese still regard *he* as the necessary foundation for all relationships, and both the concept and the term are mentioned regularly in one context or another. And as in the past, *he* embraces the whole lifestyle, from home or office furnishings and decorations to the preparation of food.

To the Chinese, harmony is not just the absence of discord. It is everything being 'right,' being in balance, and contributing to harmonious feelings. Visitors who spend any length of time in China soon learn to recognize the *he* element in virtually everything the Chinese say and do—particularly when it is a negative or irrational action that is intended to maintain harmony for the sake of harmony.

But, with all this, the historical view of the Chinese as a peaceful, tranquil people, living in harmony among themselves and nature was mostly an intellectual creation that represented a philosophical image of the Chinese— not real life.

The social system the Chinese have been forced to live under, and which continues today in only slightly weakened form, imbues the people with a potential for savage violence that negates much of their passion for harmony—because most of the programmed harmony that has existed over the centuries was involuntary and at the expense of the individuality and spirit of the people.

In every controversial situation in China, there must be a scapegoat who can be punished and thereby leave everyone else pure and unsullied, because legitimacy is based on having an unblemished reputation and maintaining public harmony. This is especially true in politics but generally applies in business as well.

In many cases, depending on the nature of the "offense," the person picked as scapegoat may not have been involved at all but is chosen—or volunteers—as a sacrifice, and punishment may be more symbolic than real.

89

黑社会

Heishe Hui

(Hu-ee-shay Huu-ee)

"The Secret Societies"

There has never been any such thing as guaranteed freedom of speech or assembly in China. Until recent times, public dissent of any kind was taboo. There were numerous sanctions, some of them horrible to contemplate, that were typically imposed to eliminate troublemakers and at the same time discourage others from doing the same kind of things.

During periods of turmoil in the Qing (Ching) Dynasty (1644–1911), just writing a private letter criticizing the government was enough to receive the death penalty if it became known to the authorities.

Because of this situation, it became customary for political dissidents to develop secret societies, originally referred to as *Tian Tu Ren* or *Heaven Earth Man* societies (Triads in English) and now more commonly known as *Heishe Hui* (Hu-ee-shay Huu-ee), or *Black Societies*. These first secret groups were vehicles for planning and carrying out programs designed to reform elements of the local, regional or national governments.

In other cases, secret societies were established to spread religious convictions that were not approved by the government. Still other groups were motivated by a combination of political and religious fever, or just to provide impoverished and powerless groups with some means of protecting themselves and bettering their living standards.

The first Triad societies apparently appeared in Taiwan and Fujian Province in the 1700s. They were made up of sailors and boat people mixed with poor townspeople who banded together for self-protection. They are said to have engaged in low-level criminal activities.

By the early 1800s a number of the Triads had grown into large organizations that contained members from virtually all levels of local society, including women. Also by this time, some of the Triad members were representing themselves as patriots, intending to overthrow the Manchu rulers, restore the Ming Dynasty, and introduce democratic principles into China.

Government leaders reacted in their usual harsh way in an effort to destroy the Triads. A regulation was issued making the death penalty mandatory for Triad leaders and calling for severe punishment for their followers. Captured leaders were strangled in public. Triad members were publicly whipped, receiving one hundred blows from a bamboo staff, then banished to lands a minimum of a thousand miles away.

From this period until the downfall of the Qing (Manchu) Dynasty in 1912 the Triads were active as both political dissidents and self-help societies, creating and sustaining their own economic base by legitimate as well as illegitimate activities.

During the latter 1800s, when the Qing Dynasty was being torn apart by internal problems and depredations by foreign powers, the Triads moved overseas with the flood of Chinese who fled their homeland to seek safety and stability in Southeast Asia, the U.S., Cuba, Latin America and elsewhere.

China's famous revolutionary Dr. Sun Yat-sen, who served briefly as the "provisional president" of the Republic of China in early 1912 after the fall of the Qing Dynasty in 1911, made use of the members of societies in Southern China, and himself had joined the Hawaiian branch of the Triad society in 1904.

But there was no place for the Triads in mainland China after the Communist takeover in 1949. Members who did not join the Communist bandwagon were imprisoned or exterminated. From that point on the overseas Triads devolved into crime syndicates, primarily preying on overseas Chinese.

When the Communist government reopened China to the outside world in the late 1970s, the Triads began re-establishing themselves on the mainland. They are now growing in wealth and influence in tandem with the economy of China and overseas Chinese communities.

90

喝酒

Hejiu

(Ho-jee-uu)

"Drinking in Culture"

The Chinese may have been the first humans to change non-alcoholic drinking from being just a nutritional necessity to being both a nutritional and recreational activity.

Hejiu (ho-jee-uu) or "drinking" is not only one of the most common social activities in China, it has become so much a part of the culture it is practically impossible for someone to be Chinese if they do not indulge in social drinking.

The most common social drink in China is, of course, tea. And in the view of many, the practice of tea drinking is one of China's greatest contributions to mankind.

Tea is brewed from the leaves of the *camellia sinensis*, or tea plant, which have been processed in one of three different ways to produce three general tea categories: green tea, brown tea and black tea.

Green tea is made from fresh leaves that have been steamed to preserve their color and prevent fermentation. Brown tea is made from leaves that have been partially fermented. Black tea is made from leaves that have been fully fermented. Several sub-varieties of teas are made from semi-fermented and fermented tea leaves.

The fermentation process of tea leaves begins with drying, which is followed by twisting and then rolling to separate the leaf cells and release the oils (which provides the taste). This step exposes the oils to the air, and initiates fermentation.

Next, the twisted/rolled leaves are fed through a wire mesh, then spread out in a cool, damp place, where they absorb oxygen and undergo further fermentation. The final step is drying by hot air to stop the fermentation process and give the tea a uniform color, taste and aroma. Brown tea results when the fermentation process is stopped early.

Tea houses, the public social parlors of China, have existed in China for several thousand years, playing especially key roles as meeting places for business and social purposes, and as stop-overs for travelers.

A ditty that suggests the ongoing importance of tea in Chinese life goes like this: Tea before you eat; tea afterwards; tea before you leave; tea when you return; tea before you start (to work); a tea break in between; tea when no one is home; tea when company comes. Tea is usually served to guests automatically.

The cheapest and most common tea is a mild brown version, called *oolong* in Cantonese, which is served by most families and restaurants the way Westerners provide water.

Beijing and Shanghai style restaurants often serve a green tea that has been dried over hot charcoal, then mixed with rose, plum, lychee and jasmine essence.

Chiu Chow (also called Swatow) restaurants often specialize in a strong, bitter-tasting black tea called *Tek Kwanying* or *Iron Buddha*. It is served, in thimble-sized cups, before the meal to clear the palate and after the meal to settle the stomach.

Jasmine tea (*shangpin*), served in many higher class restaurants, is one of China's most aromatic teas.

The Chinese claim that their tea-drinking is one of the reasons very few Chinese are fat (including those who are well-off enough to over-eat rich foods every day).

They say that the tea they drink with meals combines with the fatty oils in the food, and "leaches" the oils out of the body, dramatically reducing the calories their bodies absorb.

Visitors to Chinese homes are generally served tea immediately or soon after their arrival, but etiquette calls for them to refrain from drinking the tea until the host has mentioned it at least twice and usually three times.

One of the more interesting facets of tea-drinking etiquette in Hong Kong and adjoining Guangdong Province has to do with getting your restaurant table teapot refilled and thanking the waiter or waitress.

When the teapot is empty, or low, and you want more tea the custom is to leave the lid slightly askew as a signal that you want it refill. When the waiter or waitress refills your cups or the teapot the custom is to tap on the table three or four times with your fingers.

This way of expressing appreciation is said to have derived from the *k'ou-t'ou* (kow-tow), or kneeling down and touching the forehead to the floor before high-ranking government officials.

Although the British quickly became addicted to drinking Chinese tea they were shocked and horrified at the idea of kow-towing to Chinese officials. When some early diplomats and traders were informed that they had to perform this ritual when meeting officials they threatened to go to war against China.

A note to tea-makers: Never let the water continue to boil after it begins to bubble and steam. Continued boiling causes the water to lose its oxygen, and gives the tea a flat taste.

Drinking alcoholic beverages is a skill the Chinese have been honing for several thousand years, and visiting businesspeople are strongly advised not to try to outdrink them or even match them glass for glass.

People who like drinking, can "hold their liquor" and not suffer hangovers or any diminishing of their abilities may choose to play the drinking game, but it is wise even for those with iron stomachs and heads to pace themselves when jousting with Chinese.

For everyone else, drinking modestly or not at all is the best course no matter how forceful the Chinese host might be. Explaining that you cannot drink for some reason or that you can drink only a little, is acceptable.

A common way of begging off is to say, *Sui bian* literally *As one pleases*, but in this case meaning *I'll take just a sip*. Soft drinks are also common when multiple toasts are called for.

Maotai, China's most famous and most powerful drink (it is about 50 percent alcohol) is made from sorghum, and comes from Maotai City in Guizhou Province.

China's institutionalized drinking toast is *Ganbei!*, which is the equivalent of *Bottoms up!*, *Cheers!*.

91

Heng
(Hueng)

"Hanging In"

One of the most fascinating things about China's traditional culture is its relationship to nature, and the use of natural phenomenon in allegories to explain the mysteries of life as well as provide guidelines for leading a harmonious existence.

In addition to making such explanations memorable, this device contributes immeasurably to bringing out practical applications of rules to live by, humanizing them and making them personal.

Flowers, for example, known as much for their fragility as their beauty, are often used to illustrate characteristics that seem to be exactly the reverse of their fragile image, particularly in reference to human qualities.

One piece of the puzzle of humanity that China's early sages contemplated at length and frequently compared to flowers was the importance of *heng* (hueng), which literally means *continuing* and refers to enduring—to the endurance that is necessary to cope with obstacles that stand in life's way.

Heng, noted the sages, underlies the whole of the cosmos, from the galaxies in the heavens to the smallest piece of matter—all continue in one form or another, and in doing so, constitute what we know as eternity.

By its nature, *heng* is never a static condition, and because of this people are advised to make sure they are centered in their thinking, that the foundations for their efforts are solid, and that their goals are worthy; otherwise, disappointment and possibly failure are inevitable.

On more practical terms, guidelines implicit in the *heng* symbol include a positive family relationship, being wary of embracing the new without mature consideration, avoiding extremes, making sure your goals are realistic, being courageous and aggressive when such qualities are called for, and remaining calm in the face of the unknown and adversity.

As always, one of the *heng* messages that is central to responding properly to the opportunities as well as the threats of life is to work continuously to elevate your own standards of behavior, to know yourself, to conform to the highest ideals of society, and to regularly renew yourself by participating in rituals that nurture the spirit.

For at least the last two and a half millennia the Chinese have been steeped in the philosophy of *heng*, but only a few of the qualities promoted by the concept have ever been or are now readily discernible in most Chinese; not because of any inherent propensity to ignore the lessons but because they have lived in a political and economic system that made such behavior impossible.

The only facet of *heng* that the Chinese were able to absorb was simply endurance itself; the ability to survive under often inhuman conditions and continue to perpetuate themselves. The hope is now growing in China that people will be able to take more advantage of the wisdom of *heng*.

92

和平演变

Heping Yanbian

(Heh-peeng Yahn-bee-enn)

"Resisting Peaceful Evolution"

One of the greatest fears of the original Chinese Communist Party leaders, particularly the older generation who took part in the revolution from the early 1920s on, was that "spiritual pollution," already present in China and continuing to seep in from the West, would limit the success of the Party in communizing China and thereafter be one of the ongoing dangers the country would face.

By "spiritual pollution" Mao Zedung and the other CCP leaders were referring to any political and economic ideology other than communism and socialism, as well as any religion and any other social beliefs or practices having to do with human rights, individual rights, individualism, and so on.

The CCP spent a great deal of its time and resources on programs designed to exterminate all manifestations of "spiritual pollution" in China, and to maintain barriers against unacceptable ideas coming in from the outside. These programs were based on either executing people who had been "spiritually polluted," or sentencing them to brain-washing and years of hard labor in prison.

Much less conspicuous than these programs and the fear that generated them was something that was labeled *heping yanbian* (heh-peeng yahn-bee-enn), which translates as *peaceful evolution*, but means something altogether different from what it suggests on the surface.

In its Chinese Communist Party context *heping yanbian* refers to what the CCP leaders saw as attempts by the United States and other Western countries to surreptitiously destroy Chinese communism and transform the country into a democratic, capitalistic society by such "peaceful" measures as withholding economic cooperation, and subtly introducing capitalist concepts into the country by both direct and indirect methods.

By the end of the disastrous Cultural Revolution in 1976 it had become obvious to Party stalwart Deng Xiaoping and other more moderate Communist leaders that rather than continue to fight *heping yanbian* they should welcome it and do everything they could to speed it up, but only on their own terms and at a pace of their own choosing.

This gradual awakening of Deng and other CCP members to the inherent weaknesses of the Communist system, and particularly to the spin that Mao Zedung had put on the ideology, finally resulted in a series of government "reforms" in 1978 that marked the beginning of the end of the Chinese experiment with communism.

The response of the Chinese people to this piece-meal introduction to *heping yanbian* was an astounding example of both their resilience and talents. In less than ten years China was well on its way to becoming an economic superpower.

Heping yanbian is not only transforming the economy of China, just as Mao feared it would, it has already transformed the Communist Party itself.

93

洪

Hong
(Hung)

"The Bottomline"

In the West, morality is generally divided into black and white, and from the religious viewpoint there is little appreciation, understanding or tolerance for shades in between. Still, on a day-to-day basis, Western morality is as variable and as circumstantial as expediency requires.

Christianity, for example, teaches very strict standards of behavior, and yet Christian societies tolerate an astonishing variety of behavior that completely disregards its own teachings. Again generally speaking, there is also a public and a private morality in the West, and the two are often diametrically opposed to each other.

Part of this dual-and-expediency approach to morality results from the fact that Westerners are culturally conditioned to look only at the surface of things, and to ignore or gloss over everything else—as if the world was one dimensional.

The Chinese say that it is because of this "shallow" approach to life, that Westerners habitually make fast decisions and are constantly changing their minds.

Confrontations between Westerners and Chinese are therefore inevitable, because the Chinese are programmed to think, to see and to react in holistic terms; to look beyond the surface into the depth of things; to carefully and slowly consider all angles, all eventualities, and to base their behavior on fundamentals rather than surface signs.

Of course, not all Chinese are dedicated to or are expert at holism and there are frequent aberrations in their behavior on an individual and mass basis. But their traditional culture is based on holistic thinking, and begins with the fundamental positive-negative nature of the cosmos.

One of the things this means in practical terms is that the Chinese generally take longer than Westerners to make decisions and often complicate things that are basically simple by considering and giving precedence to factors that are not relevant at that time.

Hong (hung) is a word that is especially meaningful to the Chinese. It means *profundity*, and refers to the Chinese penchant for looking at things in depth.

It often seems that the Chinese are obsessed with *hong*, wanting to see everything and understand everything before they will move—something that just as often endlessly frustrates Western businesspeople and diplomats.

One of the things that both businesspeople and diplomats are advised to do when presenting any kind of proposition to the Chinese is to anticipate every question the Chinese side could possibly have, and answer them before they are asked.

In any event, successful cross-cultural communication requires substantially more *hong* than Westerners are used to, and is therefore a factor that must be taken into consideration in any dealings with Chinese.

94

后门

Hou Men

(Hoe-uu Mane)

"Using the Back Door"

Bureaucracy is one of the most enduring—and deadly—of the many things supposedly invented in China. More than three thousand years ago, the governments of the various kingdoms of China were administered by a cadre of bureaucrats who had already mastered all of the attitudes, skills and behavior for which the breed is known today.

But that was not all that Chinese bureaucrats had going for them over the millennia. They functioned and thrived in a political system in which they and the rulers they served had absolute power over the lives of the people beneath them.

The common people of China had no inalienable rights that were guaranteed by law. Broadly speaking, they were looked upon and treated as property of the state. Their primary function, as seen by the bureaucrats and rulers, was to create the wealth necessary to support the government on as high a level as possible while they were allowed to keep only enough of what they produced to survive.

Within this environment, the ordinary people of China were forced to develop many skills to deal with the elite officials who ran the local and national governments. These skills ranged from knowing when and how to bribe officials, to operating an "underground economy" that allowed them to surreptitiously improve their own standard of living.

Access to this unofficial world, whether it involved a government official or the supplier of some needed goods or services, was through the *hou men* (hoe-uu mane) or *back door*, a term that has exactly the same connotation as its English equivalent, but was—and still is today—far more meaningful and important in China that it is in most Western countries.

In earlier times, the use of the *hou men* was often vital to simple survival. There were so many regulations restricting the behavior of ordinary people, and the sanctions used to enforce these regulations were so severe, that it was virtually impossible for the people to survive without resorting to the *back door*.

The *hou men* continues to be one of the busiest portals in present-day China. Bureaucracy continues to reign supreme, limiting the rights and choices of the people and forcing them to do as they have always done—go behind officialdom to get as much out of the system as they can.

Outsiders dealing with China learn very quickly that they too must utilize the *hou men* for both personal and business purposes, and the more such doors one discovers or develops, the more effective the dealings can be.

Of course, there is always an element of danger in using the *hou men* so the newcomer is advised not to rush in before establishing a relationship with one or more trusted Chinese who can guide you through the intricacies of the system.

Knowing the right protocol to approaching and using one of China's back doors can be as important as the door itself.

95

怙

Hu
(Who)

"Obsession with Power"

Until the introduction of a few democratic principles into China in the late 1970s and 1980s, the Chinese had never experienced the kind of personal freedom that Americans and many other people take for granted.

China's age-old social customs as well as its authoritarian government prescribed and controlled virtually every aspect of thought as well as behavior. Ordinary people had no political power whatsoever, and were totally subject to the will of government authorities.

Men on every level of Chinese society traditionally used their superior social status to lord it over their wives and children. But outside of this narrowly restricted area, common men had practically no control over their day-to-day lives or their destiny.

Because of this the Chinese—men in particular—became obsessed with achieving *hu* (who) or *personal power*—a factor that was eventually to change the course of China's history.

Until the last decades of Imperial China, however, the only legitimate way a man could achieve any real degree of *hu* was to become a government official—and this was absolutely impossible for well over ninety percent of the population.

Throughout much of China's history this situation led to periodic peasant rebellions, to the appearance of provincial warlords, to secret societies, and eventually to the migration abroad of several million Chinese.

And it was overseas that the Chinese obsession for *hu* was to come into its own.

Outside of the cultural and political chains of China, this obsession for personal control fueled an extraordinary drive that has made overseas Chinese one of the most accomplished and affluent groups in the world.

Among the characteristics that are typical of overseas Chinese, again men in particular:

a. They feel they cannot reach their full potential working for others.
b. They are determined to be their own boss, to have their own company.
c. Once they have their own company they are obsessed with keeping power in their own hands.
d. As they age and approach retirement, they are equally obsessed with passing their companies on to their families.
e. They keep a low profile in order not to attract undue attention to themselves.

While obsession with *hu* has contributed enormously to the success of many overseas Chinese businesspeople, there are also built-in handicaps. These range from weak generational links that often damage and sometimes destroy family-owned companies; refusing to bring in professional outsiders to manage companies that have grown too complicated and too large for one person to handle; and internal power struggles that are endemic in Chinese families.

As one overseas Chinese tycoon put it: "Chinese are like grains of sand. They never stick together."

Another factor that plays a role in *hu*-dominated overseas Chinese businesspeople is that most of their business is done through personal networks that are almost always generational. When their generation passes from the scene, these business relationships also disappear.

This is not always detrimental to their businesses, however, because if the next generation coming on line is competent, it can make the changes that are necessary to keep up with the times.

Now that mainland Chinese peasants, workers and businesspeople are free to give vent to their obsession for *hu*, it is acting as a powerful stimulant for economic growth in China.

More and more of the successful descendants of overseas Chinese are also taking their business know-how, money and motivation back to the mainland, further contributing to the expanding wealth of China.

Hua
(Whah)

"The Glory Seekers"

First-time visitors to China are often seeking to confirm images of the country that are decades if not centuries old, and may come away sorely disappointed when they discover that the reality of present-day China is quite different from what they expected.

Even the physical artifacts of traditional Chinese culture, the pagodas, shrines and palaces, often turn out to be disappointing, either because of their scarcity (thousands of them were destroyed during the so-called Cultural Revolution between 1966 and 1976), or because they are far less imposing than imagined.

The one thing that generally lives up to visitor expectations, however, are the Chinese people themselves—their overwhelming numbers, their ethnic diversity, the beauty of the children, the survival of many of the folkways that date back centuries, the startling ways they mix the old and the new, and their views of themselves and the world at large.

It is probably impossible for an outsider to truly and fully see the Chinese as they see themselves, or get close to approximating the view they have of the outside world. Such a feat would require that the outsider literally become Chinese.

And because the outsiders' own cultural programming results in them looking at China as a mirror image of themselves, they are often surprised and frustrated when their vision turns out to be false.

Many visitors to China take it for granted that the great mass of rural poor would readily give up their identities as Chinese in exchange for a better life. Surprisingly, that is generally not so. The typical Chinese farmer is as proud of his racial identity and cultural heritage as the successful business-person or high-level government official whose life is as different from his as night and day.

The racial, cultural and national pride that imbues the typical peasant of China is normally a quiet pride, but one that continues to reflect the former glory of China. The term *hua* (whah), which means *glory*, is still today combined with the ideogram for person to mean *the people of China*.

The original meaning of *hua* was *radiant* or *glorious*. Using it with the character for person to refer to the people of China signifies a vainglorious self-image that may be out-of-place to the foreigner but is still meaningful to the Chinese.

The visitor to rural China who sees the primitive conditions in which people live may find it difficult to believe that they could view themselves as *the glorious people*, but the feeling is there, below the surface, rooted in the virtues of the traditional Chinese family system and in the certainty that their gods are the superior gods.

Visitors who are inclined to take a superior approach to the Chinese in general, whether in a social, technical or economic sense, are likely to create an even deeper sense of resentment, and complicate their relations.

华侨

Hua Qiao
(Whah Chee-ah-oh)

"The Overseas Chinese"

Genealogy has always been of special importance in China because one of the main pillars of society from the dawn of Chinese history has been ancestor worship. This practice made it essential that families keep precise records of their predecessors, and some present-day families claim they can trace their ancestry back two thousand years or more.

In southeastern China, especially in Guangdong Province, genealogy has been of particular importance since the mid-1900s because family records have become something akin to treasure maps leading to great wealth.

Hundreds of thousands of family records in this region of China have been used to confirm kinships with the millions of Chinese who live outside the country—the now famous *Hua Qiao* (whah chee-ah-oh) or *overseas Chinese*.

The number of *Hua Qiao* whose ties go back to some of these villages now exceeds the stay-at-home populations of the districts.

Because of the tradition of ancestor worship that binds them to their native places, most overseas Chinese have maintained the feelings of kinship and loyalty alive for generation after generation.

From the first months and years following the outflow of Chinese immigrants in the 1700s and 1800s, money and gifts of all kinds have flowed back to China. By the 1970s this flow of money from overseas Chinese in the United States, Singapore, Hong Kong and elsewhere had become a virtual flood.

Hua Qiao, virtually all of whom originally lived in hostile environments in their adopted homelands, were well-prepared from cultural experience to keep a low profile in order not to attract official or public attention, to keep information about their activities and companies confidential, and mostly to engage in businesses that were typically operated beyond the view of the public, in such categories as sub-manufacturing, assembling, wholesaling, finance and transportation.

Today many of the richest men in Southeast Asia are of Chinese ancestry, and virtually all of these modern-day taipans have taken advantage of the opportunities offered by the opening of China to foreign businesses. Their investments run the gamut, from hotels to oil fields.

Some of the wealthiest of these *Hua Qiao* have become godfathers to their native places, bestowing parks, schools, hospitals and other facilities featuring the latest technology on villages and towns that had changed very little since their ancestors left.

Since the 1980s overseas Chinese have been one of the most important sources of investments helping to transform China's economy, and because of the importance of these investments to China the national government has enacted a variety of laws favoring them, treating wealthier overseas Chinese visitors with hospitality and pomp that is normally reserved for heads of state.

Some regions that have been particularly enriched by investments from their overseas relatives have built special hotels for them and go to other extremes to welcome them and cater to them during their visits.

More and more *Hua Qiao* are becoming active in China as business entrepreneurs, lawyers, scientists, teachers, translators and interpreters, providing the cross-cultural talents that are essential for China to become a full-fledged member of the international community.

98

Huei
(Hway-ee)

"Raising Money from Friends"

One of the key factors behind the independence and economic success of so many overseas Chinese is that families and close friends cooperate in taking care of personal matters as well as in financing business enterprises.

The traditional Chinese way for an individual or a family to raise money for some business project is to form a *huei* (hway-ee), or *financial syndicate*, typically with ten to twelve members who pay a predetermined amount of money into a pool for a set period of time, often twelve months.

If each participant in a 10-person *huei* puts in $1,000, the founder of the syndicate can borrow a total of $10,000 the first month. Thereafter, the other members bid to borrow the monthly total of $10,000. Whoever agrees to pay the highest interest on the money gets the loan.

The total of the money in the pool may fluctuate each month, depending on how much interest the winning bidder pays and whether or not the other members choose to reduce their monthly payment by the amount of the interest, or pay the full amount and let it build up.

The winner of the monthly bid becomes a *dead* member, meaning he or she cannot bid again and thereafter must pay the full $1,000 each month. If there is no bid, a drawing is held among the *live* members and the winner gets all of the money paid in that month.

Variations in the total amount in the pool determines the interest the investors earn. The longer one waits before bidding—or winning a drawing—the more interest one earns because there are more "dead" members paying the full amount.

In a twelve-month *huei* the person who bids during the seventh month can usually get the money without paying any interest. Those bidding after the seventh month earn interest. The final borrower does not have to bid and earns the most interest.

The most profitable of the *huei* are those in which there are six or seven people who need the money as quickly as possible. Those who don't need the money or can wait until after the seventh month generally earn interest rates that are substantially higher than those paid by banks.

There are risks in *huei*. A winning bidder may take the money and run. Members may drop out and not make the monthly payments. Because of this, virtually all Chinese *huei* are limited to family and clan members who can be trusted.

Historically, *huei* have been especially common in overseas Chinese communities because their members were not accepted by local indigenous business communities and had no other way of raising money.

The concept of the *huei* is also used by large-scale Chinese entrepreneurs as well as by long-established and wealthy Chinese business groups. They prefer the confidentiality and control that comes with raising funds "inhouse."

99

会友

Hui You
(Whe yoe-ou)

"The Bridegroom Brotherhood"

Wedding ceremonies in China have undergone a number of changes since the infamous Cultural Revolution (1966–1976). Prior to that war against all of the old traditions, weddings were generally held in neighborhood ancestral halls and involved family members and close friends.

One of the primary features of weddings was the institution of *Hui You* (whe yoe-ou), which can be translated as *Brotherhood of the Bridegroom*.

Each *hui you* was made up of a few of the life-long friends of the groom. In addition to helping the groom prepare for and get through the wedding, the members of the brotherhood maintained a close relationship with the newly married man thereafter, coming to his aide on other important life-cycle occasions.

The chief member of the *hui you* had to be an older married man whose parents were still alive and who preferably had a son of his own. The more economically successful or socially prominent the head man was, the more the young bridegroom could benefit from being associated with him.

Soon after the end of the Cultural Revolution the *hui you* tradition was resumed, but it has since been conspicuously modernized in keeping with other changes in Chinese society.

In today's *hui you* the main man must still be an older, married friend of the family, but the number of brotherhood members has been expanded to include as many as 20 or 30 of the bridegroom's friends, co-workers and cousins, and once the wedding is over the group disbands.

In addition to helping with the physical arrangements of the wedding and following banquet, the brotherhood members also buy, at their own expense, such things as wine and cigarettes to pass out to wedding guests, and are in charge of arranging for transportation (minibuses and taxis) for the bride and groom and their relatives.

Becoming a member of a *hui you* can be costly because as personal friends of the groom members are expected to buy especially nice gifts, and the wider their circle of friends the more often they are invited to serve as groom aides. It is considered both a duty and an honor, however, and few ever refuse.

More importantly, *hui you* now play a major role in the enormous amount of networking that goes on in China—serving as a virtually unending source for new contacts.

Foreign visitors, especially businesspeople, are prized as wedding guests because they add a special international element from a social viewpoint, and offer the possibility of foreign connections that can be especially valuable to the families and the *hui you* members.

Some of the ritualistic symbols that were a traditional part of Chinese weddings, such as an umbrella, a stick of sugar cane, rice and a head of lettuce, are still seen, but few of the young people involved in weddings are knowledgeable about the origin or meaning of such rituals.

The umbrella and rice are to protect the bride from being attacked by a golden rooster while en route to the groom's house; the cane stick is symbolic of a long marriage; and the head of lettuce suggests fertility and good fortune because the pronunciation of the word for lettuce, *shengcai,* sounds like the Chinese words for fertility and fortune.

During the wedding banquet, dumplings are boiled and the newlywed couple is asked to taste the first dumpling together. The dumpling is deliberately undercooked, which in Chinese is *sheng* a pun on the word for *fertility*. The couple is supposed to say *sheng* so they will have children to pass on the family traditions.

100

户口

Hu Kou

(Huu Kow)

"Reach of Big Brother"

In 1955 the Chinese government inaugurated a new nationwide system known as *hu kou* (huu kow) or *household registration*, to keep track of everyone in the country. In addition to identifying all members of each household, the system also distinguished between residents in rural areas who were required to grow their own grain for personal consumption, and urban residents who had to buy their grain from state-run stores.

One of the immediate effects of the new policy was a dramatic reduction in the mobility of the population. Urban residents could buy rice and other grains only at designated stores with stamps that were not transferable to other people or usable in other stores. Farmers, required to raise their own grain, were not issued grain stamps and therefore could not buy grain anywhere.

To further proscribe mobility, the government decreed that anyone wanting to move had to get approval from the Public Security Bureau (PSB). This permission was routinely denied except for better-to-do people who could afford to bribe local PSB officials.

One of the key criteria for approving a request to move was the availability of a job and housing for the petitioner—or an official document attesting to the fact that a specific individual or family had agreed to exchange jobs and or houses with the petitioner.

Not only did all the members of every household have to be registered with the PSB, any change in the household, including short-term visitors, had to be reported to the local security police.

Grain rationing was relaxed in 1979, and millions of farm residents began flocking to cities and new industrial park areas, looking for factory work.

But the *hu kou* was still used as a method of control. It was still necessary for everyone to be registered as a member of a recognized household in order to qualify for school, work, new housing and various services.

Most new housing was allocated through the individual's place of work. New housing, when available, was allocated to families that needed additional space, and to newly married couples.

Once a family or newly married couple had been promised an apartment in a new building they could not apply for space anywhere else even though they had to wait for months or years for the new apartment building to be completed.

If newly married couples were unable to find housing, they had to remain registered as dependents of their respective parents. In this case, if they had a child, the child was registered as a dependent in the household of the wife's parents.

After 1978 the introduction of some elements of free enterprise into the Chinese economy and the relaxation of CCP controls over the movement and occupation of people resulted in enormous pressures against the *hu kou* system.

It was simply impossible for the CCP bureaucracy to keep some 300 million family registrations up to date by hand (there were no computers). Members of families could not take copies of their *hu kou* with them when they traveled or moved, which meant they had no officially acceptable identity papers. In addition, the certificates were easy to alter, making false and improper entries common.

In the mid-1980s the Chinese government began issuing personal Identification Cards, *Sheng Fen Zheng*, to all individuals. These cards were imprinted with photos of the individuals, encased in plastic, and looked very much like American driver's licenses.

These I.D. cards must be renewed every 10 years until the individual reaches the age of 60. Thereafter, they are for life.

In addition to personal I.D. cards, Chinese who are in school have school I.D. cards. Employees have *danwei* or workplace I.D. cards. There are other I.D. cards that designate rank and class, which are needed when shopping and traveling.

Chinese bureaucrats, uniformed police, Public Security Bureau agents, and virtually everyone else in any position of responsibility, including clerks in state-owned retail stores, have the right to demand to see anyone's identification.

Regularly encountering people who demand, "Your papers!" sometimes raises the specter of Nazi and Fascist regimes of the past.

In the meantime, the traditional *hu kou* system continues in effect, with each household expected to keep its family registration up to date.

101

计

Ji

(Jee)

"The Key to Success"

In the late 1950s and early 1960s one of the bestselling books in Japan was *The Art of War*, written by the famed Chinese military strategist Sun Tzu around 500 B.C.

Japanese businessmen, already nurtured on the Confucian principles of China, readily grasped the relationship between modern-day business and war, and adopted Sun Tzu's treatise as a management bible.

When I wrote about this phenomenon in a trade magazine in 1959, it drew derisive smiles and laughter from many American and European businessmen who were then importing enormous quantities of Japanese-made goods. They were looking into a one-way mirror that reflected only their own perspectives.

The opening paragraph in *The Art of War* is just as appropriate to business as it is to war, and requires the substitution of only one word to cover the essence of business management. It says: "The art of war [business] is of vital importance to the State; the way of life or death; the road to safety or ruin. It is essential that it is seriously studied."

Sun Tzu's book on the art of war is very small; well under ten thousand words. It consists of thirteen chapters, the longest of which is less than one thousand words. Each of the chapters expounds upon one key principle that is vital to waging war, or business, successfully.

The second principle in the book is *ji* (jee), or *planning* (the first principle is *si* [suh] or *knowledge)*, without which it is unlikely that any battle or business plan can succeed.

While Sun Tzu emphasizes the importance of precise, detailed planning, he puts equal emphasis on the importance of being flexible (which applies as much to business as it does to war). Here is the way he makes his point:

As water shapes its flow according to the ground, an army wins by relating to the enemy it faces. Just as water retains no constant shape, in war there shall be no constant condition. Thus, the one who can modify his tactics according to the enemy situation shall be victorious and may be called the divine commander.

Present-day Chinese are just as dedicated to *ji* as their ancient ancestors, and because they automatically equate business with war they take the planning stage very seriously.

Whether or not business (or political) plans devised by the Chinese appear rational and sound to outsiders is another matter. Since they are designed to serve the cultural values and national interests of the Chinese they are not likely to please anyone except the Chinese.

Westerners wanting to do business in China would do well to steep themselves in the teachings of Sun Tzu. If nothing else, letting their Chinese counterparts know they are aware of Sun Tzu can be an advantage.

There is no single key to being successful in doing business in China. There are many keys, and therein lies a significant part of the challenge.

These keys include all of the well-known axioms, such as know your own company and its products, know what you can do and can't do, know as much as possible about the political and economic environment of China, and be especially attuned to the cultural and social factors that motivate and control the Chinese.

One aspect of this cultural awareness is the simple but subtle fact that the Chinese judge potential business partners by their after-hours behavior as well as their behavior in board rooms.

It is therefore important for foreign businesspeople to comport themselves with reasonable dignity when consorting with their Chinese counterparts in restaurants, bars, golf courses or wherever.

102

Jia

(Jee-ah)

"All in the Family"

Western executives who have experienced the Japanese way of doing business have an advantage in understanding the nature and behavior of Chinese companies and government enterprises—although there are characteristics of Chinese management that are totally different from the Japanese way.

During the heyday of Japan's emergence as a world-class economic power Japanese companies were generally patterned after the Confucian concept of a family. And, of course, all of the Confucian-based concepts applying to Japanese management, then and now, were imported from China and adapted to fit the Japanese scene.

The top person in the company played the role of the father (or mother). Employees were hired for life (among larger companies), and management was more or less based on the kind of parent–child relationships that were typical of traditional Confucian-oriented families.

In the meantime, totally different political and economic systems in China have put a distinctive coating on the traditional concepts of Confucianism, giving them characteristics that are unique.

The ideal Chinese corporation, of whatever size, is still patterned after the *jia* (jee-ah) or *family* of ancient China, and most Chinese commercial enterprises are, in fact, run very much like extended families. *Jia* is the ideogram traditionally used in China in reference to military organizations.

Jia is one of the key words in Sun Tzu's famous handbook on fighting and winning wars. He relates it to the structure of the organization, staffing each of its sections or units with capable officers, making sure there is communication and harmony among the units, forming alliances with other armies, and reacting effectively to external factors.

In present-day China, commercial as well as government enterprises are hybrid organizations created out of a combination of Confucianism, communism and socialism, with the result that they have practically none of the strengths that were built into Sun Tzu's *jia*, and many of the weaknesses that are inherent in all three systems.

Outsiders wanting to do business with Chinese enterprises must deal with the organizations as if they were independent kingdoms of their own, with relationships more often based on personalities than on objective principles, and the need for ongoing diplomacy to keep the relationship on track.

Diplomatic maneuvers must go well beyond the head of the company to include upper and middle managers in order to keep them all friendly and cooperative. Having lower level managers on your side can mean the difference between success and failure.

Generally speaking, it is necessary to deal with Chinese companies as if they were large, close-knit families.

103

漸

Jian

(Jee-enn)

"The Tortoise Wins"

Every outsider who has ever had any intimate contact with China, either personal, business or political, has encountered the concept of *jian* (jee-enn) which I have likened to the "tortoise syndrome."

If, as Einstein said, time slows down when you move very fast (and if you move fast enough it stops altogether or even reverses itself), one might be tempted to say that the Chinese have been moving at near light speed since day one.

But in this case, reality is just the reverse. The Chinese long ago learned how to slow time down by moving slow—not fast.

Jian, which means *developing*, is often used to refer to a point or period in time when things should be approached in a slow, deliberate, traditional way. But the overall sense of it seems to be that all of life should move at a slow, stately pace, and that any attempt to accelerate things can be anywhere from foolish to fatal.

Numerous examples, such as business negotiations, political moves, marriage, changing your occupation, and so on are given as occasions when a *jian* approach is the best one. A meditative, tranquil attitude is an integral part of taking the slow road, and when combined with persistence and high principles, has the best chance of success.

As always, however, the Chinese concept of *jian* is broad and deep and is applicable to a variety of situations, beginning when you are young and just starting out, when it is normal for you to be criticized whether you are moving fast or slow. The proper *jian* reaction to this is to learn from the criticism and use it to help you achieve success over the years.

As you move up the ladder of success, if you are guided by the principle of *jian* you can avoid becoming overly confident and putting your accomplishments at risk; you stay flexible enough that you can side-step problems and either duck or retreat in the face of danger, but you maintain your balance and your gradual ascent.

On the next level of success you may encounter jealousy and envy in addition to the usual challenges, but if you hold fast to your course even these people will come around and eventually want to share in your success. To divert jealousy, you need to *jian* (establish) a network by sharing your fame with others and thanking them for your success although they may not have done anything to help you.

If you remain faithful to the dictates of *jian* and achieve the highest level of success you will be accepted by all, admired and emulated, and held up as an example for others to follow.

Jian is not just about surface factors or minor elements that might impact on your situation. It incorporates the deepest social, political and economic values of the times, and calls on you to take all of these into consideration in your planning and behavior.

Finally, *jian* implies that whatever the circumstances of the times, taking a *developing* mode is the safest and best way to achieve your goals. Of course, it can be said with a great deal of accuracy that China has been in a constant *jian* mode since the middle decades of the Qing Dynasty.

健

Jian
(Jee-enn)

"Vim and Vigor"

China has been famous for some two thousand years for its scholar-bureaucrats and for the value placed on learning. In contemporary times, stories of the academic success of young Chinese students in the United States and other Western countries have become commonplace.

The cultural and practical esteem accorded to learning in China contrasts sharply with the still all-too-common attitude in the United States that education in general and studying in particular is somehow an imposition and, where lower class boys are concerned, sissified.

Many American adults who should know better congenitally fall into the trap of programming their children to discount the value and importance of education by portraying attendance in school in a negative fashion—as a bother and a pain but something that kids have to do because it is the law.

Such seemingly harmless remarks as telling kids how lucky they are when they don't have to go to school (because the teachers are on strike or the school is closed because of some other emergency), reinforce the image of school as an unpleasant chore, if not outright punishment.

This perverse image of school and study apparently originated in early America when most work and life in general was very simple, and success was more a matter of practical experience, physical strength, and often expertise with a gun. In this environment, being studious was generally looked upon as being unmanly.

In traditional China, on the other hand, education was an almost sacred treasure. The *only* way to social and financial success was through education, and achieving the level of learning necessary to advance up the social and economic ladder required extraordinary perseverance and *jian* (jee-enn) or *vigor*.

Jian conveys both the respect that the Chinese have for learning and the concept that if a person wants to succeed in life the one thing that must be pursued most vigorously is education.

It was recognized in ancient China that the ability to read and write was the means to power and wealth. Just the nature and number of the ideograms that had to be mastered to become literate in Chinese made it a formidable task that required several years of vigorous effort—and this was before formal education could actually begin.

Combining the concept of *writing* with *person* and *becoming established in life* in a ideogram to mean *vigor* was a very Chinese thing to do.

In China today most children continue to be impregnated with the idea that getting an education takes precedence over everything else, and they are constantly exhorted to demonstrate *jian* in their studies.

105

贱

Jian

(Jee-enn)

"Sexual License"

Male chauvinism has been one of the primary characteristics of Chinese culture since the beginning of the country's recorded history, and probably goes back to the first Chinese Adam and Eve.

Among the masses, women were traditionally seen and used more or less as brood stock and labor, with practically no personal rights. Men on all social levels perpetuated the belief that education was not suitable for women, and presumed that all of their needs were fulfilled by serving the interests of the family.

Officially, the sexuality of women was seen as something that was there for the perpetuation of the family, and for the lower classes, as virtually nothing else. But among the affluent and those in power the sexuality of women was also regarded as a "heaven" for pleasuring men.

The ideogram the Chinese created to denote sexual license, *jian* (jee-enn), is made up of the character compound that depicts three women, suggesting either that sexual license was thought of in terms of rich men who could afford to keep several concubines or female slaves to whom they had sexual access, or illicit affairs.

The pattern for sexual license among the well-to-do in dynastic China was set by the emperors, some of whom had harems numbering in the hundreds. One emperor is recorded as having "used" nearly one thousand girls ranging from the age of eight to the late teens.

This custom of "using" concubines and female slaves was carried out on a smaller scale by court officials, and by government bureaucrats down to the local level, as well as by regional warlords, and better-off landowners.

A number of China's most famous historical novels are based on sexual themes as lived and imagined by upperclass men, but there is very little reference to lusty behavior among common people. Although it is also said that sex was the *only* recreation for men in rural China.

As elsewhere, prostitution has apparently existed in China from the earliest times, waxing and waning with the political and economic conditions. During periods of war and famine, the number of girls sold into prostitution or concubinage rose in proportion to the crisis.

The Communist regime that took over China in 1949 made a determined effort to eliminate prostitution, multiple wives and female sex slaves, and in the early decades was mostly successful. But old habits die hard, and it was not long before Communist officials themselves began to take advantage of their power to consort with many women.

In present-day China sexual pleasures are no longer taboo to the lower classes. Young people date and carry on pre-marital affairs much as they do in most other countries. Married men of means often have liaisons with available women.

Some wives of well-to-do men who spend many nights away from home have their own lovers. Prostitution exists in the major industrial cities and elsewhere, despite frequent crackdowns. Finally, after millennia, sexual license is alive and well in the Middle Kingdom.

Foreigners visiting or living in China are advised to exercise special discretion if they chose to carry on, or attempt to carry on, sexual liaisons with Chinese. Many government officials, on all levels, still consider such fraternization as a dangerous threat to China, and have been known to take arbitrary measures against the parties concerned.

In terms of sexual views and behavior, foreign playboy types rate the young women of Taiwan as being the most liberal. They say that it is possible for attractive, affluent foreign males in Taiwan to have sex with almost any single woman they choose to court.

106

将功赎罪

Jiangong Shuzui
(Jee-ahn-gung Shuu-zuu-ee)

"Bitter Toil"

Slaves and indentured laborers were common throughout the millennia of Imperial China because of the economic benefits that derived from having workers who did not receive wages.

From its earliest years, the Chinese Communist Party has also used forced prison labor, known as *jiangong shuzui* (jee-ahn-gung shuu-zuu-ee) or *bitter toil*, but the CCP had more than economic reasons for doing so.

One reason for the use of *jiangong shuzui* was to take enemies and potential enemies out of circulation, punish them, and thereafter keep them under absolute control. Another reason was the immediate practical value of having the advantage of millions of workers producing wealth for the new Socialist society at a cost that was far below what would have to be paid in a free economy.

The third and most important reason was psychological—the belief that being forced to work like a slave from dawn to dusk for year after year, and being subject to severe punishment for any kind of unapproved behavior, plus incessant indoctrination, would mold the people into ideologically pure "Socialist workers" who would thereafter be perfect Communist citizens.

As has since been graphically demonstrated, only the first of these premises, *laogai sheng chan* or *labor reform production*, proved to be valid. Prison labor production now accounts for a significant percentage of China's national economy.

The enterprises making up this segment of the Chinese economy—farms, factories, mines—are known as *laogai qiye* or *labor reform enterprises*, a euphemism for prison labor.

The CCP began establishing prison work groups long before it took power. As of 1932 there were over 900 such groups in Jiangxi Province, where Mao Zedung and his troops were headquartered. That same year, the use of prison labor was made an integral part of the overall Communist Chinese manifesto and thereafter prison farms and prison factories were established wherever the Communists were able to assert themselves.

The stated purpose of the Chinese gulag was to *punish and reform* all anti-Communist and anti-Socialist elements in the country. This included landlords, businesspeople, most teachers and intellectuals, and people with any Western experience or democratic ideals.

People in all of these categories were lumped into one huge group and labeled *class enemies*, or *enemies of the people* by the Chinese Communist Party.

There were several code words used to designate "class enemies." These included the following:

She an fan (she ahn fahn) = *Alleged counterrevolutionary*
Si fan (suh fahn) = *Movement against reactionary thinkers*
Fangeming youpai (fahn-guh-meeng yoe-ou-pie) = *Counter-revolutionary rightists*
Huai fenze (H'wie fun-t'say) = *Bad elements*

In 1953 the CCP established a policy known as *duoliu shaofang* or *keep more, release less*, pertaining to ordinary criminals who had completed their sentences. This policy called for releasing 30 percent of the convicts and extending the sentences of the rest—a measure designed to maintain larger and more stable prison populations for the sake of production.

In 1957 the CCP decreed that imprisonment in a forced labor enterprise was an administrative procedure, not a criminal proceeding. It was therefore not necessary to go before a judge to convict people before sentencing them to hard labor.

In 1964 the policy regarding releasing prisoners was changed again to *se liu, sebu liu* or *keep four, release four*, meaning that half of the inmates whose time was up were to be released. Under this policy, those kept included those who had not "reformed," those without jobs waiting for them on the outside, those without homes, those whose homes were near large cities on the coast, or near national borders.

The CCP used proven Communist techniques for identifying suspects and victims. A PSB agent was assigned to every company and organization, class or what have you in the country. Each of these entities was required to have a permanent standing Communist Party committee.

If this committee was dissatisfied with the attitude or productivity of any member of the company or other group, it was expected to report that individual to the PSB agent, who would then have the person arrested and sentenced to a forced labor prison.

Parents were encouraged to report unruly, lazy children to the PSB for incarceration in labor "reform" prisons—something that reached its nadir in the 1980s.

The sentences of individuals were routinely extended two or three times. In the early decades the only justification needed was a report by a prison cadre that the individual was in need of additional reform. Later a kind of review office was established.

Over the years numerous euphemisms were used in reference to prisoners, including *personnel* and *students*.

In the early 1990s, it was estimated that there were between eight and ten million people confined in *jiuye* or *forced job placement* (FJP) enterprises. All of them lived in the enterprise compounds and were organized in military-type groups. They had no say-so in their jobs, location or housing. Families that had urban household registration cards were allowed to live in some forced job placement compounds.

The *jiuye* system of sentencing people to hard-labor prisons is still flourishing in China. The pay of FJP workers is said to average from 60 to 70 percent of that of workers on the outside.

Jiuye inmates are given two weeks of paid leave each year to visit their families or relatives. Punishment for failure to return from home-leave is severe.

交流

Jiaoliu
(Jee-ah-oh-lew)

"No Communication in China!"

A very successful overseas Chinese businessman once made the remarkable comment that the Western concept of communication—being skilled in the exchange of opinions and information between people—is virtually alien to the Chinese.

This gentleman said that the Chinese never think of or talk about *jiaoliu* (jee-ah-oh-lew) or *communication* in that sense. He explained that instead of communicating information or orders directly to their co-workers or subordinates, Chinese managers in business and government talk in general terms and give hints of what they want done.

He said it was left up to staff members to "guess" what they are supposed to do and how to do it; that everyone was constantly being tested by this technique, and if they wanted to survive they would work much harder and much longer in an effort to satisfy their bosses.

A major part of this rationale is said to derive from the overwhelming need the Chinese have for avoiding confrontation and maintaining a harmonious facade.

Another part of this kind of behavior is no doubt related to the traditional Chinese philosophy that the head people in a company or other enterprise should be somewhat aloof, and distant; and not given to baring their plans or their souls to others.

The Chinese frequently use the term "mysterious" in listing the ideal qualifications for a leader in any field.

Some China experts say the Chinese language itself is a major obstacle in communicating directly and clearly. They say it is too imprecise; that it lends itself to ambiguity and uncertainty, and leaves gaps that the hearer must fill in by "guessing."

It often seems that the ideograms with which the language is written are, in fact, more like "key words" or headlines than fully completed sentences, and that the hearer must indeed have a significant fund of information and substantial cultural insight to correctly interpret speech as well as the written word.

Whatever the cultural or linguistic reasons, the fuss made over difficulties in communicating effectively in Chinese is sufficient that foreigners in China should take special care to be as clear and as comprehensive as possible.

At the same time, there are clear signs that the Chinese are not only capable of but very good at communicating directly and unambiguously to foreigners when they want to—meaning that the ambiguity that typically marks Chinese communication is a cultural custom, not an inherent characteristic of the language or the thinking processes of the Chinese.

This dual ability of the Chinese—being exceptionally skilled at using ambiguous speech as well as being equally capable of communicating clearly and precisely—gives them an advantage when dealing with foreigners that should also be taken into account.

108

Jiaoshu Yuren

(Jee-ow-shoo Yuu-rune)

"Learning the Chinese Way"

Very early in its long history Chinese civilization evolved into what amounted to two distinct cultures.

The overwhelming majority of Chinese were farmers whose lifestyles remained simple and generally primitive from one millennia to the next.

Then there was a much smaller group—around 10 percent of the population—of elite scholar-administrators, military officers and successful merchants who lived in comfortable surroundings, if not finery; were well educated for the times; and enjoyed the arts, literature, and a sophisticated cuisine.

This split-level civilization was maintained for century after century by both design and coincidence. Social classes were more or less permanently fixed by birth and by law. About the only avenue of upward social mobility was education, and this was strictly controlled by economics, custom and natural barriers presented by the ideographic writing system.

Learning how to read the thousands of ideograms with which the languages of China were written was an exceedingly difficult, time-consuming ordeal. All formal education was strictly reserved for males. Most education was oriented toward preparing for civil service examinations and careers in government.

The subject matter of the civil service examinations was confined to the philosophical and moralistic writings of the ancient sages, particularly Confucius. All of the textbooks involved in studying for the examinations were written in classical Chinese, not vernacular speech.

Very few farm families could afford to support sons and pay to have them tutored for the 20 to 30 years of intensive study necessary to pass the examinations. Education was not deemed proper for female children, who were destined to spend their lives subject to the needs and whims of their fathers, brothers, husbands and mothers-in-law.

In this milieu, teachers were among the most esteemed people in Chinese society. They were seen as paragons of selflessness who spent their lives in acquiring knowledge and an understanding of the human condition, and passing it on to their students.

Teachers were not seen as just conduits of knowledge. They were also seen as providing the moral insights and guidelines necessary for the proper functioning of society. The widely used term *jiaoshu yuren* (jee-ow-shoo yuu-rune) meant "teaching book and teaching people how to live."

Students looked upon teachers as their second parents, and felt deeply obligated to them for the rest of their lives.

But from 1949 until the later part of the 1970s, CCP leaders, particularly Mao Zedung, saw this respect for and loyalty to teachers as an untenable threat to the Party. In Mao's mind, the only loyalty permissible was to the Party.

As a result of Mao's thinking, China's famous student–teacher relationship was virtually destroyed during the infamous Cultural Revolution (1966–1976), when Mao ordered students to smash all of the old traditions of the country.

It was not until the generation of youth born after the Cultural Revolution began entering school that massive efforts were begun to rehabilitate the image and reputation of teachers.

It is doubtful that China's teachers will ever regain the exalted image they had for more than four millennia because the policies and programs of the Communist Party did succeed in breaking the hold that Confucianism traditionally had on the Chinese mind-set.

Present-day Chinese are much too independent minded and individualistic to stand in awe of their teachers.

家族

Jia-Zu

(Jee-ah-T'su)

"The Fifth Cousins"

Legend has it that Chinese civilization developed from one hundred families, which, anthropologists speculate, migrated to the area of the Yellow River in central China from what is now northern China or Siberia.

As the story goes, these families, whose names were recorded, developed into clans that have been continued down to the present times. In any event, family-clan groups have been the defining structure of Chinese society since the civilization entered the pages of history.

History now notes that the ethical system prescribed by Confucius in the 5th century B.C. resulted in China's family unit being precisely arranged in hierarchical order with the father exercising supreme power. Thereafter this system was cast in Confucian stone and eventually became the official foundation for society.

Because of the nature of China's government—an authoritarian bureaucracy under an emperor who ruled "by divine right"—the general population had no say-so in the makeup of the government or its laws. People were subject to the laws as well as the personal whims and idiosyncrasies of those in power.

In this draconian environment, the family was of critical importance to the immediate as well as the long-term survival of every Chinese. The family was the sanctuary of the people. The only people that family members could trust to have their interests at heart were other family members.

China's district policemen, magistrates, regional mandarins and court officials looked out after themselves, their families and friends, and generally treated the common mass as taxpayers and suppliers of goods and labor whose few rights could generally be ignored with impunity.

Obviously, the bigger the individual family the greater its ability to support and protect its members. Thus the *jia-zu* (jee-ah-t'su) or *extended family* became the key to both survival and success for families on every level of society. And just as obviously, those at higher levels had more to lose and more to win than those lower down.

The *jia-zu* is of considerably less importance now than it was throughout China's pre–open market history, but it is still a key factor in Chinese life, often more so among overseas Chinese than some of their more successful brethren back home.

Peek behind the facade of almost any Chinese enterprise and you will likely find layers and generations of families and relations that extend outward to second, third and even fourth or fifth cousins—and again particularly so in such places as Hong Kong, Singapore, Taiwan, Bangkok and other centers of overseas Chinese.

The *jia-zu* concept and practice may appear to many non-Chinese as an obsolete holdover from tribal days, but it still has many advantages, some of which are sorely needed in many other societies as well.

Foreigners doing business in China learn very quickly that one of the best ways to recruit reliable and loyal employees is to ask senior, trusted staff members to recommend their relatives or the relatives of other employees.

继承

Jicheng
(Jee-chung)

"Dividing Up the Money"

China's traditional *jicheng* (jee-chung) or *inheritance* system has had a great deal to do with the continuation of the family business system and with the fact that large conglomerate-type organizations were non-existent in pre-modern China.

In the traditional Chinese inheritance system, all property was equally divided among the heirs, with preference going to sons. One of the obvious results of this system was that the sole ownership of any business could not survive the death of the owner unless there was only one heir.

In the past, this system worked against the development of large family-owned conglomerates over a period of two or more generations because individual members of each succeeding generation preferred to take their inheritance and build their own businesses.

Since most mainland Chinese families can now have only one heir by law, the role that inheritance plays in business will change dramatically over the coming generations. But overseas Chinese continue to have large families and therefore several heirs in each family.

While most young overseas Chinese are still passionate about building their own companies and being their own boss, some, especially those who inherit large companies in which there is a cadre of non-family professional managers, are choosing to keep their inheritances intact.

Another problem that continues to plague companies owned by overseas Chinese is known as the *Third-Generation Syndrome*. This refers to the propensity for grandsons who have inherited successful and often large companies to end up destroying them because they do not have the goals, drive, connections and skills of the founding grandfathers and their own fathers.

In the meantime, the family-operated cottage industry and sub-contract system that existed in China for more than four thousand years, and was resurrected by the government in the 1980s following the failure of communism, is still going strong in other Asian countries as well.

In fact, the huge export industries developed first by Japan and then by Hong Kong, Taiwan, Korea, Singapore and other Southeast Asian countries were not the work of large corporations but of hundreds of thousands of tiny, small and medium-sized companies—some of which developed into huge multi-national conglomerates as their national economies grew.

All of the great corporate names of Japan, Korea and other Asian countries—Hitachi, Hyundai, Samsung, Sony, Toyota, etc.—were built on the backs of dozens to hundreds of small sub-contractors and still today depend on networks of small manufacturers and assemblers for their existence.

As long as China's *jicheng* system contributes to generational entrepreneurship its pluses should outweigh its minuses.

111

激动

Jidong

(Jee-dung)

"Soothing Ruffled Feelings"

We Westerners pride ourselves on being logical and objective, and keeping our emotions under control—especially when it comes to public and business relationships. We are conditioned to keep our private thoughts and affairs separate from our professional lives; to be impersonal in our judgments and actions.

In direct contrast to this, the foundation of the Chinese world is *jidong* (jee-dung) or *personal feelings*; everything derives from personal relationships, and is taken personally. Every Chinese relationship, whether personal or business, is charged with an extraordinary degree of emotion and *human feelings* that must be considered and dealt with in an acceptable manner.

This contrast in the personal as well as business behavior of Westerners and Chinese frequently results in misunderstandings and friction of one kind or another that all too often leads to ill-will, mistrust and acrimonious accusations.

The very first thing that the Chinese typically do when they meet new people *whom they want to meet, for whatever purpose*, is to do everything they can to put the relationship on a personal basis as quickly and as solidly as possible; to establish deep emotional ties with the individuals concerned because that is the only way they know how to interact with others.

Problems arise, for both sides, when the Chinese personal-emotional approach encounters the foreign objective-logical approach. Like magnets, they repel each other.

But the emotional element in the makeup of the Chinese does not exclude logical, pragmatic thinking and behavior. They can be just as practical and as logical as the occasion demands—and the situation allows.

This ability to combine emotionalism and pragmatism gives Chinese an advantage over Westerners whose upbringing and education is designed to wean them from emotional behavior.

Like chameleons, the Chinese can change their position and their commitments in order to fit the changing environment. Or, they can bring about a change in the environment itself in order to give themselves an advantage.

Westerners who have not been initiated into the ways of the Chinese are first mystified and then frustrated by having to deal with attitudes and behavior that shift from one position to another, particularly when the positions are diametrically opposed.

Given this situation, it is dangerous for foreigners to base their business ventures with Chinese companies and government organizations on the personal relationships they believe they have developed with individuals. These relationships can be, and often are, ignored or turned off when it is expedient.

The only rational recourse outsiders have is to do everything possible to build relationships with Chinese that are based on solid business considerations as well as personal contacts so that they can withstand attempts to alter the relationships or subvert them altogether.

节

Jie

(Jee-eh)

"Road to Good Fortune"

One of the most remarkable theories about the nature and susceptibilities of the human mind and body is that the body and mind respond immediately and directly to every iota of information or energy that comes its way, through sound, smell, sight, or touch, and that this "input" begins long before birth.

This theory holds that there are two kinds of programming that are constantly being fed into the human mind and body from outside sources. One kind that has a neutral or beneficial effect, and another kind that has a negative, harmful effect.

Not surprisingly, the beneficial programming the mind and body are subjected to according to this theory is made up of pleasant, pleasurable things that soothe and satisfy, and include such things as viewing the beauties of nature, listening to good music, enjoying the company of family and friends, achieving highly desired goals, and so on.

Obviously it is unpleasant, disturbing and destructive things that have a negative impact on people; all of which we know very well. But what is unknown, says the above theory, is that every one of these negative messages is not only permanently imprinted on our minds, they are also permanently impressed into our muscles and body structure.

In other words, every negative message we ever get, intended as well as unintended, adds a measure of stress to our bodies as well as our minds, building up destructive energy. The mind becomes more and more cluttered and eventually ends up in turmoil. The muscles of the body tighten up, losing their elasticity.

It is said that when a person undergoes a deep physical massage to relieve muscle constrictions the action often releases subconscious memories, causing them to flash across the conscious mind like streaks of lightning.

The Chinese have a word for releasing this kind of stress from the mind and body: *jie* (jee-eh), which means *liberation* or *deliverance*; and they also have their own way of accomplishing this process.

Rather than depend on physical therapy to relieve stress, the Chinese recommend a mental process (which may be combined, however, with the slow-motion exercise known as *Tai Ji Quan*).

Look inward, say the Chinese, recognize both the existence and source of the stress, then consciously and deliberately cleanse yourself of the stressful factors—which range from personal mistakes made in the past, grudges against people, anger, desires for revenge, irrational opinions, unrealistic obsessions, frustrations caused by bureaucratic barriers, to trying to do more than you are capable of doing.

The secret to staying stress-free, according to Chinese wisdom, is to prevent its build-up by immediately engaging in the process of *jie* when you are confronted by a negative situation.

This is often one of the first lessons newcomers in China should put to use, since they invariably run into one frustrating situation after the other.

节

Jie

(Jee-eh)

"Staying Within Limits"

Excessive behavior, in one way or another, seems to be a natural human characteristic that distinguishes people from virtually all other life forms. Over the course of human history, one of the primary challenges to all societies has been how to curb this characteristic without bringing destruction down on themselves.

Chinese philosophers addressed the problem of excessive human behavior under the heading of *jie* (jee-eh), or *limitations*, in which they noted that it is only through limitations that the human race, and all nature in general, survives. They advocated *zhong yong zhi dao*, or *the middle way is best*.

The famed *Book of Changes* points out that nature itself sets the first line of limitations, determining where and how life survives, and providing guidelines for mankind to follow. But it adds that mankind itself must set the defining limitations that establish standards of behavior that give meaning to human life.

In the Chinese context, all order in the affairs of humans begins and ends with *jie*—in setting social, political and economic limitations; and not surprisingly, a great deal of the disorder that has afflicted China was the result of limitations that went too far in attempting to control the thinking and behavior of people. The Cultural Revolution was an example of *jie* carried to the ultimate extreme.

Obviously, the ideal society is one in which limitations meet but do not exceed the intellectual, emotional and spiritual needs of people. China has therefore never been an ideal society because its limitations from the dawn of Chinese history have been excessive—designed to control the attitudes and behavior of people for political expediency; not for fulfilling their needs or nurturing their full potential.

Despite all of the wisdom accumulated by the great sages of China, including *I Ching* itself, the governments of China have never put people first. Those in power have always put themselves first, order second, and the people last.

This failing is in itself a *jie* that the Chinese have imposed upon themselves, apparently because the limitations under which they traditionally existed prevented them from developing a society based on democratic principles.

It is only now that the Chinese are reaching a point where the concept of limiting the limitations set on personal freedom and personal responsibility is beginning to transform the society.

Jie has been used for centuries in reference to all kinds of undesirable situations that are exacerbated by too many limitations or too few. The advice given directly, or that is inherent in *I Ching* references, is aimed at achieving a "limitations balance" that results in the all-around behavior that is considered ideal in the Chinese context.

Outsiders in China must learn a great deal about the various *jie* in order to function effectively. There are various limitations having to do with age, for example, that are especially meaningful to the Chinese.

For example, having a conspicuously younger businessman or businesswoman in charge of older people in a company or organizational hierarchy still ruffles the cultural feathers of the Chinese, and must be handled with special care.

阶级

Jieji

(Jee-eh-jee)

"The Unleveling of China"

One of the most contradictory elements of communism was the concept of a classless society in which everyone was socially, economically and politically equal—a point that was a major tenet of the preachings of Communists in China and the former Soviet Union.

But of all the world's Communists, the Chinese should have known that attempting to create a level society went against the grain of humanity.

Basic to the Chinese concept of social beings is the fundamental idea that people are *not* created equal and that the circumstances of their birth, upbringing and environment inexorably widens the gap separating them.

The attempt by the Communist Party of China to homogenize Chinese society despite historical evidence that it could not be done cost the people dearly.

But efforts to smash the foundations of Chinese life and create a "new man," epitomized by supreme leader Mao Zedung's so-called Cultural Revolution, were not altogether in vain. They were the bricks that broke the Communist camel's back. They not only failed to homogenize the society, they also made it starkly clear that the country could not survive without multiple *jieji* (jee-eh-jee) or *social classes*, as well as economic *and* political levels.

In today's China there are five classes established by law: peasants, workers, soldiers, leaders and cadre. Peasants live in rural areas and are primarily farmers. They are legally barred from moving to towns or cities, but many break the taboo and join the floating millions seeking work in other industries. They can, however, move to other rural villages without official permission. Many peasants who continue to live in their rural villages work part-time or seasonally in nearby factories. Workers live in towns and cities and engage in labor not related to farming.

People who are born into peasant or worker-class families and registered as such at birth stay in their respective *birth classes* for life, regardless of their educational level or what they do for a living.

Cadre are members of a special class that overlaps the other classes. They are peasants, workers, bureaucrats or soldiers who have distinguished themselves in their occupations, and received *cadre* status from the government.

Although the *rank* of cadre does not indicate social level or degree of affluence, it brings with it a number of highly prized privileges, including the coveted right to ride in "soft" class coaches on trains.

Leaders, who also may be members of the other classes, are more or less the equivalent of China's managerial class. They are also usually university educated, and may also have been awarded the status of cadre.

All people in China are supposed to carry identification cards that, among other things, designate their class. When buying train tickets or tickets for other forms of transportation it is necessary to show these I.D. cards. See **Hu Kou**.

Interestingly, prices for various services in China, including train fares, are based on social class as well as the quality of the services concerned. The higher your social class the more you must pay. Foreigners pay the highest prices of all—not because they are considered the highest class, but because they are presumed to be the most affluent.

There is growing cross-over among peasants, workers, soldiers and bureaucrats, and the "class" lines are blurring—particularly the lines distinguishing peasants and workers.

Further, the class loyalty and submissiveness that was once required of both peasants and workers is fast disappearing. Hundreds of thousands of farmers are now conspicuously more affluent than many workers, causing increasing discontent among the workers because they regard themselves as socially superior to peasants.

Indications are that China's legally designated social classes will continue to become more and more blurred, and that in the future social status in China will be determined by educational level, occupation and money.

计划生育

Jihua Shengyu

(Jee-wha Shung-yuu)

"Bringing Up Little Emperors"

Shortly after the Communists gained power in China in 1949, economists and others began warning that the country would soon face irreversible problems if it did not quickly implement a *jihua shengyu* (jee-wha shung-yuu) or *family-planning* program.

These observers noted that a number of fundamental changes brought about by the new government, including a dramatic drop in infant mortality because of improved health care, an equally significant rise in life expectancy, the closing of hundreds of monasteries, convents and houses of prostitution, combined with the pressure on families to have large numbers of sons, would result in a dangerous jump in the population which was already well over half a billion.

Taking these warnings to heart, the government enacted laws on birth control and abortion in 1953 and set up birth control study groups in 1954. Zhou Enlai, one of the key figures in the founding of the People's Republic of China, began personally urging limitations on childbirth in 1956.

But in 1957 Chairman Mao Zedung accused China's most influential population control advocates of being rightists for wanting to weaken the country by reducing its population, and purged them from their positions.

From 1957 to 1974, the years of the disastrous "Great Leap Forward" and the first eight years of the "Cultural Revolution," little was done to stem the tide of newborns.

In 1974 Chinese women were averaging between four and five children. The government increased its pressure on families to have fewer children, and many of those in urban areas cut back on the number of their offspring for both economic and social reasons.

By 1976 Chinese families were still having from three to four children each. By 1980 the fertility rate was 2.2 percent but the population figures continued to spiral upward.

It was announced at the National People's Congress in September 1980 that thereafter most Chinese families would be limited to one child and that family planning would be an integral part of the nation's long-term development strategy.

However, minority groups and families who lived in remote, scarcely populated areas were exempted from this measure.

The population continued to bulge upward and by 1982 had passed the one billion mark. Investigations revealed that in 1981 some six million families had a second child and that nearly two million families that already had five or more children added one more to the total.

When the results of the 1982 census became available the government instituted absolutely draconian measures to bring the burgeoning population under control. IUD insertion was made compulsory for women who had already had one child. In families with two children, either the husband or the wife was forced to undergo sterilization.

In one 14-month period in 1981 and 1982, 16.4 million women had tubular ligations and four million men had vasectomies. In many instances, the roving sterilization teams were accompanied by armed guards for protection.

Many pregnant women were forced to have abortions; some families resorted to female infanticide; others to selling female babies. Demographic data suggests that around 200,000 female infants were *gotten rid* of in just one year during the early 1980s.

Newly married couples were required to get written permission from their workplaces or the local population control office before they could have their one allotted child. Family-planning cadre assigned to workplaces were responsible for keeping records of the monthly periods of female employees.

Parents who had more than one child, or more than was allotted to them, were fined and lost various entitlements, including the right to larger housing and education for their children.

But having several children, particularly sons, was one of the most deeply ingrained of China's cultural imperatives, so being limited to just one child was a sacrifice of enormous proportions, especially to the country's peasant families.

By the early 1990s, China's fertility rate was down to about 1.4, but with some 22 percent of the world's population and only 7 percent of its arable land, the population problem was far from over. Still, the government began trying to shift from outright coercion to trying to convince couples that they did not need more than one child to ensure their economic future.

In 1994 the standing committee of the National People's Congress approved legislation that went well beyond population control. It called for the use of enforced abortions, sterilizations and marriage bans to avoid the birth of "abnormal" children.

The new bill, aimed at people who are likely to pass on congenital illnesses or defects to their children, prohibits people with hepatitis, venereal disease, and mental defects from marrying.

Pregnant women diagnosed as having certain infectious diseases or abnormal fetuses are required to halt the pregnancies.

When this new bill was passed China's Public Health Ministry said it was necessary because from 300,000 to 460,000 congenitally disabled children were born in the country every year—a situation that brought "unhappiness and economic burdens to hundreds of thousands of families and lowered the quality standards of the population."

In 1994 the government announced new measures to prevent young couples below the legal marriage age—22 for men and 20 for women—from living together. The new regulations allow the government to separate unmarried couples under the marriage age, and to prohibit any marriage the government considers unsuitable.

In remote regions of the country the government is also engaged in an ongoing battle against bride sales, bigamous marriages and marriages between close relatives.

Families that have only one child, particularly when the child is a son, have become notorious for spoiling their offspring, and the news media regularly refers to these spoiled boys as "little emperors."

晋

Jin

(Jeen)

"Staying on the Bandwagon"

It goes without saying that when unprincipled, immoral people or nations become powerful they represent a great threat to both their own societies and the world at large because they invariably use their power to sustain and strengthen themselves at the expense of others.

Chinese wise men recognized this human failing millennia ago and sought to overcome it by establishing a positive philosophical base, along with precise, practical guidelines, for the exercise of power.

The philosophy created by these wise men was founded on the premise that the accumulation of power does not take place within a vacuum but within a society, beginning with the family unit and expanding outward and upward, and that it was beholden upon those accumulating power to maintain correct/moral relations with their families, people at large, and their governments.

This very wide and very deep concept is subsumed in the single word *jin* (jeen), which is translated as meaning *progress*, but goes far beyond that simple process to incorporate the idea of *progress with total social responsibility*—or to give it more of a Chinese twist, *progress with heart*.

Within the Chinese concept of *jin*, principled people of progress have the love, understanding and support of their families, giving them a strong, stable base. They are keenly aware of the social environment within which they operate and are dedicated to working in harmony with society to make sure that it benefits equally from their efforts. Furthermore, they are also just as aware of their political responsibilities and make sure that they meet them fully so they will also have the understanding and cooperation of the authorities.

Unfortunately, until recent years the political environment in China made the application of this wonderful philosophy impossible within mainland China itself, and it was able to flower only among overseas Chinese in such places as Hong Kong and Singapore.

Now, a growing number of overseas Chinese business tycoons are following the ancient dictates of *jin* in their projects in China, thereby helping to speed up the political and social revolutions in their homeland.

Sometime around the 1960s—some say following the publication of Rachel Carson's landmark book *Silent Spring*—the sentiments expressed in *jin* became the subject of serious debate and decision in the U.S. and elsewhere outside of China, and the concept of socially and politically constructive progress has been gaining adherents ever since.

But the world at large still has a long way to go in understanding and accepting the message of *jin progress*—because it is no less than a total philosophy involving the whole of human behavior.

Jing
(Jeeng)

"What Really Satisfies"

For more than four thousand years an elite minority of the Chinese people sustained a system that did *not* meet the needs and aspirations of more than 90 percent of the population. The minority was able to do this by keeping the masses illiterate and by using whatever brute force was necessary to maintain themselves in power.

This situation created a great and profound dichotomy between the best of Chinese thinking and Chinese behavior, and the disparity becomes more and more conspicuous as one delves deeper into the well of Chinese wisdom.

In fact a well, *jing* (jeeng) in Chinese, is one of the primary symbols of the great storehouse of knowledge and wisdom educated Chinese accumulated during the first three millennia of their civilization.

Jing, in this case translated as the *source*, goes far beyond the general sense of knowledge or wisdom. It includes the nature of people in the cosmos and the meaning of humanity in the broadest and deepest sense.

China's early philosophers correctly divined that people cannot be truly satisfied or fulfilled if they break faith with their true nature and allotted role in the cosmos, and that in order to know their nature and role they must constantly return to the *jing*, the well of humanity.

In its Chinese context the *source* contains all of the wisdom that mankind needs to direct it to the right path and to keep it there—in analyzing and shaping one's own character, in relationships with others, in business, or in any other human endeavor.

The root principle of the philosophy of *jing* is that evil will not, cannot, exist in tandem with humanity. Applied humanity cancels out all evil, leaving only the good.

On a practical level, *jing* provides perfect guidelines for interacting with one's family and friends, for dealing with strangers, for the operation of social enterprises, for engaging in business and conducting politics.

To be true to the *source*, all behavior in these areas must harmonize with one's humanity. The criterion is always whether or not it conforms to or conflicts with humanity.

Therefore, in the Chinese context the greatest challenge facing mankind is to discern its own humanity, and thereafter be true to it—again, something that the Chinese themselves have not been free to do because of irrational political philosophies.

To make *jing* work for you, the philosophers say, do not depend only on your own perceptions and opinions, but seek the wisdom of others; put yourself into situations where your wisdom and talents are challenged, and keep your eyes and ears open for opportunities to use your talents.

Once you have had enough experience to begin to understand humanity and evaluate your own life and goals, the next step is to apply your growing insights to your own life as well as your outside activities, and to share your knowledge of humanity with others.

Hopefully, the China that is now emerging will be able to make use of this ancient wellspring of wisdom.

经济特区

Jing Ji Te Qu

(Jeeng Jee Tay Chu)

"The Capitalist Enclaves"

In 1966 the government of Taiwan, with help from the United States, designated the southern port of Kaohsiung as an export processing zone, where manufacturers and assemblers involved in exporting had special advantages. The enterprise was so successful that two more zones were established in 1969.

The message sent by this success was not lost on mainland China's nearby coastal provinces of Fujian and Guangdong. But China was then embroiled in the decade-long Cultural Revolution and they could do nothing about it.

In April 1979, some three years after the official end of the Cultural Revolution, Premier Deng Xiaoping recommended to the Central Committee of the CCP that special export zones be established in Fujian and Guangdong. Whether or not this was done on his own initiative or was suggested to him by Party officials from the two provinces is unknown. In any event, three months later the Central Committee gave its approval to the concept, authorizing four such zones.

The districts chosen were Zhuhai near Macao, Shenzhen near Hong Kong, and Shantou and Xiamen, which are opposite Taiwan. The PRC then went Taiwan one better by greatly expanding the advantages and assistance offered to foreign businesses to get them to set up factories in the zones. The PRC also changed the name from *Chu Kuo Tegu* or Special Export Zones to *Jing Ji Te Qu* (jeeng jee tay chu) or *Special Economic Zones* to reflect their much broader mandate.

As the saying goes, the rest is history. There were the usual problems with bureaucracy and personnel who had no experience in working to Western standards. But the motivation and the opportunities were so great that the four zones quickly developed into economic powerhouses, eventually becoming the tail that wagged China.

Shenzhen, in particular, mushroomed into a huge city of highrise office buildings, industrial parks, residential apartments, retail shops, restaurants, nightclubs and bars—a perfect clone of nearby Hong Kong.

These islands of capitalism not only became China's primary economic engines, they also brought with them the social ills that the PRC had fought so hard to eradicate from China—street crime, prostitution, conspicuous consumption, popular Western entertainment, individualism and a strong distaste for Communist thought and bureaucratic red tape emanating from Beijing.

Despite these problems, however, there was no way the CCP could discount the contribution that the *Jing Ji Te Qu* were making to China's economy, and in January 1984 the concept was expanded to fourteen more coastal areas and the island of Hainan. This was followed by other moves in the direction of capitalism, including the designation of a number of "Trade and Investment Promotion Zones."

In subsequent years the Special Economic Zones came in for periodic storms of criticism from more conservative CCP members because the success of the zones also spawned an equally conspicuous growth in corruption involving businesspeople and Party officials—including some officials in the higher echelons of the Party hierarchy in Beijing.

The Special Economic Zones have continued to set the pace for China's economy and have become key factors in forcing the CCP to convert more and more to a market-driven economy.

Still, the CCP maintains that it will never allow the development of a fully *ziyou shichang* or *free market* in China.

技术交流

Jishu Jiaoliu

(Jee-shuu Jee-ah-oh-lew)

"Technical Exchange Ploys"

China's undisputed position as the *Central Kingdom*—meaning the most civilized and advanced country in the known world—for more than 3,000 years, resulted in the Imperial Court and the ruling class in general developing a self-centered view in which all others were expected to defer to China, and to pay the Central Kingdom both tangible and intangible tribute.

Another facet of early Chinese culture was that knowledge was something that belonged to all, that people with special knowledge were obligated to share it with others without any thought of recompense.

This did not mean that those with knowledge were expected to teach without being paid. But the pay that teachers received was not given in exchange for their knowledge. It was given to sustain their livelihood, which is philosophically quite different.

Because of this enduring concept of knowledge as being there for the taking, and that teachers are conduits of knowledge, not the owners of it, the Chinese have traditionally had difficulty accepting the Western concept of patents and copyrights.

In the traditional Chinese context of things, the idea of an individual personally *owning* the process of how to do something, or exclusive rights to written words, was not only alien, but preposterous.

The idea of *paying* someone, any amount of money, for the right to make use of an idea or process struck pre-modern Chinese as the height of absurdity.

The Western concept of patents and copyrights is certainly well-known in present-day China, and there are laws detailing and protecting such rights. But the concept is still not fully accepted and is often not followed.

One of the aspects of this ongoing cultural difference is that in *jishu jiaoliu* (jee-shuu jee-ah-oh-lew), or *technological transfers*, from foreign companies, the Chinese do not automatically put a limit on the scope of the transfer, as is common in the West.

They generally expect to get *all* of the technology or rights involved, regardless of what the contract says, and will typically presume that they can go as far as they want in using the technology.

A more recent factor in both technological transfers and investments in China is an addition to the old "tribute" mentality. Now, instead of expecting gifts and other favors from other countries as tribute, there are strong feelings that the Western world *owes* China because the West is rich and is seeking to get richer by taking advantage of the huge Chinese market.

It is therefore important that foreign companies seeking to transfer technology to Chinese enterprises be aware of this philosophical and pragmatic difference, and address it thoroughly, and diplomatically, in their negotiations.

就业

Jiu Ye

(Jee-yuu Yeh)

"Forced Job Placement"

On September 7, 1954 the Chinese Communist Party Congress proclaimed a new category of convict labor under the heading of *Jiu Ye* (jee-yuu yeh) or *Forced Job Placement* (FJP).

At first, the only people sentenced to forced labor periods were ordinary criminals who had completed their original sentences and were then immediately sentenced to FJP—often in the same prison and working at the same job. Sometimes these new terms were for a specific number of years; other times they were indefinite, depending on the whims and needs of the various prison authorities.

In 1961 the *jiu ye* policy was changed to also include people who had been imprisoned in *lai jiao* or *re-education through labor* facilities as *class enemies*—a subterfuge that came about because the CCP decided to establish fixed terms for *lai jiao* prisoners, and this new policy made it possible for the government to keep these people as enslaved workers indefinitely.

All the local "Labor Reform Organ" had to do to reclassify prisoners as *jiu ye*, and thereby keep them in the gulag system, was to apply to the local office of the Public Security Bureau. Although the prisoners had completed their penal sentences, they had no say in the matter.

It is estimated that during the first three decades of the Communist Chinese gulag system some 40 million convicts, most of whom were "class enemies" rather than criminals, were re-sentenced into job-placement servitude.

There was a natural tendency for successful factories and farms to want to keep the *forced job placement* workers assigned to them because they provided cheap, and eventually experienced, labor. As a result during the early decades of the system very few people were released. About the only exceptions were those who became too old to work, became infirm, managed to prove that they had been falsely accused, or could convince sympathetic officials that they were fully reformed and were no longer a threat to the government.

Some prison factories and farms, often depending on their location and the kind of facility they had, allowed the families of incarcerated prisoner-workers to join them. On the average, contact with the outside was limited to letters and monthly visits of 20 to 30 minutes.

Forced-labor prison farms and prison factories continue to play a major role in China's system of justice and political control, as well as in overall economic production.

Many non-prison factories in China provide housing inside of walled compounds for their workers and their families. The compounds have gates and guards, and people are checked in and out—and since the facilities are basic and the employees are generally not free to change jobs, the overall impression the outsider gets is that they are only a little better than FJP prisons.

开放政策

Kai Fang Zhengce

(Kie Fahng Chung-t'seh)

"Open Door Policy"

China's history with its neighbors has not been a happy one. Several times during the long age of Imperial dynasties the country simply closed its doors to the outside world—one time keeping them closed for nearly 300 years.

In the latter part of the 1800s, Japan, Russia, Great Britain, Germany and other European nations vied with each other to obtain both territory and influence in China, threatening the very existence of the country.

Although the United States had an active and growing interest in China during this period, it was not a party to the attempts to carve the country up into pieces.

On the contrary, the U.S. urged these foreign powers to follow a *kai fang zhengce* (kie fahng chung-t'seh) or *open door policy* in regards to China rather than continue using threats and force to stake out exclusive rights to portions of the country.

But there was no power behind the American proclamation and it was ignored. Then an anti-Christian, anti-foreign rebellion broke out in China in 1898 (the Boxer Rebellion). In August 1900 the U.S. contributed soldiers to an army of Japanese, Russian, French and British troops that entered Beijing and suppressed the rebellion, earning the wrath of most Chinese.

U.S.-Chinese relations deteriorated further in 1905 when stories of the mistreatment of Chinese laborers in America came to the attention of the just-established Qing Ministry of Foreign Affairs.

The Ministry refused to renew the country's immigration treaty with the U.S., and in June 1905 Chinese merchants in all of the major east coast port cities declared a total boycott on American goods in support of the Ministry's action.

The U.S. forced the Qing Court to issue a proclamation calling for an end to the boycott, but Chinese officials in the cities concerned posted the notice upside down as a signal that it had been issued under duress, and the merchants ignored it.

Finally, the boycott began petering out in October of that year—marking the U.S.'s first trade war with China, and the first references to *kai fang zhengce* or *open door policy* in regards to China—by the U.S. rather than China.

The next official reference to China opening its doors to the West, and the first time the reference was made by China, came from Deng Xiaoping, the successor to Mao Zedung and Zhou Enlai, in 1978.

Up to that point, the official policy of the People's Republic of China (PRC) was that the United States was the primary source of the "spiritual pollution" that the government was determined to keep out of the country.

This "spiritual pollution" included the concepts of democracy, capitalism, human rights, individualism, emphasis on sexuality and sexual relations, popular music, prostitution, street crime, and so on.

Deng recognized that the policies and programs implemented by the CCP up to that time had failed, and that the only way China could compete with the West was to once again open its doors to Western technology and investments

After months of acrimonious debate, Deng prevailed. The government announced that thereafter in would welcome technology and investments from the West, would participate in more international organizations and allow large numbers of students and professionals to go abroad for study and training.

In January-February 1992 Deng visited the Shenzhen Special Economic Zone near Hong Kong, and was astounded by what he saw. One of his comments was that China should "blaze new trails boldly, not mince along slowly like a woman with bound feet."

A short while later, the government-approved newspaper *Renmin Ribao* blared the headline: "Opening Up to the World and Using Capitalism."

The accompanying article castigated those who were opposing economic reforms.

In May 1992, Deng sponsored the preparation and distribution of Central Document No. 4, which extended the "open door policy" from the Pacific coast regions to the entire country. In short order, dozens of other cities were given status similar to the special economic zones.

As usual, when the Chinese use *kai fang zhengce* it often means something entirely different from its English translation, and must be approached with the Chinese connotation in mind. In brief, the term means the door is open only to what serves the goals of the PRC.

坎

Kan
(Kahn)

"Facing Danger"

There are some people who seem to be under a perpetual cloud of bad luck and suffer one kind of emotional or physical injury after another. A character in the American cartoon strip *Lil Abner* drawn by Al Capp that was popular for decades captured the essence of this common human tragedy. The cartoon character had a small cloud with a lightning bolt flashing through it perpetually ensconced over its head.

Some people attribute this constant state of bad luck to external cosmic forces (fate!) over which they have no control—sometimes saying they were born under an unlucky star or their mother was bewitched, and so on.

Other people, both men and women but particularly women, have such poor self-esteem and confidence that they blame themselves for the insults and injuries they suffer. Women seem especially vulnerable to this malady because of the negative influences of chauvinistic societies.

But there is another kind of evil influence, which regularly bedevils people of both sexes and all ages, which the Chinese denote with the word *kan* (kahn), meaning *danger* of a very real and substantial kind.

Kan refers to dangers that are inherent in the environment one lives in, personal as well as professional, and relates to bad decisions or negative actions that continuously—or time and again—make matters worse.

Chinese wisdom recognizes that most of us are confronted with dangerous situations now and then when we are not at fault and the situations cannot be avoided. The sages say these occasions should be met calmly and deliberately and used to increase self-awareness and appreciation of the good things in life.

The key to combatting *kan*, according to the sages, is to confront the situations directly, maintain your principles and integrity no matter how much pressure there might be to compromise, and continue acting with complete confidence.

Among the strategies suggested by the sages for contending with *kan*:

a. Stop whatever it is you are doing that isn't working and you know isn't right, and start over again.
b. Do not try to solve a major problem or achieve a major goal in one giant step but approach it in small, consistent increments.
c. Assume a low profile and stay out of harm's way until the situation changes for the better.
d. Do just enough to keep yourself afloat while waiting for better times.
e. Be satisfied with modest success.

By persevering in the face of *kan* you set a valuable example for family members and others, who will then support you in your endeavors and contribute to your chances for success.

Most personally caused "environmental dangers," add the sages, are a result of people giving in to desires that are not valid or worthy. The solution, the sages note, is for people to re-examine their values and motives, and raise them to where they are above such actions.

But much of the *kan* that has hexed the Chinese throughout much of their history was not brought on by their own personal failings. Rather, it was an unavoidable result of a social system that was based on the deliberate use of *environmental dangers* to control behavior and severely punish any deviation from the established norm.

Now, with the gradual growth of personal freedom in China, the people at least have more of a choice in following the advice of the sages to avoid bad luck.

123

炕

Kang
(Kahng)

"Hot Times in the Cold North"

For all of their practical experience and pragmatic approach to most things in life, the Chinese—and their cultural proteges, the Japanese—have some remarkable blind spots in their attitudes and behavior.

I first became acquainted with this cultural incongruity during the first winter I spent in Japan in the late 1940s, when I often thought I was going to freeze to death.

I very quickly became aware that traditional Japanese homes, including those in the northern regions of the islands where below freezing temperatures are the winter norm, were built as if they were in the tropics.

Rather than construct homes to ward off the freezing cold of winter, the Japanese built them to contend with the high humidity of summer. Houses were designed and constructed to encourage the flow of air through them. Outside walls were thin, and most interior partitions were made of almost sheer paper.

No attempt was made to heat homes in winter, no matter how low the temperatures. The only concession the Japanese normally made to cold temperatures were small charcoal-fired ceramic pots called *hibachi* (he-bah-chee), which warmed only the hands, and, in the homes of the better-off, sunken (and covered) fire-pits in the main family room, called *kotatsu* (koe-tot-sue), that warmed only the feet and legs—a situation that changed rapidly with the coming of affluence and Western housing concepts in the 1960s and 1970s.

There was some conjecture that the earliest Japanese had migrated to the islands from the tropical regions of Southeast Asia and the Pacific, and had brought their *tropical* style of housing with them. That may be so, but it is more likely that the traditional practice of not heating their homes came from southern China.

While the scene in China is now also changing, someone ages ago, apparently arbitrarily, drew an east–west line through the center of China and designated the southern portion as hot and the northern part as cold.

There has never been any question about it getting cold in the northern portions of China and in the higher elevations of the west. But whoever decided that it does not get cold enough in the southeastern and southwestern regions of China to warrant heating homes during the winter months must have read an early tourist brochure.

The dividing line between north (cold) and south (hot) China is the Yangtze River (known by most Chinese as the Chang Jiang or *Long River*). Crossing this river has traditionally been a momentous event—like crossing an international border or the equator—with all of the emotional nuances and barriers that used to divide the Yankee North and the Rebel South in the United States.

For whatever reason, the traditional custom was for families north of the hot–cold line who could afford it to heat their homes in winter by an ingenious system called *kang* (kahng), which was one of the earliest (if not the first) central heating systems ever devised by man, with little or nothing being done to heat homes in the southern zone.

The *kang* consisted of a fireplace from which the heat (and smoke) was channeled into a network of flues beneath the floor, thereby heating the home from the bottom. The fireplace thus served the dual role of cookstove and heater.

Still today foreign travelers in China who have occasion to be guests in private homes during the winter months are struck by the arbitrary division of China into hot and cold zones, pointing out that they often came close to freezing in the so-called hot zone in the south, and just as often suffer from heat prostration in *kang*-equipped homes in the north.

Poorer Chinese, no matter where they live, have traditionally attempted to keep warm in winter by putting on more clothing; not by fully heating their homes or workplaces.

Some of the most comfortable homes in China, winter and summer, are those situated in natural caves and man-made underground locations, where temperatures are in the comfort range the year around. An estimated thirty million Chinese live in caves.

124

看相

Kan-Xiang
(Kahn-She-ahng)

"Face-Reading for Fun and Profit"

Face-reading is as old as humankind, and is a universal art that all of us practice virtually every day with varying degrees of skill. We all know and respond to facial expressions that indicate fear, anger, merriment, pleasure and other moods, and we know from experience that such facial characteristics as unusually large eyes or big noses have an important influence on our lives.

But there is a great deal more to face-reading than these obvious signs. The face reveals facts not only about a person's mood, but also about his or her character, health, personality, sexual inclinations, popularity, ability to make money, social status and life expectancy. And just as one's face influences his or her life, life in turn changes our faces—for better or for worse.

Face-reading is primarily based on the size, shape, position, quality and color of certain facial features. Before one can *read* these signs, however, there are other factors that must be taken into consideration—the most important of which is the strength of the *vital power* of the person whose face is to be read.

Everyone is endowed with what might be called a "battery" that gives off a kind of energy that the Chinese call *qi*. The strength of this divine-like power varies greatly in individuals. In some people it is very feeble, and as a result they have dull eyes, dull faces and usually lead colorless lives. In others, this light may shine with startling brilliance, and such people tend to lead extraordinary lives.

Ages ago Chinese astrologers, healers and scholars in other disciplines began cataloguing facial characteristics and relating them to intelligence, ability, behavior in general, health, success, longevity, and so on.

As long as 2,000 years ago *kan-xiang* (kahn-she-ahng) or *face-reading* had become both an art and a profession. The Chinese learned that there are three facial *zones* that send different *messages* and are closely related to one's age.

These zones are the forehead, the middle of the face from the eyebrows down to and including the nose, and the mouth and chin. The top zone relates to intellect, the middle zone to diligence and perseverance, and the lower zone to health and compassion.

During youth the forehead is the most important part of the face. In middle age the middle part of the face predominates in its signals. The mouth and chin are the most important indicators during old age.

Many of the messages sent by the face are obvious enough to just be common sense. Some are more esoteric. A person with a triangular face tends to be intellectual and a dreamer. A square face denotes an athletic or physical character. Round-faced people tend to be adaptable, practical and methodical. Women with round faces are usually gregarious and sociable.

High, wide foreheads are indicative of intelligence. An older person with a high, wide forehead that has several well-defined parallel lines (wrinkles) is exceptionally intelligent, with a stable character. People with a single, vertical wrinkle between their eyebrows are usually very strong-willed, very stubborn. People with large ears, especially if they also have long, large earlobes, are generally very long-lived. People with wide mouths and full lips are more sensual than people with small mouths and thin lips.

Interestingly, strong, straight eyebrows are very masculine, and when women make up their faces with such eyebrows they give a very mixed message to men. People with prominent, hooked noses are better at making money than those with small, straight noses, and so on.

Altogether, there are more than 115 *kan-xiang* points observed and catalogued by the ancient Chinese—all of which are just as valid today, regardless of one's racial or ethnic background, as they were millennia ago.

Chinese businesspeople, government officials and others make regular use of face-reading in judging the people they deal with. Outsiders dealing with the Chinese would be wise to inform themselves of some of the key principles of *kan-xiang*.

125

考虑

Kaolu Kaolu

(Cow-lew Cow-lew)

"We're Looking Into It!"

It often seems to outsiders that government bureaucracy in China operates on the premise of "make everything complicated, go slow, and do as little as possible"—which should not be surprising since Chinese bureaucrats have had some four thousand years to refine and polish their way of doing things.

Every ill or disadvantage ever attributed to bureaucracy is rampant in China, and while most of the pitfalls and problems are classic Chinese, others can be traced to the legacy left by communism, particularly the sloth virus that it carries.

A huge area of the problems encountered in dealing with any part of the Chinese government results from the circumstantial nature of Chinese ethics. Since policies and procedures can be, and routinely are, changed at the whim of a new bureaucrat or to counter any coincidental situation that arises, lower ranking government workers say and do as little as possible in order not to be caught with their necks sticking out.

Furthermore, Chinese laws and regulations are often deliberately written in such a way that there are a number of possible interpretations. One of the reasons given for this is that the laws may not work, so it would be unwise to make them too precise. Another reason given is that they are just a test to see what will happen.

In the commercial sphere the deeply rooted Chinese custom for the founder, president or manager of an operation to retain all authority and to personally direct everything, leaves employees with little or no leeway in responding to customers.

Knowing that any assumption of decision-making authority would get them into serious trouble with the boss, employees habitually pass the buck.

This combination of sloth and fear of sticking their necks out has penetrated and colored the psyche of many shop and company employees in China. But it is the most conspicuous in government-run enterprises, where there are no traditions of customer service.

All of these influences, and more, have resulted in *kaolu kaolu* (cow-lew, cow-lew) meaning *we're looking into it*, becoming one of the most commonly used phrases in China.

What is not explicit in *kaolu kaolu* is the time-frame involved. It is, in fact, timeless. Depending on the subject and purpose, it can mean days, weeks or months—or that nothing at all is going to be done.

Where relatively minor things are concerned, most Chinese accept a *kaolu kaolu* response without questions or objections because they are afraid of irritating the person who responded, getting on their bad side, and thereafter never being able to get anything out of them.

Foreigners on the receiving end of a *kaolu kaolu* reaction should exercise similar caution. If the matter is important and cannot be dropped, it is usually better to bring in an influential go-between.

126

考试

Kaoshi
(Kah-oh-she)

"The Great Exams"

China's Imperial Court was apparently the first government to institute the practice of making scholarship the basis for all government service—a program begun during the short-lived but important Qin (Chin) Dynasty, which began in 221 B.C. and ended in 207 B.C.

Other dramatic changes instituted by Emperor Qin included the merging of dozens of feudal states into a unified country, the division of China's society into five vertical classes—the aristocracy, scholars, military, merchants and peasants—establishment of a uniform legal code, burning of most of the books based on the teachings of past philosophers (in an effort to break with traditions of the past), and the beginning of construction on the Great Wall.

From the Qin Dynasty onward, scholars from all over China gathered at the capital once a year to participate in the *kaoshi* (kah-oh-she) or *examination* system.

From the Han Dynasty, which began in 206 B.C., until the Southern and Northern dynasties of the Three Kingdoms period (A.D. 221–581), the examinations consisted of formulaic essays on the art of governing. Then the scope of the *kaoshi* was greatly expanded to incorporate rhetoric and literature as well as statecraft, and a system of grades and degrees was established.

During the illustrious Tang Dynasty (618-907), the grading system and degrees awarded was made more complex. In Western terminology there was a bachelor's degree (*tong zi*), a master's candidate degree (*xiu chai*), a master's degree (*ju ren*), and a doctor's degree (*jin si*).

By the Ming Dynasty, which began in A.D. 1368, the *kaoshi* had grown into a huge decentralized bureaucracy of its own. The road to government service began with taking the test on a provincial level, where examinations were held during the eighth lunar month. Successful candidates who wanted to qualify for higher office could then go on to the capital to participate in more difficult tests given during the second lunar month each year.

While the *kaoshi* system guaranteed that China would have a large class of scholar-administrators who were steeped in the classic philosophy and statecraft of the past, the system probably did more to delay the advent of universal education and mass literacy in China than any other factor.

Only males were allowed to study for the tests, and only those who came from relatively well-to-do families could afford to take the 20 to 30 years required to master the test subjects. The textbooks studied by the candidates for degrees were written in classical Chinese, which was so different from ordinary speech that it was like learning a second language—and effectively barred virtually everyone else from gaining the same knowledge as the elite class of scholars.

Kaoshi continued to hold sway in China until just before the collapse of the last dynasty, the Qing (Ching), in the fall of 1911. From that time until the victory of the Chinese Communist Party (CCP) in 1949 and the beginning of the People's Republic of China, the country was in a state of perpetual chaos. Obtaining government jobs was a matter of connections and appointments.

In the new Communist regime, qualifications for civil service in China were based on ideology and political correctness as well as connections instead of ability—a system that eventually became a total farce.

In 1977 university entrance examinations began again after a 10–year hiatus, and this signaled the return of *kaoshi* standards. In the late 1980s different departments in the government began their own civil service examinations, as a *test* to see if they could upgrade the quality of their employees. It is expected that the *kaoshi* system will once again eventually be applied to all civil service workers in China.

客气

Keqi

(Kuh-chee)

"Rituals Versus Laws"

Some 2,500 years ago Confucius said that any society that depended primarily upon laws to control the behavior of its citizens would eventually be torn apart by its own internal violence.

Confucius went on to say that the more laws a nation has the less likely its people will be to obey them, the more rapidly the entire society will become lawless, and the more law enforcement will be required to sustain any semblance of civilization.

Looking back at more than 2,000 years of Chinese history that preceded him, Confucius learned that the most peaceful and progressive epochs in China's history had been the periods when the rulers and their administrators were virtuous (were interested only in the welfare of the people), and the people were willingly cooperative and industrious.

Confucius learned that these peaceful, progressive epochs were not marked by laws but by good manners and high standards of morality and ethics—by cultural attitudes and behavior that he called *rituals*.

Building on these historical precedents, Confucius began teaching a social system based entirely on prescribed rituals; on ethics and etiquette for all human relationships, personal and private as well as public and professional.

As the centuries passed, other social philosophers added to Confucius's ritual-based system. It gradually permeated Chinese culture, and was adopted and promoted by the Imperial Court as the official doctrine of the state.

Successive rulers and the elite of China continued to follow and foster the precepts of Confucius down to modern times because his system promoted a passive, peaceful, cooperative populace.

The fact that the Confucian system achieved its goals by denying individuality, making women absolutely subservient to men, and being anti-human in many other ways was totally ignored by the elite of China because it served to protect and preserve their exalted status.

Confucian rituals ruled China until inroads by Western political and social philosophies led to the downfall of the dynastic form of authoritarian government, and the eventual ascendancy of the Chinese Communist

Party which regarded Confucianism as its blood enemy and set out to destroy it.

One of the key facets of the Confucian system that humanized it to a great extent (because it was a fundamental requirement for any civilized culture) and has survived both Western influences and communism, was *keqi* (kuh-chee) or *courtesy*.

Keqi remains a hallmark of the behavior of most Chinese, and is one of their primary cultural assets, not only in helping to maintain a high standard of decorum in the world's most crowded country, but also in their international business and political affairs.

A frequent response to excessive thanks or praise is *bu keqi*, or *let's not be so formal*.

客人

Keren

(Ku-wren)

"The Honored Guest"

One of my favorite stories about the character and psychology of the Chinese has to do with their traditions of thrift, and how these traditions often conflict with other attitudes and behavior.

This particular story involves a very stingy man who attempts to maintain his self-image as a gentlemen of means but does so in such an extreme manner that it presents a scenario that is both sad and hilarious.

One day the man takes a short trip away from home on some kind of errand and leaves his teenage son in charge of the household. When he returns home he asks his son if anything happened. The son replies that one of his father's friends stopped by to pay him a visit.

The father questions the son sharply about how he welcomed the visitor, demanding to know if he served him any refreshments. The son, knowing his father would be very angry and punish him if he admitted to having served anything to the guest, replied that instead of having actually served the visitor anything, he had drawn him a picture of a pie.

Upon hearing this, the father began to slap and berate the boy, shouting, "You fool! Drawing him a *piece* of pie would have been enough!"

In contrast to this stingy fellow, and other examples of common Chinese behavior, particularly the wooden, unbending reaction one encounters so frequently in offices and stores, the Chinese are rightly known as being extraordinarily solicitous toward and generous to *keren* (ku-wren) or *guests*.

The treatment of guests is one of the most impressive and endearing qualities of the Chinese—and, in fact, it often goes so much further than what visitors expect that it becomes embarrassing and sometimes stifling.

Much of the hospitality the Chinese traditionally extend to guests is motivated by their sense of "face"—of not wanting to appear too poor or too selfish to uphold their reputation and make a good, positive impression.

Unlike the man in our story above, most Chinese will ordinarily go to more trouble than they should and spend more than they should on guests. While part of this is a cultural thing, another part of it is nationalistic—a deep-seated desire to uphold the honor and face of China.

But an equally important facet of Chinese hospitality is that outside of bureaucratic workplaces they are a genuinely friendly, gregarious and curious people. They are fascinated by new things and are drawn to meeting and getting acquainted with foreigners. It often happens that Chinese who meet foreigners by chance, on buses or trains or in the streets, will invite them into their homes and treat them as honored *keren*. On these occasions it is common for the Chinese to speak candidly about their fears and their hopes, and to exhibit the other qualities that have traditionally endeared the average Chinese to foreign visitors.

129

怕输

Kiasu

(Kee-ah-suu)

"The Gimme Generation"

Kiasu (kee-ah-suu) is a Hokkien term, with a slightly derogatory nuance, that was originally used by officers in the Singaporean armed forces to describe a new recruit who tried extra hard to impress his superiors during basic training.

The term quickly spread to the civilian population of Singapore when three ex-servicemen created a *kiasu* cartoon character based on the image of a gung-ho, eager beaver who couldn't get enough of anything fast enough.

The cartoon was a runaway success and spurred a mini-franchise conglomerate that included a magazine and a series of Mr. Kiasu books with such titles as *Everything I Also Want, Everything Also Must Grab*, and *Everything Also Number One*.

McDonald's (Singapore) produced a Kiasu Burger (chicken with extra lettuce, extra sauce, and forty-seven sesame seeds on extra long buns) that resulted in long lines of customers waiting to make like Mr. Kiasu.

Hotels also got on the bandwagon by giving the character a positive image and using it to promote their facilities and services—in "we have everything individuals, couples, or parents and kids could ever want" messages.

Singaporean commentators say the *kiasu* cartoon became a huge success because it fits their character. "Although we are one of the smallest nations in the world, we try to be the biggest and best in everything that we do—the biggest airport, the biggest port, and so on," said one.

The *kiasu* character was also accepted by Singaporeans as a sign that they could laugh at themselves; that although they were still driven to excel, they were beginning to loosen up, relax and slough off some of their feelings of insecurity.

Hokkien residents of Singapore still use *kiasu* in its original derogatory sense. The Singapore government lectures local businesspeople on being less selfish and grasping like Mr. Kiasu, and encourages them to be more courageous and willing to take risks for the benefit of the tiny city-state.

Kiasuism has made it on an international level, having appeared in *A Dictionary of Political Terms in Singapore*, published by the Ohio University

Press, and described in the humor magazine *Witty World* as *incisive, relevant, without being offensive.*

Like so many things in China and among overseas enclaves of Chinese, the term *kiasu* is likely to have a short life, serving as a symbol of the fundamental changes taking place in the traditional Chinese character, and soon being replaced by something else. The cynicism and humor expressed in the term will surely live on, however, as they have been a Chinese trait for millennia.

In mainland China, the desire for instant gratification will also surely grow and survive well into the future.

130

Kuai
(Kwah-ee)

"Year-round Resolutions"

Among the most conspicuous traits of the Chinese is their dedication to achieving a task once they have made a commitment—and for ages the building of the Great Wall has been symbolic of Chinese persistence in the face of great challenges.

More contemporary examples of the persistence of the Chinese is their ongoing battle with nature, including dealing with periodic floods and droughts, the annual dust-and-sand storms blowing off the Gobi Desert, and the challenge of feeding a billion-plus people from fields that have been cultivated for up to five thousand years.

Perhaps the most memorable example of the perseverance of the Chinese, however, has been in their surviving the many man-made disasters that have ravaged the country time and again, from the dynastic wars of the past to the political and cultural revolutions of the 20th century.

This strength of purpose and will is addressed in the forty-third of China's *64 Commandments for Living the Life of the Superior Man*. But this element, as well as several others, often appears to be a contradiction in traditional Chinese behavior.

The forty-third commandment, *kuai* (kwah-ee), which is translated as *resolution*, calls upon the Chinese to be forthright and candid in their public statements and in pursuing their goals, particularly when they face competitors or enemies of one kind or another.

But in reality, the pattern of behavior that is the most common in China often seems to be just the opposite of this rule.

Another facet of the same guideline calls on the Chinese to be completely open about the information they accumulate and to share it freely with everyone. But this, too, has traditionally been just the opposite of actual Chinese behavior.

It is much more characteristic of the Chinese to be secretive about their wealth, the information they have collected; even the extent of their learning and abilities when dealing with strangers and other outsiders, including their own government officials.

The reason for this seemingly contradictory behavior is simple enough. Revealing such information has always, one way or another, presented a danger to individual Chinese and often to China as well.

In its proper usage, *kuai* refers to making a firm public resolution to pursue the course of action that you believe is correct regardless of the danger that may be involved. This entails being sure that your way is the right one, letting everybody—your family, friends, associates and enemies—know that you are resolved to persevere, and then do so calmly and with the greatest confidence.

The lesson of *kuai* can be applied by foreign companies and countries in their dealings with China in order to avoid such illegal or immoral involvements as giving in to hints and demands for bribes, or attempts by private enterprises or government agencies to force unfair agreements.

Letting your Chinese counterparts know that you are familiar with this key cultural concept may help you avoid some of the attempts to ignore it.

131

筷子

Kuai Zi

(Kuu-aye Tzu)

"Small Piece Picker-uppers"

Despite being forced from ancient times by the social and political values of their culture to frequently defy logic and rationality in their behavior, the Chinese are among the most pragmatic of all people.

The number and variety of inventions made by the Chinese over the centuries is a powerful testament to their practicality and ability to think logically. Neither tradition nor laws could completely stifle the inventive bent of every observer and tinkerer.

One of the most practical and insightful of all Chinese inventions was the abacus (*suanpan*), developed some time during the early Ming dynasty. This simple looking device was the world's first mechanical calculator or *computer*, and is still widely used in China (as well as in Japan, Korea and other Asian countries) alongside of modern electronic calculators.

Another Chinese invention that predates recorded history and is still used by virtually all of China's billion plus people, as well as by the Japanese and Koreans and a growing number of other people around the world, is the *kuai zi* (kuu-aye tzu).

Ages ago the ancestors of modern-day Chinese went from using one stick to poke at fires and the things they were cooking to using two sticks in parallel with each other to grasp, manipulate and pick up pieces of food—a significant advance in the culinary art.

In concert with this advance in cooking came the practice of rendering larger chunks of meat or whatever into smaller pieces so they could be picked up more easily with the hand-held sticks.

Eventually these two sticks were christened *kuai zi* which translates as *small piece picker-uppers*.

Over the centuries these *small piece picker-uppers* came to be used as eating utensils, and were produced in smaller more stream-lined versions made of wood, bamboo and ivory. Eventually, *kuai zi* were spread around the world, mostly by Chinese immigrants.

Somehow, someone, probably an Englishman, or maybe a sailor out of San Francisco, decided that calling the two sticks *kuai zi* or *small piece picker-uppers* was just too much, and he began calling them *chopsticks*. I'm sure it was a man who did this because a woman would have been more imaginative.

Today the Chinese still call chopsticks *kuai zi*, and Westerners call *kuai zi* chopsticks.

Having myself been trained to eat with *kuai zi* at a tender age, I can fully understand and appreciate why they are so important to the Chinese. Like virtually all Chinese, I feel very strongly that eating Chinese food with knifes and forks is some kind of sacrilege.

Not only do knives and forks seem to clash with the character of Chinese food, they also appear to adversely affect its taste. Learning how to eat Chinese food with *kuai zi* is one of the easiest and most delightful ways that one can begin an introduction to China's culture.

Kuei
(Kway-ee)

"Overcoming Contradictions"

The Chinese, perhaps more so than any other people, have been weaned on the concept of the duality of all things in nature and the infinite number of *kuei* (kway-ee) or *contradictions* that this makes inevitable.

In the Chinese cosmos, virtually the whole of life consists of a continuous series of contradictions which each individual must come to terms with in order to survive and make progress toward any goal.

Kuei, they say, exists in all human affairs because individuals have their own unique viewpoints, and the ongoing challenge is to bring the opposing parts together without force so that they merge of their own accord and become stronger.

Again, the sages of China teach that to be successful in resolving the *kuei* of life one must first overcome the dualities of human nature, to see things objectively and clearly, and then deal with external contradictions.

Among the personal attitudes named by the sages that individuals must overcome in order to deal effectively with external contradictions are prejudices of all kinds, unpopular political beliefs, attachments to individuals or groups that act as handicaps, and being overly nationalistic.

They also observe that seemingly insoluble contradictions, in either business or political matters, do not always mean the two parties cannot reach an agreement; that if both sides work conscientiously toward a compromise the results often end up being a stronger union than if there were no differences to begin with.

Not surprisingly, one of the first guidelines for dealing with contradictions in one's personal life or in public endeavors is to exercise patience, to apply gentle persuasion or pressure here and there, but let the opposing forces evolve at their own speed—a characteristic of Chinese behavior that is recognized world-wide.

Another key guideline is to become objective enough in one's own thinking to see the swirling mass of contradictions, on whatever level, as the natural state of things, and just as a man and a woman have to accommodate the natural contradictory elements in their nature in order to come together in sexual union, the same applies to all other matters.

A third guideline is to maintain the integrity of your own well thought-out principles, regardless of the strength or intransigence of the opposition—and if you are right in your thinking you will win, or so say the Chinese.

China's wise men make a point of emphasizing the importance of establishing close, cooperative relationships with others of like mind in whatever course of action one chooses to pursue.

Having insight into the concept of *kuei* can be a valuable asset to foreign businesspeople and diplomats dealing with Chinese.

133

Kun
(Koon)

"Bad Days"

It goes without saying that if even a tiny percentage of all the Chinese who had lived over the millennia—a figure estimated to be well in excess of ten billion—had followed the teachings of the great masters, China would have been a totally different country for the last two or more thousand years.

Reading the Chinese classics leaves one with the powerful thought that China's sages recognized practically all if not all of the conditions of mankind—negative, neutral and positive—and said about all that could be said about them.

In fact, in the accumulated wisdom of China there seems to be an answer to every question, and precise guidelines for overcoming every problem.

Yet, history starkly demonstrates that most Chinese never heard the word, and most of those who did were powerless to make use of it—or chose not to for a variety of reasons.

One of the words that *all* Chinese were intimately familiar with, however, was *kun* (koon) or *adversity*—a condition that invariably follows peace, prosperity, progress and all other positive things as surely as night follows day.

Chinese philosophers taught that because *kun* was a natural phenomenon people should not look upon it as their own bad luck or punishment from the gods, but as nature's way of tempering itself and all things in it, and to take advantage of it to develop their own character and spur themselves onward to greater efforts.

The key to surviving and growing during adversity, said the sages, was willpower and adhering strictly but quietly to the principle of truth; to let your actions speak louder than your words. By such actions, they added, adversity could be turned into success.

The sages also admitted, however, that there are occasions, as during most of the history of China, when there is nothing people can do to overcome *kun* and have no choice but to endure it.

If the adversity continues for a long time, they add, it eventually leads to loss of spirit and the will to fight (again, exactly the case in China for much of its history), and it all comes down to simple survival.

The Chinese have survived because their natural fertility was the one thing that the governments up to the middle of the 20th century did not try to deny them.

Among the few things the majority of Chinese have inherited from their long and sometimes glorious history is an inner strength and a reservoir of unfulfilled needs and unused dreams that could eventually propel them into the front ranks of mankind.

While the outside world is salivating at the prospects of getting big pieces of the Chinese market, it should not forget the importance of adding some of its own wisdom to the cultural stock of China—particularly ethics based on universal good that would contribute to diminishing the presence and power of *kun* in Chinese life.

134

坤

Kun
(Koon)

"In Harmony with Nature"

This term *kun* (koon), or *natural response*, is one of the key foundations of all Chinese philosophy. It has to do with meeting all of the challenges of life, overcoming or merging with them, and achieving the fullest potential of one's being.

In the Chinese context of things, *kun* was the first principle that manifested itself immediately following the Big Bang—creation itself—and should therefore be brought into play at the beginning of all human endeavors.

Just as the cosmos must be true to its own nature, in tune with all of its own forces, *kun* points out that to succeed, all human endeavors must also be in tune with the times and their events.

By *natural response* is meant the ability of a person to be totally receptive to all external forces and to respond with words and actions that are in perfect harmony with those forces—including situations when silence and non-action are the best of all responses.

In order to be completely receptive and be able to respond naturally, the way a mirror accepts and reflects an image, it is, of course, necessary that one be fully self-aware and able to eliminate one's own ego from all responses.

There are several levels of human endeavor in which the application of *kun* differs. At the lowest level is recognition that any beginning carries with it the seed of deterioration, and the need to prepare for it.

The second level of involvement calls for elimination of all pretense, prejudices and intolerances, and being totally candid and honest in all responses. The next set of guidelines calls for the suppression of personal ambitions and for doing one's best to benefit others.

From this point on, all endeavors should be marked by quiet modesty and discretion to avoid calling attention to one's self, and encouraging others to extend themselves, resulting in benefit to all.

Once a person has mastered the ability to respond naturally to both internal and external affairs, the weakness most likely to re-occur is an outbreak of personal ambition, which, if it is allowed to run its course, could spoil much or all of what has been accomplished up to that point.

The principle of natural responsiveness is certainly not unique to the Chinese. But for foreigners to apply it successfully to relationships with the Chinese requires a great deal of insight into Chinese culture, particularly their values and motives.

It is also vital that the outsiders concerned have a great deal of skill in accomplishing cross-cultural communications because they have to get down to and encompass the visceral level of human emotions.

135

功夫

Kung Fu/Gong Fu

(Koong Fuu)

"The Power of Chi"

Geographically, China is totally unlike the image that most Westerners have of the country. Only some 10 percent of the huge landmass is tillable, and even a smaller percentage of the country lends itself to the rice paddies that we tend to see in our mind's eye.

Most of China is forbidding mountains. There are over one hundred mountains in China that are over 7,000 meters high. Other huge areas consist of jungles, vast deserts and seemingly endless, and mostly barren, plains.

Historically, the rugged, inhospitable nature of so much of the land effectively separated the different racial and ethnic groups, and made traveling within China a major and generally dangerous undertaking.

Among those who traveled despite the dangers were Buddhist priests whose mission it was to seek out distant lands and establish temples where they could practice their faith and provide spiritual services to the people. Priests in the more contemplative sects of Buddhism habitually chose the most remote—and scenic—sites for their temples. In early China mountains had special significance because it was believed that spirits dwelled there.

It was this impulse and mission that led monks in the year A.D. 495 to the high Zong Yue Song Mountains in what is now Shanxi Province, where they founded the *Shaolin* or *Temple of the Little Forest*.

In the middle of the 20th century the *Temple of the Little Forest* was to become famous the world-over as the place where the martial art known as *kung fu* (koong fuu) (or *gong fu* in Mandarin) was discovered and developed. The term literally means *skilled man*.

It is believed that the *kung fu* concept was originally a philosophy and not a martial art, and that it was brought to the Shaolin temple by a monk named Tat Mo, who came to the temple from India to teach Buddhism.

To carry out their personal missions, newly ordained priests of Shaolin were sent out to wander a world that was filled with danger.

The mountains throughout the settled portions of China had traditionally been infested by outcasts, misfits, renegades and others who could not or would not conform to the laws and customs of the mainstream of society, and opted for lives in the wild mountains. Banditry was a popular profession, and a robe was not enough to protect a defenseless priest.

After generations of being preyed upon by these mountain cutthroats, the priests of the Shaolin temple developed a style of defense and offense that was based on using *qi* (chee)—the cosmic energy that brings life to the body—instead of weapons. Over the centuries, several other *kung fu* schools appeared, some of them based on less violent maneuvers and blows, and some using such weapons as pikes, wooden staffs and swords.

The Shaolin temple school of *kung fu* is said to have undergone a major revival in the 16th century, its fame spreading throughout the country. The original moves and blows were consolidated into a total of 170 basic actions divided into five groups, patterned after the defensive and offensive movements of cranes, dragons, leopards, snakes and tigers.

The secret discovered by the Shaolin priests that made their style of *kung fu* such a devastating weapon was how to concentrate the energy of a blow beneath or behind the point of impact by compressing it and then releasing the blow with blinding speed. The great *kung fu* fighter Bruce Lee described the difference between a *kung fu* blow and a boxer's punch in terms of an iron ball at the end of a chain and a man's fist at the end of his arm.

The boxer's blow is low in energy because it is released slowly and because much of the energy remains in the boxer's fist, arm and body. Whereas a *kung fu* blow, executed with lightening speed, delivers virtually all of the compressed energy, as if the hand was a free-moving iron ball.

Lee said that a boxer's blow generally affects only the surface of the body it strikes, whereas the energy from a *kung fu* blow "explodes inside" the target's body, causing much more pain and damage—like an anti-tank shell that penetrates the metal skin of the tank, then explodes.

Another way of fully appreciating the impact that can be delivered by a *kung fu* blow is to consider the fact that a very fragile straw can be driven into a slab of wood, as if the straw was a rigid piece of metal, by a high-speed wind. The secret of the deadly power of *kung fu* is thus in the speed of the blow, and the area of the body targeted.

One of the primary keys to becoming proficient in *kung fu* is, of course, practicing form and speed, which is why one sees students of the art spending hours jabbing the air (which, when done with great speed, produces the whooshing sound that is characteristic, albeit exaggerated, of *kung fu* movies).

Kung fu is now a national sport in China and considered a national treasure. There are numerous styles of the art, all of them generally based on the actions of cranes, snakes and tigers when engaged in combat. Now, rather than being practiced as a defensive or offensive martial art, it is practiced to enhance physical fitness and spiritual awareness.

The Chinese say that the *real* name of this art is *gong fu* not *kung fu*; and that *gong fu* refers to martial arts in general, and means *outstanding achievement.*

136

孔夫子

Kung Fu-Zi

(Koong Fuu-T'zu)

"The Master Sage"

Kung Fu-Zi (koong fuu-t'zu), a man who was to have more influence on more people than any other human being (or god) to date, was born in the village of Qufu in Shandong Province in the year 551 B.C. He died in 479 B.C., at the age of seventy-two.

Kung's father died when he was a child and his mother when he was in his teens. Thereafter he worked at a variety of "despised" jobs, eventually becoming a bureaucrat in a number of dukedoms, and finally a teacher and advisor to the rulers of small kingdoms.

An avid student of the past, Kung, known to the Western world as Confucius, devised a system of social and political ethics based on filial piety, kinship, loyalty and righteousness. The key to his philosophy were the relationships between ruler and subject, father and son, husband and wife, elder and younger brother, friend and friend.

Kung taught that all wisdom begins with self-knowledge. He also taught that men should not serve, and people should not obey, unworthy rulers, and that superior people should provide moral examples for the masses.

Confucius was a prolific writer and editor and is credited with compiling a number of works that long after his death were published as the *Wu Jing* or the *Five Classics*—two on history, one on rituals, one on poetry, and the *Yi Jing*, or *Book of Changes*, which covered cosmology and divination.

In the A.D. 12th century, a collection of sayings by Confucius and Mencius (the famous 4th century B.C. philosopher), and some selections from a ritual classic on human nature and moral development, were published in four books under the heading of the *Analects*. Thereafter the *Five Classics* and the *Analects* became the primary subject matter of China's famed national examinations for government service, which were held annually until the beginning of the 20th century.

As time passed Confucianism became rigidly defined in hierarchical terms in which rulers had absolute rights over their subjects, husbands over wives, and parents over children, and took on the aura of a state religion.

In A.D. 1670 the court of Emperor Kangxi, who ruled the Qing (Ching) Dynasty from 1661 to 1722, issued a set of 16 maxims, known as the *Sacred Edict*, that were based on summaries of Confucian values and ethics. The edicts were published in book form for general distribution and thereafter, like Mao Zedung's Little Red Book in the 20th century, became the bible of official social and political thought in China.

In addition to the vertical structure of society, the maxims emphasized obedience to superiors, hard work, thrift and generosity.

Music was one of the key disciplines used by Confucius in his teachings on morality and ethics. He was not the first to understand the power that music has on the human mind and spirit, but he was the first to make music a significant factor in the education of moral man.

Confucius considered music—specifically what Westerners would call chamber music—an echo of the harmony between the individual hearing the music and the cosmos, and said that the purpose of music was to contribute to social and cosmic harmony. He added that the goal of *all* art forms, including literature, should be to display and promote social harmony with the cosmos.

Confucius understood that just as cosmicly harmonious music, literature and other arts can enhance the quality of human life, those that are not in tune with the cosmos can also be used to debase and destroy the quality of life—witness the state of many of these arts in the world today.

The Confucian system was based on a very practical kind of morality. There were no abstract principles of good and evil. Instead, there were precise rules of conduct designed to control all behavior in a precisely structured hierarchical society.

Confucianism was hardly a religion in the Western sense. There is no god, there are no priests, shrines or churches. There is no proselytizing. The Chinese have never run around claiming to be Confucianists.

Confucianism began as a simple social ethic. Over the centuries it absorbed many of the tenets of Daoism and Buddhism, and by the 14th century, had become a full philosophy. Its purpose was to provide for a very high degree of social order by combining an absolute, stern degree of carefully defined virtues and graceful manners.

The primary control sanction in the Confucianism system was shame, backed up by swift, sure punishment for anyone who failed to live up to its expectations. Everyone was conditioned from childhood to behave properly to avoid bringing intense shame on themselves, on their families, or on their relatives and neighbors.

But by the end of the Qing Dynasty in 1912 many Chinese intellectuals had turned against the teachings of Confucius, blaming them for most of the profound weaknesses inherent in Chinese culture, and for China's inability to defend itself against inroads and attacks by foreign powers.

Radical revolutionist-writer Chen Duxiu wrote in 1916 that Confucianism was totally incompatible with the Western concepts of equality and human rights, and should therefore be discarded.

Mao Zedung, the primary founder of the People's Republic of China, and his followers made a dramatic but only partially effective effort in 1966 to eradicate Confucianism from China by unleashing the "Cultural Revolution."

While this 10-year orgy of destruction failed to exorcise Confucianism from Chinese culture, it nevertheless had a fundamental impact in that it helped to legitimize many social concepts that were diametrically opposed to Confucian thought—beginning with the equality of men and women.

Still, Mao did not give up on his efforts to eliminate Confucianism in China. In 1973 he approved of a campaign initiated by the CCP to further discredit Confucian thought by having well-known Party-line writers flood the more popular magazines with essays condemning Confucian thought.

Today both mainland and overseas Chinese, realizing that much of what Kung taught is universal and eternal truth, are trying to salvage and modernize the Confucian principles and practices that are pro humanity and therefore worth saving.

拉关系

La Guanxi

(Lah Gwahn-she)

"Extending Your Social Credits"

There is an old saying in China that you cannot clap with a single hand, a reference to the fact that getting things done depends more on a web of connections than any other factor.

The importance of connections in China derives from a historical lack of rule by law, impartial judgments and behavior based on universal principles.

In the Confucian concept of the world, virtuous rulers (who were also presumed to be wise and benevolent), including regional and local magistrates, did not need to conduct themselves according to precise, immutable laws. Instead, they were expected to make the right decisions based on their own standards of morality and ethics.

But this system led to corruption becoming institutionalized in China, creating a society in which the only thing an individual could depend upon was personal connections.

There were, and still are, two kinds of connections in China—direct connections, meaning members of one's own extended family and other relatives, former classmates, ex-teachers, co-workers and others one has gotten to know personally; and indirect or "associate" connections, referring to people whom your direct contacts know.

Using indirect or associate connections is known as *la guanxi* (lah gwahn-she) or *pulling (one's) connections*.

Both direct and indirect connections work in China because the custom has been ritualized and sanctified as the *right thing*, the *moral thing*, to do. Anyone who does not respond as expected loses *face*, is regarded as immoral or uncivilized, and is no longer trusted or respected.

The effective use of *la guanxi* is a subtle and sometimes dangerous exercise. It requires that your direct contact have current and precise information about his or her relationship with the person that you want to meet or need something from.

If the relationship is not strong enough—if the *social debt* owed by the indirect contact to the direct contact is not sufficiently large to warrant a favorable response—the effort may result in some irritation or anger, and fail.

Asking a direct connection to use his or her contacts on your behalf naturally puts that person on the spot. If you misuse or abuse the connection, it could destroy the relationship between the two connections.

Because of the personalized nature of most social and economic relationships in China, making and maintaining connections is an overriding necessity that is pursued with considerable intensity, significantly influencing the behavior of people, including inducing them to lie and to be excessive in their praise of others.

Foreigners find that making their way in China is also greatly enhanced by using *la guanxi*, but they must be even more careful to avoid abusing or misusing indirect connections.

劳动教养

Laodong Jiaoyang

(Lah-oh-dong Jee-ah-oh-yahng)

"Re-education Through Labor"

Mao Zedung, the primary founder of the People's Republic of China, believed that China could not be converted to a Communist state as long as there were property-owning, capitalistic middle and upper classes in the country, and his aim was to totally destroy these classes.

It was also Mao's belief that confiscating the property of the middle and upper classes and forcing them to become common laborers on farms and in factories, combined with intense re-indoctrination programs designed to eliminate their middle and upper class attitudes and behavior and replace them with approved Maoist-Communist thoughts, would create the perfect Socialist society.

Mao labeled this brain-washing process *laodong jiaoyang* (lah-oh-dong jee-ah-oh-yahng), or *re-education through labor*.

In its efforts to achieve these goals the CCP operated outside the constitution and the law by the simple expedient of labeling its actions *administrative*.

The CCP followed the dictum of *kuai bu, kuai xun*, or *swift round-up, swift interrogation* followed by immediate imprisonment or execution. People by the hundreds of thousands were arrested, interrogated and sentenced without formal legal procedures.

China's Public Security Bureau operated more or less like the local police, state police, FBI and CIA, all rolled into one, but virtually without restraints.

Judges and courts were viewed as representatives of the government, not the accused, and were expected to uphold what was later to be called the Four Cardinal Principles of the Communist Party (adhering to socialism, the dictatorship by the Party, the leadership of the Party and the thought of Marx, Lenin and Mao).

Ordinary people were treated to the same process and punishment as that applied to those guilty of genuine crimes. Both were sentenced to prison labor camps or factories, where mental and physical torture were routinely used to brain-wash inmates and turn them into zombie-like workers.

Prostitutes, juvenile delinquents, people refusing to work or accused of being lazy, were also sentenced to hard labor.

By Mao's death and the winding down of *the Great Proletariat Cultural Revolution* in 1976 the *laodong jiaoyang* program had lost momentum and begun to lose its force, but in the previous twenty-five years it had wreaked social and cultural havoc on China, caused immeasurable suffering, and contributed to the death of millions.

While not practiced on a revolutionary scale today, the *laodong jiaoyang* concept remains one of the primary principles of the CCP system, and is still used to *reform* both ordinary criminals and people accused of being *enemies of the people*—meaning anyone who says or does anything not approved by the CCP.

Especially during anti-crime campaigns, the laws are ignored by the courts. Hundreds to thousands of people are rounded up and sentenced to *re-education through labor*—a process known in Mao jargon as *mass-line* justice.

劳改队

Lao Gai Dui

(Lah-oh Guy Dwee)

"Thought Reform Camps"

When the Chinese Communist Party (CCP) defeated the Nationalist forces in 1949 and became supreme in the country, the aim of Mao Zedung and his Communist associates was nothing less than to brain-wash the half billion (soon-to-be one billion) Chinese; to totally erase all of the old beliefs and customs and replace them with Communist-Socialist thinking and behavior.

One of the ways chosen to accomplish this extraordinary goal was to label all who were not even eligible to join the Communist Party—landlords, businesspeople, professionals, intellectuals—as "class enemies" and "anti-Socialist elements" and create a nationwide system for reducing these millions of people to the level of farmers and laborers.

Mao established six criteria that were used as guidelines for identifying and labeling people as enemies of the state who were therefore subject to forced conversion to his way of thinking. These six guidelines were as follows:

1. Everything that is said and done must contribute to unite the people, not divide them.
2. Every word and action should directly and positively contribute to the transformation of China into a Socialist state.
3. Every word and action should contribute to the consolidation and strengthening of the power of the democratic dictatorship.
4. Every word and action should contribute to strengthening democratic centralism (the concentration of power in the hands of the Communist leaders).
5. Every word and action should contribute to the strength of the Communist Party leadership.
6. Every word and action should contribute to international social unity and the unity of peace-loving people around the world.

Mao added that anyone who did not speak and act in accordance with these guidelines was an enemy of the people and should be dealt with through dictatorial methods based on enforced hard labor.

Mao explained that by dictatorial, he meant Lenin's definition—a form of government based upon the use of force that is unrestricted by any law.

To transform the attitudes and behavior of millions of Chinese who had been conditioned by one of the world's most definitive and powerful cultures for more than four thousand years was an undertaking of gargantuan proportions.

But Mao and his Communist colleagues were up to the task. Copying the idea of convict labor camps from the Soviets, they established and institutionalized a system known as *lao gai dui* (lah-oh guy dwee), literally *labor reform teams*, but in actuality referring to prison farms and prison factories. (Slaves and indentured laborers were common in Imperial China.)

There were six divisions in the *lao gai dui*: regular hard-labor prisons, re-education-through-labor camps, disciplinary production camps, detention centers, juvenile offenders' camps, and forced-job-placement camps.

In addition to sentencing ordinary criminals to one or the other of these prison facilities, the Communist government of China also sentenced millions of others—landlords, teachers, students, businesspeople, artists, writers, doctors, lawyers, architects, journalists—to the *lao gai dui* for periods ranging from a few years to life.

Although there were so-called maximum periods of imprisonment established for various offenses, prison authorities were empowered to extend the sentence of any prisoner who resisted the brain-washing and conversion to Communist-Socialist paragons, or just showed indifference or lack of enthusiasm.

Prison authorities routinely extended the sentences of prisoners on the recommendations of staff members of the prison farms and factories.

All prison labor farms and factories in China were given two names—one that was kept secret from the public at large, and one that was for public consumption. The first name was the real name of the prison factory or prison farm. The second name was that of an ordinary farm or business enterprise, which was used to conceal the true nature of the farm or factory from outsiders.

During the Cultural Revolution from 1966 to 1976, all levels of the Communist Party organization, as well as the student Red Guard brigades, were authorized to establish—and fill—different kinds of labor camps. Among the names used in reference to these facilities were *Bases for the "Sent-Down"* (meaning intellectuals, landlords and others forcibly exiled to rural areas from cities), and *May 7 Cadre Schools*, in reference to the first large-scale student uprising in China on May 7, 1919.

From the 1950s until the 1980s, there were several thousand of these "labor reform" prison camps and factories throughout China, with an estimated peak population of around 40 million.

Hongda (Harry) Wu, himself an inmate on prison labor farms and prisoner-operated factories for 19 years, estimates in his book *Laogai—The Chinese Gulag* that as late as the early 1990s there were some 4,000 detention centers, 1,500 prison factories, 80 juvenile offender camps, 600 reform-through-labor camps, and 990 convict labor camps in China.

Convicts in all of the various kinds of prisons, whether farm prisons, factory prisons, or whatever, were organized on military lines, with squads, platoons, companies, battalions and brigades. The leaders of these units, especially the smaller ones, were other prisoners who had been fully converted by brain-washing techniques or had special knowledge or skills.

Many prison wardens preferred to assign hardened criminals to be in charge of these thought-control and work units because the criminals were tougher and stricter disciplinarians.

By the 1980s the production in China's *lao gai dui* had become so important to the national economy that it was vital to the government to see that it continued. Hundreds of the prison factories had begun exporting to the United States and other countries.

As the production of the slave-labor factories and farms became more and more important in the overall economy, and the international community began complaining about China's use of slave-like labor, the government began gradually improving the working conditions and compensation of the inmates.

Labor reform enterprises were given more freedom and encouraged to transform themselves into fully commercial businesses, with special emphasis on exports.

But these reforms were incompatible with Deng Xiaoping's *Four Cardinal Principles*, and created new tensions and turmoil. Efforts at political conversion and thought-control were reduced dramatically and in some enterprises, especially in regions more distant from Beijing, they were suspended altogether. Most people, by this time, had simply stopped listening to the barrage of Communist-Socialist ideology.

Profits had become more important than reform ideology to both the people and the government, and were epitomized in Deng's famous announcement that "To get rich is glorious!"

In 1994, the Chinese government agreed to let American officials inspect a number of export-oriented factories suspected of using prison labor.

China has consistently used semantics to deny that there are any political prisoners in the country. They are called *fangeming-fenzi* or *counter-revolutionaries*.

The use of prison labor in China is monitored by a group in the U.S. called the Laogai Research Foundation.

劳教

Lao Jiao

(Lah-oh Jee-ah-oh)

"The Brave New World"

When the Chinese Communist Party became supreme in the country in 1949 its leaders were acutely aware that they were in the minority and that virtually all of the people in the middle and upper classes would choose some form of democracy and capitalism if they had a choice.

But the Communists were determined to either eliminate or convert to Maoist communism everyone who opposed them. During the first years of the regime, dozens of thousands of the higher profile members of the Nationalist forces and their allies, along with large numbers of landlords and intellectuals, were rounded up and executed.

After the main brunt of this blood-bath ended, the CCP began considering other ways for handling the millions of people whom it considered an ongoing threat to the CCP and its goals.

One of the measures ordered by the CCP in 1957 to help achieve this goal was the establishment of a network of *lao jiao* (lah-oh jee-ah-oh) or *re-education through labor* work camps (meaning either prison farms or prison factories) in all of the prefectures, autonomous regions and both large and middle-sized cities of the country.

Each of these entities was responsible for setting up its own local prison facilities "as needed," in accordance with the size of their populations. The total number of such camps was later estimated at around 600.

Thereafter, hundreds of thousands of middle and upper class workers and professionals were arbitrarily classified as enemies of the people, rounded up, and sentenced to various terms in the *lao jiao*, with the length of their sentences depending on their social class, occupation or profession, whether or not they had ever had any connections with foreigners, if they spoke English or some other foreign language, and so on.

This blanket categorization covered practically every educated and professional person in the country, making it possible for local Communist authorities to get rid of anyone they suspected or disliked or wanted to get out of the way for any other reason.

The CCP justified this flagrant violation of the very concept of law by proclaiming that it was a government administrative action and not a judicial punishment, and was therefore not subject to any legal procedures.

Local offices of the Public Security Bureau did not have to file any kind of report to the courts or to PSB headquarters. They could simply arrest and consign people to prison as they saw fit.

Once imprisoned, every individual was subjected to intense brain-washing that continued until they died or until they could give the answers wanted by their interrogators and convince the prison cadre that their conversion was sincere. Thereafter, they were forced to work for 10 to 12 hours a day, six days a week.

According to Harry Wu, who survived the Chinese gulag, the CCP regime used "secrecy, isolation from the outside world, spreading of superstitions, repetition of lies, distortion of truth" and other methods in its brain-washing system.

Because both workers and prison camps had daily production quotas, and the resources allotted to each prison· facility was determined by its productivity, there was enormous pressure on both the inmates and their keepers.

Since records of the individual *lao jiao* were not made public, there is no way of knowing exactly how many people were incarcerated in the prison camps during the early decades of the Communist regime, but estimates are that the figure was in excess of 20 million.

Prior to the establishment of the "labor re-education camps" there were between 20 and 25 million landlords and well-to-do farmers in China. By 1980 these two groups had disappeared.

The *lao jiao* system still flourishes in China, with the length of the sentences handed down determined by the class and political background of the accused, and by whether or not the government chooses to make an example of the individual by imposing an especially long sentence.

141

老师

Laoshi
(Lah-oh-shur)

"The Honored Teacher"

For more than 4,000 years of China's history, the Chinese were taught to revere learning and to hold the teachers of knowledge and wisdom in the highest esteem.

There was no profession more honored than that of the sage who unselfishly devoted his life to study, contemplation and teaching. Leaders surrounded themselves with wise men, and the affluent engaged teachers to tutor their male offspring, often retaining recognized scholars for life.

The Chinese word for ordinary teacher or professor, still used today all the way from kindergarten through university, is *laoshi* (lah-oh-shur), which literally means *elder role model* and traditionally incorporated all of the esteem with which the Chinese viewed people of learning.

Given such an extraordinary tradition over such a long period of time, what happened in China between 1949 and 1976, particularly during the early years of the so-called Cultural Revolution (1966–1976), beggars the imagination.

In 1966 Mao Zedung, chairman of the Communist Party, set the country's millions of high school and university students against all teachers and "intellectuals" in the country, ordering the students to destroy every vestige of the "old" culture.

The young people of China were so frustrated at the Confucian restraints under which they still lived, at the ongoing political morass that had plagued the country for more than 100 years, and basically at the failures that had racked China for so long, that they went on a frenzied rampage, humiliating, torturing and sometimes crippling and even killing their teachers and professors, making a mockery of everything that the Chinese had held dear for so many millennia.

For nearly 10 years being a teacher in China was a frightening and dangerous thing.

It was not until Mao died in 1976 that rationality began returning, and the CCP admitted that China could not survive and prosper without *laoshi* and an educated population.

And although *laoshi* again resumed their traditional roles in Chinese society, they were unable to regain all of the prestige that had once been theirs. Too many of the traditional concepts had been destroyed by the Maoist regime and by students and their worker-allies during the Cultural Revolution.

One lesson the Chinese learned during the Cultural Revolution was that having an education did not guarantee personal or financial security, and that connections were just as important if not more so, than a high school or university diploma.

Cynicism about the value of a higher education and the role of *laoshi* has continued to spread in China. It will probably be well into the 21st century before economic factors return education to its exalted position, and result in complete rehabilitation of the teaching profession. See **Wenhua Da Ge Ming**.

142

老外

Laowai
(Lah-oh-wie)

"The Outsiders"

China has an extraordinary emotional impact on foreigners who spend any extensive length of time there. Much of life appears to be one contradiction after the other; a seesaw that is in constant motion. Things are often either positive or negative, satisfying or frustrating; seemingly without a balance or middle road.

Generally speaking, foreigners cannot predict what is going to happen in China, and this unpredictability can be enormously upsetting to those who do not quickly learn to accept things as they are and bend with the wind.

Much of the Chinese behavior that strikes outsiders as contradictory or irrational, that makes things far more complicated and subtle than the outsider thinks they should be, results from the Chinese having less control over their private and professional lives. They must conform to some degree to a variety of regulations and customs that are unknown and invisible to outsiders.

Another key factor in the emotional impact that China has on foreign residents is that no matter how long they may have been in China, whether years or a lifetime, they remain *laowai* (lah-oh-wie) or *outsiders*.

For most foreigners this inability to merge themselves into the local scene and become one of the crowd, to not be stared at or singled out for special treatment or discriminated against for no reason other than the fact that they are not Chinese, is a burden that eventually becomes unbearable.

Another aspect of culture shock that afflicts most foreign residents of China is that, generally speaking, they cannot take most of the common things of life for granted. Things that they expect to be done are not done, or become undone. Things that they automatically assume will not be done are sometimes done.

Often just when foreigners in China think they have things all figured out, they come apart. People whom they have gotten to know, to like and to trust, do things that are the reverse of rational expectations.

The inability of the Chinese to see non-Chinese as anything but *laowai* is primarily based on racial characteristics. Since racial traits are immutable, there is simply no way the outsider can become a Chinese.

But despite all of the inconsistencies, irrationalities and unpredictability of life in China for *laowai,* or perhaps because of them, there is a charm, an attraction, in the way of China that has a subtle effect on most foreigners who live there for any length of time.

China changes the fundamental values and expectations of most long-time foreign residents, and they often do not realize that these changes have taken place until they leave the country. Some who leave China find that their own culture is no longer exciting or satisfying. They either go back to China or spend the rest of their lives wishing they could.

老乡

Lao Xiang

(Lah-oh She-ahng)

"Pull of 'Native Place'"

People everywhere are familiar with the idea of having an emotional attachment to the place where one was born and raised. I recall vividly the extraordinary emotional rush I felt from visiting my birthplace in a tiny isolated valley in the Ozark Hills of southern Missouri after an absence of forty years.

There was only one family still living in the valley, and the house in which I was born was gone. But when I stood on the very spot where my home had been, I wanted to shout like Alex Haley, the author of *Roots,* when he finally discovered the African village where his ancestors came from.

The older, more conservative and stronger the culture, the more powerful the attachment to one's birthplace is likely to be. But in the case of Chinese this attachment has even deeper and more significant roots.

For more than two thousand years, China's social, economic and political systems literally bound most people to the places where they were born. A form of ancestor worship brought with it a religious obligation to look after the tombs and spirits of one's forebearers, further strengthening their ties with their *lao xiang* (lah-oh she-ahng) or *native place*.

Daily life in China was traditionally centered on the extended family and interacting closely with one's neighbors. The survival and welfare of each individual was intimately connected with the fortunes of the family, the neighbors, and the land in the immediate vicinity.

Local dialects and accents, diets, the forms of local recreation and entertainment, intermarriage within the district, wariness toward outsiders, all combine to give *lao xiang* special meaning to the Chinese, especially to those in rural areas.

When the Chinese Communist Party took power in 1949 virtually every political, social and economic program the CCP inaugurated was in direct opposition to the concept of *native place*, and all that it meant to the people.

The most destructive of these programs were "forced job placement," under which people were forcibly transferred to jobs in distant parts of the country, and the huge, nationwide gulag system of prison farms and factories that were filled with political prisoners.

In the early 1950s the CCP struck another serious blow to the *native place* concept by abolishing all of the native place associations and guilds.

But most Chinese still today are attached by a cultural umbilical cord to the place of their birth, or if they are overseas Chinese, to the place where their ancestors came from.

This attachment continues to play a significant role in the thinking and behavior of the majority of all Chinese, and has a discernible social, economic and political impact on the life of the nation.

Loyalty to one's *lao xiang*, to cultural habits that distinguish that area, and to other people from the same district, divides the main body of Chinese into a multitude of groups that are the same racially but otherwise different enough that it is necessary to be aware of the differences and take them into consideration when dealing with people on an individual or collective basis.

Not surprisingly, a hierarchy exists that divides the district and regional groupings of Chinese into higher or lower ranks. Some are more acceptable than others. Employers will not hire workers from some districts. People from some districts will not marry people from certain other areas. There is deep-seated enmity between some villages and districts that regularly results in violence. Blood feuds exist.

Because of the ingrown, localized nature of Chinese culture over the generations and the virtual absence of exposure to people from significantly different mores, the Chinese became super sensitive to anything or anybody that was different from what they were used to. Some of this prejudice was benign, but when the Chinese felt threatened in any way it instantly became malevolent.

The majority of rural Chinese continue to be extraordinarily prejudiced in their view of and reaction to Chinese from other districts and regions. Even among the Chinese who go out of their way to be friendly toward and associate with foreigners for personal or business reasons, this prejudice lies just below the surface and is liable to flare up without warning at the most unpredictable times.

144

Li

(Lee)

"The Importance of Ritual"

One of the old literary names for China was *Li I Chih Pang* or *The Land of Ritual and Right Behavior*—an extraordinary reference to the role that ritual has played in the history of the country.

In the traditional Chinese context, the concept of ritual encompasses all forms of man-made social behavior, from the simplest to the most elaborate. Ritual, notes psychologist-Sinologist Michael Harris Bond of the Chinese University of Hong Kong, unites and bonds the ethics and bipolarity of Chinese thought.

In other words, the Chinese concept of *li* (lee) or *ritual* goes beyond manners and mores to embrace the whole of human relationships, beliefs and behavior in their cosmic setting.

Rituals encompassing both religious and secular affairs had been at the heart of Chinese life for centuries before the time of Confucius in the 6th century B.C. He removed virtually all of the supernatural elements from the rituals he taught, emphasizing instead the importance of concentrating on worldly affairs and establishing a foundation for harmony on all levels of society.

Confucius taught that without ritual there could be no peace or prosperity in society, since ritual served as both the source of knowledge about right behavior and the vehicle by which it was expressed.

The thrust of Confucius's teachings was to provide an ethical foundation for government based on ritualistic relationships between ruler and subject, and between all individuals in society.

In the centuries following the time of Confucius his concepts of *li*, with numerous additions by later philosophers, gradually permeated and colored the whole pattern of Chinese life, perpetuating a vertically arranged chauvinistic system in which personal freedom and choice among the masses virtually ceased to exist.

While Confucius's own views recognized human individuality and the importance of the self, he believed that the interests of the state took precedence over individual rights which, he said, should be sublimated for the benefit of the whole through the observance of *li*.

Rituals are still a significant part of the lives of all Chinese, but they have long since lost most of the extreme public formality that was characteristic of earlier times—the kowtow being one of the most conspicuous forms of behavior that died with the end of the last dynasty in 1912.

Present-day Chinese etiquette, in fact, often clashes sharply with Western ideas of ethical and genteel behavior. Examples of the latter are frequently seen in television shows that are crude by Western standards.

A TV show I recently saw involved an extended family that had been separated for some years. In a funny skit, a girl recognizes her male cousin by the tone of his fart. He gleefully demonstrates his joy at being recognized by farting several additional times in rapid succession.

145

Li
(Lee)

"The Right Behavior"

In Western dictionary terms *etiquette* is defined as: (a) any special code of behavior or courtesy; (b) prescribed forms of conduct in "polite" society; (c) the standards to be observed by one who makes claims of "good breeding;" and so on.

While there seems to be general agreement that "etiquette" refers to the *way* "cultured" people conduct themselves in their dealings with others, none of these definitions make any specific reference to whether or not the Western concept of etiquette has a moral base.

In fact, Westerners have always tended to see etiquette as a class thing; as being something above and beyond the lower classes; and as something that applied only to a style of behavior; not one's essential character.

In other words, the politest, most decorously behaved person imaginable could in actuality be the world's greatest scoundrel putting on an act—which is often the case.

Good manners are obviously still an important skill in the upper levels of Western society, but they are taught less frequently and less thoroughly than in the past, particularly in the United States, and have less and less to do with morality or the character of people.

The Chinese concept of *li* (lee) or *etiquette* goes far beyond style. It evolved over the centuries from deep-seated philosophical contemplation of the relationship between man and the physical and spiritual cosmos. The goal of this contemplation was to divine the "correct" behavior for man—correct in the sense of what was "moral," meaning that it contributed to rather than detracted from cosmic harmony.

Chinese etiquette began as religious ritual, and was spread among the people as a religious observance. It was a system of moral behavior, not a style of manners, and it applied to every man, woman and child, regardless of their social level.

But Chinese *li* did not emerge pure and simple in a vacuum. It came about in a hierarchically structured society of inferiors and superiors, and within the context of an authoritarian government in which the emperor, court officials and others of high rank were treated with all the reverence and posturing associated with "proper" behavior toward exalted beings.

There was a strong element of both class and culture in traditional Chinese etiquette, but only in the sense that the higher the class and the better educated the individual, the higher the standards of etiquette they were expected to follow.

There were standards for the lower classes as well, and very severe sanctions if they failed to live up to these standards, particularly when meeting and interacting with higher level government officials.

Etiquette, and Chinese style morality, are still of prime importance in today's China in formal and personal situations. For the outsider to function effectively with Chinese it is necessary to know not only some of the key forms of expected manners, but also some of the philosophy that is rooted in their traditional behavior.

In public situations, however, the fabled politeness of the Chinese has become a victim of the Communist nightmare. People out in public are often rude to strangers, and it is common for them to curse each other at the slightest provocation.

廉

Lian

(Lee-enn)

"The Perfect Man"

China has been in the throes of political, social and economic revolution for more than two hundred years; a period of time that is not exceptionally long by Chinese standards but one that is now changing China more fundamentally and dramatically than any of the many other revolutions it has experienced over the past five thousand years.

There is no doubt that the China of the future will have a more democratic society and an economy primarily run by market forces. What is still very much in doubt, however, is how much of the virtue of its traditional culture will be retained in this new China.

Obviously much of China's traditional culture will disappear altogether because it is totally incompatible with practically every principle of democracy and free enterprise. But many of the values and beliefs that molded the Chinese into a distinctive people reflect philosophical and physical truths that are eternal, and hopefully will survive this mother of all revolutions.

One of the philosophical truths that has been recognized in China for millennia, but has hardly been used because of political circumstances, is the importance of *lian* (lee-enn), or *moral integrity*.

In some instances, Chinese use the term *lian* in reference to "face" or reputation, but it is most often used in reference to the kind of behavior expected from an ideal civilized human being.

Lian remains a key word in China today. One of the highest accolades that can be paid to anyone is to say that he or she is a person with *lian*. This means he or she is a person who can be trusted to say and do the right thing regardless of the circumstances or temptations.

Of course, the "right thing" in the Chinese context may be quite different from what it is in a Western sense, and this difference must be recognized in order to avoid serious misunderstandings.

The ultimate for a person with *lian* is to be civilized (moral) in a universal sense and across cultural lines—an advanced state of moral development that is far more common among overseas Chinese than mainland Chinese.

Truly *lian* people are usually well up in their years, have had successful lives as parents and in some line of work—whether as businesspeople, bankers or farmers—have nothing else to prove, and are motivated only by a sense of goodwill.

These are also people who are representative of the best in China's traditional culture—wise in a way that allows them to see the reality of any situation, and to make decisions that are free of personal hang-ups.

Westerners dealing with China are advised to seek the help of people who are widely recognized as having *lian*, and are therefore able to act as resistance-free conduits between their respective cultures.

面子

Lian
(Lee-enn)

"The Importance of 'Face'"

Americans and many Europeans are weaned on the concept that every person is responsible for his or her own behavior, and a great deal of effort is made to ensure that Western children develop a keen sense of individuality and personal worth.

When Americans in particular end up as social misfits who cannot get along with others and are prone to violence, we often (mistakenly) attribute much or all of their misbehavior to lack of self-esteem.

In China, on the other hand, the cultural practice for more than four thousand years was to downplay the concept of the individual and emphasize the supremacy of the family and the group.

Extraordinary effort was made to homogenize people, to condition them to think alike and behave alike. Individualism was considered immoral and non-Chinese.

Within the framework of this system, the important thing was group-esteem, not self-esteem. The sense of self was blurred to the extent that it virtually did not exist. Practically speaking, no one could make decisions on their own for themselves alone.

On top of this factor, Chinese society functioned on the basis of personal relationships rather than objective customs and laws. There were laws, but they were designed to preserve and serve the government, not to protect the people or to make it possible for them to conduct their affairs based on a foundation of legal rights and practical expediency.

Every person, every group, had to develop and nurture an extensive network of personal connections in order to get things done. Their livelihoods and often their lives depended upon having this kind of "social credit." Anything that besmirched their "face" had a decidedly negative effect on their ability to use their "social credit," and was therefore very serious.

Individuals thus became almost totally dependent upon others for their values and their standing in society. Concern about their own face was essentially the only area or thing about which they had personal control.

This social system led to an obsessive sensitivity about one's *lian* (leenn) or *face*. Any slight of any kind that made people feel bad or look bad reflected not only upon them but also on their families and groups, and was treated as a major insult that called for quick apologies—and in more serious situations, some kind of retribution or revenge.

Rather rare Chinese who were not as sensitive to slights or insults as the typical person were known as *hòu pífū*, or *thick-skin face*.

Chinese concern with *lian* is as strong today as it was during the Imperial days, if not stronger. Society in general, including all commercial enterprises, still depend upon "social credit" and "face" as the primary ingredients in all relationships.

In a society where trust and loyalty are the bedrock of all relationships, loss of face can make one an untouchable. Some Chinese define face as *social connections*.

In addition to protecting one's own face and that of others, it is especially important to "give face" to others from whom you want continued goodwill and cooperation. In Western terms, this means treating them with special respect or honor.

Outsiders dealing with the Chinese may now and then be exempted from the demands of *lian*, but generally speaking it applies to everyone involved with China. Without "face" and a "bank full of social credits," survival and success in China is practically impossible.

临

Lin

(Leen)

"Things Are Looking Up"

Chinese beliefs include a variety of tenets that Westerners tend to view superficially and to regard as superstitions. On closer examination, however, these beliefs often turn out to have solid foundations.

One such belief has to do with cycles in human affairs, in this case the timing or beginning of auspicious events, which comes under the heading of *lin* (leen), translated as *promotion* when used in the sense of something moving ahead.

Lin is concerned with the common sense belief that there are good and bad times for beginning anything new, particularly in promoting one's self, in the sense of a job promotion, or one's ideas.

When a state of *lin* exists—meaning that the timing is good—success is virtually guaranteed as long as your motivations and goals, even though based on self-interest, are pure.

All *lin*-enhanced endeavors are based on self-interest and inspiration, but must be conducted in concert with others who share your views and enthusiasm, and must benefit them as well.

What is so special about a *lin* opportunity is that most or all of the external circumstances that influence human behavior are in your favor. People like you, respect you and want to help you. Instead of resisting your ideas and plans they will support you.

Where business or political matters are concerned you might say that all of the planets are lined up in your favor, providing you with the perfect opportunity to consolidate your position and make significant gains—or to make extraordinary contributions to the goals of your friends and associates.

On the male-female front, you can also make great progress in your relationships because the object of your affections is receptive and allows you to take the lead.

Success that occurs during a time of *lin* results in you being able to discern the reality of things with much greater clarity, and significantly increases your spiritual and physical strength—but all of this can be lost if you do not continue to be tolerant and caring toward others.

The sages advise that you should extend special effort to make your enhanced physical and spiritual strength a permanent part of your character because the period of *lin* will end and you will be faced with remaining steady during a new cycle of decline.

Accepting and following this advice, the sages add, will result in you achieving the highest levels of authority and provide you with opportunities to benefit others by sharing your knowledge and experience.

Other advice offered by the sages is that once you attain a pinnacle of power you should let others carry out your plans, and if you have chosen your associates well, you will achieve even higher goals.

149

领导

Lingdao

(Leeng-dah-oh)

"Leaders and Managers"

The Western image of an ideal political leader or corporate executive is someone who has a strong personality, a good grasp of the matters at hand, conceives and implements policies, makes timely and firm decisions, and stands up for the people under him or her.

In China the primary qualities expected in a leader or executive is someone who is good at establishing and nurturing personal relationships, who practices benevolence toward his or her subordinates, who is dignified and aloof but sympathetic, and puts the interests of his or her employees or followers equal to or above his or her own.

The Chinese assume that *lingdao* (leeng-dah-oh), *leaders*, and *lingli* (leeng-lee), *managers*, will automatically make good, benevolent decisions to avoid harming themselves and their families, thereby losing face. In other words, for cultural reasons rather than reasons based on managerial theories.

Furthermore, virtually all authority in China is bound up in individuals; not their offices or titles. The power these individuals exercise comes from the personal relations they have with those around them and the image of virtue and goodwill with which others view them.

None of this means that the individuals concerned are qualified to be executives or leaders. It often happens that people in such positions are there for what turns out to be all the wrong reasons.

And not surprisingly, such people are prone to surround themselves with subordinates who do not question them or make any attempt to guide them, and to keep their staffs in the dark as much as possible.

In fact, it is characteristic of Chinese management that top executives do not share all of their thinking or their plans with subordinates, preferring to keep them guessing and forcing them to work harder in order to look good because they don't really know what or how much they are expected to accomplish.

Keeping staff and employees in the dark is also a vital factor in executives, bureaucrats and politicians maintaining their power.

It is also common for both political leaders and business executives to abuse or compromise the integrity of their subordinates by using them to achieve purely personal goals.

Westerners who automatically assume that this philosophy of personalized management is incompatible with modern industry should be wary of jumping to conclusions. Some of the most successful companies in Hong Kong, Taiwan and Southeast Asia were built on personalized management and show no signs of slowing down.

Authority in China has always been conceived of as a personal thing, and has always been exercised in a personal manner, with all of the inconsistencies and abuses that such an arbitrary system suggests.

Generally speaking, China's government leaders, bureaucrats, and businesspeople as well, also automatically assume an extraordinary degree of righteousness and authority based solely on the awesome length and weight of Chinese civilization—another factor that their foreign counterparts must deal with.

150

历书

Lishu

(Lee-shuu)

"Keeping Up with Spirits"

In 1589 China's Imperial Court published a revised version of the famed Daoist canons, stating in the new edition that charms, worn or carried on the person, would keep *xian* (she-enn) or *spirits* under control and ward off evil.

This proclamation greatly increased the popularity of *fu* (fuu) or *charms*, and encouraged a custom that had already been common in the country for ages.

Jade is probably China's best-known good luck charm. The popularity of precious stone as a charm goes back several thousand years. It is believed that jade carved into the shape of a dragon symbolizes power and strength; jade tigers attract good fortune from the god of the Western Paradise.

One of the more popular of the Daoist charms listed in the new issue of the canons was a slip of paper bearing some auspicious words written by a temple priest while he was in a trance. These charms were placed in lockets or medallions made of silver or gold.

There are many other special charms in the Chinese world of the supernatural, including a number that are illustrated in the annual *Lishu* (Lee-shuu) or *Almanac*, one of the oldest and most influential periodicals in China.

The *Lishu*, already in use by 2200 B.C., and still a popular bestseller today in Taiwan, Hong Kong and Southeast Asia, is a combination calendar (both Eastern and Western), horoscope, weather forecast, and the latest updates on *feng shui* orientations (for the placement of buildings, landscaping, furniture, doors, etc.).

Other kinds of information in the almanac include rules of etiquette, lists of family names, and philosophical suggestions for successful business management.

The cover illustration of the annual *Lishu* remains the same year-after-year—a farmer and his oxen. But the details of the drawing differ each year, and represent the weather forecast for the year.

If the oxen is red that indicates it is going to be an unusually wet year. If the farmer is wearing shoes it means the weather is going to be dry. If the farmer is wearing a hat, the forecast is for a cold spring.

The size of the oxen in relation to the farmer, the shape of its tail, belly and head—all have a specific meaning relating to the weather of the coming year.

In overseas Chinese communities *Lishu* sell just as well, if not better, among city dwellers as they do among farmers because urbanites use them for fortune-telling.

Knowing something about the *Lishu* and the role it continues to play in Chinese life can be helpful in forging and keeping good relations with Chinese.

龙之梦

Long De Meng
(Lung Duh Mung)

"The Dragon Dream"

One of the differences between the Chinese and Japanese that is especially conspicuous today is the residual strength of the cultures among Japanese and Chinese who leave their home countries and spend time abroad.

Anyone who has spent any considerable amount of time in Japan is acutely aware of the strength of Japanese culture as long as the Japanese are inside its web in their own environment. But, remarkably, when the Japanese step outside of this web and spend as little as three years in the West, they lose much of their Japaneseness, shedding their cultural veneer as if it were a skin.

Furthermore, Japanese who settle abroad as permanent residents very quickly assimilate into local cultures and within one generation can hardly be distinguished from the people of their adopted land.

The attitude and behavior of the Japanese-American residents of Hawaii and California at the outbreak of war between Japan and the U.S. in 1941 was a stark and surprising example of how easily and quickly the Japanese adopt new cultures, values and loyalties.

The Chinese, on the other hand, do not give up their cultural identity so easily. Many Chinese who are three and four generations removed from their ancestral homeland still feel and act culturally as Chinese.

Stan Shih, founder of Taiwan's huge ACER Group of companies, says that the ongoing strength of Chinese culture is based on what he calls the *Long de Meng* (lung duh mung) or *Dragon Dream*. He describes this dream as resulting from Chinese children being impregnated with knowledge of the former greatness of China, which provides them with a challenge and the motivation to exert almost superhuman effort to live up to and maybe re-capture the glories of China's past—at least for themselves and their families.

Shih was not too optimistic about the future of mainland China, how-ever, observing that the Chinese did not yet know how to handle personal freedom. He said: "The Chinese [who have freedom of choice] are not easy to organize. Everyone wants to be the head of the chicken!"

But mainland Chinese dream the *Dragon Dream* as often and as clear-ly as overseas Chinese, and there is no doubt it will become more and more of a factor in helping them regain many of their past glories. In Chinese mythology, dragons are not fire-breathing monsters—except when some-one steps on their tails. Then their fury knows no bounds. Chinese dragons are revered for their power and grandeur, and have long been used as a sym-bol for the emperor.

履

Lu
(Luu)

"Watching Your *P*s and *Q*s"

One of the most conspicuous features of Chinese civilization has been the style and role of personal etiquette—how the people greeted each other, their manner of interacting with each other, how they ate and behaved in general, and so on.

In the traditional setting of the Imperial dynasties, this personal behav-ior was closely related to morality because the more stylized and refined the manners, the higher the morality attributed to the individual, the more they were respected, and the more influence they had—a syndrome that is, of course, well-known in the West.

But there was a significant difference between the typical social behavior of the ordinary Chinese and the common people of the West because all Chinese were conditioned to follow a precisely prescribed highly stylized form of behavior that had existed for centuries and was an integral part of the common culture.

Lu (luu) or *conduct* was an overriding theme in the lives of the Chinese for more than three millennia, becoming as much a part of their national character as the principles by which they lived.

Conduct was recognized by Confucius and other Chinese sages as the outward manifestations of one's education and character and therefore a measure of one's socialization and value as an upstanding citizen.

They were also wise enough to know that strict physical conditioning in manners was an integral part of the process of absorbing the principles behind the etiquette.

Lu was so important in Chinese culture that it was one of the first ten of the elements treated in the classic *Book of Changes*, which Confucius is believed to have edited. The book equated proper conduct with correctness in values, motivations and goals but at the same time it dealt with day-to-day affairs in a very practical manner designed to keep people out of trouble and give them an advantage in their endeavors.

In essence, the *Book of Changes* says the path to success, whether social, economic or political, is paved by maintaining a calm, dignified demeanor at all times.

More specific advice for achieving success, from the lowest level up, includes not taking advantage of friends or acquaintances, not becoming obligated to others, doing things in moderation, keeping your expectations under control, staying modest and exercising caution in your endeavors. But, the sages add, if you are sure of your goals and methods, make a strong commitment to them and do not waver.

Other *lu* principles that are important to the Chinese include overcoming some of your own weaknesses, such as prejudices or incompetence, allying yourself with people who are both competent and of good character, learning from them, and thereby raising your own standards.

Despite much less emphasis on *lu* in present-day China, once a personal relationship is established the level of dignified conduct remains high enough to distinguish the Chinese from most other people.

153

旅

Lu

(Luu)

"Guidelines for 'Travelers'"

A strong feeling that we do not really belong in our present time and space has struck most of us at one time or another. It seems that this phenomenon may be universal in the human psyche because it has been mentioned over the ages by people in diverse cultures.

In China this phenomenon was recognized as a fundamental human characteristic by the first philosophers and became institutionalized under the term *lu* (luu), which means *traveling*.

Traveling in this context does not mean physically going from place to place. It refers to an intellectual and spiritual attitude that prevents people from staying with one thing or with the same people for extended periods of time.

The *traveling* person seems incapable of putting down roots, and is more like a butterfly, flitting from one place to another, searching, tasting and testing, unable to make commitments.

Most people go through a short time of *lu* in their younger, formative years, but once they mature the *traveling* generally ends.

Some people, however, are born *travelers*, and the condition is life-long. In others the time of *traveling* by mature adults may be a phase that lasts for only a few years or even shorter periods during specific situations. It is to these two groups of people that the Chinese sages addressed themselves.

Not surprisingly, people who are *traveling* are advised to not make any long-range plans or commitments (because they will "move on" before the goals are accomplished), to keep a low profile, to stay modest in their aims, to not mislead others by making promises that will not be kept, to remain sensitive to the needs of others, and to be generous in helping others.

If the *traveler* holds to these guidelines, add the sages, he or she will have the best chance of living a happy and useful life.

On a practical level *travelers* are also advised to avoid getting hung up on trivial matters and to focus more on the broad picture, recognizing and acknowledging their own character, but viewing it with dignity and self-confidence.

One of the problems that lifelong *travelers* who finally achieve some success must live with is the strong feeling that they have not yet arrived; have not done enough or all that they are capable of doing. The only response to these second thoughts is for such people to constantly remind themselves that they must also be modest and generous in setting standards for themselves.

Until recent times, few Chinese have had the opportunity to indulge themselves in *traveling* except in the purest intellectual sense because their lives were decided for them by the state and their work units. Growing individual freedom is changing this, and will contribute to a more varied and interesting China.

Knowing that most foreigners who come to China to live and work will be there for only short periods of time, the Chinese tend to treat them like *lu* and be reluctant to make long-term commitments to them.

Overcoming this syndrome requires a great deal of extra effort by outsiders to convince their Chinese associates that their commitments transcend time and distance.

154

律

Lu

(Luu)

"Your Worst Enemy"

It is a well-known piece of folk wisdom that people are often their own worst enemies, particularly when it comes to establishing and maintaining harmonious and supportive relationships with others.

People who are afflicted with this perverse quirk in their characters and personalities just as often blame others for their own failings. They are unable to see that it is because of their own shortcomings that they cannot get along with, inspire, or lead others.

Virtually all of China's great philosophers recognized this common human failing and commented at length about the importance of self-realization, observing that awareness of one's own character and perspectives was essential before one could understand and deal appropriately with the world at large.

Sun Tzu, China's great military strategist, was even more concerned about this weakness because failing to recognize and overcome one's own failings could lead to defeat in war, death, and the fall of the state.

In his famous book *The Art of War*, Sun Tzu made coming to terms with your own weaknesses through unrelenting *lu* (luu) or *discipline*, the third element is his thirty-six strategies for victory (the first two were planning and foresight).

It was Sun Tzu's position that a military commander could be well trained in the art of war and know *how* to defeat his country's enemies but not be able to do it if he was not aware of and in control of his own weaknesses.

Sun Tzu listed the faults that are the most detrimental to a general as recklessness, cowardice, quick temper, concern about his personal reputation, and being too compassionate toward his men.

In contrast to these failings, Sun Tzu said the superior general had the virtues of wisdom, sincerity, benevolence, courage and strictness. He added that it was imperative that a general lead by example, and that it was therefore just as important for a general to be disciplined as it was for his men.

Lu has been a major factor in Chinese culture since well before Sun Tzu's time. The rigid social structure and the extraordinary demands of the highly refined etiquette system made parental discipline during childhood and self discipline throughout the remainder of life a key component in Chinese society.

To become educated in China meant learning how to read and draw several thousand intricate ideograms and achieving familiarity with a number of equally intricate philosophical systems, all of which required an enormous amount of self-discipline.

Simply existing in crowded, highly organized China in earlier years demanded a degree of discipline that went well beyond what most Westerners regard as rational. While life in present-day China is far less restricted than it was during the dynastic eras and the heyday of the Communist period, it still requires extraordinary self-discipline to cope with the crowds and the idiosyncrasies of the culture.

Foreigners in China invariably find that they must dramatically increase their level of personal *lu* in order to function effectively.

155

乱

Luan
(Luu-enn)

"The Greatest Fear"

Throughout most of their history, the people of China were secure in the certitude that theirs was the greatest, the best, and the most enduring of all countries, and there were numerous valid reasons for such beliefs.

Geographically, the huge landmass of China was protected on the east by a great ocean, on the north by the harsh vastness of Siberia, on the west by the vast reaches of the Gobi Desert and the great barrier of the Himalayas, and on the south by the jungles and mountains of the upper Indo-China peninsula.

With more than four thousand years of minutely detailed history and a record of achievements that dwarfed all of the rest of the world combined, it was simply beyond Chinese comprehension that any other nation might have equal or greater claims to glory.

China's book of history is filled with the rise and fall of many dynasties, and marked by the violence of wars and practically every natural disaster known to man, but for most of this great expanse of time China was a land of peace and relative prosperity.

The main social, economic and political principle of China over these ages was, in fact, peace and harmony—not based on personal choice, but on a minutely structured and rigidly controlled system designed to prevent *luan* (luu-enn) or *disorder* and preserve the family, village, work unit and dynasty that existed at that time.

One of the most important facets of this control system was a stylized form of personal behavior that became so pervasive and culturally powerful that it took on the trappings of a cult.

Any behavior that was outside of a precisely sanctioned norm was regarded as a threat to society that could lead to widespread disorder and dire consequences for everyone.

Within this environment, the Chinese developed a pathological fear of *luan*, causing them to go to extra extremes to ensure that everyone upheld the highest standards of behavior.

This Chinese abhorrence of disorder has been put to the ultimate test time and again since they began to have regular intercourse with the outside world on terms that they could not control. But avoiding disorder continues to be one of their most important guidelines in their daily activities, whether personal or business.

Chinese attempts to avoid *luan* often include withholding information, misrepresenting facts, stonewalling, refusing to take some action, lying and so on—which just as often runs counter to the rationale and behavior of Westerners, and results in considerable misunderstanding, friction and ill-will.

When faced with a situation in which the Chinese appear to be motivated only by their desire to avoid upsetting the order of things, regardless of how irrational or meaningless the behavior might be, about the only direct recourse is to politely but firmly persist and hope that you can wear down their resistance and get whatever it is you are after.

If time and other circumstances permit, often the most effective method for overcoming this kind of impasse is to bring in a third party connection, a *guanxi*, to act on your behalf.

156

乱

Luan

(Luu-enn)

"Fighting to the Finish"

Because of a deeply embedded philosophy and practice of harmony, complemented by a built-in abhorrence of chaos and strict enforcement measures, there was traditionally little violence in China in normal situations and times.

Still today people are generally safe from personal violence in the byways and streets of Chinese cities.

One of the more telling reasons why China is usually safer than most other countries, is that when arrested those who are responsible for committing crimes and perpetuating violence are dealt with quickly and harshly.

A long sentence in prison or quick execution by a bullet in the back of the head are common forms of law enforcement. As one Chinese taxi driver was quoted as saying, "We don't have many repeat offenders."

However, when the Chinese do fight among themselves it is likely to be a *luan* (luu-enn) fight, meaning "a fight to the finish," often with revenge extracted from the losers in particularly cruel and gruesome ways.

The reason for this *luan* kind of behavior is that there has never been a philosophy of compassion, of forgiving and forgetting in China, and such a philosophy is still alien to most Chinese.

But the relatively few periods of mass violence in feudal China invariably occurred when the local or national governments became so oppressive the people rebelled; or when the governments became so weak they could not enforce the draconian laws and practices on which their rules were based.

China's dynastic governments, which ruled the country from before 2000 B.C. until 1912, generally had long lifetimes as dynasties go—most of them from 200 to 400 years—before internal corruption or destruction by outside forces brought them down. And none of the dynasties gave up without a fight. The Mongol invasion of China in A.D. 1280, which ended the Qin Dynasty, is said to have cost the lives of over thirty million people.

Most large-scale violence in China in recent years resulted from severe, compulsive competition between groups for the rights to extremely limited resources. Factory workers or farmers who perceive that their livelihood is being threatened will often react like urban gangs fighting over turf or for primacy in certain rackets.

In addition to this, the beliefs and etiquette that once prevented most individual acts of violence in China are gradually breaking down. The struggle to get an ever larger piece of the capitalist pie is also increasing competition. There factors are resulting in violence of all kinds becoming more common.

Like other countries that have not yet come to terms with freedom of thought, aggressive individuality and the personal turmoil that results when age-old restraints disappear, the Chinese now face the challenge of coping with growing social disorder.

Given their history, chances are the short-term reaction will be a continuation of the traditional *luan* philosophy, resulting in ever-expanding execution fields.

157

伦理学

Lunlixue

(Loon-lee-shu-eh)

"Ethics Chinese Style"

Wall Street Journal editorial writer Andrew B. Black once wrote: "China has no soul!" He might also have said, "China has no ethics"—at least in the Western sense. A Taiwan Chinese says of his own countrymen, "Very few people can or want to distinguish between right and wrong!"

These are harsh judgments, but all of them are true enough that they are a vital factor in any matter having to do with Taiwan or mainland China.

All of pre-modern China's social and political institutions were fashioned to conform to the dictates of autocratic rulers who answered to no one and were primarily concerned about preserving and enhancing their own status.

In this environment of dictatorial rule by individuals, *lunlixue* (loon-lee-shu-eh) or *ethics* were not based on universal principles of good and bad, but on the circumstances of the moment—a system that is generally referred to as "situational ethics" in Western terms.

To Westerners who have been nurtured on logic and empirical reasoning, situational ethics are not ethics at all, but a facile way to avoid rational, practical behavior. Westerners who are confronted for the first time with all of the twists and turns of situational ethics tend to regard such behavior as unfair, devious, dishonest and oftentimes stupid.

But in the traditional Chinese context of ethics and morality, changing the rules and behavior to fit the situation was not unethical or immoral but good sense. Their definition of ethics was strictly personal.

The first premise in understanding and dealing with Chinese *lunlixue* or *ethics*, is the fact that they were never based on so-called absolute truths or immutable principles.

Western ethics divide good and bad into separate categories. There are degrees of good and bad; but what's good is good and what's bad is bad, without exception. Without this kind of foundation, it would be impossible to make workable laws to protect people.

In contrast to this approach, traditional Chinese ethics were not based on the recognition of good and bad in a secular or religious sense. They were based on the concept of preserving harmony among and between all of the levels of society, *as decided and administered by the government*.

In other words, ethics in China were whatever the prevailing government said they were, meaning that they were arbitrary and circumstantial, often depending on the whim or idiosyncrasies of any number of individuals on different levels of government.

On a personal level, ethics were based on expediency as well as feelings rather than principles. Said a Chinese critic: "In the old way, the custom was to avoid upsetting people at the expense of righteousness and justice. The primary obligation was to avoid friction, even though it was at the expense of honesty, rationality and personal feelings."

Forced to suppress their individuality and to exist in an environment ruled by situational ethics, the Chinese developed split personalities—one marked by feelings of profound inferiority, and the other by extreme arrogance.

In their inferior mode the Chinese bowed, scraped and smiled to everyone who had influence. In their arrogant mode, they became tyrants who could be as unfeeling as the worst savage.

This cultural conditioning remains very much in evidence in China today, especially in the attitudes and behavior of many government officials who appear to be in a permanent arrogant mode, narrow-minded and selfish. Much of the behavior of lower ranking government employees, particularly their treatment of the public, is so callous that it verges on the sadistic.

In recent decades substantial progress has been made in injecting varying degrees of Western style ethics into the political, social and economic systems of China. But it will no doubt be several generations before the circumstantial ethics of the past can be purged from the culture.

Further, growing individual freedom at the expense of the old family system and Confucian morality has a negative as well as a positive side for the Chinese. Virtually all of the things that were once taboo in China, and were punished by the severest sanctions, are now common—selfishness, greed, rude manners, dishonesty, distrust and disobedience.

In the meantime, Westerners dealing with Chinese will have to continue accommodating themselves to Chinese programming in situational ethics—and how far this accommodation has to go, or should go, varies with the circumstances.

Foreign businesspeople, politicians and diplomats who are not familiar with this facet of Chinese culture are at a serious disadvantage, and just knowing about it is not enough to overcome the disadvantage. It takes considerable experience and the development of special cross-cultural skills to achieve an acceptable balance between Chinese ethics and Western ethics.

The aspect of China's situational ethics that is generally the most difficult for Westerners to deal with is its fundamentally one-sided nature. Fairness, in the Western sense, is not an inherent factor in Chinese culture. It is not a normal part of Chinese thinking.

The goal of Chinese businesspeople, politicians and diplomats is to win. It is not to be fair or generous or philanthropic. It is to gain and keep the upper hand. The Chinese are past masters at putting on faces to fit whatever situation is at hand, to disarm their counterparts or competitors, to disguise their intentions, to weaken their adversaries, to give themselves every possible advantage.

This is not to say that there are no fair-minded, objective, generous Chinese. But they are rare—and in the eyes of other Chinese are no longer *Chinese*.

The best that foreigners can do in attempting to deal with the Chinese on an equitable basis is to have their own programs and priorities in order and in writing, clearly and comprehensively, and be prepared to spend whatever time, energy and money it takes to reach an agreement.

How successful you might be and how long it takes to achieve that success depends on whether or not the Chinese will compromise on enough of their desires and demands. In the Chinese context, food, money and the interests of China come before Western style ethics.

Another word of warning: The Chinese will do their best—and their best is very good—to persuade you, one way or the other, to give concessions. If you give a concession just as a gesture of goodwill, without getting anything in return, you have willingly stepped into the quicksand of Chinese culture.

Veteran old China hands who are bilingual and work with Chinese managers and employees in companies that are run Chinese style say that putting up with traditional *lunlixue* is time-consuming and adds directly to the expense of doing business. They add that it will change only if and when Western style management practices are adopted by Chinese companies.

158

逻辑

Luoji

(Luu-oh-jee)

"Behind the Chinese Face"

Marco Polo and other early visitors to China do not seem to have complained very much about the way the Chinese think and behave. They were apparently so impressed by the power and accomplishments of the people of the Middle Kingdom that they did not question their methods.

The complaints were to come later, first from Westerners who had gone through the Industrial Revolution and looked upon the feudal institutions and rituals of China as primitive anachronisms, and now from business-people and diplomats who are trying to understand and work with the Chinese as equals.

Much of the reactionary behavior of the Chinese often strikes Westerners as infantile, irrational and self-defeating, or as not making sense for some other reason. These charges most frequently occur in business and political situations where the foreign side wants to introduce a new element into Chinese behavior.

Westerners are constantly being frustrated by the failure or refusal of Chinese to instantly see and respond positively to such "logical" suggestions or requests, particularly when the benefit to the Chinese side appears totally obvious.

On many such occasions the immediate reaction of Westerners is to presume that the Chinese are non-receptive because they are dumb or because of racial, political or other reasons that should have nothing at all to do with the situation at hand.

Some or all of the above may be true, but generally such resistance results from a different kind of *luoji* (luu-oh-jee) or *logic*. Outside of scientific inquiry, Chinese and Westerners often think on different cultural channels.

It is natural for the Chinese to accept and tolerate diversity and contradictions in human affairs as well as in nature. The Chinese goal or ideal is to accept all things and then to reconcile them into a unified whole—something that generally drives Westerners batty.

It is also natural for Chinese to consider things that appear to others as being inconsequential or totally unrelated to the question or proposition at hand. This also sets Westerners on edge.

In many instances, the term *fuzzy logic*, invented by an American computer programmer in reference to the unpredictable and often unknown factors that impact on behavior and natural phenomena, could very well be applied to Chinese thinking.

In addition to leaving room for unknown and unpredictable natural phenomena in their social, business and political relationships, most Chinese also consider the role of the supernatural in human affairs, and do not become overly concerned about pinning everything down in precise terms.

Again this is not to imply that Chinese cannot or do not think in perfectly clear, Western style logical terms. But most interpersonal relationships in China are based on fuzzy logic.

It is therefore important for outsiders to keep in mind that in any situation calling for reflection and action, the Chinese do not automatically react in a purely logical manner or in accordance with any existing law—as Westerners tend to expect.

The Chinese reaction is more likely to be based on what they feel is least likely to disturb their personal world, or on what will benefit them—and China—the most without causing problems.

Foreigners who attempt to deal with Chinese businesspeople or government bureaucrats on a strictly logical basis will find themselves detoured or blocked at virtually every turn.

In Chinese terms, human feelings take precedence over logic, and anyone who insists on always behaving in a logical manner is viewed as cold, hard-hearted and troublesome.

159

麻将

Majong
(Mah-jong)

"Noises in the Night"

One of the best ways to experience the sights and sounds of China and get a sense of the essence of Chinese life is to stroll the back alleys and lanes of its villages and cities, for much of the life of China is out in the open, visible for all to see.

There is also a fascinating difference between day and night life in China, and to even begin to understand the character and personality of the Chinese it is essential that one experience the night-time scene of bars, cafes, sidewalk food stalls, restaurants, tea and entertainment houses. (With an early rising time, however, most Chinese are in bed well before midnight, except on holidays.)

One of the most nostalgic and meaningful of the night-time activities in China is the game of *majong* (mah-jong), the basic meaning of which is "Sparrow of 100 Intelligences." One can often hear the clicking of the *majong* tiles from behind closed doors.

Majong, which originated in China early in the Sung Dynasty (A.D. 960–1279), is similar to the Western card game of gin rummy, in that the goal of the game is to collect combinations of sequences and sets of identical tiles. But it is far more complicated than rummy because there are many more possible combinations, and it requires a lot more concentration and experience to play well.

A *majong* set is made up of one hundred and thirty-six tiles, and there are usually four players. Play begins with shuffling the tiles (accounting for the distinctive clicking sound emanating from majong parlors), and arranging them in four lines, or "walls," seventeen tiles long and two tiles high.

In a *majong* set there are three "suits" of thirty-six tiles each, made up of bamboos, circles and Chinese ideograms; and seven categories of four tiles each, made up of red dragons, white dragons, green dragons, east wind, south wind, north wind and west wind.

Players throw dice to determine the number of tiles they get on the first draw. The player with the highest dice score gets fourteen tiles and discards one, while the other players draw thirteen tiles. The game then proceeds much like rummy, but with more elaborate rules. Four rounds complete a game.

Originally *majong* tiles were made from pieces of paper. Later they were made from bamboo and then the shin bones of cattle and sometimes ivory. Most tiles today are made of heavy plastic.

Majong has traditionally been a gambling game, but in recent years it has also been gaining in popularity as a parlor game played by both men and women for entertainment.

Majong games are often major social events, some of them lasting for several days. Westerners who know how to play the game often find it provides them with a door into the inner circle of their Chinese friends and business contacts. Interestingly, *majong* was once so popular in the United States that one and one-half million sets were sold there in just one year alone—in 1923.

This extraordinary phenomenon came about because American businessman Joseph C. Babcock, who lived in Shanghai, introduced the game into the U.S. in 1920.

It quickly became such a fad that people all over the country bought Chinese robes to wear while they played the game, and some went to the extent of turning rooms in their homes into "*Majong* Rooms," redecorating them in Chinese motifs.

Some of the sets sold in the U.S. at that time cost as much as five hundred dollars (almost as much as a Model T Ford). But the craze was over by 1925.

During the heyday of the *majong* fad in the U.S., Babcock exported so many *majong* sets from China that the Chinese makers ran out of the cattle shin bones used to make them.

Babcock quickly arranged for several million shin bones to be exported to China from cattle slaughter houses in the U.S.

In China today when someone wants to get a *majong* game going they frequently use the colloquial phrase, "Let's build a Great Wall."

骂街

Ma Zhan / Ma Jie
(Mah Chahn / Mah Jee-eh)

"Fighting with Your Mouth"

When I first began visiting Hong Kong and Guangdong Province in Southeastern China in the 1950s I was repeatedly surprised and unnerved by what I perceived to be angry shouting matches between Cantonese speakers, including family members who were working together.

It wasn't long, however, before someone explained that it is necessary to speak louder than usual in order to communicate effectively in Cantonese because that language has nine different tonal levels that must be enunciated clearly to get the desired meaning across.

I also learned that all other Chinese languages are tonal as well (but with fewer tones), and require exceptionally precise, clear pronunciation or they become unintelligible. Rather than being taken as exotic or sexy, speaking Chinese with an accent can get you nowhere or in trouble.

The tonal nature of China's languages, combined with the gregariousness of the Chinese, makes China a very noisy place. In restaurants and other public places the din is generally enough to drown out any conversation that is not virtually shouted.

There is one other common category of shouting in China that has nothing to do with the nature of the languages, however. It has to do with the propensity of the Chinese to engage in *ma zhan* (mah chahn) or *mouth fights*.

In pre-modern China harmony took precedence over virtually everything else. There were very strong cultural taboos as well as administrative laws against physical violence. Both parties in a physical fight were automatically guilty of disturbing the peace, and liable for severe punishments.

But the density of the population in China's urban areas, and the extreme pressure on the Chinese to follow a very detailed form of etiquette when interacting within one's *own* group resulted in a high level of repressed frustration that could be set off by a minor annoyance when it involved a stranger.

It therefore became common for people to vent their anger in prolonged and loud *ma zhan*—*verbal battles*—instead of coming to blows. Much of this verbal battling was for show—playing to the crowd—and ended when the parties felt they had gained or preserved "face."

More serious confrontations between clans, warlords and other large groups that ended up in violent battles involving all sorts of deadly weapons were almost always preceded by long, loud verbal exchanges when the two groups came face to face. A number of individuals on each of the opposing sides took turns shouting accusations and insults in a formalized manner.

Both *ma zhan* and actual physical confrontations are becoming more common in China as the restraints imposed by the traditional culture continue to weaken, and competition for space and economic advancement heat up.

On the international front, this factor will most likely have a profound influence on the future behavior of Chinese businesspeople and diplomats, as they become less restrained in their actions and reactions.

Visitors in China today are more apt to witness a modernized version of *ma zhan* known as *ma jie* (mah jee-eh). *Jie* means *across the street*, so *ma jie* refers to people facing each other across a street and engaging in verbal battles—something that happens regularly in China's crowded cities.

Adjusting to the din of restaurants, tea shops and other public places, including streets, is one of the accommodations that foreigners visiting or living in China must make in order to feel comfortable and enjoy themselves.

美

Mei

(May-ee)

"Beauty in a Chinese Eye"

My earliest mind's eye image of China was created by paintings of mountain spires standing like magical sentinels, deep gorges and waterfalls, the banks of narrow, tree-lined streams being enjoyed by robed travelers, and broad rivers decorated with lonely boatmen fixed in time.

There was always something about this image of China that was mysterious, deep and subtle, that went beyond my experience with Western art; something that suggested a two and maybe three dimensional view that was new to me, and therefore provocative.

Other images have since been added to this view of China; images that reflect the more mundane world of squalor, callousness and pain; but always in the background is a reflection of *mei* (may-ee), or *beauty*, that is so compelling it has a hypnotic effect.

Closer examination of the *mei* of traditional arts and crafts of China reveals an intimate relationship with nature. Those done by masters reflect the innermost essence of the things they represent, an essence that is rooted in their cosmic natures.

Further study shows that the *mei* of China is based on the order and beauty of the universe; on the attempt of the artist or craftsman to attune the human mind and will to the harmony of the heavens, and produce tranquility.

To the Chinese, beauty is not in the eye of the beholder, as it so often is in the West. In Chinese aesthetics, an object must accurately reflect nature in its pure cosmic state to be truly beautiful, and it is up to the viewer to develop the aesthetic ability to see, understand and appreciate the portrayal of this relationship.

It is the harmonious chord of nature struck by Chinese art that gives it its power to still the mind and soothe the spirit—a chord that is the music of the universe.

China's traditional arts and crafts, known and revered world-wide for many centuries, are among the most conspicuous of the many features that distinguish Chinese culture.

Chinese ceramics, drawings, paintings, lacquerwares and carvings, in fact, all of the arts and crafts of China are imbued with a distinctive essence that sets them apart from the indigenous cultural artifacts of other countries.

While nature is the model for the shape and style of Chinese artifacts, there is something else; a force emanating from the materials and the finish, that adds a spiritual quality and a distinctive style that is uniquely Chinese.

In addition to these qualities, there is also a special ambience radiated by Chinese arts that is very sensual—a sensuality that adds significantly to their appeal, working its magic even on people who have had no aesthetic training.

By combining the artistry of nature, the spirituality of their materials and a subtle but powerful sexual quality, the Chinese are able to produce a kind of beauty that is classic and eternal.

The power of Chinese *mei* is that it does not attempt to aggrandize itself but lies quietly on and below the surface, luring and inviting the viewer to merge with it. Chinese beauty evokes excitement, but always in conjunction with tranquility and harmony.

One piece of Chinese art in a room is often enough to create a tranquil but subtly sensuous mood. Several well chosen pieces create a haven that resonates with harmonious tranquility and sensuality.

Chinese paintings, calligraphy and other drawings are stylized to concentrate beauty in one small area. A single symbol is often used to suggest the whole cosmos. And delving into the cultural content of these symbols is one of the doorways to understanding China.

Businesspeople who are in economic competition with China should bear in mind that once the Chinese reach the point that they are creating their own industrial designs, their long aesthetic traditions will give them a formidable advantage.

Contact with China also affords visitors an opportunity to increase the depth and breadth of their aesthetic prowess and incorporate some of this new experience into their own creative efforts.

Visitors should be aware, however, that many of the products produced for the tourist trade are cheaply made imitations, or are products embellished with artistic motifs that are not compatible with the item or its use.

Learning enough about Chinese art and handicrafts to discern the difference between fake and genuine is part of the pleasure of the Chinese experience.

For the last two centuries China's traditional aesthetics have suffered one blow after the other, from within and from without. In more recent decades these onslaughts have been administered by self-styled political extremists who deliberately set out to destroy the old culture and create a new one.

Of course, this is not the first time that attempts have been made to re-make China in some other image. The Mongols, Manchus, European free-booters and missionaries, all failed. But this time things are different. The Chinese are changing themselves, freely and aggressively.

What this means to the ancient traditions of *mei* remains to be seen.

Few foreigners can come into close contact with the serenity of Chinese art without being deeply moved, and this pleasuring of the senses is one of the enduring attractions of Chinese culture.

美国

Mei Guo

(May-ee Gwoh)

"The Beautiful Country"

There is some evidence which indicates that Chinese traders and perhaps other Chinese travelers as well visited the North and South American continents centuries before Columbus.

Some of this evidence consists of references in records kept by the Chinese. Other evidence is comprised of Chinese-type artifacts discovered on the west coasts of North and South America.

In any event, long before the great voyages of the European explorers that led them to America and to Asia, the Chinese had already experienced several eras of exploration and foreign trade with countries as far away as Africa.

One of these later expeditions that took place in A.D. 1405 consisted of sixty-two ships, one of which was 444 feet long and 180 feet wide. The combined crews, clerks and buyers numbered 27,870.

Government officials and others in China were aware of the thirteen American colonies some time before Americans declared their independence. Chinese scholars and others who opposed the Manchu-dominated Qing Dynasty, were tremendously impressed with the American Revolution, and looked upon George Washington as a great hero.

Over the next several decades, the Chinese image of America became larger than life and took on the aura of a promised land in which there were mountains of gold and everyone was rich.

The lushness of the great expanse of the American continent, with its huge forests, grass-covered plains, thousands of rivers and super-abundance of wild life, led the Chinese to name the United States *Mei Guo* (may-ee gwoh) or *Beautiful Country*. As with most Chinese names for foreign countries, *Mei Guo* is partly phonetical for *America* and partly attributable to appropriate characters.

Despite the horrible experiences of many of the first Chinese immigrants to the U.S. in the mid-1800s, despite the "Yellow Peril" banning of additional immigration from China in the early 1900s, U.S. efforts to prevent the Chinese Communist Party from taking over China, and all the political rhetoric that has since marred U.S.-China relations, most Chinese have continued to think of America as the *Mei Guo*, and to be fascinated by Americans and the United States.

Today, *Kan Dan Shan* or *Talking about the Big Mountain* is a favorite pastime in China, and especially in Hong Kong where the people have been massively exposed to American news media, movies and television since the 1950s.

America is still both a role model for Chinese seeking freedom, and a mecca for those wanting to leave China to study, to prosper in business, or simply to escape the stifling social and political chains that prevent them from realizing their dreams.

Americans should keep in mind that the attraction that the U.S. has for the Chinese (and others) is not the American lifestyle, but the personal freedom we enjoy and the opportunities offered by a free society. Many of the Chinese who come to America continue to live in the Chinese way and in enclaves of other emigrant families.

163

没门儿

Mei Men Er

(May-ee Mun Err)

"No Way, Buddy!"

From the beginning of China's history down to recent times the successive Imperial Courts followed the practice of *Yu Min Zhengce*, or *Policy of Keeping the People Ignorant*.

It was automatically assumed by the succeeding dynasties of old China that ordinary people should not receive formal education and that governmental affairs were just that—affairs of the government and not of the people.

Yu Min Zhengce went beyond just ignoring the idea of educating the people or keeping them informed, even on a need-to-know basis. It was an aggressive policy under which universal education was opposed and the governments took special measures to prevent the people from learning even routine information about governmental affairs.

The rationale for the philosophy of keeping the great mass of people illiterate, and complete separation between the citizenry and the government, was simple. China's political administrators believed that the less people knew, the easier it would be to control and use them.

When the last Imperial dynasty fell in late 1912 and a new constitutional form of government was established early the next year, the policy of keeping the people ignorant was dropped but very little changed because most of the population could not read the newspapers and magazines that were available, and there was no other means of getting detailed information to so many people.

When the Chinese Communist Party came to power in 1949 it co-opted the ancient practice of keeping the people in the dark, and enacted even stronger sanctions to prevent "state secrets" from becoming known to the public. It also exercised total control over all news media and publishing to make sure that the media and books served the goals of the Party. Access to universities and to the best schools is still strictly controlled by the Party.

This environment, from both dynastic and Communist times, conditioned the people to try to protect themselves by saying as little as possible when questioned, never volunteering any information, and generally reacting in either a neutral or negative way in virtually all situations.

One of the most commonly used self-protecting ploys was to respond with *mei men er* (may-ee mun err) to requests. *Mei men er* literally means there is *no gate*, or *no entry*, and is used to mean there is no way that whatever you have requested is going to be or can be done.

Bureaucrats are especially notorious for their habitual use of *mei men er* regardless of the circumstances or validity of whatever request is made. The worst offenders use the term simply to avoid having to do anything, without any thought of their official responsibilities to the public or the merit of whatever is requested or proposed.

This is another of the many situations in China where logic, objectivity and common sense often do not apply. Usually the only way around "no gate" barriers is through personal connections.

164

没意思

Mei Yi Si

(May-ee Eee Suh)

"I'm Not Interested"

Old China hands are constantly preaching that two of the most important talents the outsider must have in order to cope with the customs and idiosyncrasies of China are patience and persistence.

Of course, this is a given, but it addresses only part of the problem and does not always provide the solution. There is a seemingly unending stream of situations in which something more than patience and persistence is needed to accomplish even routine goals in China.

On these occasions the challenge is to divine the true nature of the hang-up or obstacle, and then determine a course of action designed to bypass or overcome the barrier.

Some of this divination is a cultural skill that one develops over a period of time, making it possible for you to pick up on enough subtle cultural cues to know intuitively at least part of what is going on behind the stonewalling or the turn-down or whatever.

Another part of the "knowing what is going on process" is simply hard knocks experience. After dozens of encounters with bureaucrats and service personnel you learn to anticipate a variety of common reactions, and go in armed with a strategy and tactics to circumvent them.

One of the most common signals that you may be facing a fuzzy logic situation is when your question, request or presentation, is met with the ambiguous *mei yi si* (may-ee eee suh), which in its simplest form means *what you are talking about is of no interest to me*.

The same comment may be an invitation for you to "make" the situation of interest to the individual concerned by offering them some special consideration.

Another possible interpretation of *mei yi si* is *I'm not going to get involved because doing whatever would be required of me would complicate my life*.

Still another possible meaning of *mei yi si* is *what you are asking is impossible because we don't do things that way here and you are wasting my time and your time*.

The same expression may also be used when the person who is in charge of whatever it is you are talking about is not in—and chances are you will not get a definite answer about when he or she will be in.

Generally speaking, it is unwise for foreigners to use this phrase in Chinese unless they are absolutely sure that it expresses the connotation they want, and will achieve their purpose without causing them future problems. It could be construed as an insult, particularly with regard to a summary view of that person's life or career. It is stronger than saying, "He is dull" in English.

Part of the problem of dealing with this kind of language subtlety is that the Chinese do not expect such behavior from foreigners and might take it the wrong way regardless of how culturally correct the usage. The Chinese do not like people who are more clever than they are, and flaunt it

165

没有

Mei You

(May-ee Yoe-ou)

"We Just Sold the Last One"

To hear expatriate residents and regular visitors to China tell it, the original Great Wall, which was designed to keep barbarians out of the celestial empire, has been replaced by a "Great Saying" that is designed to frustrate the aims and goals of virtually everyone in China, foreign as well as Chinese.

This "Great Saying" is *mei you (may-ee yoe-ou)*, which literally means *not have*, but in usage covers a wide range of topics and meanings that are a reflection of present-day Chinese attitudes and behavior.

In its simplest form *mei you* does mean *there isn't any* or *there are none*. But things are seldom that simple in China. It may also mean: *there are some in the backroom but we don't have any up here; there may be some in the backroom but I'm not interested in finding out; we just sold the last one in stock but will have some more later; the maker has discontinued that product; it's lunch time now so I can't help you; we're getting ready to close up so I can't help you;* and so on.

Other examples of the misuse of *mei you* that occur regularly, particularly where foreigners are concerned, include ticket vendors saying no more tickets/seats are available, hotel clerks saying there are no vacant rooms, waiters saying a requested dish is not available, etc., when the statement is not true and there is some other reason for the denial that may or may not be valid. Taxi drivers who do not want to accept a fare will throw out a *mei you*, particularly when the would-be passengers are foreigners and especially if there are several of them with lots of packages.

It is often advisable for tourists and businesspeople who are going to need transportation several times during a day to reserve the same taxi for the entire day.

It sometimes appears that foreigners are especially singled out by Chinese tradespeople and bureaucrats for the *mei you* treatment, and often that is exactly the case.

Some Chinese, particularly in large cities where shops and other travel related facilities are regularly inundated by tourists, resent foreigners, and go out of their way to be rude and unhelpful.

Some of this resentment is nationalistic, but more likely it is because the individuals concerned have become fed up with having to deal with overbearing, patronizing and fawning tourists who buy worthless goods and otherwise throw money away as if it were scrap paper.

Generally, however, the visitor from abroad should not take such incidents personally. The *mei you* syndrome is endemic in China because it is a deeply entrenched part of the Chinese way of coping with an existence that is usually boring, generally does not reward special effort, and is often dangerous to anyone who stands out.

Often a Chinese person will begin a request for a particular dish in a restaurant or item in a store by using the expression *mei you*, much as one might say in English, "I don't suppose you have any..."

没有办法

Mei You Ban Fa

(May-ee Yoe-ou Bahn Fah)

"You May As Well Forget It"

Foreign businesspeople beginning negotiations with their Chinese counterparts, in government or in private industry, soon learn that Chinese negotiators play hardball, particularly when the foreign side initiated the contact.

Despite all of the initial hospitality and formal protocol that are such a conspicuous part of Chinese behavior, the white gloves come off in negotiating sessions—in part because the Chinese believe that is what the foreign side expects.

Another reason for this approach to doing business with foreigners is that China has been taken advantage of by foreign governments and foreign companies so many times in the past two centuries that the Chinese tend to have a national phobia about the dangers of doing business with outsiders.

Some of the tactics Chinese negotiators use are out-in-the-open and blunt. They have no qualms about demanding concessions that are obviously unequal and give them a significant advantage. Other ploys are couched in cultural terms that may be transparent to experienced negotiators but are likely to be misleading and frustrating to novices.

One of the more common cultural tactics the Chinese use when responding to approaches initiated by outsiders is to announce *Mei you ban fa* (may-ee yoe-ou bahn fah), which translates into ordinary English as *no way*—ostensibly meaning there is no way that the deal can go through; that it's over.

But *mei you ban fa* has a variety of other interpretations as well, and the challenge is to figure out which one and deal with it.

One of the more common uses of *mei you ban fa* is when the negotiator explains that he or she is exhausted and maybe frustrated as well—because the talks are not progressing rapidly enough to suit him or her—and he or she wants to stop. All indications may be that the negotiator is breaking off the talks altogether, but he or she may also be using the move as a threat to bring pressure against the other side.

Mei you ban fa is also used in a similar manner but without the excuse of being exhausted or frustrated. On these occasions it may be pure bluff—the Chinese side wants to force the foreign side into making some concession or concessions.

Another variation of this ploy is for the Chinese side to explain that government regulations make it impossible for them to accept the conditions being offered by the foreign side.

In more casual situations bureaucrats and others may resort to *mei you ban fa* when the subject concerned is not within their responsibility and they don't want to bother with it.

Obviously there is no single answer to countering a *mei you ban fa* situation. The best general advice is to remain calm and focused, and, in both business and political negotiations, to reemphasize the mutual benefits to be gained.

167

没有关系

Mei You Guanxi

(May-ee Yoe-ou Gwahn-she)

"That Doesn't Compute!"

Someone once said that the Chinese language was not constructed to communicate but to make it possible for the speaker to "politely escape" from any obligation or responsibility for knowing anything or doing anything.

This may be a bit extreme, but it certainly captures one of the feelings that comes with trying to reach an understanding with the Chinese, and get things done.

There are literally hundreds of words and expressions in Chinese, in daily use, that are not complete or precise, and can be interpreted in a number of different ways that on the surface appear totally unrelated.

For ages the Chinese have made a virtual cult of using poetic and allusionary terms in their writings and daily conversations, with the result that their languages abound in such terms and their ordinary speech can sound something like a code to outsiders.

Mie you guanxi (may-ee yoe-ou gwahn she) is a phrase that can be especially perplexing to the uninitiated foreigner. Its literal meaning is *there is no connection/no relationship*, but it is used in a number of ways that require considerable stretching of the imagination.

It is commonly used to dismiss a situation, in which case it has the meaning of *don't worry about it,* or *forget it.* It is often used, with a casual shrug of the shoulders, to mean *no problem,* or *it doesn't matter.* It may also mean *you don't know what you are talking about, but that's all right because you cannot be expected to know.*

In a further extension, *mei you guanxi* may mean something like *There is no way you can do what you want to do or are trying to do because you don't know the right people—so you may as well forget about it.*

This is another common Chinese saying that is especially frustrating to foreigners because typically no one makes any effort to explain a *mei you guanxi* response. Western philosophy is based on "why" and "why not."

For many foreigners in China, hearing *mei you guanxi* without an explanation is like a red flag being waved in front of their faces.

About the only immediate recourse to a *mei you guanxi* is to instantly put the situation on a totally personal basis, explaining what a serious problem it is for you, that it is causing you great suffering or loss (or both), and that the wonderfully kind and thoughtful person you are talking to is the only one who can help you.

This approach must be done without anger, and with all of the sincerity, modesty and humility one can muster. And, not surprisingly, it most often works where young women are concerned. Younger men are the next most likely to come forward with an explanation or some kind of help.

Any sign of arrogance or superiority is the kiss of death. Many Chinese delight in cutting foreigners down to size.

Meng
(Mung)

"Paying Your Dues"

China's age-oriented culture often clashes with the egalitarian and merit-oriented way of the West. Traditionally in China men were not considered mature until they reached their mid-thirties or so, and positions of authority were generally attainable only by people in their senior years.

Merit-related business management is becoming more common in China today, but in business, the professions and government service, a significant percentage of pay and promotion are still primarily based on seniority, and resistance to meritocracy remains substantial.

China's traditional seniority system grew out of both common sense and the hierarchical structure of society in which the superior position of parents, particularly fathers, was fixed by law.

Age naturally brought experience and wisdom, and since virtually all practical and technical knowledge was passed from one generation to the next through personal instruction and apprenticeship, older people had a natural lock on positions of power, prestige and economic advantage.

In China today, in situations where technological knowledge and skills takes precedence over seniority and the human relations experience that comes with age, many young people in China are vaulting over their elders in earning power, but tradition remains strongly in favor of age.

One of the aspects of traditional age and experience-related wisdom that remains valid, and is especially vital in present-day China, is contained in the word *meng* (mung), which means "inexperience" but is not specifically related to age.

Meng refers to new situations that develop that are outside of the range or depth of one's knowledge and experience regardless of age, and cannot be resolved no matter how skillful or successful one might be in other areas or how hard or diligently one tries.

When such occasions occur, say China's sages, the first challenge is to recognize that you do not have the ability to resolve the problem; and the second challenge is to have the modesty to admit it and seek help from someone who has the necessary knowledge and experience.

Fully aware that many people have a contrary nature, the sages warn that you should be humble in seeking advice and guidelines from those who are in a position to teach you something; that you should not argue with or question your advisors or try to force them to prove themselves.

This kind of behavior, the sages say, indicates a weakness in your own character, and will very likely alienate those whose knowledge and insights you sorely need. As usual, the sages counsel that you use *meng* situations to improve your own character and enhance the quality of the relationships you have with other people.

The sages add that if you are the advisor and are confronted by antagonistic seekers of advice, don't waste your time with them.

Chinese businesspeople and others typically take a *meng* mode in order to encourage foreign engineers, scientists and other technical experts to reveal as much information as possible.

169

門卫

Men Wei

(Mun Way-ee)

"Keepers of the Keys"

Chinese history has been a long drama marked by periodic wars between states, by frequent battles among warlords, by violent clan feuds, by the ongoing presence of burglars in urban centers, and by bandits in rural districts.

This threat from disorder and violence has made the Chinese extraordinarily sensitive about security. Centuries ago it became common for upperclass propertied people to surround their homes with high walls and to install sturdy doors and barred windows in their houses.

Many Chinese homes today, especially in Hong Kong and other cities where people are relatively affluent, have outer doors made of thick steel.

In olden days the gates to affluent homes and official buildings were manned by armed guards. Today many private as well as public buildings have *men wei* (mun way-ee) or *door guards* who keep track of who comes and goes, and in the case of factories and other locations, exercise considerable control over who gets in. These positions of power, which are an essential part of the internal communications in China, are often held by pensioners who are out to make a bit of money on the side.

During the early paranoic period of the Communist regime, the "ogres" served not only as doorkeepers but as spies as well, reporting on everyone who entered and left the buildings. It was especially dangerous for female Chinese to visit the rooms, apartments or offices of foreign men because it was generally presumed that they were there for sexual purposes—something that Chinese law expressly prohibited.

Many buildings, particularly school and factory dormitories and private apartments, had curfews requiring that their doors be locked at 10 P.M. or some other early evening hour. Residents who did not have an understanding with the doorkeepers of these buildings could be stranded on the outside, and visitors who stayed over-time in the buildings could be locked inside.

Still today China's doorkeepers are a force to be reckoned with. They can be strict and unfriendly, depending on their personalities and attitudes—about politics, foreigners, etc. Numerous buildings still have curfews. Residents or visitors who are unlucky enough to have to deal with such individuals have no choice but to use diplomacy, flattery, other forms of guile, and sometimes a steady stream of gifts to get on the right side of the door at whatever time is desired.

China's modern-day doorkeepers have a traditional precedent in the famous *Men Sheng* or *Door Gods*—the images of fearsome looking military figures printed on paper and pasted alongside of temples, palaces, public buildings and homes to keep evil spirits out.

170

明夷

Ming Yi
(Meeng Eee)

"Keeping a Tight Rein"

Westerners have traditionally thought of the Chinese as being inscrutable because they could not "read" their faces or other non-verbal communication cues, and because the Chinese were not forthright or candid in expressing their opinions.

This image was not just a figment of the Westerners' own imaginations. The fact is that the Chinese have traditionally gone to great lengths to maintain neutral or passive facial expressions, and to reveal as little as possible about their inner thoughts and positions verbally or otherwise.

Both of these characteristic Chinese traits were a practical defensive response to the various dangers that were inherent in their society over the millennia. Always subject to punishment from superiors who became angry or were irritated in any way, the Chinese conditioned themselves to be as neutral and as non-threatening as possible.

This concept of personal control of one's thoughts, actions and appearance is contained in the key word *ming yi* (meeng eee) or *censorship*, in the sense of self-censorship—something the Chinese were programmed to do from childhood.

In the annals of the sages, *ming yi* is presented as one of the most important "skills" a person must have to survive and succeed in an ever changing and always dangerous society.

The message of *ming yi* is clear and simple: in times of uncertainty, friction, competition, opposition or conflict, conceal your thoughts, hide your feelings, downplay your intelligence, stay friendly, smile—but never give up your convictions or your goals and persevere in subtle ways until you get what you want.

One of the most common and successful ploys of *ming yi* is to pretend that you are in agreement with your adversaries, and that you go along with whatever plans they have. But all the while you remain passive, waiting for them to fail and for circumstances that will give you the advantage.

Ming yi also teaches that evil is nothing new or strange; that it is as much a part of the cosmos as good, and that the superior people accommodate themselves to evil when necessary but do so without losing their own virtue.

The Chinese believe that victory and success comes to the person who stays quietly in the background, does not explain or reveal his or her motives or tactics, is never overtly forceful, never brags, and never openly competes with anyone—a description that fits the character and personalities of many Chinese tycoons.

Business and political success, continues the *ming yi* philosophy, are unlikely to come or to last very long for people who struggle openly to manipulate factors to their advantage. The best and most lasting success is that achieved behind the scenes, without the public being aware of it; thereby assuring you of the safety of anonymity.

Westerners dealing with China often find it to their advantage to adopt some of the ploys of the *ming yi* approach, especially in political matters.

171

名字

Ming Zi / Ming Pian
(Meeng Tzu / Meeng Pee-enn)

"You're Nobody Without Them"

Chinese history indicates that Lui Chin, an Imperial Court eunuch-regent, some time around A.D. 1500 became the first person to use *ming zi* (meeng tzu), or *name cards*, in the way they are used today.

Prior to that time, China had a well-developed postal system through which officials and others exchanged letters and various documents. All kinds of announcements, some of them printed on small rectangles or squares of paper, were also common.

But Lui took this form one step further and created his own personal name card. In keeping with his station and artistic tastes, he did not settle for a simple white card inscribed with his name, title and address. His was a large vermillion card enclosed in an equally colorful envelope. For a long time after this, white cards were used only in expressions of mourning.

In the intervening centuries *ming zi* have become an essential tool of business as well as personal relationships in China, not only because of the immediate practical value that others are familiar with, but also because of the special problem of getting names right in China.

It is said that during much of China's history there were fewer than five hundred family names in the country, of which thirty were clan names. A recent Statistical Bureau report says there are now approximately 5,662 surnames in China—with some 300 million families.

Other sources indicate that 90 percent of all Chinese share only 100 family names, and approximately 60 percent of all Chinese share only 19 names.

An estimated 10 percent of all Chinese are named Zhang (Chang), which means archer or bowman. Wang and Li (Lee) are the two other most common names.

Virtually all Chinese have middle names as well as first names, but in mainland China the practice is to run the first and middle names together as if they were one word, when they are written in Roman letters. In Taiwan, however, many people choose to separate (or connect!) the first and middle name with a hyphen. In the remote Mongolian regions four-character names are common, while two-character names were popular during the Cultural Revolution as a sign of "austerity."

Because of the confusion that is inherent in a situation where you have over 100 million people with the same last name and tens of millions of others with the same family name, name cards that include a person's first and middle name, company, title, division or department, telephone number, fax number and address, play a vital role in China.

The most common method used by the Chinese to cope with this very serious name problem when making verbal references to individuals is to combine their place of work, department and title with their name.

In business situations, titles are commonly used in place of or in conjunction with names as a means of pinning down the individual concerned. Using titles is also a traditional way of paying respect in Chinese society.

If the individual is not employed, the name plus the home address may be used.

Visitors should make sure they have name cards of their own, and that if their names are rendered in Chinese (something foreign businesspeople do fairly often to make it easier for their names to be pronounced and remembered), they must choose which of the languages to use if they also have them transcribed into Roman letters. Generally it is best to use Mandarin.

It is also useful to be aware of the fact that the Taiwanese often use different ideograms than mainland Chinese when writing the same names.

When proffering your name card, it is the height of etiquette to use both hands, and to present it "right side up" so the individual receiving it can read it without having to turn it around or over.

172

民主

Minzhu

(Meen-juu)

"The Long Wait"

Contemplating Chinese history since the late 1800s, I am reminded of the United States in the 1960s when young white Americans began to believe and act on the idea that they could not trust anyone over the age of 30 to change things for the better.

Just as they charged, it seems that by the age of 30, adults generally have so much invested in the status quo and have become so conservative and fearful that they resist change out of hand. Or they have become so disillusioned that they accept the idea that things cannot be changed and content themselves with getting as much out of the system as they can.

White American youth were slow in picking up on this wisdom and doing something about it because they had always had freedom and both social and economic choices.

The protests and demonstrations they staged in the 1960s were acts of conscience, not desperation, and they inspired changes that helped to re make American society, bringing it much closer to its own democratic ideals and laws.

Oddly enough, the youth of China became politically conscious and active far earlier than their American counterparts, and they did not start with a foundation of democratic laws and traditions. They started from 5,000 years of despotism

Minzhu (meen-juu) or *democracy* has never been know in China and is still a dream.

In the 1880s, Chinese university students were in the forefront of those demanding that the Imperial system be abolished and democracy introduced into China. Hundreds of them went to Japan, the U.S. and Europe to study Western political science and prepare themselves for becoming revolutionaries.

The first large-scale political demonstrations by Chinese students occurred in 1919, resulting in dozens of them being massacred. Other demonstrations followed, almost always with the same result—the leaders killed or imprisoned.

War between Nationalist Chinese forces and Communists and then war with Japan greatly reduced student political activities during the 1930s and 1940s, although there were demonstrations of note in 1932, 1936, and 1948.

When the Chinese Communist Party took over the country in 1949 its policy of converting or exterminating everyone with any democratic ideals totally eliminated pro-democracy demonstrations for several years.

But the worst depredations of the Communists did not kill the dream of *minzhu*, and the first post–People's Republic of China student demonstration was staged in 1957.

Then in 1966 CCP Chairman Mao Zedung and his backers converted the frustration of China's whole mass of students to their own purposes by ordering them to literally destroy all of the old traditions and every vestige of democratic thought in the country—a horror that lasted for nearly 10 years.

It was to be 1986, almost exactly 10 years after this so-called Cultural Revolution, before the next major pro-democracy demonstration took place. Then in 1989 came the mother of all of China's student demonstrations for democracy—resulting in the infamous Tiananmen Square massacre.

The sacrifices made by Chinese students were not in vain. *Minzhu* is still a magic word in China, and little by little it is changing the evil essence of the CCP.

民主墙

Minzhu Qiang

(Meen-juu Chee-eeng)

"Democracy Wall"

There is, perhaps, nothing more poignant or encouraging in the history of China than the dreams and sacrifices linked to the phrase *Minzhu Qiang* (meen-juu chee-eeng) or *Democracy Wall*—a term that reverberated around the world in 1989 and left echoes that can still be heard today.

After the death of Mao Zedung in 1976 and the end of the holocaust known as the Cultural Revolution, criticism of the Chinese Communist Party (CCP) began to resurface, particularly in the form of *zi bao* or *wall posters*, or *da zi bao*, "large character posters."

Beijing University students, poets, writers and other intellectuals began pasting their protest essays and poems on a section of a wall just off of Beijing's famous Tiananmen Square, near the former Forbidden City and adjoining the residential area where many of China's political leaders live.

Before long, this section of the wall came to be known as the *Minzhuguo Qiang* or *Democracy Wall*, and became a focal point of the unrequited desires of the people of China for respite from the anti-human policies and programs of the CCP.

This was not China's first *Minzhu Qiang*, however. The first *Democracy Wall* appeared on the campus of Beijing University in 1957 during the heat of the "Hundred Flowers" campaign initiated by Mao Zedung.

This was the short-lived, disastrous campaign Mao created to shake up the CCP by inviting both CCP members and the public in general to criticize the Party and make recommendations for its improvement. See **Da Yue Jin, Gongchan Dang, Gongchanzhuyi**.

There were also *Democracy Walls* in Guangzhou (Canton) and numerous other cities around China, but none achieved the prominence of the one in Beijing for obvious reasons—for there, the protesters were posting their inflammatory messages on the very doorsteps of the "gods" of the CCP.

One of the most famous posters to grace Beijing's Democracy Wall was put up on December 5, 1978, by a young man named Wei Jingsheng. Entitled "The Fifth Modernization," it was a take-off on Premier Deng Xiaoping's Four Modernizations campaign for transforming China (agriculture, industry, national defense, and science-technology).

Wei's "Fifth Modernization" was "Democracy."

Prior to posting the *zi bao*, Wei had learned the hard way that the philosophy and practices of the CCP were both immoral and inhuman. He began as an ardent socialist and served as a Red Guard. Then he himself became a victim of the system and was imprisoned, beaten and abused for having "impure thoughts."

As a result of his experience, Wei saw clearly that to achieve true socialism, a free and democratic society was absolutely essential. The year after he posted his famous "Fifth Modernization" poster, Wei was arrested, charged with espionage, and sentenced to 15 years hard labor.

On April 1, 1979 the CCP issued an edict prohibiting the hanging of politically oriented wall posters anywhere in the country. Only totally benign posters that had been approved by the police could be posted on any wall.

A short while after Democracy Wall was shut down by the government, a young man appeared at the wall, quickly pasted up a poster and disappeared into the crowd.

The poster was entitled "For You," and was signed "Ling Bing," which means *Icicle*.

The poem, as quoted by David Goodman is his *Beijing Street Voices: The Poetry and Politics of China's Democracy Movement* (London, 1981), read:

My friend,
Parting time is pending.
Farewell—Democracy Wall.
What can I briefly say to you?
Should I speak of spring's frigidity?
Should I say that you are like the withered wintersweet?

No, I ought to talk of happiness,
Tomorrow's happiness,
Of pure orchid skies,
Of golden wild flowers,
Of a child's bright eyes.
In sum we ought
To part with dignity,
Don't you agree?

This was not to be the end of Democracy Wall, however. Ten years later it came close to bringing the Communist Party down.

See **Tiananmen Guangchang**.

那里那里

Nali, Nali

(Nah-lee, Nah-lee)

"Where? Where?"

Some two and a half millennia ago the great sage Confucius taught that ritualized etiquette, morality and prosperity were inseparable.

Wise man that he was, Confucius understood that for a society to sustain itself and prosper in an orderly and peaceful fashion it was essential that people be taught a fundamental philosophy of life based on respecting and obeying properly constituted authority, following precise rules of conduct, and treating other people the way you would like to be treated.

Confucius also understood that human beings are emotionally, spiritually and intellectually influenced by music, and taught that music should be a part of the education and life of every individual.

Of course, Confucius was referring to "good music"—music that soothes, nurtures and inspires, and thereby helps mankind transcend its animalistic side.

The teachings of Confucius eventually became the bedrock of Chinese culture, but during the course of China's long history after Confucius a number of different philosophies were taught by other masters, some of them creating contradictions in Chinese culture that still today confuse and sometimes frustrate foreigners visiting and working in China.

One of these contradictory philosophical tenets was that existence is a mirage; that nothing is real; that everything we see, feel and do is a figment of our collective imaginations. This being so, say the Daoists and others, it is best to do nothing, and whatever one does makes no difference in the grand scheme of things because nothing is real in the first place.

A Confucian concept that remains very much in force in China today, however, is the importance of humility. Confucius recognized that pride, particularly in people in power, was one of the deadliest of sins and invariably led to corruption and the misuse of power. Confucius also recognized that compliments, particularly when paid to undeserving people, fed the fires of pride, and should therefore be used sparingly.

Since accepting compliments, deserved or not, is itself symptomatic of pride, it became customary in China for people to respond to compliments with some comment such as *Nali? Nali?* (nah-lee? nah-lee?), or *Where? Where?*—figuratively meaning, "I have done nothing to deserve your compliment."

Another commonly used term to ritually side step compliments is *bu hao* (boo how), which literally means *not good*. In this sense, it means something like, *I'm not good enough to deserve your praise.*

Still another way the Chinese typically demonstrate humility and modesty is to politely refuse offers of refreshments, gifts and other favors two, three and sometimes four times before graciously accepting them. One of the highest terms of praise used in recommending a person is a reference to how "humble" he or she is.

Foreigners entertaining, hosting or offering gifts to Chinese should keep this etiquette in mind, politely repeating the offer every minute or so until it is accepted.

Outsiders dealing with China should practice using *nali nali* or *bu hao* to counter some of the compliments routinely used by the Chinese to soften up other people, especially potential business partners.

By politely and humbly side-stepping compliments, you avoid some of the social obligations that often go with accepting the praise of others.

南洋华侨

Nan Yang Hua Qiao

(Nahn Yahng Hwah Chee-ah-oh)

"Those Who Went South"

Chinese immigration into the neighboring countries of Laos, Vietnam, Cambodia and Thailand, as well as to the Philippines, Malaysia, Singapore and Indonesia began more than a thousand years ago and thereafter went in spurts based on political and economic upheavals in the homeland.

None of this early immigration of the Chinese was approved by the government, and those who left were referred to as *Nan Yang Hua Qiao* (nahn yahng hwah chee-ah-oh) or *Short-term Visitors to the South Seas*— even though there was no expectation that they would ever return.

These earliest Chinese emigrants were more or less regarded as traitors for having abandoned their homeland, and had no official standing either in China or in their host country. They had no recourse to any kind of protection from China, and were left on their own.

Because of their own proclivities to stay together in regional and linguistic groups, and the pressure to band together to defend themselves against hostility from most of the host countries (Malaysia was something of an exception), these "visitors" maintained both their Chinese culture and their spiritual and intellectual attachments for the homeland for generation after generation.

In the earlier centuries virtually all of the Chinese who migrated to Southeast Asia and the South Seas were from the Canton, Hakka, Chiu Chow, Hokkien, Yunan, Kiangsu, Chekiang, Hupei and Shantung regions in southern China.

Despite their unofficial standing and the discrimination the Chinese "visitors" encountered in these host countries, their traditions of family cohesiveness, group effort, diligence, frugality and self-preservation instincts gave them an extraordinary economic advantage over the native populations.

By becoming small-scale manufacturers, wholesalers, exporters, importers, agents and financiers, the Chinese immigrants gradually become key players in the economies of all of the countries of Southeast Asia.

In Indonesia, for example, ethnic Chinese make up less than three percent of the population, but they control somewhere around 70 percent of all private business capital in the country. In the Philippines, ethnic Chinese account for only around one percent of the population, yet they own and manage around 35 percent of the domestically owned business in the country.

In Malaysia, where some 37 percent of the population is ethnic Chinese and there are laws mandating that native Malays own a minimum of 30 percent of all domestic business, Chinese Malays own around 70 percent of the domestic-owned enterprises.

In Thailand, where ethnic Chinese make up about 10 percent of the population, it is estimated that they own some 50 percent of the financial industry, and 90 percent of the manufacturing and wholesaling-retailing industries.

The astounding economic success of the ethnic Chinese in every Southeast Asian and South Pacific country that they migrated to, despite the racial, political and social obstacles they faced, is an extraordinary testimonial to the power of Chinese culture.

Now, thousands of the most successful of these *Nan Yang* "short-term visitors" are using their wealth and know-how to help modernize their ancestral homeland.

内部

Nei Bu

(Nay-e Boo)

"Privileged Information"

Throughout pre-modern Chinese history it was the philosophy of the Imperial Courts that keeping the general population ignorant of governmental and national affairs was not only the prerogative of the government but was something that was absolutely necessary to ensure social and political stability.

When the Chinese Communist Party took over the country in 1949 it continued the traditional policy of keeping the people in the dark. But it didn't stop there. It made being in possession of, asking about, or revealing "state secrets" to others a very serious offense.

What made this policy particularly onerous for both Chinese and foreigners alike was that it was applied to such things as the unemployment rate, the number of people in prison, even weather information.

Practically all statistical information about the country as well as how the country was being run—and sometimes by whom—was classified as *nei bu* (nay-e boo), literally meaning *internal* or *inside* and used in reference to "privileged information"—or information that only people in "need to know" positions were authorized to have.

This Communist Party obsession with keeping information of all kinds confidential made it both difficult for ordinary people, particularly business-people, and especially those involved in foreign trade, to make informed decisions, and greatly hindered the recovery of the economy following the end of the Cultural Revolution in 1976.

But the so-called "reforms" that were begun by the Communist Party in 1978 and continued the 1980s—meaning reductions in political control of the economy and the adoption of many capitalist practices—included a significant reduction in the government's efforts to operate behind closed doors.

By the early 1990s vast amounts of information about China were readily available to scholars, journalists and businesspeople. But it was still necessary to exercise extraordinary caution in how one used such information.

Journalists daring to write articles that were critical of Communist leaders and their policies were still subject to arrest and imprisonment on charges of spying and revealing classified secret information.

Businesspeople who got into conflicts with their partners or suppliers, particularly when they were state-owned enterprises, were also still subject to similar charges.

While such incidents are no longer common, the threat is still there, and dealing with the problem is not always a matter of abiding by the laws of the land, since local authorities often interpret laws to suit their purposes.

Such charges are invariably made under the cloak of "administrative actions" rather than through the courts, and are therefore virtually indefensible.

内参

Nei Can

(Nay-e T'sahn)

"Keeping People Pure"

Throughout most of China's history, books and virtually all other sources of secondary knowledge were essentially reserved for the small elite class of scholar-officials and the few private individuals who were both educated and affluent enough to buy them.

Although books were being printed in China as early as the 10th century A.D., their distribution and use was further limited by a government policy that knowledge was a dangerous thing.

Because of this policy, the commercial printing of a number of China's most famous books was prohibited, resulting in them being laboriously copied by hand and distributed privately for hundreds of years after they were first written.

Some of these pioneer books, particularly those that are pornographic, are still not legally available in China.

Generally speaking, the Chinese traditionally have had to depend more upon social and cultural "telepathy" for their information than on government announcements or any kind of public news media.

One of the aspects of this public information vacuum was that printed news, in poster or any other format, was always as brief as possible—generally nothing more than stark headlines which were often themselves misleading.

In order to grasp even a nominal portion of the story behind these headline announcements it was necessary for the Chinese to know all the possible nuances of the various "code words" used and to be able to fill in between the headlines.

During the heyday of communism in China (1949–1976), dozens of books and publications were banned altogether or placed on the *nei can* (nay-e t'sahn) or *restricted publications* list—often at the behest of intellectuals rather than the government. Other books were cut, black-lined or had pieces of paper pasted in them to prevent readers from being able to read certain passages.

The rationale for restricting the availability of these books to scholars and other privileged people was that they were "inappropriate for the general public." This meant that they contained political ideas, criticism or sexual material that either government officials or some group of intellectuals thought would be harmful to or mislead the public.

When these *nei can* books did exist in China they were kept in restricted areas of libraries and stores. Only people with special "passes" were allowed into these "Inner Reference" rooms. China's present-day government still practices censorship as well as obfuscation on a grand scale. And although it is becoming more and more difficult for the government to control what is printed and distributed, its power for obfuscating official news and laws is undiminished.

Veteran expatriate businesspeople in China are constantly cautioning newcomers not to take anything the government says at face value, and not to presume that newly passed laws are going to be enforced.

It is commonly accepted in China that anything the government denies is usually just the opposite, and by the same token, that nothing is official until it is denied.

内行

Nei Hang

(Nay-e Hahng)

"Red Carpet Treatment"

Among the grandest historical images of Imperial China were the great court dinners staged in Xian, Beijing, Nanjing and other capitals, for special occasions (when over 100 chefs would be employed), and massive audiences for visiting notables that would include thousands of elite honor guards and courtiers in attendance.

These events were remarkable manifestations of traditional Chinese hospitality as well as the Chinese love for colorful pageantry, and have been carried over into modern times.

From the end of the Qing Dynasty in 1912 until the 1970s, however, civil wars, revolutions and World War II put a stop to most of the conspicuous entertainment and hospitality for which China had been famous.

But Mao Zedung, founder of the People's Republic of China, re-established the ancient Chinese custom of welcoming foreign heads of state with huge banquets when he entertained American President Richard M. Nixon in the Great Hall of the People in 1972.

Such ostentatious hospitality was not limited to China's political leaders, however. All Chinese, on whatever level, have traditionally treated visitors to banquets great and small, and have long since been masters of *nei hang* (nay-e hahng) or laying out the "red carpet" for visitors. *Nei hang* by itself means something like *master specialist* in reference to someone who is especially skilled at something.

When China began opening its doors to foreign investment and foreign trade in 1978, the number of visitors, both businesspeople and government officials, skyrocketed—causing such a demand for master chefs that a large college was established to train hundreds of people each year in the fine art of Chinese cuisine.

By the mid-1980s government and commercial enterprise spending on banquets for foreign visitors had spiraled to several billion yuan a year, making it one of the largest items in the country's national budget.

Despite attempts by China's government leaders to control spending on *nei hang*—by putting a cap on how much could officially be spent per person and limiting who was authorized to stage lunch and dinner parties—banquets continued to grow in number and importance. Generally, these evening banquets consist of several courses of increasingly more exotic food, punctuated by toasts of strong white wine, such as *mao tai* or *fen zhiu*.

Today putting up with and surviving *nei hang* treatment in China is another barrier that outsiders have to surmount in order to deal effectively with their Chinese counterparts.

While most of the *nei hang* treatment many foreigners receive in China is aboveboard, legitimate and enjoyable, a lot of it is over-done and is used insidiously to gain advantage.

It is therefore sometimes advisable to draw a line, not only because of one's health but because some degree of reciprocity is expected, and can easily get out of hand.

Chinese naturally expect to be treated with a degree of conspicuous hospitality when they travel abroad.

痞

Pi

(Pee)

"Up Against a Wall"

Almost everyone has had the experience of reaching stalemates or dead ends in their private lives as well as their work. Some of us experience nothing but dead ends and stalemates—caught forever in a quagmire of circumstances, many of which are often of our own making.

The Chinese refer to this unhappy state as *pi* (pee) or *stagnation*, a period of time when nothing works correctly because all of the forces that control or impact on life, both internal as well as external, are at an unyielding impasse.

During periods of *pi*, growth stops and decay gets the upper hand, providing the perfect environment for the rise of people who are inferior and unscrupulous, causing further decay and problems.

The Chinese have had a great deal of experience with *pi* over their five-thousand-year history, to the extent that it was listed as number twelve in the sixty-four things that have to do with human affairs.

According to the Chinese sages of old, since any kind of real progress is impossible during periods of *pi* the only meaningful recourse is to do nothing—to move back from the front lines of turmoil and wait until the time of stagnation reaches its nadir before doing anything.

This philosophy is vintage Chinese, and may be one of the reasons why so many incompetent Imperial regimes lasted for so many years.

One of the worst periods of *pi* in recent Chinese history was the great Cultural Revolution that began in 1966 and finally petered out in 1976. Virtually every man-made evil the wise men of ancient China ever warned about rose up like vengeful monsters, turning child against parent and friend against friend, bringing a kind and degree of destruction and death that had not been seen in China before.

One of the most destructive factors always inherent during a period of *pi* is lack of communication. Even when communication is attempted, people either won't listen, choose to misinterpret what they hear, or deliberately misinform others to achieve their own goals.

Specific Chinese advice for dealing with *pi* includes holding quietly to your principles, responding to opportunities or calls for help only after things begin to change for the better, remaining cautious even after things begin to improve, and moving forward boldly to implement great progress only when things really begin to come together.

Hopefully, the rationalization of Chinese culture now going on will eventually eliminate much of the ill-fated psychology of *pi* because it is more often than not used as an excuse to delay taking positive actions that would shorten cycles of stagnation.

180

偏见

Pianjian

(Pee-enn-jee-enn)

"The Prejudice Mongers"

In moments of unusual candor, usually brought on by extreme frustration, many Chinese will blurt out that the Chinese are the most prejudiced people on earth. This is no doubt an exaggeration, but the Chinese rate high among people who are conditioned to look down on everyone else, including other Chinese with whom they have no close ties.

The racial and cultural *pianjian* (pee-enn-jee-enn) or *prejudices* of the Chinese should not be surprising, given the fact that until recent times the overwhelming majority of the people "lived in a well," and had been told for millennia that they were superior to other people.

As far as most Chinese ever knew throughout most of their long history every human being had black hair, an epicanthic fold in the eyes, a slightly yellowish skin and was relatively short in stature and slender in build.

Trying to imagine what the Chinese must have thought when they first saw a huge man with red hair and green eyes or a tall blonde woman with blue eyes and pale white skin, is virtually impossible.

American Bill Holm who taught in China for a year, came home and wrote a book called *Coming Home Crazy*, has red hair and green eyes and is about the size of a football linesman. He reports—good-naturedly—in his book that as far as the Chinese are concerned, only wolves have green eyes.

But it does not take green eyes and red hair to attract attention and set tongues clacking in China. Very subtle differences in accents, dialects, food, clothing, manners, or whatever, of other Chinese who live only a few kilometers away are enough to bring out the built-in prejudicial nature of the Chinese.

Nowadays the prejudicial syndrome of the Chinese is much more apt to be aimed at other Chinese than at Caucasians, but the Chinese still have extreme difficulty in controlling their prejudices toward black people who are in China.

During the 1980s a number of African nations sent students as well as military personnel to China for training on university campuses and in urban centers, causing high tension and numerous clashes between the Chinese and Africans.

In the recent past the Chinese have gone into *pianjian* frenzies during controversies involving black students from African nations, but this too is fading.

Probably the biggest prejudice problem facing foreign employers in China is when they inadvertently mix Chinese groups that cannot stand each other because of language, food preferences and behavioral differences.

As the Chinese get further and further out of their "cultural wells" they will no doubt develop enough tolerance to get along among themselves, but this will probably be two or three generations in coming.

In the meantime, foreign companies setting up businesses in China should keep the possibility of a *pianjian* problem in mind when they start hiring factory workers and office staff. It can be quite serious and should not be ignored.

181

皮包公司

Pibao Gongsi
(Pee-bah-oh Gung-suh)

"Briefcase Companies"

Anyone who has ever spent any time in Hong Kong or in any other capitalist Chinese enclave appreciates the entrepreneurial and hawking ability of the Chinese.

But when the Chinese Communist Party (CCP) assumed power in China in 1949 both street-peddling and entrepreneuring were banned. Large numbers of people who had followed these professions were imprisoned or shot.

Some 30 years later, after the CCP had practically destroyed the country's economy, it reversed itself, partially lifted the ban and began encouraging private enterprise within some segments of the population, including farmers.

Entrepreneurs and peddlers appeared as if by magic. The results were remarkable. Just one example: a few years later a group of farmers in an outlying province chartered a plane for a shopping spree in Beijing.

A decade later China was well on its way to becoming an economic superpower, despite the fact that less than half of the population had been freed to participate in the burgeoning market-driven economy.

Among the new breed of entrepreneurial go-getters who are helping to transform China into a free market are the so-called *pibao gongsi* (pee-bah-oh gung-suh), or *briefcase companies*—meaning brokers and other middlemen whose only tangible assets are a briefcase and name cards.

Far from being interlopers who force their way into situations where they are not wanted, most of the *pibao gongsi* perform a valuable service by seeking out business opportunities and acting as facilitators between companies that do not have the requisite personal ties.

Pibao gongsi can be particularly useful to foreign enterprises in their first approach to the Chinese market, and especially so to companies that cannot afford to open offices in China and staff them with experienced bilingual personnel.

Of course, there are good and bad "briefcase companies" so it is important for the foreign side to find out as much as possible about such prospective agents before making any kind of agreement with them.

Generally, the best way to approach the challenge of qualifying a *pibao gongsi* is to get recommendations from foreign corporations who are already successfully operating in China, from commercial attaches in embassies, foreign chambers of commerce, corporate lawyers who are active in China, accounting services, and from personal contacts in Chinese universities or other institutions.

Pibao gongsi that should be avoided include those whose business relationships are based solely on bribes, keeping in mind that some gift-giving and favor-doing is normal and necessary.

182

皮蛋

Pidan

(Pee-dahn)

"Eating Chinese Culture"

In earlier times visitors demonstrated their respect, awe and sometimes fear of Imperial China by bringing gifts for the emperor, members of the Imperial Court, and other high personages they expected or wanted to meet.

Abiding by a very strict formal etiquette in all meetings with members of the Imperial Court and ministries was also an essential requirement for foreign visitors, with the most notorious of these requirements for Imperial audiences being the kowtow, which required that individuals get down on their knees and touch the floor or ground with their foreheads.

When Europeans began visiting China and were confronted with the kowtow it was a shock to both their dignity and feelings of superiority. Some were so incensed that they were expected to bow down to a "heathen emperor" that they talked of showing the Chinese what's what with the force of arms.

The Chinese no longer expect visitors to lower themselves to the floor, but they still expect that they come bearing gifts and that they demonstrate both goodwill and friendship toward China in a variety of other ways.

One of the most interesting tests of both appreciation for Chinese culture and friendship for China (the latter meaning that one is willing to go well beyond the half-way point to prove friendship), is whether or not one can eat a *pidan* (pee-dahn).

A *pidan* is a so-called 1,000-year-old egg. Of course, a *pidan* is not one thousand years old, although it looks like, smells like and tastes like it could be.

Pidan are "cultured" by coating with them with a layer of lime and clay for six to ten weeks. The lime soaks through the eggshell, turning the egg white to a bluish brown, and the yolk to a dark green.

I compare the taste of a well-aged *pidan* to something like a cross between an overripe avocado and old fish. Many Chinese and foreign afficionados like to eat the eggs before they are fully aged, when the white and yellow are still runny. When eaten at this stage, I recommend that the uninitiated have several good-sized slices of ginger handy to pop into the mouth with the egg—and follow the ginger with a slug of beer or some other potent brew.

Not being able to stomach a *pidan* does not mean you cannot develop a satisfactory relationship with Chinese or do business with them. But downing a mucky "1,000-year-old" egg with gusto will certainly raise your stock in everyone's eyes.

Actually, there are many other things on a typical Chinese menu that are more challenging than *pidan*, things whose names alone are enough to discourage most newcomers to Chinese cuisine.

Declining such delicacies should be done with diplomacy and self-deprecating humor to avoid hurting anyone's feelings.

183

偏袒

Pientun

(Pee-unn-tuun)

"Living with Flexible Laws"

One of the many things about China that conflicts with Western attitudes and behavior is the deeply entrenched custom of interpreting laws to fit the situation. China has many laws based on right and wrong, but when it comes down to enforcing those laws or dispensing justice in whatever form or fashion, the authorities concerned often treat them only as general guidelines or ignore them altogether.

This practice creates problems for Chinese and foreigners alike because it is impossible to predict how any individual official is going to interpret a law. In foreign trade, the laws are often "adjusted" in ways designed to give China an advantage over the foreign side.

In general business affairs within China, laws are used to give one side an advantage over another, to provide some extra benefit to an agency or to an individual, and so on.

In China it has not been laws but human feelings, including of course selfish desires, that have traditionally been the basis for both social and business relations. The Chinese have never looked upon laws as being a sensible or effective method for controlling the behavior of people.

Confucius went so far as to say that the more laws a nation has the less law-abiding a people will be, and that nations that base their survival on laws will eventually be torn apart by their own internal violence because people will give up any personal attempt to conduct themselves virtuously and do anything they think they can get by with—a scenario that pretty accurately describes American society today. For generations the Chinese have had the motto, *Fa lu shi huo de*, or *The law is a living thing*. Resisting codification, this flexible concept of legal codes is very different from the Western approach.

Since the take-over by Communists in 1949 the Chinese government has been passing one law after the other, but they are all *pientun* (pee-unn-tuun) or *flexible laws*, as far as enforcement is concerned. At the same time, internal strife is increasing rather than decreasing, and may yet fulfill Confucius's prophecy for China as well.

Ordinary Chinese still prefer to resolve issues through human interaction rather than through laws. But human feelings are arbitrary and unpredictable and the individuals concerned often cannot make rational decisions. So it is often necessary to bring in third parties as intermediaries in order to resolve many conflicts.

The Chinese approach to resolving disputes, and in interpreting *pientun* laws, has been called the "mother-father" approach, meaning that decisions are based on instinctual parental feelings of what is best for the individuals concerned, or, in the case of government officials, on what is best for the government officials themselves, for that particular government agency, the national government, or the nation as a whole.

All foreigners who become involved with China to even minor degrees invariably encounter *pientun*. Businesspeople who become deeply involved generally find that they have to learn how to cope in an entirely new kind of legal environment.

184

拼音

Pin Yin

(Peen Een)

"Spell That Again!"

Talk about culture shock! The languages of China, combined with the ideograms used to write them, constitute one of the most intriguing, aesthetically pleasing, and yet frustrating and forbidding communication systems ever devised by man.

The fact that Mandarin (Putonghua), Shanghaiese, Cantonese, Hokkien and the other primary languages of China are tonal in character and are the devil to pronounce, pales beside the number of ideograms one has to learn to be fully literate in reading and writing any one of the languages.

If you include all of the technical, scientific, medical and other specialized terms, there are well over 100,000 *han zi* (hahn tzu) or *Chinese characters* in the Chinese writing system. There is no record of anyone every having memorized that many ideograms, but it is necessary for the average educated person to know at least 3,500 *han zi* to function efficiently in Chinese society, and that in itself is a formidable task.

This problem is further compounded by the existence of tones in the various Chinese languages. Many of the same words have several meanings, depending upon whether they are pronounced with a high tone, low tone, rising tone or falling tone, or some combination of these tones (Mandarin, the "national" language has four tones; Cantonese has seven tones).

Language experts say there are only around four hundred sounds to pronounce the five thousand ideograms and all of the additional ten to twenty thousand compounds making up the daily spoken languages of China.

This means there are not nearly enough sounds or syllables for each one of the ideograms to have its own exclusive sound. So what do the Chinese do to surmount this problem? They don't really surmount it, they just pronounce many of the characters with exactly the same sound.

Some sounds (written in different ways) have dozens of meanings. This means it is vital for the speaker to use the right sound, in the right tone, in a context that makes the meaning clear—or as clear as possible.

This problem is compounded when you write Chinese in the familiar ABCs, and is a challenge that the Chinese and foreigners alike have struggled with for centuries.

Finally, in 1958, the government of China announced that the romanization system known as *pin yin* (peen een) or *phonetic transcription*, was the one and only official system for writing Chinese in *luomahua* or roman letters. It was put into universal use in 1979. It is taught in elementary schools nationwide, and appears on most street and shop signs.

At first encounter, the *pin yin* system of writing Chinese appears even more irrational than the English system of spelling. From the viewpoint of English letters and sounds, there appears to be little or no rhyme or reason to a number of *pin yin* spellings. X, for example, is sounded as an S or Sh; Q is pronounced as if it were Ch.

Looking at many Chinese words written in roman letters there often appears to be no hint at all on how they should be pronounced. But after studying with someone who knows how to pronounce the odd looking spelling, it all gradually comes together (how long this process takes depends upon the individual).

It pays even the short-time casual visitor to learn how to pronounce some of the more common Chinese name-places, however. Not being able to pronounce the name of the hotel, shop, restaurant or other typical destination you want to go to can be a serious inconvenience.

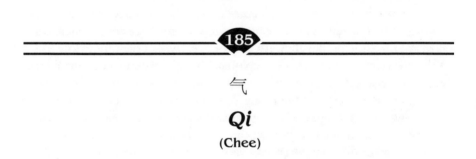

185

气

Qi
(Chee)

"Plugging into Cosmic Power"

In 1971 in Kamakura, Japan I was introduced to a man named Nahum Stiskin who had just written a book called *The Looking Glass God—Shinto, Yin-Yang and a Cosmology for Today* (John Weatherhill Inc., Tokyo).

By that time, I had been in Japan for some twenty years, and thought I was fairly well versed in the origin and tenets of Shintoism, Japan's indigenous animistic religion, as well as in the Chinese principles of *yin* and *yang*.

I was so astounded by the book that I read it three times within the first few days, bought ten additional copies to send to friends, and engaged in several long discussions with the author.

Stiskin was a recent graduate of Brandeis University with a degree in Western philosophy. Following his graduation he had studied the Chinese principles of *yin-yang* for two years with a Japanese Orientalist in the U.S., becoming so intrigued that he moved to Japan in 1969 to delve deeper into the philosophies, arts and sciences of the East.

In brief, the theme of *The Looking Glass God* was that Shintoism was an expression of pure human intuition, and was a revelation of the origin and essence of all matter in the cosmos and the relationship between all forms of life and matter.

Stiskin told me that he became aware of the deeper meanings of Shintoism and the *yin-yang* concept when he began studying the ancient Chinese ideograms originally used to define and describe Shinto and *yin-yang* precepts. He was, he said, equally astounded when he realized that Shintoism was based on physics that the Western world was just now in the process of discovering.

Both *yin-yang* and Shintoism account for the *qi* (chee) or *energy* that suffuses the universe, noting that it is the force that results from interaction between the dualistic nature of matter, the positive and negative.

Several thousand years ago wise men in China came to the conclusion that there was a special "force" or "current" that infuses and flows through all things in the universe, animate as well as inanimate (a concept that also occurred to the Greek philosopher Pythagoras in the 6th century A.D.).

According to Chinese theory, it is this force that empowers everything in the universe, providing the life-essence for every last thing, from the stars and planets to the atmosphere, oceans, people, plants and animals.

In this theory, all matter, in whatever form, radiates some of this cosmic force as currents of energy. People, trees, flowers, water, even rocks, cast a field or "aura" of energy that affects everything around them. Note how trees that are too near other trees or solid objects naturally bend away from them.

The Chinese called this cosmic energy *qi*, and it is the foundation for much of their philosophy and science. The root meaning of *qi* is *vapor*, by which is meant the *matter* (energy) that forms all life.

Qi, say the Chinese, is what brings ordinary matter to life and what determines its nature, its health, its life span, and its influence on its environment.

Acupuncture, the Chinese method of treating health problems by inserting needles into the body, is based on *qi*. The Chinese say that when the *qi* of the body becomes unbalanced, or when the cosmic force is not flowing properly, illness results.

The Chinese long ago identified a "network of *qi* lines" in the body, and discovered that inserting needles into these lines at key points had a specific effect on the flow of energy along the lines, either stimulating or redirecting the energy.

They also discovered that the *qi* network in the body was directly connected with key body organs, from the brain and the eyes to the spleen and liver, and so on. A needle inserted in an earlobe, for example, would affect the condition of some other part of the body.

Feng shui, the ancient Chinese art of placement, is based totally on the flow of *qi* from the surrounding environment—mountains, hills, rivers, lakes, the ocean, trees, and other structures, including items of furniture.

Since the flow of *qi* may have either a positive or negative influence on other things in the vicinity, depending on its directional relationship, the Chinese attach great importance to making sure that gates, doors, buildings, furniture or whatever face in a direction that allows for the smooth flow of positive *qi*.

The extraordinary power of the martial art *kung fu* derives from *qi*— from knowing how to concentrate it and then release it with such force that it is like an explosion.

In Chinese usage, *qi* refers to a spiritual kind of energy that is reflected in one's appearance as well as behavior. This energy, which is fixed at birth, may be negative or impure, with the result that the individual will have a bad character regardless of how benign or supportive the environment.

The "magnetism" that is often present in unusually successful people is *qi*. In some people it is so powerful that they do, in fact, attract like a magnet. The extraordinary energy that some people exhibit in their work or play is a function of *qi*.

Another way of thinking of the power of *qi* in people is to liken it to electricity produced by a battery. Some people have weak batteries; others have powerful ones. If a person's "battery" becomes too weak or is short-circuited, illness results. Some people have so much *qi* that they cannot channel it into positive pursuits, and are constantly making waves.

To the Chinese the amount and kind of *qi* a person has determines his or her success or failure in life. When meeting a person for the first time they automatically measure the strength and quality of the individual's *qi* as the basis for judging the person's character and worth.

One of the reasons why the Chinese find it difficult to judge the character of Westerners is that they cannot read their *qi* across the cultural gap that separates them.

This presents a problem that cannot be eliminated without first eliminating its cultural roots. The only practical recourse is for both sides to be conscious of the problem and learn how to work through it.

Knowledge of the concept of *qi* and its influence on people and the environment in general can be a valuable asset for anyone interacting with the Chinese.

See **Feng Shui, Kung Fu, Qigong**.

乾

Qian
(Chee-enn)

"Power of Creativity"

The *I Ching*, or the *Book of Changes*, might be described as China's book of knowledge, or perhaps more aptly as *The Sixty-Four Commandments of China*. However it may be described it is something like the philosophical and metaphysical bible of China.

The book began as a guide to the natural changes that affected the daily hunting, fishing and farming pursuits of the first Chinese, much like almanacs of more recent times in the West.

As the centuries passed, the whole stock of knowledge accumulated by succeeding generations of Chinese was absorbed into the book in condensed and often very esoteric symbolic forms.

Eventually the book was standardized into sixty-four hexagrams, with accompanying essays to explain them. The hexagrams and their explanations purported to cover all of the affairs of man—social, political, economic, ethics, etc., serving not only as guidelines for behavior, but also predicting the future outcome of both positive and negative behavior.

The first and what might be considered the most powerful principle covered by the *Book of Changes* is *qian* (chee-enn), which means *creativity* or *creative power* as it applies to human affairs.

Looking at the hexagram that represents *qian*, it is tempting to make a comparison with the biblical Garden of Eden in which the only inhabitants,

Adam and Eve, are perfect human beings (a state that apparently lasted for only a brief period of time!).

And viewing China from the outside it is tempting to say that the first and most powerful principle in the Chinese philosophy of human behavior is the one *least often* encountered—in the past or now.

A person imbued with *qian* is endowed with the wisdom and insights to know himself or herself, to understand the innermost feelings and aspirations of others, to attract dedicated disciples, and the ability to transform the world around him or her through creating honorable and fair organizations and laws that will carry out his or her dreams.

Many of the emperors and would-be conquerors of China in the past may have begun with such lofty goals, but it was not long before they became victims of their own ambitions, resulting in their dreams of heavenly kingdoms on earth turning into new nightmares.

Uncontrolled ambition after the achievement of great success is, in fact, the only weakness that the person with *qian* is warned about. But all the person has to do to achieve success in the first place is follow the dictates of his or her principles and allow his or her inner strength to express itself.

There are numerous examples of contemporary Chinese in Hong Kong, Singapore, Kuala Lumpur and elsewhere in Southeast Asia who have *qian*. Time will tell if the evolving political and economic situation in China will allow people endowed with this ancient concept to thrive in their own homeland.

Chinese scientists in the U.S. and elsewhere outside of China have also repeatedly demonstrated extraordinary creativity, achieving an impressive number of breakthrough inventions.

One example that quickly comes to mind is Yan Ran-Hong, a native of Taiwan who went to work AT&T Bell Laboratories as a 28-year-old rookie on the semiconductor research staff in Aberdeen, New Jersey.

Yan was working on silicon microchips. While watching his first-ever snowfall one morning he noted that the snowflakes did not stick to the sides of cars. It immediately occurred to him that vertically "doping" silicon wafers with a "snowfall" of boron atoms could dramatically change the speed of the chips. He was right, and his fresh insight resulted in an enormous boost to the efficacy of the tiny semiconductor devices.

Why was Yan able to come up with what industry experts immediately saw as a common sense solution to an old problem? Yan explained that it was "mind-set." Westerners are conditioned to think in straight, orthodox lines. Chinese look at puzzles or problems from all angles.

Once mainland Chinese are free to unleash their holistic thinking processes, their long-suppressed creativity could astound the world.

187

Qian

(Chee-enn)

"Everything in Moderation"

At first glance, the Chinese concept of the cosmos as made up of carefully balanced powers may appear to be both esoteric and extraneous. But it is, in fact, fundamental in all things, from the behavior of the stars to interpersonal relationships.

One of the most important facets of this cosmic balance is expressed in the term *qian* (chee-enn), which means *moderation* or *modesty*—a concept that has played a key role in Chinese life since ancient times.

In the 6th century B.C. the great sage Lao Tzu, the founder of Taoism (or Daoism in modern-day Mandarin Chinese), spoke at length on *qian*, emphasizing that it was one of the most essential ingredients in living in harmony with one's self and with others, and that without it one could not become truly civilized.

A master observer of human nature, Lao Tzu wrote in his book *Tao-te Ching*:

> He who shows himself is not luminous.
> He who justifies himself is not prominent.
> He who boasts of himself is not given credit.
> He who brags does not endure for long.

All of China's sages, from Confucius to modern-day Lin Yutang, have recognized the role of moderation in human affairs and have made it one of the pillars of their preaching. All of them recognized that it was the excesses of mankind, and especially of leaders, that led to immorality, violence and destruction.

Qian, the fifteenth element in the *Book of Changes*, was traditionally one of the first lessons taught to all Chinese, and was especially important to ordinary people because any kind of excessive behavior was not only culturally taboo, it was politically unacceptable.

Recent changes in both the cultural and political environments of China have greatly weakened the concept of personal moderation, especially among the younger generations. Avoidance of personal displays of power and aggrandizement is still seen as the standard for moral behavior, but with such displays themselves no longer being punishable offenses, immoderation is becoming rampant.

However, outsiders dealing with upper level Chinese businesspeople and bureaucrats should keep in mind that unnecessarily conspicuous displays of wealth and power give a negative image. One example of how important *qian* is at home and in the office: works of art or valuable antiques are kept in cabinets or boxes, not hung or displayed. The collector shows them privately to friends and other connoisseurs.

This does not mean that the Chinese are not impressed by wealth and power. Quite the contrary. The foreign businessperson who maintains an office in a 747 jumbo jet, flies into Beijing several times a year and conducts business in the plane at Beijing International Airport, gets all the attention and cooperation he or she expects.

Foreigners dealing with China should keep in mind that they will get along much better with their Chinese counterparts and make more progress faster if they display a keen sense of *qian* in all comments and behavior.

The wealthier and more powerful people are the more the Chinese expect them to embody the concept of *qian*. This does not mean that they cannot live well. It is a matter of attitude and style.

188

Qian
(Chee-enn)

"Taking on Challenges"

No one knows better than the Chinese that life is filled with one obstacle after another; that no sooner is one problem solved than another one arises.

As far back as the third millennium B.C., educated Chinese were already spending a great deal of time contemplating the *qian* (chee-enn) or *obstacles* that people confront during the course of their lives, and trying to come up with sound advice that would help them cope.

These early contemplations by the Chinese, which went to the depth of human psychology, quickly revealed that many of the seemingly insurmountable problems people faced were of their own making. They also learned that most of the *qian* arose from the particular path or profession chosen by individuals themselves, and therefore could not be blamed on anyone else.

When the obstacles encountered were self-made, the sages advised that one should take advantage of the opportunity to self-reflect, analyze the motives that led to the problems, and attempt to remedy one's own weaknesses.

The ancient Chinese were also wise enough to realize that many of the problems that people face are the result of inhibitions; of not having the confidence or courage to do what they know should be done, even when they know how to do it. The solution to this handicap was obvious, said the sages—recognize and admit your inhibitions and work to overcome them.

In the case of genuine institutional obstacles, the advice of the sages was to emulate flowing water when it meets a barrier. The water doesn't give up or turn back. It slowly builds up, and eventually either goes over, around or through the obstacle.

Another suggestion was to enlist the aid of others, putting together your own team or group or joining an existing group, whose combined talents and strength will allow you to achieve your goals.

Because almost everyone almost always faces a variety of obstacles, *qian* became one of the sixty-four elements affecting mankind that is addressed in *I Ching*, the *Book of Changes*.

As in all the other elements, the *I Ching* recognizes five levels or categories of obstacles, and comments on each one of them. The reactions advised begin with going nothing and waiting until circumstances are in your favor.

Extraordinary measures to counter extraordinary barriers are advised on the next level. If the situation threatens you or those close to you with the loss of security or existence, however, the advice is to reconsider your goals and strategy.

If you are satisfied that the risks are worth the danger, *I Ching* advises that you bring in allies. If you exhibit great spirit in your pursuit of your goals, continue the sages, your allies will be inspired and extend further efforts to help you. The final piece of advice: if you and your allies are doing all that you can do and you still face insurmountable *qian*, seek the help of wise men.

189

气功

Qigong
(Chee-gung)

"Breathing Your Way to Health"

Unlike certain Indian yogis, the Chinese do not claim that people can live on cosmic energy alone, but they have copious evidence proving that a certain type of breathing, called *qigong* (chee-gung) or *deep breathing*, has truly remarkable health benefits, some verging on the miraculous. Visitors to China are often charmed by the spectacle of older men and women in parks slowly turning, raising and rotating their arms in unison. They are practicing *qigong.*

China's famous philosopher Lao Tzu (also known as Dao Ze), who was born in 604 B.C., postulated that all life is the result of a vital energy or cosmic force that he called *qi* (chee). Just as electricity gives "life" to electronic and mechanical equipment, *qi* in Lao's terms is the spark than animates all living things, from the smallest bacteria to plants, animals and man.

The practice of *qigong* is said to have been promoted by Hua Tuo, (died in A.D. 208) one of China's medical pioneers, during the end of the Han Dynasty and beginning of the Three Kingdoms period, after he discovered that measured deep breathing practiced regularly dramatically improves one's peace of mind, general health and longevity.

In addition to *qigong*, Hua is also noted for developing an oral anesthetic for use in surgical operations—but his accomplishments were to be his undoing.

Hua was called in to treat Cao Cao, ruler of the state of Wu, for a severe migraine headache. Following a successful treatment, Cao Cao requested that Dr. Hua give up his practice and join the army as the emperor's personal physician. Dr. Hua declined. The imperious ruler had him executed.

Over the centuries, Daoists added a mystical side to *qigong*, detracting from its legitimacy. But people who practiced the exercise properly were able to achieve remarkable results in both physical and mental activities—feats that were often beyond what is recognizable or explainable in scientific terms, and sometimes resulted in them being regarded as practitioners of black magic.

In any event, the physical and mental benefits of *qigong* were indisputable, and the practice of deep breathing for its health benefits became institutionalized in Chinese life.

At present, an estimated 50 million Chinese engage in *qigong* as part of their daily routine, and it is used by a growing number of therapists in the treatment of a wide range of ailments and diseases, from high blood pressure to cancer.

Carefully monitored results of the use of *qigong*, often involving patients who had failed to respond to treatment by both Western trained doctors and herbal doctors, were so dramatic that in the 1980s the Chinese government sponsored the establishment of the China Qigong Science Research Center in Beijing, where *qigong* masters and scientists are working together to discover the scientific basis for the benefits of the practice, and to develop it into an independent science.

Now, instead of Daoist devotees and fringe healers, medical doctors and scientists are the leading advocates of *qigong*. In the mid-1980s one such group of professionals founded the private China Qigong Training College in Beijing to train *qigong* specialists, and to research and write a series of textbooks covering the history, theory, and practice of *qigong*.

Each year the *qigong* college graduates between 300 and 400 practitioners who then return to their own home villages and towns to set up clinics and schools.

Administrators at the China Qigong Training College say they regard *qigong* as one of China's national treasures, and believe that it will become a universal life science during the 21st century.

There are several *qigong* "schools." One school combines controlled breathing with very light physical exercises. Another emphasizes meditation on the body nodes, particularly the "body center" about three inches below the navel, during the breathing exercises.

A third school, said to have been founded by the famous but ill-fated Dr. Hua, emphasizes breathing plus exercises based on the movements of the crane, bear, deer, monkey and tiger.

190

奇迹

Qi Ji

(Chee Jee)

"Avoiding the Fall"

Success in any field of endeavor is something like a sexual climax. People tend to lay back, relax and rest on their laurels. And that, say the Chinese, is when things start going to pot. They believe that nothing except change is constant, and that success that is not followed by careful nurturing inevitably leads to decline.

The Chinese term for the fall after the rise is *qi ji* (chee jee), which means *after the end*. The compound is incorporated into a series of warnings that are basic to becoming and staying successful—and is important enough to be number sixty-three in the hexagrams making up *I Ching*, or *Book of Changes*, the bible of the Chinese way.

The *qi ji* hexagram relates to a number of tendencies or elements that can be positive or negative, depending on your reaction to events. There are five variations of the hexagram and six readings, all of which warn of inappropriate behavior, and advise on what you should do to overcome the dangers inherent in the situation.

One of the most interesting of the variations of *qi ji* described in *I Ching* is one in which the situation is said to be like being in the eye of a typhoon—you can see what is happening all around you but are unable to affect it in any way. The practical-sounding advice when you are in the eye of a hurricane is to stay cool and don't do anything to endanger yourself.

Among the lessons to be learned from the *qi ji* factor: to accept responsibility for the actions you initiate because they will almost always go awry if you don't; to not give up in the face of problems or extra responsibilities occurring from worthwhile actions you set in motion; to take small steps and go about your work carefully; to avoid grandstanding; to take pleasure in the simple things of life; to be honest with yourself and others; to not blame others for your own shortcomings; and to enlist the help of good people in your efforts to succeed.

According to the precepts of *I Ching* it is impossible to avoid the decline that occurs after a person or a thing reaches a state of equilibrium. The point is to dispassionately view the changes that began immediately upon achieving success, and take steps to counter those that would have a negative impact.

As in so many other areas of life, say the Chinese, the secret to being prepared for what happens after success is knowledge that is carefully analyzed to provide a basis for foreseeing coming events, followed by equally careful planning to counter whatever contingencies occur.

The goal of being prepared in this manner is not to prevent things from changing—that is generally impossible, especially for any length of time. The aim is to stay aware of *qi ji*—of what is happening once you succeed, and change with the circumstances.

Foreigners dealing with China are constantly faced with attitudes and behavior deriving from the Chinese desire to avoid *qi ji*, but the rationale they are following is often not obvious, and just as often results in misunderstandings and ill-will.

Qing
(Cheeng)

"Clearing Up Cobwebs"

Chinese traditions of intuitive calculation and scientific research, which go back more than four thousand years, were for the most part restricted to the narrow, static interests of the state and to the small, elite class of educated men who had the time to be curious and the resources to pursue their curiosity.

This system greatly limited the potential of the Chinese for achieving new insights and invention, but it nevertheless resulted in many discoveries, from philosophical truths to technology that changed the way people in all industrialized societies work and live today.

At the same time it imbued educated Chinese with a virtual obsession to understand the nature, function and promise of all things.

Chinese concern with understanding the things about them was expressed in the name chosen for what turned out to be the country's last

Imperial dynasty, the *Qing* (cheeng), founded in 1644. *Qing* means *clear*, *lucid* and *pure*, and is generally translated into English as *clarity*.

An enlightened and ambitious dynasty during its earliest decades, the Qing government set out to rebuild virtually the whole infrastructure of China, from great cross-country canals and roads to monuments and museums. The construction projects going on at any one time during this era numbered in the thousands and involved millions of workers.

But one thing the elite of the Qing Dynasty could not cope with was the arrival of industrially advanced Europeans in the early 1600s and the impact of their culture of militant expansionism. During the last half of the dynasty, China roiled with rebellions and revolutions, and from attacks by England and other foreign powers.

It was not until the beginning of the Communist dynasty in 1949 and the conversion of China into an industrial-military power that the scientific bent of the Chinese was allowed to bloom, and it was not until the failure of communism was undeniable in the 1980s that the latent Chinese trait for clear thinking and creative activity was partially unleashed.

Original references to *qing* related to human character, with the admonishment, from such sages as Confucius, that not only families and larger social units but kingdoms as well would eventually fall if they did not maintain the purity of their characters—an indictment that is once again coming true in the Middle Kingdom.

In current usage, *qing bui* means *clear conscience*, and *qing chu* means *clearly understood*. Both are very common expressions.

As political freedom and economic opportunities expand in China, a second *Qing Dynasty*—and this time one that is much more people oriented— could be in the offing. Outsiders can help speed the process this time, rather than hinder it as they did in the past, by keeping their own standards of conduct on the level of *qing*.

请客

Qingke / Yanjiu Yanjiu

(Cheeng-kuh / Yen-jew Yen-jew)

"Wining and Dining to Win"

The Chinese are famous—or infamous—for their hospitality. Individuals and families will routinely shower visitors and guests with a variety and volume of food and drink that costs far more than what they can afford—and is more than their guests can possibly consume.

This cultural syndrome is mostly fueled by pride and a deep-seated fear of losing face from giving the impression they cannot afford the cost of a sumptuous banquet, are not sufficiently cultured to follow a ritualized protocol, or are not *Chinese* enough to uphold the honor of China.

There is another factor, probably of equal importance, in why banquet style meals are so common and popular among the Chinese. Over the millennia the greatest day-to-day challenge to most Chinese was to make sure they had enough food to eat to ward off starvation.

This stark reality resulted in the Chinese developing what might be called an obsession about food. In addition to eating anything that was nutritious and not poisonous, they became acutely conscious about preparing food to make it both palatable and attractive; and eating the various dishes in the proper *yin-yang* order to ensure both physical and spiritual harmony with the cosmos (and therefore good health).

Eating with family and friends also became an institutionalized ritual to demonstrate and nurture filial piety, parental responsibility, devotion to friends, loyalty, success, appreciation, and Chineseness.

Still today, no matter how poor the Chinese, they will splurge for food on special occasions. The more successful and larger a Chinese family, the more conspicuous the role played by food.

Chinese businesspeople and government officials in particular use food and drink as one of their primary tools in creating and sustaining cooperative relationships with other people—a process known as *qingke* (cheeng-kuh), which, by itself, means *invitation* or *invite a guest*.

Bureaucrats on all levels are especially notorious for annually spending huge sums on expensive banquets to entertain visitors.

To the Chinese sharing a large meal is the fastest and most effective way of demonstrating goodwill and friendship, getting acquainted with and bonding with people.

Qingke, which is used in the sense of "wining and dining," is also used as a means of impressing and softening up would-be business partners, subtly getting them to lower their defenses and making them more susceptible to being manipulated.

A significant goal of *qingke* is to put business (and political) relationships on a personal, friendship basis rather than a quid pro quo arrangement, in keeping with the Chinese way of basing relationships on changeable circumstances rather than constant factors.

Outsiders who accept *qingke* hospitality from their Chinese counterparts or suitors, and do not return it, should be aware that they are playing the game according to Chinese rules and are expected to be more pliable and forgiving in the relationship.

Another key expression often used in association with building up influence with a government official is *yanjiu*, which can mean either cigarettes and wine or "research discussions."

When businesspeople and others extend an invitation to officials they make a point of saying the phrase twice (*yanjiu yanjiu!*), in a humorous manner, so that the officials will clearly understand that in addition to a banquet meal accompanied by business discussions, they will be given cigarettes and wine as gifts.

权

Quan
(Chuu-enn)

"Lessons in Being Boss"

Over the centuries the Chinese were so conditioned to obeying their social superiors and government officials without question that it became an ingrained habit, passed on from one generation to the next. Eventually it got to the point that most Chinese felt lost and virtually immobilized if they were not given precise duties and instructions by someone with *quan* (chuu-enn) or *authority*.

One of the many negative facets of this system was that it was dangerous to question the experience or ability of people in authority, so mediocrity often flourished unchecked on every level of government and commercial enterprise.

In his usual forthright fashion, however, military strategist Sun Tzu (5th century B.C.) took both incompetent generals and leaders to task, and laid down a number of principles for evaluating them that have been transformed into modern-day management and corporate take-over wisdom.

Among the key points that Sun Tzu made and their application to business:

1. When a commander orders his army to advance or retreat without knowing what the results will be, he is a bad commander and should be removed. The same goes for a business manager who orders a move into or out of a market or a product line without knowing what the consequences will be.
2. A politician who tries to administer an army the same way he runs a bureaucracy is doomed to failure. The ex-bureaucrat or academic who tries to run a business without any experience in the marketplace is likewise courting failure.
3. Giving authority to military officers who are not familiar with the need to be flexible in the field, because of favoritism or any other reason, is a recipe for disaster. Misusing managers in this fashion in business can result in numerous mistakes and undermine the confidence of the entire organization.
4. Not staying in touch with his commanders in the field leaves a general blind and unable to make the right decisions. The same goes for top-level executives in the business world—especially when the "commanders" are stationed overseas and need to react quickly to circumstances.
5. The general who is primarily interested in advancement and fame puts his personal interests above that of his commander-in-chief and country, and is therefore a threat to the country. Business executives who behave like prima donnas or hired guns with big reputations to keep intact are a threat to the companies they head—as is so often demonstrated in the United States.

Summing up some of Sun Tzu's insights in the use of authority in business: executives who are ignorant of the product or market concerned should not make decisions concerning them; executives should not try to manage both staff and line functions with the same approach; executives should not assign tasks to individuals who do not have the experience to handle them.

Sun Tzu adds that it is critical for people in authority to be flexible and capable of managing change. He also advises that they be quiet, calm and mysterious—which is generally just the opposite of Western, especially American, businesspeople and politicians.

曲艺

Quyi
(Chuu-eee)

"People Propaganda"

As in most ancient cultures, oral storytelling became a vital part of the lives of the Chinese very early in the history of the country. The art was a recognized profession by 475 B.C., but no doubt had been common for thousands of years before that.

During the first millennia of China's history *quyi* (chuu-eee), or *storytellers*, focused on history, legends and myths. The formal recognition of *quyi* troupes dates from the Song Dynasty (A.D. 960–1279). By the Yuan Dynasty (A.D. 1271–1368), they had begun to comment on current affairs, resulting in an Imperial edict prohibiting critical commentary of any kind.

By the year 1600 large troupes of *quyi* had become so prominent that they were regularly invited to perform at the Imperial Court. This stimulated the proliferation of *quyi* genres throughout the country, each with its own distinctive style.

By the beginning of the Qing Dynasty in 1644 there were *quyi* in every part of the country, and they had once again become very political, attacking warlords and the central government, and fomenting revolutionary thoughts in general.

Not one to miss a bet, Mao Zedung in the 1920s incorporated hundreds of *quyi* into the propaganda efforts of his revolutionary Red Army, totally controlling the content of their stories. Six issues of the *Red Army Daily* published in July 1930 printed more than twenty *quyi* scripts in full.

Following the beginning of war with Japan in 1937, China's Communist Party virtually took over the *quyi* profession, enlisting the services of many famous writers to prepare scripts attacking the Japanese.

Several *quyi* performed at the inaugural ceremony of the People's Republic of China (PRC) in Beijing on October 31, 1949. Soon after establishment of the PRC, the government issued new guidelines for *quyi* stories, using them as a tool to glorify the exploits of heroes of the Communist Party and promote the Communist ideology.

Backed by Mao and other top-level government leaders, *quyi* flocked to Beijing from all over the country. *Quyi* scripts were printed as books, published in newspapers and magazines, and broadcast over the radio. In 1951 the noted revolutionary artist Li Bozhao founded a national *quyi* magazine called *Shuoshuo Chang-Chang*. Other *quyi* periodicals quickly followed suit.

When the Korean War started in 1951 the Chinese government dispatched several of the country's most famous *quyi* artists to the front lines to boost the morale of the Chinese troops that had been sent in to help North Korea. Two of the storytellers were killed in the fighting.

In May of 1951 Zhou Enlai, China's popular foreign minister, issued a government document officially establishing guidelines for *quyi*. The document said in part: "They can be consciously used to give rapid reflection of reality, so due importance should be attached to them. In addition to the production of large numbers of new scripts, many old scripts that contain historical stories and old legends with which people are familiar should be transformed and used."

This official recognition resulted in an avalanche of writers and artists taking up the *quyi* profession. Many of the old masters who had served during the war against Japanese and then against Chiang Kai-shek and his Nationalists became active again, and the next 17 years were a new golden age for *quyi*.

But the so-called Cultural Revolution that Mao instigated in 1966 brought disaster to the *quyi*. During the first years of the Cultural Revolution *xuan chuan dui*, or *propaganda teams*, of musicians, actors, dancers and acrobats toured the country spreading Mao's latest principles and rhetoric in two-hour-long evening shows, often performed outdoors. But later hundreds of the better known storytellers were persecuted, troupes were disbanded, publications were stopped, scripts were burned.

When this decade of chaos ended in 1976 the Association of Chinese *Quyi* Personnel (ACQP) was established and the profession gradually came back to life. The *quyi* section of the Ministry of Culture was reactivated, and its provincial equivalents also resumed their activities.

Shortly thereafter the ACQP was renamed the Chinese Quyi Artists' Association. The national magazine *Quyi* resumed publication, and was soon followed by other publications. *Quyi* books began appearing, and the *Chinese Encyclopedia* brought out a volume devoted solely to *quyi*.

Today China's *quyi* artists compete with TV, but they appear to be holding their own. Present-day *quyi* performers play several parts, and audiences typically participate by instantly voicing their approval or disapproval of performances—from the content of the stories to the facial expressions and gestures of the artists.

Much of the success of *quyi* artists depends upon their skill in using language and behavior to accurately depict the characters they are imitating. Instant audience feedback lets the performers know when they are successful in their efforts.

Soon after the relaxation of Communist controls in 1978 another kind of storytelling, the *xiang sheng* or *comic dialogues*, quickly became popular, first in the underground and later in more public areas. These satirists specialize in short anecdotal stories that spear the stupidity and irrationality of Chinese Communist Party officials.

The *xiang sheng* use a rapid-fire series of puns called *cross-talk* to build to a comic crescendo that can be extremely funny. Their programs are often broadcast on trains and on marathon television shows.

仁

Ren
(Rune)

"Chinese Benevolence"

People who go to China for business or other professional reasons are often overwhelmed with the hospitality extended to them. This hospitality just as often goes beyond sumptuous feasts and drinking parties to include very generous contributions of personal time for sightseeing, shopping and so on.

This is not a recent phenomenon. Visitors to China over the last four centuries have reported voluminously on the spontaneous kindness of individual Chinese, particularly toward uninvited and unexpected foreign guests.

This characteristic Chinese trait, expressed in the term *ren* (rune), which is translated as *benevolence* or *human heartedness*, is often traced back to Confucius, the master sage himself, who regarded it as the first of the four virtues he said were innate in human beings (the three other virtues he named were righteousness, propriety or etiquette, and wisdom).

But like so many other aspects of the Chinese way, *ren* was not a universally practiced custom among the Chinese. Generally speaking, demonstrations of kindness were strictly limited to family members, kin, friends, and "foreign" guests *after* a personal relationship was established.

Because life for most Chinese throughout history has been marginal, their compulsion to survive limited their kindness to those with whom they had a personal relationship. They could not afford to be benevolent to everyone they encountered. There were simply too many people. Generally, their obligations began and ended with those within their family or group.

Foreign strangers in China have traditionally been in a special category, however, because they were rare, because being kind to them would not later complicate the lives of those involved (except in times of political turmoil), and because it was a matter of personal as well as national face.

Another factor in present-day Chinese reactions to visitors from abroad is purely selfish. Many people see contact with outsiders as a possible source of some kind of advantage: as a connection they might be able to use to improve their lot in terms of business or as a chance to emigrate. Some people pursue this possibility so aggressively it puts visitors in positions that are untenable.

Dealing with this kind of situation puts a special burden on some visitors that sometimes results in ill-will on both sides. The only recourse visitors have is to explain as quickly and as fully as possible the limits of their goodwill.

There is every reason to believe that growing affluence and individual freedom in China will dramatically expand the ability of the Chinese to practice *ren* indiscriminately and help eliminate much of the callousness that now degrades the culture. Eventually this mostly latent trait could help bring the mass of Chinese closer to the ideal society Confucius envisioned.

Having been made extraordinarily sensitive to *ren* by the lack of it in their own society, the Chinese are quick to recognize the presence or lack of it in others.

Government officials in particular are known to take advantage of the benevolence of others, especially Americans, as one of their regular diplomatic ploys.

忍

Ren

(Rune)

"The Patience of Job"

Television has done to China what more than forty centuries of time failed to do—create a consumer mentality in the hundreds of millions of Chinese farmers, and make them hunger for things of fashion and convenience, rather than just bellies full of rice and vegetables.

Until the 1980s and 1990s, the lives of China's farmers had changed little for more than two thousand years. The seasons and the generations changed, but the lifestyles and hardships remained the same.

One could not hurry the crops or the seasons, or the passages of life. There was no sense of urgency to do things faster or better or differently. Life passed at a leisurely pace.

In this environment, *ren* (rune) or *patience* was taken for granted. Anyone who displayed impatience, unless there was some kind of emergency, was considered to be acting in a dangerous and immoral manner. Confucius admonished that things done in haste could not be done well.

The more worthy the challenge facing the Chinese the more important it was to avoid errors and oversights by doing it slowly and carefully. The truly cultured Chinese, by definition, could not be one who was in a hurry to accomplish things.

This long tradition of slow, deliberate contemplation and action and the avoidance of any semblance of haste naturally had a profound impact on the character of the Chinese, and although significantly diminished today, is still visible and still a factor to be dealt with.

Both businesspeople and bureaucrats in China generally resist any attempt to rush them, and constantly preach to foreigners that they must practice *ren*; that things cannot be hurried in China.

Actually, things *can* be hurried in China when those in power decide there is sufficient reason to do so, but patience is one of the many keys to surviving and succeeding in the Middle Kingdom.

Because the Chinese are so sensitive to signs of impatience, and especially to overt attempts to speed things up, it is necessary to handle such situations with a great deal of subtlety and tact. The most ethical approach is to enlist the help of a third party who has influence with the people involved.

Often the fastest and most effective approach, however, is to offer some kind of special, personal incentive to the people who are in a position to speed up the process—in other words a bribe; something that has been an integral part of the Chinese system since bureaucratization of the government over two thousand years ago.

In its Chinese context *ren* also incorporates the concept of tolerance, in the sense that the Chinese are conditioned to put up with any number and kind of annoyances or incongruities without complaining.

The reason for the development of this distinctive trait was that complaining about anything in China has always been a dangerous thing to do, and the philosophical foundation of the culture included an overpowering dose of fatalism.

When in China foreigners must set time-related and result-oriented goals for themselves that relate specifically to the Chinese environment. As ex-teacher in China, Jon Weston, noted: "If you expect results found in Western countries, you will go mad!"

热闹

Renao
(Rue-nah-oh)

"Having a Hot Time

Renao (rue-nah-oh) or *excitement* of a purely benign nature has traditionally been rare in China. The lives of most Chinese were so circumscribed by crowding, laws, rituals and the demands of earning a livelihood that the kind of adult participation sports and personal experience activities that have been available to other people for centuries were virtually non-existent.

Particularly in rural China, where most of the people have always lived, there were few if any practices or games—except for sex—that dealt with the deliberate pursuit of excitement for whatever purpose. Among all Chinese, even behaving in an excited manner was frowned on.

In earlier times, any day-to-day excitement in China was more likely to be violence of some kind—either natural or man-made. For one thing, executions have long been used as public spectacles by Chinese authorities, primarily to serve as warnings but also much in the way that Rome used gladiator fights to satiate the unrequited blood lust of the people.

Traditionally the closest thing to recreational excitement for the average Chinese were annual festivals that were primarily spectator events. On rare occasions traveling acrobatic teams and circus-type performers would visit rural areas.

The success of the women's volleyball team, which won the Olympic gold medal in 1980, initiated a new passion for spectator sports in arenas as well as on television. It now includes soccer, basketball, ping-pong and badminton.

Accidents and visitors from the outside, particularly non-Chinese visitors, have traditionally drawn instant crowds—a phenomenon that still occurs today in provincial areas. In large cities, even minor incidents can draw huge numbers of people in a matter of minutes.

Life in China was not devoid of pure, personal pleasures but what did exist was generally limited to more personal activities such as eating and drinking with family and friends, and sex.

There is apparently nothing the Chinese love more than having meals and drinking sessions with friends that are marked by *renao*, which literally means *heat* and *noise*, and is used to describe a gathering that is warmed by lively conversation and loud laughter.

This kind of pleasurable experience is obviously not unique to China, but it is of special importance because it is one of the few ways the Chinese throughout the ages were permitted to loosen up, let their hair down and enjoy themselves.

But even this opportunity was greatly diminished by the fall of China's last Imperial dynasty in 1912, and the eventual victory of the Chinese Communist Party in 1949. During the first three decades of the Communist regime there was almost no levity in China—no carefree meetings of family or friends with light-hearted banter; no loud, joyous communion of souls and spirits. The country was filled with fear, betrayal, brutality and death on an unbelievable scale.

Now, *renao*-impregnated gatherings at tea houses, restaurants and hotel lounges are one of the most common sights in China.

198

人家

Ren Jia

(Rune Jee-ah)

"Maintaining Family Ties"

In Chinese philosophy all human things begin with the family, which must be established on a firm foundation of "the natural order." This traditionally meant that the father was head of the family; that each member knew his or her position, role, and responsibilities; and that the survival and prosperity of the family took precedence over individual interests.

The importance of the family in the Chinese social system is expressed in the well-known saying, "Bring the family to its proper order and all social relationships will be correctly established."

In Chinese homes children were taught filial piety both directly and indirectly. Those who attended schools were required to study a series of four books on filial piety that included a treatise which had been in use for more than two thousand years.

The family is one of the key hexagrams in China's classic *I Ching* or *Book of Changes*.

Relations between the father, mother and children in a Chinese family were ideally based on affection and respect, and on the recognition and acceptance of the family as an indivisible unit that would survive and prosper if it was functioning properly—and could bring ruin to all of the members if it did not function as intended.

The traditional Chinese family has been described as a combination welfare state and police state. It was organized to be as economically self-sufficient as possible and to police its own members, primarily by the threat of shame, physical punishment and expulsion out into the cold, cruel world.

While extended families and communities acted as collectives or unions in many respects, each family was still an independent entity responsible for its own survival. Rivalry between families (and communities) was therefore intense, greatly limiting cooperation.

Anthropologists say that neither Chinese villages nor urban districts were communities in the Western sense of voluntarily sharing responsibilities, looking out for each other, and cooperating in joint efforts such as street cleaning, or staging social events or recreational activities.

These latter functions, when they existed, were more likely to be carried out by associations involving relatives, birthplace, language and occupation.

The emotional, intellectual and spiritual restraint that had to be exercised by the lower ranking members of a Chinese family systematically resulted in the buildup of friction and infighting. But since life outside of the family was a dangerous no-man's land, discontented members generally had no choice but to swallow their frustrations and get along as well as possible.

All institutions in China, the government on all levels, commercial enterprises of all kinds, and all professional groupings were theoretically patterned after the core social unit of the family. The paramount political leader was ideally seen as and behaved like a father whose actions were based on his love and respect for his "family."

By the same token, the "leader-father" expected total obedience and cooperation from his "children." When they disobeyed or were lax in their duties, it was up to him to punish them.

In the traditional Chinese context, any organization, from the country itself down to the smallest enterprise, will function at its best if it is run as a family unit, because its members will be bonded together by *ren jia* (rune jee-ah) or *family ties*, that transcend individual goals, and will sacrifice themselves for the survival and prosperity of the whole.

Still today the *ren jia* concept is a major factor in every facet of Chinese society, and must be taken into consideration in dealings with the government, private enterprise, and individuals. Government officials are especially susceptible to approving or disapproving business deals on the basis of whether or not there are any advantages to their families.

Company executives and managers still tend to see themselves as "parents" of their employees, and generally fashion their approach to management on the basis of parent-child relationships. Business owners are acutely sensitive to *ren jia* in all of their dealings, particularly in terms of who they employ as managers, in delegating authority and in relations with other companies.

However, family ties are often stronger among overseas Chinese than they are among mainland Chinese. Shortly after taking over the country in 1949 the Chinese Communist Party began a systematic campaign to sever the ties binding families by requiring that large numbers of urban husbands and wives live apart, usually in widely separated areas, on enforced work assignments that lasted for as long as twenty years or more.

This policy was adopted because the leaders of the Chinese Communist Party (CCP) believed that the traditional ties that bound families together would hinder the acceptance of the Communist ideology. Their idea was to eliminate all vestiges of family loyalty and replace it with loyalty to the CCP and the state.

Then during the so-called "Great Leap Forward" in 1958–1960 most of the country's farmers were forced to join communes that operated very much like civilian service corps in which all household responsibilities, from cooking to child-raising, were pooled. Mothers and fathers often saw very little of their children, or their relatives.

Finally, during the 10-year "Cultural Revolution" most of China's urban families were further split, with millions of them being sent to distant rural areas to work as farmers and laborers.

Thus for nearly thirty years, virtually every social and economic program initiated by the CCP was designed to destroy the family as it had existed from the beginning of China's history.

In the meantime, the social and economic challenges faced by overseas Chinese made their traditionally close-knit family ties all the more important to their survival and success.

199

人情

Ren Qing

(Rune Cheeng)

"Appealing to the Heart"

Feudalism in China did not begin to end until the victory of the Chinese Communist Party (CCP) in 1949. From the dawn of Chinese history until that time, ordinary people had no say in government. Without political power, they had no way to defend themselves directly, or demand anything of anybody with official standing.

Among the various indirect ways the people developed to protect themselves and get things done, bribery, in one form or another, was probably the most common and most effective. Behaving in a humble, obsequious manner was another ploy that became entrenched in the culture.

When the CCP took over in 1949 it eliminated some of the feudal customs that had burdened the Chinese since the beginning of their history, but the Party tightened controls over other areas of personal behavior and added numerous limits to the options people had.

The use of bribery to grease the wheels of China's newly communized bureaucracy slowed down for the first few decades, but by the 1970s it was even more rampant than it had been during the heydays of the Imperial dynasties.

In the "brave new world" of Communist China today, practically nothing can be accomplished without bribery or personal connections—for which one often pays dearly in reciprocal favors.

When the Chinese are not in a position to offer a bribe or some special advantage, and yet want something that can be obtained only through a connection, another cultural ploy that is frequently brought into play is the *ren qing* (rune cheeng), or *appeal to the heart*.

Ren qing refers to asking someone for a favor when you are not in a position to reciprocate, so you do so by appealing to the other person's ego, vanity, compassion, sense of responsibility to their fellow man, etc.

Generally speaking, the most effective *ren qing* appeals are those that are aimed at individuals' egos, combined with the fact that petitioners are voluntarily putting themselves in a position that obligates them to return the favor some time in the future.

Many Chinese who are in power positions dispense favors left and right, including when they are unsolicited, in order to build up a bank of favors they can call on later.

In keeping with the Chinese way of having long memories and carrying obligations over from one generation to the next, if you receive a favor from someone and do not return it before they die, surviving members of their family or their descendants have a right to collect from you or from your family.

Foreigners in China frequently find themselves in positions where they are expected to extend favors because they have—or the Chinese assume they have—so much more to offer than the Chinese. If these *ren qing* requests are reasonable and doable, the foreigner, like the Chinese, can build up valuable "reserve" sources of future favors.

200

人情

Ren Qing

(Rune Cheeng)

"Human Feelings First"

One of the most fundamental and crucial differences between the histories of China and most European countries has to do with human feelings and social order, and with man-made laws pertaining to what Westerners, particularly Americans, refer to as "human rights."

In Europe and the United States social and political philosophies evolved in the direction of government by laws designed specifically to protect and preserve human rights within the context of a stable, well-ordered society.

Despite a growing number of contradictions in American and European laws, combined with irrational interpretations that turn many of them into farces, they have served to create some of the most benign and "human" societies seen so far.

In China, on the other hand, social and political philosophies took the direction of guaranteeing social order by suppressing personal freedom and human rights in the interest of the state. Generally speaking, the people of pre-modern China had obligations and duties, but no human rights in the usual Western sense.

Approved conduct in China was not based on immutable principles of good or evil from the viewpoint of religion or the individual, but on what was constructive or destructive to its social and political systems.

While the overriding aspects of the Chinese system were therefore inhuman from the Western viewpoint, its inhumanity was substantially mitigated by the concept of *ren qing* (rune cheeng), or *human feelings*, which was confined and limited but was nevertheless an integral part of the system.

Not having immutable laws to protect them or to guide them (except in their duties to others and to the state), and yet recognizing their individuality—intellectually, emotionally and spiritually—the Chinese made *ren qing* the basis for virtually all decisions and behavior that were not precisely covered by Imperial law—and even these laws were interpreted on the basis of "personal" feelings by those who could get by with it.

Ren qing continues to play a vital role in Chinese behavior, in their private lives as well as in business and the professions. It is almost always the final criterion in their definitions of right and wrong, acceptable or unacceptable, regardless of any law, custom or precedent.

Foreigners dealing with Chinese commonly encounter situations that result in misunderstandings, friction and often ill-will because the Chinese are coming from the viewpoint of *human feelings* in *their* cultural context, and the foreigners are following established patterns of behavior based on laws or policies that do not take *ren qing* into consideration at all or to the extent that it satisfies the expectations of the Chinese.

There is no simple solution to this cross-cultural problem because neither side can quickly or easily shed its cultural skin. The only recourse is to be aware of the different set of values, let your Chinese counterparts know you are aware of them, and work closely and sincerely with them to accommodate the feelings and expectations of both sides.

In addition to Westerners who work with Chinese keeping *ren qing* uppermost in their minds, it also helps to make regular direct references to "human feelings" in discussions and other interactions with employees as well as customers, suppliers and government officials.

人权

Ren Quan
(Rune Chu-enn)

"Inhuman Rights"

Traditional Chinese legal philosophy did not recognize that people had inherent *ren quan* (rune chu-enn) or *human rights.* According to traditional Chinese thinking, people had no rights except what the state gave them, and the rights that the state extended to people could be changed or withdrawn at any time.

Throughout Chinese history, human rights have been a monopoly of the state and have been treated as privileges to be used by the government to reward or punish people on the basis of their behavior.

In theory, this philosophy was not as dreadful as it appears to Westerners. Chinese philosophy presumed that the selflessness and goodwill of government leaders would protect the people from any abuse of power, and that the power of the government would be used only for the benefit of the people.

Reality, however, was quite different. The people of China have traditionally been held in bondage to the state; with very little difference between the Imperial Court system of government, the intervening military dictatorships, and the first decades of the Communist government.

Shortly after the Communists took over China in 1949 the new government classified the Western concept of *ren quan* or *human rights* as "anti-Communist," and prohibited any use of the term or discussion of the concept.

As always, the survival and power of the government took precedence over the rights of the people—a concept that is, of course, common to all societies, but in China the relationship was totally one-sided. All rights were vested in the government.

From the beginning of the Communist regime in China its laws were primarily designed to spell out and emphasize the duties of the people to the state; not to guarantee freedom of thought or action by individuals or by groups.

The Chinese Communist Party did, in fact, pass a few laws and edicts that purported to guarantee a number of personal, individual rights to the people. But about the only one of real note was a 1950 law that prohibited forced marriages.

Generally speaking, the constitution that China's Communist Party leaders created, and the laws they passed pertaining to the rights of people and limiting the actions of the government, were little more than a sop to the rest of the world and to the people of China.

It is the publicly stated policy of the CCP to ignore any law that interferes with its dictatorial powers to run the government and the country as it sees fit, and to imprison or execute anyone who threatens its policies.

However, continued economic progress and the appearance of a large, affluent middle class in China is inevitably eroding the power of the CCP to deny human rights to nearly one quarter of the earth's inhabitants.

At this point in time, however, most Chinese do not clearly understand the meaning of *ren quan*, particularly as the term is used in the United States. In fact, the concept is absolutely meaningless to many people.

Attempts by the American government to force the PRC to accept and follow the American concept of human rights is an admirable undertaking, but it will no doubt be at least one and maybe several generations before the concept becomes a part of the Chinese conscience.

As one Westernized Chinese said: "During more than 4,000 years of history, human rights have never been a part of the Chinese experience. It is not going to happen overnight."

软席

Ruan Xi / Ying Xi
(Ruu-enn She / Eeng She)

"Looking for Loose Seats"

The appearance of the first railway line in China, a short one built near Shanghai in 1876, created a furor. Most Chinese in the area thought it disrupted the harmony of nature and man, and demanded that it be removed. The governor of Shanghai gave in to these demands the following year, bought the line from its investors, and had it destroyed.

By 1896 China still had only 370 miles of railroad track (compared to 182,000 in the U.S.), but after 1900 this new form of transportation expanded rapidly, primarily financed by foreign groups.

Traveling by train in China today is an adventure that is often well worth the inconveniences and various challenges that are encountered, but just as often this applies only to hardy souls who want to experience the country in the raw.

With several million of China's one billion-plus people on the road at any given time, both accommodations and space on trains are almost always premium and sometimes nonexistent. For foreigners, just buying tickets can be enough to discourage an Indiana Jones.

Some ticket outlets have special windows reserved for foreigners. Most do not. Some outlets sell tickets only for future use. Some windows sell tickets only for specific classes. If you do not read or speak Chinese, getting to the right window and buying the right ticket can be a formidable experience.

Generally, it is advisable to have a Chinese connection buy your tickets in advance—and start your own raw experience after you get on the train.

Accommodations on Chinese trains are divided into *ruan xi* (ruu-enn she) or *soft seat* and *ying xi* (eeng she) or *hard seat* categories; along with *ruan wo (soft sleepers)* and *ying wo (hard sleepers)*. A fifth category is called *shan xiao*, which can be translated as *hard stand*—a standing or squatting only ticket.

"Soft" refers to Chinese style first class; hard refers to Chinese style second or third class. The hard seat category, for example, is "third-world third class" by most world standards. Among other things, there is no padding on the seats.

The fifth category of ticketing on Chinese trains (and boats), *sanxi piao*, literally *loose seating*, is designed for people who have little or no money, and authorizes them to stand, sit or squat in open areas between the coaches, and in freight cars that are not completely filled with merchandise.

Dining cars are reserved for passengers with soft seat, soft sleeper and hard sleeper tickets. All others have to fend for themselves, carrying their own food or buying from vendors at station stops. Those with hard sleeper tickets must provide their own hot-water pots for making tea.

Traveling on China's trains gives one a new way of looking at hard and soft—and a new appreciation of some of the problems facing a country with over one billion people.

新人类

Sam Yan Lu

(Sahm Yahn Luu)

"New Human Beings"

Taiwan Chinese differ from their mainland brethren in both subtle and conspicuous ways. In some respects Taiwan Chinese often appear to be more traditional than mainland Chinese. In other ways they are so much more Westernized—or perhaps modernized would be a more appropriate term—that they are a different people.

Earlier exposure to the outside world and its much smaller population and size resulted in sweeping cultural changes in Taiwan while mainland China was still locked in the multiple straightjackets of feudalistic traditionalism and communism.

Younger Taiwanese Chinese began to develop a burning desire for personal fulfillment in the early 1970s. Utilitarian values began to take precedence over cultural values. They rapidly became consumption oriented. The sacrifices their parents had made were ancient history.

By that time it was already being said of Taiwan Chinese born after 1960 that they had no respect for traditions or their elders and were concerned only about making as much money as possible.

Prior to the 1970s, Taiwanese, like their mainland Chinese relatives, were not encouraged to seek personal satisfaction or happiness. They had little if any "inner world" they could enter for solitude or contemplation. They were conditioned to put the family first; to do things for others, not themselves.

Taiwanese architect Carl Shen lived in the United States for eighteen years. When he returned home in the 1980s he said he felt like the sand that ancient Greeks put between temple columns as abrasives. After the sections of the columns were joined they were then rotated until the sand had smoothed the surfaces and resulted in a tight fit. He said he was being ground between American and Chinese cultures but was unable to achieve a smooth fit.

Shen and other Taiwanese describe the post-1960 generations of Taiwanese as *sam yan lu*, which is Cantonese for *new human beings*.

Said one Taiwanese: "Before, children had only ears and no mouths. Now, more and more children in affluent families are 'all mouth'—spoiled brats."

Shen noted one plus factor in favor of the younger generation of Taiwanese. "They are very much aware that age does not necessarily equate with knowledge, wisdom or useful experience."

Shen added: "The piety of this new generation is more associated with the material world than the spiritual. They pray for success and riches, and if they don't get it they curse the gods.

"But, this 'cash game' is terrifying to some. We are grateful for progress, but the pursuit of money has poisoned society. The young have no sense of ethics; no interest in traditional culture. They eat fast, play fast and live for the moment."

Mainland China is on the same slippery road of cultural change as Taiwan. It will take decades longer to transform the more than one billion mainland Chinese into *xin ren lei*, but the change is inevitable. *Xin ren lei* is Mandarin for *new human being*.

204

三纲

San Gang
(Sahn Gahng)

"The Three Bonds"

The core of China's original ethical system is said to have been based on *san gang* (sahn gahng) or *three bonds*—the bonds between ruler and subjects; between fathers and sons; and between husbands and wives, in that order.

In this traditional ethical system the obligations owed by inferiors to superiors were not reciprocal. Inferiors had no inalienable rights. They were expected to sacrifice their individuality and their lives in service to those above them.

Superiors were expected to be virtuous, and to treat their underlings with suitable compassion befitting their superior stature. But as always, the corrupting influence of power and privilege was generally stronger than any virtue, and only the rare policeman, magistrate, mandarin or Court official lived up to these expectations.

Chinese ethics were designed to serve an authoritarian social system in which the population was divided into specific classes. Ethical behavior consisted of paying the proper respect to those above you, and fulfilling precisely defined obligations to your family, to the larger group your family belonged to, and so on up to the emperor.

Thus Chinese ethics were not based on any concept of universal human rights, equality, fairness, majority rule or any of the other democratic principles that developed in Europe and the United States. Chinese ethics were strictly relational, and subject to change with circumstances.

More often than not, people on each level in the social hierarchy took advantage of those below them in whatever way they could. On a personal level, this meant that fathers took selfish advantage of their sons, wives and daughters, and sons took advantage of their younger siblings.

The lower one was in the family hierarchy, the fewer rights and personal options, and the more people one had to obey and serve. The lowest status in the family was that of the youngest female child.

There was a plus side to *san gang*, however. The three bonds infused each family with the power of cohesive cooperation as a unit, adding greatly to its chances of survival and potential for success.

Changes wrought in China by the Communist Party and by the growing influence of Western attitudes of equality and individuality have dramatically altered the role and importance of *san gang*, on a family as well as national level.

The ruler-subject bond has been sundered. In families, wives no longer regard themselves as inferior to their husbands. Neither sons nor daughters docilely obey their fathers. But the underlying foundation of *san gang* is not dead. The bonds binding Chinese families are still strong and still contribute to the stability and strength of Chinese society.

三铁

San Tie

(Sahn Tee-eh)

"The Three Irons"

The ultimate dream of the Chinese Communist Party (CCP) was to totally eliminate all of the ills of capitalism, competition, commercialism, and excess consumption by creating a Socialist state which provided cradle-to-grave welfare for the masses, and kept all political and financial power in the hands of the Communist Party.

Mao Zedung, the first chairman of the CCP, and his colleagues were determined to forcibly transform China into this Socialist "paradise" in just a few years by exterminating all hard-core dissidents and literally brain-washing the rest of the country—eliminating all other beliefs and practices, and then physically and mentally programming the people to accept and follow the philosophy and policies of Mao and the Communist Party.

The economic foundation of this Socialist paradise was to be based on *san tie* (sahn tee-eh) or the *three irons*—lifetime employment, guaranteed wages and guaranteed positions for managers.

In the earlier stages of consolidating the Communist regime in China—from 1949 to the mid-1970s—the CCP was able to partly implement all of the *three irons*, but at a horrible cost to the people and the country.

At various times during this 25-year period up to 20 million people were incarcerated on prison farms and in prison factories, and more than 100 million were forcibly assigned to jobs in distant cities and regions of the country, away from their families.

Following the death of Mao Zedung in 1976 and the disaster brought on by his grand finale, the so-called Cultural Revolution, CCP leaders began disowning the philosophy and policies that had nearly destroyed the country. They began cautiously introducing free-market principles into the economy.

By the mid-1980s, the drive for economic success had resulted in the government backpedaling on the *three iron* guarantees, and increasingly using its dictatorial powers to force people away from guaranteed employment, wages and positions.

This new change was another shock to China's workforce, particularly those employed in state-owned enterprises. Their fear of unemployment brought on work slowdowns, threats of strikes, the murder of managers, and a growing number of suicides.

Once again, the CCP had painted itself into a corner from which there was no easy or quick escape. Resistance by the workers became so fierce that the government had to back off from its new policy of "smashing the three irons."

But over the next decade, as the economy improved and both employment opportunities and income rose dramatically, *san tie* became less of a national issue and more of a local and individual concern.

Most of China's workforce is still under the protection of the *three irons* but neither the government nor workers are chained to them.

三信危机

San Xin Weiji
(Sahn Sheen Way-e-jee)

"Three Crises in Faith"

By the early 1980s China's economy was on the verge of collapse. The traditional Confucian moral values that had stabilized and sustained the country for millennia had virtually disappeared, and the Chinese Communist Party publicly recognized that it had failed to convert the country into a Communist-Socialist paradise.

This failure was subsumed under the heading of *San Xin Weiji* (sahn sheen way-e-jee) or *Three Crises in Faith*—that is, "no faith in socialism, no faith in Marxism or Maoism, and no faith in the CCP leadership."

Acknowledging this failure, Deng Xiaoping, the last of the Long March leaders to assume the mantle of "emperor," began introducing carefully selected capitalistic elements into the economy, including the segment made up of the nationwide gulag system of prison farms and prison factories.

During the disastrous Great Leap Forward and the famine of 1959–1961, the CCP had arrested hundreds of thousands of people as a preventive measure to protect itself, sending most of them to prison farms. One such farm, the Qinghe, had 100,000 inmates, according to Hongda (Harry) Wu who was an inmate there during the latter part of this period.

Wu said that during this time, rations for prisoners at Qinghe consisted of two corn buns a day, and that inmates were reduced to eating insects, rodents, snakes, tree bark, roots and grass. He added that the living space allotted to each inmate in the farm's dormitories was only 60 centimeters wide.

Now, Deng's new policy resulted in the prison farms and prison factories being given more leeway in their treatment of prisoners, and in encouraging the facilities to transform themselves into fully commercial enterprises with special emphasis on exports.

Efforts at thought control and political conversion were also reduced dramatically, and in some enterprises suspended altogether. Profits began taking precedence over reform ideology. This new government swing was epitomized by Deng Xiaoping's famous announcement that "To get rich is glorious!"

Hundreds of thousands of newly released "Forced-Job Placement" (FJP) workers transformed themselves into *getihu* or *household* entrepreneurs who were permitted to operate on their own or to employ up to seven people.

These reforms were incompatible with Deng's Four Cardinal Principles, creating new tensions and turmoil. As usual, conflicting messages from the CCP contributed significantly to growing demands for more democracy and other political reforms.

Finally, students from Beijing University and other schools began gathering in Tiananmen Square. Initially these gatherings were small but they soon grew into a major outcry for democracy, resulting in the now infamous massacre in 1989.

By the early 1990s the Party line of the government had moved even further away from the earlier rigid Communist-Socialist policies of Mao Zedung and Deng Xiaoping himself in order to accommodate more and more capitalistic elements and allow the CCP to maintain the facade of its legitimacy.

While the "reforms" initiated by the CCP as a result of the *San Xin Weiji* resulted in almost miraculous improvements in China's economy, the "three crises" themselves did not disappear. The reforms and their results served only to reinforce the widespread dislike of socialism, Maoism and the CCP leadership.

商人

Shangren

(Shahng-rune)

"Making of a Businessperson"

In Imperial China merchants were generally regarded as unethical and immoral because the nature of their calling required them to take advantage of other people—their labor as well as their needs.

Because it was believed that people who engaged in business could not live by the principles of Confucian morality, they were officially ranked near the bottom of the social classes. In addition, the Imperial government enforced a variety of licensing requirements and taxation schemes in an effort to prevent them from becoming rich and powerful—first because it was believed that accumulating riches was wrong, and second because anyone with wealth could become a political threat.

During the first two millennia of China's recorded history there were no legal codes protecting businessmen, no banks, no commonly available and reliable currency; in fact, none of the services needed to support large-scale businesses.

Despite these disadvantages, however, a wealthy and powerful merchant class rose during the long and illustrious Chou Dynasty, which began in 1030 B.C. and lasted for nearly eight hundred years.

Some hundred years later, during the early decades of the even more famous Han Dynasty (206 B.C.–A.D. 220) the Imperial Court prohibited private enterprise altogether, ending nearly a thousand years of fairly free economic growth.

As Imperial power declined during the 17th and 18th centuries, aggressive Chinese businesspeople once again began doing exactly what the Imperial Court had long feared. They became rich and powerful (and their successors eventually helped to bring an end to China's last Imperial dynasty in 1912).

But during the 18th and 19th centuries there was no substantial effort by these early Chinese entrepreneurs to build large-scale national companies because there was neither the motivation nor the necessary managerial experience.

Natural talent in any area outside of the studies sanctified for entry into government service was still not encouraged by the government or the social system in general. Exceptional ability and ambitions were regarded as dangerous.

The economic strength of early China was based on the existence of hundreds of thousands of self-employed craftsmen and small businesses tied together by wholesalers and a vast network of village and town markets that were served by an equally large number of river boats, barges and coastal ships—all functioning with very little government interference.

However, because of the arbitrary nature of the government and no solid foundation for the protection of property and other assets, businesspeople kept most of their profits in cash or other valuables. Corruption among government officials was widespread on all levels, making it even more precarious for commercial enterprises.

All of these things, combined with China's Confucian-oriented social system, made it impossible for the country to develop into an industrial power.

Then in 1949 along came the Communists who tried to do the Imperial dynasties one better by outlawing virtually all forms of private property as well as private enterprise. Businesspeople became the lackeys of Communist bureaucrats.

But when Communism failed to deliver any kind of paradise, private enterprise became the catchall slogan for reinventing China. Among other things, the government made it legal for individual families to become entrepreneurs, admitting once and for all that without the energy, diligence and willing work of the people no amount of government planning could rebuild the country.

In today's China to be a *shangren* (shahng-rune) or *businessperson* is an honorable calling, and for the first time in the history of the country, most people would rather be in business than in government.

Despite the aura of modernization that surrounds typical Chinese businesspeople today, however, they are still Chinese in most of the ways that count. They still reflect varying degrees of personalism and paternalism, feel insecure and threatened, and are constantly on the defensive because from one day to the next they do not know what the government is going to do.

Business management in China and among overseas Chinese continues to be based on a mixture of traditional cultural factors. Companies are seen as, and more or less operated as, social organizations.

Rather than conduct their businesses on the basis of product, price and market research, the Chinese still depend primarily on personal networks to provide them with stable sources of raw materials, power, market information and sales outlets.

Generally, Chinese managers do not manage by giving direct, verbal orders to their subordinates. They are more likely to "hint" at what they want, rather than to command. Reasonableness takes precedence over reason.

Where personal interactions are concerned, the Chinese have been culturally conditioned to approach problems indirectly. They are not taught or trained to communicate openly and directly.

Instead, they are taught to "feel" the thoughts and wishes of others. In inferior-superior situations this brings a great deal of pressure to bear on subordinates to "guess" what superiors want and to try to please them.

As one veteran expatriate businessperson says, "The Chinese teach and manage more by example than they do by direct orders or explicit instructions. Workers expect to find out what is going on by a process of gradual osmosis."

The stability of a Chinese company is primarily based on the traditional Confucian-oriented vertical relationships between people, a high degree of paternalism, and trust founded on mutual obligations and reciprocity.

Lines of authority in Chinese companies—as well as in government agencies—are seldom clear-cut, and in many enterprises, particularly those still managed by their founders, very little if any authority is given to middle and lower level managers.

Because of this cultural factor, most lower and middle level managers prefer not to make decisions on their own, and habitually resort to *qing shi* or *requesting instructions* from higher-ups.

In government enterprises and state-run companies, this system also contributes to the tendency for bureaucrats to automatically say no to things that come from below them, and yes to anything that comes down from above.

It is therefore a major challenge for most Western businesspeople to deal effectively with their Chinese counterparts. The problems of cross-cultural communication, differing values and goals, plus differences in morality, require extraordinary perseverance and adaptability.

In their more candid moments, some Chinese businesspeople will readily confess that they are opportunists to the core, take every advantage they can, and do whatever is necessary to succeed. They add that the only rule in playing the game of business is not to get caught.

Another factor is that many Chinese still expect foreigners to have a "tribute mentality" that calls for them to go more than halfway in working out joint ventures or other business relationships with China.

升

Shen

(Shune)

"The Spirit of Things"

One cannot escape the spirits in China. They are everywhere. But this should not be surprising, since several billion Chinese have lived and died in the past five thousand years, and all of those who have passed on continue to exist in their own special form and place.

The ancient Chinese belief that only the body dies and the soul lives on was the basis for China's ancestor worship. Much of the traditional attachment of the Chinese for the birthplace of their ancestors came from the belief that 70 percent of the spirit of the deceased resided in the tomb (and the remaining 30 percent resided in the ancestral tablet kept in the home).

Spiritualism is alive and well throughout most of China despite the efforts of the Chinese Communist Party from 1949 to the 1980s to eradicate the practice.

To use the words of noted Chinese-American author Bette Bao Lord from her haunting book *Legacies: A Chinese Mosaic*, the Chinese "cannot outrun the shadow of their ancestors."

In addition to the *shen* (shune) or *spirits* of ordinary people the Chinese pantheon is crowded with the spirits of god-like saints who range from the

Eight Immortals to the Five Hundred Saints, plus numerous other dieties of the land, sea and air.

The Eight Immortals, seven men and one woman, were originally historical characters who became saints by virtue of their good deeds and sacrifices. After their deaths they gradually became invested with supernatural powers, and have long since been used as symbols of longevity and immortality.

In addition to its role in divination and geomancy, spiritualism continues to play a significant role in the everyday affairs of many Chinese. In some rural areas, when children die and when adults who had not married die, it is still the custom to find the spirits of unmarried dead of the proper sex and right age and ceremoniously unite the spirits in wedlock.

In some instances this practice is carried out by the parents of a newly deceased child without the knowledge or cooperation of the other set of parents whose child died earlier, causing a great uproar if and when the deception is discovered.

Today long-time urbanites in China are less attentive to the spirits of their departed ones, but many still carry on the traditions of revering their ancestors.

There are also still occasional incidents of older people suddenly running across traffic lanes in front of speeding cars, hoping the cars will "cut off" the line of demon spirits thought to be following them.

Most Chinese are still especially concerned about spirits during funerals, particularly evil spirits, and many funeral ceremonies include bands that play very loud music to frighten devils away.

It was believed throughout much of China's history that the spirits of one's ancestors continued to be interested in and exercised influence over the living. And in earlier times, the spirits of the dead were regularly consulted before decisions of state were made.

Now, people are more likely to consult with astrologers to guide them in their behavior. A significant proportion of the population of China refers to astrological advice for virtually every major decision they make, and some follow astrological signs for mundane decisions as well, including such things as the best days for getting haircuts or making trips.

See **Zhanxingxue**.

209

圣

Sheng
(Shung)

"Romance of the Sages"

In most countries any list of famous historical figures is generally weighted in favor of military heroes and political leaders—and often they are one and the same; the military victor in war becoming the political chieftain in peace.

In fact, throughout the history of most of the world it seems that military power and the ability to use it effectively has been the defining factor in the growth and character of the larger societies.

China, however, is a conspicuous exception to this rule. The Middle Kingdom has had its wars and military heroes, but far fewer than most other countries in terms of the length of its history, its size and its population.

Unlike the Romans, Arabs, Spaniards, British, French, German and other empire builders of the past, the Chinese were not obsessed with spreading their influence beyond their borders or conquering the world. They looked inward instead of outward, and were satisfied with what they had.

The Chinese prized intellectual accomplishments and refined behavior more than they did physical prowess and aggressive action.

One of the key reasons for this fundamental difference in the character of the Chinese was religion. The so-called religious beliefs of the Chinese—animism, Daoism, Buddhism and Confucianism—did not foster aggressive behavior as did Islam, Christianity and other proselytizing religions.

The beliefs of the Chinese simply did not include the concept of converting the rest of the world to their way of thinking. Instead they emphasized self-discipline and peaceful harmony on a cosmic level but only in their own society.

Generally speaking, the Chinese were motivated and inspired by *sheng* (shung) or *sages*, not by religious or military zealots. Rather than being culturally conditioned to conquer and assimilate—or destroy—they were programmed to protect and preserve their own system, and to ignore everybody else.

Again generally speaking, the Chinese made knowledge and wisdom the foundation for both political power and wealth. The most revered figures in Chinese society were its wisest men—the *sheng*.

Among the best-known of the hundreds of scholar-sages produced by China: King Wen (?-1066 B.C.); his son, the Duke of Chou (1066-771 B.C.); Ze Dao or Lao Tzu (604-550 B.C.); Confucius (551-479 B.C.); Tzu Chung (399-320 B.C.); Mencius (371-289 B.C.); Mo Tzu (479-438 B.C.).

The role of the sage has greatly diminished in Chinese life today, with the desire for money and power taking precedence over knowledge and wisdom.

But in both politics and business, successful people who are perceived as sages are able to yield extraordinary moral influence that goes well beyond their direct authority.

And for the first time in China's history, businessmen-sages are usurping the power of the country's political leaders and government bureaucrats.

Unlike most of the cultural traits of the Chinese their respect for wise men is not limited to their own sages. They are equally respectful of all *sheng*, regardless of their racial or national origin—a factor that both foreign governments and corporations could use to advantage in selecting people to represent their interests in China.

210

Sheng
(Shung)

"Getting What You Deserve"

In times past, bending with the wind and being patient was an inseparable part of the character and day-to-day practices of the Chinese people. They saw things in terms of generations rather than decades or years, and were upset when anyone tried to hurry them.

Attempting to make changes or start and finish things quickly by working faster and longer hours was basically an alien concept. Their approach was based more on feelings and timing, rather than time itself.

Workers coming together in the morning on a job did not necessarily start working at a set time. They would sit around, smoke, drink tea, talk, and finally drift into work.

Doing things in harmony with both internal and external influences took precedence over doing them rapidly. In Chinese philosophy, the journey was just as important as the destination, and human feelings always came first.

A few Chinese are now as ambitious and as aggressive as typical Westerners, but the overwhelming majority remain true to their traditional character, preferring slow, incremental progress over conspicuous leaps forward.

The Chinese believe that if they move forward slowly, cautiously and in harmony with nature they may tap into the power of *sheng* (shung), which is a coming together of internal as well as external forces in a harmonious upward movement.

Sheng means *advancement* and may apply to any area of life, from personal relationships to business and politics. The key, in whatever situation, is that you work diligently in a self-disciplined manner, never wavering from your goals.

When you are in a *sheng* mode everything goes your way. People support and cooperate with you, contributing to a steady rise in your position. The biggest danger when you are on an upswing is to begin taking things and people for granted, which may result in you losing your focus and attempting to take shortcuts.

To ensure that *sheng* continues to work for you, say the Chinese, it is vital that you continuously reevaluate your own motives and methods, and that you remain modest and methodical in your efforts.

One of the key factors in getting the most out of a *sheng* period is to be flexible, willing, and able to adapt your methods and goals to harmonize with circumstances that you cannot control.

The Chinese have recognized and institutionalized the *sheng* factor in their overall philosophy and day-to-day psychology for more than three thousand years, in attitudes and actions that have long since been an integral part of their culture.

Foreigners who encounter the slow, deliberate pace of the Chinese in business, politics or any other relationship should keep in mind that there is an age-old logic behind their behavior, and that it is not always intended to impede or frustrate.

To the Chinese it is also the right way to do things.

211

肾亏

Shen Kui

(Shune Kwee)

"When Sex Appeal Fails"

In a Western setting China's huge population, traditionally collectivist society, and deep-seated male chauvinism would surely have resulted in a wide range of culturally induced psychological ailments that are familiar to Westerners.

But such is not the case in China because the Chinese have also traditionally been conditioned to internalize their psychological problems, to not talk about them, and to go to extreme lengths to disguise them and keep them hidden from view.

Western psychologists say that when the Chinese do suffer from psychiatric problems they do so in a strictly Chinese way—responding to anxiety, tension, depression, and a widespread lack of understanding comfort and acceptance, in ways that appear to be unique to China.

International psychopathological studies have identified three unusual syndromes that have existed in China for centuries and have been treated with herbal medicines rather than psychiatry.

One of these disorders is a sudden panic attack among men who believe their penises are shrinking. Another of the syndromes is acute fear of cold, especially as it applies to food in the *yin-yang* sense of hot and cold. The third syndrome, known as *shen kui* (shune kwee) is apparently the most common of the three.

Shen kui means *kidney weakness*, and refers to a combination of ailments that include sexual indifference, inability to sleep, and chronic fatigue.

Given China's philosophical and political history of forcing people, especially women, to suppress and ignore their sexuality, it would not be surprising to learn that *shen kui* was endemic to China, as some suggest.

The same psychological studies of China that identified the above three syndromes also indicated that the traditional Chinese fixation on food and on herbal medicines were manifestations of the syndromes.

After the Communists took over China in 1949 one of the key parts of the government's central planning was to assign husbands and wives to jobs in widely separated areas of the country, forcing them to live apart during much of their working lives.

This, combined with strongly enforced sanctions against premarital and extramarital sexual relations, contributed enormously to sexual frustration as a national malady, and to the spread of *shen kui*.

In the 1980s and 1990s Chinese health authorities reported that hospitals and clinics were overflowing with young women who were so sexually frustrated that they could no longer function, and that suicides among them were common.

Although there are far fewer constraints on sexual liaisons in China today, single foreigners who live in China are likely to come down with *shen kui* because intimate fraternization between Chinese and foreigners is still frowned on.

The ubiquitous television set, with its steady diet of sexually oriented advertisements and films is now the most significant influence in the sexual attitudes and behavior of the Chinese.

212

识

Shi

(She)

"Knowledge Is Power"

In the 5th century B.C. the military strategist Sun Tzu wrote: "If you know yourself and your enemy, in a hundred battles you will never fear the result. When you know yourself and not your enemy, your chances of winning or losing are equal. If you know neither yourself nor your enemy, you are certain to be in danger in every battle."

Even before the time of Sun Tzu the Chinese knew the value of *shi* (she) or *knowledge*, and had a long history of academic and scientific endeavor. During the Hsia Dynasty, from 2000 B.C. to 1600 B.C., for example, there were many technological developments that made the building and sustaining of large cities practical.

During the following Shang Dynasty (1550 B.C.–1030 B.C.), wheeled vehicles and a sophisticated system of writing became common, and irrigation for agricultural purposes was perfected.

National civil service examinations for government service, based on in-depth knowledge of Confucianism, Daoism and the works of other philosophers, were established during the famous Han Dynasty (206 B.C.–A.D. 220).

But this same dynasty also saw the implementation of a taboo against private enterprise—a chokehold on the people of China that has not yet been totally removed.

Because they recognized that *shi* is power, all Chinese leaders from the Han Dynasty until around the end of the Ming Dynasty in 1644 attempted to maintain a monopoly on education. The system made it virtually impossible for anyone except male children of upper class families to become educated.

It was not until the fall of the last Imperial dynasty in 1911 that people were more or less free to pursue any kind of education they could afford. But this freedom was to be shortlived, ending in 1949 when the Communists came to power. They turned education into a pure government monopoly that was designed specifically to inculcate the people with Communist ideology and to serve the interests of the state.

Education virtually stopped throughout China from 1966 to 1976, when Mao Zedung attempted to eradicate all vestiges of traditional thought; to wipe the minds of the Chinese clean in order to fill them with pure communism.

This great "Cultural Revolution" destroyed the lives of millions of people, adding enormously to the handicaps already inflicted upon China by the Communist ideology, and setting the country back several decades.

China's Communist Party still today tries to control the knowledge of the people, but it is gradually losing its grip on both their minds and purses. The more knowledgeable the people become, the more powerful they become.

Like their overseas relatives, most mainland Chinese are now obsessed with gaining *shi* and the freedom that it brings.

213

师

Shi

(She)

"Getting It Together"

Neither Luke Skywalker nor Obiwan Kenobe in *Star Wars* were the discoverers or the first users of "the force." That honor goes back several thousand years to priests, philosophers and military strategists in China—and to a variety of people in other ancient civilizations as well.

Early Chinese, keen observers of the world about them, took their first lessons from nature, noting the force of gravity and mass on everything from celestial bodies to water.

It was equally obvious to the Chinese that mass and the "gravitational pull" of combined effort changed the tides of human affairs in the same way that they moved and controlled planets and rivers.

This power of mass and combined effort was labeled *shi* (she) or "collective force" by the Chinese, and was integrated into the *Book of Changes* as the seventh of the sixty-four factors relating to human affairs.

Shi is not a self-creating, self-acting force in human affairs. It must be organized and channeled in the direction desired to achieve specific goals, and as usual, the first requirement for the successful harnessing of *shi* is self-discipline.

The second element in the successful use of "the force" is emptying your mind of extraneous thoughts, opening your mind to the flow of all cosmic forces, and focusing on your goals. Just as Luke Skywalker in *Star Wars* had to learn not to struggle against overpowering forces of opposition, the user of *shi* must learn how and when to slip into the energy stream of internal and external *shi* and go with the flow.

Taking advantage of the power of *shi* also requires knowledge of, and compatibility with, the prevailing social, political and economic forces, and the ability to communicate clearly on all levels with family, friends, associates and the public.

To get the most out of *shi* and achieve extraordinary goals one must also have leadership ability and a powerful vision that attracts and holds people to you, and be able to maintain this vision in the face of obstacles and setbacks.

Shi in itself is neutral. It can be used just as easily and as effectively by immoral people for evil purposes—witness the villains of mankind, from the greatest, such as Hitler, to small warlords and neighborhood gang leaders.

Foreigners are able to tap into the flow of *shi* in China, but it presents some special challenges. You must first establish personal credibility and long-term commitment to your goals, and then bring in able people who understand and appreciate your vision and want to share it with you.

At the same time you must also create and then continuously nurture a network of contacts in business and government circles that can help you overcome the various problems that are inherent in the Chinese political and economic systems.

师傅

Shifu

(She-foo)

"Addressing People"

Addressing people in China has always been tremendously complicated by the fact that there are so few surnames in all of Han China. It is said that some 60 percent of all Han Chinese have only 19 family names, and an estimated 10 percent (or over 100 million) of all Han Chinese are named Zhang (pronounced *Chang*).

This problem was further exacerbated by generations of cultural conditioning in a precise etiquette that covered physical behavior, manner of speaking and vocabulary, and was based on the social class, occupation or rank, sex, and age of the individual.

The system the Chinese devised to reduce the problems caused by this lack of variety in names and contending with all of the social and hierarchical gradations was to use titles instead of names in numerous formal as well as informal situations.

During the long ages of the Imperial dynasties, sanctions for not using or misusing an established form of address was a very serious matter, and could result in the death penalty if the person addressed was high-ranking.

After the Communists took over China in 1949 they tried to eliminate all class differentiations by encouraging the people to address each other as *tongzhi* or "comrade," regardless of their rank—or in the case of Party seniors, prefixing "comrade" to their Party title. Interestingly enough, many Chinese were offended when foreigners used this term to them or in reference to other Chinese. They regarded it as condescending.

During the Cultural Revolution (1966–1976) it also became politically correct for China's huge number of workers to refer to each other as *shifu* (she-foo) or *master worker*.

Shifu was an old word that was originally used as an honorific title for people who were, in fact, masters of some trade, from carpentry to pottery making.

But under the Communist regime the term came to be used to address anyone who worked with his hands, including clerks and waiters—and it is still used in this manner. It may be used by itself or following the individual's family name, as in Li Shifu. Since the re-opening of China to the outside world, the use of Mr., Mrs. and Miss have once again become acceptable, but it is still proper and expected for people with official titles (president, director, general manager, deputy manager, minister, and so on) to be addressed by their title or their last name plus title: Manager Zhang (Zhang Jingli); General Manager Zhang (Zhang Zong Jingli).

Among themselves, the Chinese use many kinship terms, such as older brother, older sister, sister- or brother-in-law, cousin, aunt, uncle, grandma and grandpa.

Just as common is the adding of the age-related titles *lao* and *xiao* to people's family names. *Xiao* is used when addressing someone younger than yourself; *lao* when the person is older.

Generally speaking, foreigners should not use these age-related titles unless they are actually conversing in Chinese. There is too much danger of making a mistake or otherwise offending someone.

215

噬嗑

Shi Ke

(She Ho)

"Making Things Better"

It is one of the first axioms of life in China that evil will occur whenever and wherever there is the slightest opportunity. The Chinese understand that evil is more powerful than good, and that the creation and preservation of good requires unending positive action, while evil occurs of its own accord in the absence of deliberate good.

It is also recognized in China that evil, like everything else, is cyclical, and waxes or wanes with the presence or absence of people with evil hearts because when they are present they spread evil, and if their evil is not stopped it becomes a plague that eventually sickens the whole society.

China's early sages, in their attempts to prepare people for dealing with the presence of evil in human affairs, counseled the continuing importance of *shi ke* (she ho), or *reform*, in personal, business and political matters.

Since most evil in human affairs comes in the form of misbehavior by individuals, the sages advise that one should constantly be on the alert for evil-doers, and that once identified such individuals should be quickly subjected to *shi ke*.

This philosophy, carried to its extreme, has been very conspicuous in China's recent history. After the victory of the Communists in 1949 they immediately set about to "reform" all of the millions of people in China who opposed them.

This massive *shi ke* effort included unending reorientation programs, enforced self-reflection and public confessions of wrong thoughts and wrong-doing, continuously spying on people, torture, long prison terms, and executions by the tens of thousands.

China's notorious Cultural Revolution that began in 1966 and did not formally end until 1976 was another national orgy of *shi ke*—an unbelievably cruel attempt to "reform" several hundred million people by re-education, public ridicule, torture, imprisonment, enforced hard labor, and, again, mass executions.

The early sages who made *shi ke* a key part of the overall philosophy of the Chinese did not mean for it to be used in an inhuman way. They counseled firmness but gentleness, and made a special point of noting that those attempting to bring about "reform" on a personal or social level should at all times require the same improvements in their own character and conduct.

In its original context, *shi ke* was designed to be as much of a self-improvement process as a method for eliminating unfair and immoral obstacles by reforming individuals and systems that had gone awry.

This ancient sage advice applies equally well to foreigners doing business in China. Personal problems with employees should be confronted without delay, and clear, decisive *shi ke* actions taken to eliminate the factors causing the problems.

Shi Shen

(She Shune)

"Gentlemen of China"

One of my strongest images of China is that of an older man, with a long white beard, who represents the embodiment of Chinese civilization, with all of its artistic and scientific accomplishments and all of the human wisdom it has accumulated over more than five thousand years.

This image is that of a *shi shen* (she shune), the perfect Chinese *gentleman*—a man who has come to terms with his passions and has them under control; a man who has absorbed the wisdom of the ancient masters and is at ease with the cosmos; a man who thinks the right thoughts and says and does the right things regardless of the turmoil and dangers around him.

Of course, not many Chinese have achieved this practically divine state, but the fact that millions of them over the centuries have strived mightily to reach this goal, and many came close to it, has had and still has an impact on characteristic Chinese attitudes and behavior.

It is also a fact, of course, that many of the men I have seen were more representative of the average old men of China than the eternal *shi shen* in my imagination—just old men, taking their ease, quietly living out the last years of lives that were probably mean and painful; and owing their benign expressions not to wisdom and tranquil thoughts but to a-passivity and acceptance beaten into them by a system that was fundamentally anti-human.

Still, becoming a *shi shen* has always been the goal of most Chinese men, no matter how poor they might be or how limited their formal education. It is something built into the culture; an impulse that expresses itself subconsciously in a style of behavior that conforms to the cultural expectations for all men of senior age.

The old Chinese philosophy of filial piety and respect for the aged in general has traditionally added to the image of the *shi shen*, and although this is changing it is still a significant factor, regardless of the social or economic level of the individual concerned.

Confucius advised that one of the best ways for people to improve their own character and add to their wisdom was to associate with superior people, meaning people made wise by long and varied experiences.

Outsiders involved with China should take this advice to heart, cultivating the friendship of one or more carefully selected older Chinese men and women and seeking their counsel as mentors. The benefits that can accrue from this kind of relationship can be enormous.

Studying and emulating the character of the true *shi shen* is also a door into Chinese society, and a major benefit in dealing with the Chinese in commercial and political enterprises. Older Chinese are natural mentors, and respond readily to such approaches.

书法

Shufa
(Shuu-fah)

"Learning to Be Chinese"

The making of a Chinese is one of the world's most demanding and impressive of all cultural accomplishments. Chineseness is not something that you can just grow up with and absorb naturally.

You can become *part* Chinese that way, but you cannot metamorphose into a fully complete Chinese that easily. You must deliberately engage in a tremendous amount of hard work over a period of many years to become a complete *Chinese* Chinese.

This hard work includes learning how to read and draw some five thousand ideograms—the *han zi* or so-called *Chinese characters*—with which the various Chinese languages are written.

Learning to read and draw *han zi* is one of the key things that imprints the final Chinese touch to the one billion-plus people who call themselves Chinese.

Then there are different levels of *Chineseness* among those who are programmed on the ideograms. The person who learns five thousand ideograms (there are over one hundred thousand) is arguably more Chinese than the person who learns only two thousand.

The finishing touch provided by the graphic representations of Chinese culture is *shufa* (shuu-fah) or *calligraphy*, the art of drawing the characters as "art"—one of the most distinguishing features of Chinese culture and one that has been admired in the West since the first Western contact with China.

Shufa, and the Chinese writing system in general, has also been a major source of the exotic, mysterious image that China has had in the minds of outsiders. The ideograms, in all of their written forms, are complex, and being totally incomprehensible to the illiterate, have traditionally served as a great wall, helping to obscure China from prying eyes.

Calligrapher Chan Him, at the University of Hong Kong's School of Professional and Continuing Education, says there is no mystery to Chinese calligraphy. But his explanation does little to remove the mystery.

"Calligraphy is not a symmetrical arrangement of conventional shapes. It is like the coordinated movements of a skillfully composed dance; movements that include impulse, momentum, momentary poise and the interplay of active forces combined to form a balanced whole," he said.

Chan added that the ability to do calligraphy well depends on the writer's skill and imagination in giving interesting shapes to the strokes and to compose beautiful structures without retouching or shading, with well-balanced spaces between the strokes.

Chan makes it sound easy, but it requires years of practice and some considerable artistic talent to achieve even modest ability in the art.

Taking a genuine interest in *shufa* and practicing the art on any level is one of the most effective and satisfying ways to develop personal relationships in China, and become an insider.

顺

Shun

(Shune)

"Gentleness Versus Force"

Among the many dichotomies in Chinese culture, none is more conspicuous than the contrast between the passivity and violence and between the gentleness and brutal savagery that has been so much a part of China's history.

For a culture based on order and harmony it is startling and frightening to contemplate the volume and variety of the violence that has been an integral part of Chinese life over the ages.

But once you look at the nature of traditional life in China the reasons *why* the culture could have generated and condoned so much violent and cruel behavior becomes readily understandable.

The order and harmony for which Chinese rulers strived was not based on the consent or cooperation of the people. It was imposed upon them by force of arms. Further, this order and harmony was structured in such a way that it deprived the people of free will in virtually every other area of their lives as well.

The teachings of the great sages were routinely ignored when they conflicted with the compulsive determination of the rulers of China to protect and preserve their privileged positions, which they did by denying virtually all rights to the people.

Over the millennia the great mass of Chinese had no civil rights that were guaranteed by impartial law. They were subject to officials who acted as judge and jury and had the power of life and death over them.

Dissent and infractions were severely punished; often by execution for only minor offenses. People who were arrested on suspicion or because they displeased an official were routinely tortured in some of the cruelest and most inhumane ways imaginable.

The absolute power of the rulers of China corrupted them absolutely.

The *shun* (shune) or *gentleness* for which the Chinese are famous was first of all a philosophical concept that was translated into practical reality only in a narrow, limited sense. Rather than being a universal characteristic, it was confined to specific times and categories of people.

As a philosophy, *shun* epitomized the ideal existence—one that proceeded like a leaf floating down a slow-moving, meandering stream. The leaf encountered no resistance and never had to exert any effort to stay on course because its course and that of the smooth-flowing water was the same.

But in the real world of daily Chinese life, *shun* was reserved for family, friends and guests. Strangers were either competitors or enemies or both, and any unnecessary involvement with people not in one's group not only made life more complicated but could endanger it as well.

Things have changed in present-day China, but not that much. The lives of people are still primarily controlled by their family obligations and group relations. Avoiding unnecessary contacts and involvements is still important in staying out of harm's way.

Visitors to China quickly discern the contrast between the *shun* of the personal friends they make and the mean and callous behavior that is common among bureaucrats, law enforcement agencies, and strangers in general.

This is one aspect of China that is not likely to change in the foreseeable future.

Shun
(Shune)

"The Soft Way to Success"

Just as the longest journey begins with a single step and a desert with a grain of sand, the Chinese have learned that there are many things in the affairs of society that cannot be hurried; things that can be accomplished only in slow, often imperceptible increments.

And no one knows better than the Chinese that the cumulative effect of a tiny movement or force can eventually destroy any obstacle or create something entirely new—an understanding that has played a key role in shaping their national character.

Because China's traditional culture made rapid changes and developments practically impossible, even in one's personal manners, the use of this slow, incremental force, known as *shun* (shune) or *penetrating influence*, became characteristic of the Chinese way of doing things—and is one of the elements covered in the *Book of Changes*.

Shun incorporates the nuance of *gentleness* in reference to the fact that its influence is not obvious or immediately disrupting; that it is more like a light breeze.

On the insidious side, knowledge of the power of *shun* was used in the so-called "Chinese Water Torture" in which a single drop of water was made to fall repeatedly onto a victim's forehead. *Shun* was also frequently used to get revenge on someone in such a way and over a long period of time that they were never aware of the source of their misfortune.

Generally speaking, however, *shun* was the approach used by the Chinese in all of their day-to-day personal and public affairs, especially in business and politics, in which they commonly faced powerful opposition.

There are exceptions, of course, especially among overseas Chinese and entrepreneurial types in mainland China, but most Chinese, particularly businesspeople, still today follow the age-old philosophy of *shun*.

One of the secrets for the successful use of *shun*—besides great patience—is to have a clear vision of your goals and to make a long-term commitment to achieving them. The sages add that it is often necessary to ally one's self with other, more powerful, individuals or groups to eventually achieve success.

As always, the sages say it is essential for the person using *shun* to behave in harmony with the times and environment, aligning his or her goals with the sentiments and desires of others in order to multiply his or her strength.

While modern-day political leaders of China have frequently ignored the lessons of *shun* and resorted not only to abrupt but violent actions, it is easy to recognize the "penetrating influence" syndrome in the behavior of most Chinese, even though most of it is not defined as such.

Being aware of the *shun* syndrome might help outsiders develop a bit more patience in their dealings with the Chinese.

讼

Song
(Sung)

"Knowing When to Run"

In the hierarchy of things that impact on human affairs, the Chinese list *song* (sung) or *conflict* as number six (after creativity, response, overcoming difficulties in starting things, inexperience, and waiting for things to settle down).

Song refers to any of the multitude of things that create conflict in people's lives, whether the cause is internal or external. But the primary emphasis is on opposition from others who disagree with your philosophy or are in economic or political competition with you, when you have no way of responding directly with any hope of success.

When you are first confronted with this kind of opposition, the sages advise that you avoid any kind of conflict because trying to argue with or fight with the opposition directly would only make things worse.

In the second stage of such opposition, the advice from the sages is the same—keep your pride under control, back off and wait for the circumstances to change. The third level of advice is the same—forget about material success and status because they are meaningless if they bring disaster down on you.

As long as the forces of opposition arrayed against you remain strong and you are uncertain about the righteousness of your own goals, the sages counsel continued restraint. If you are sure of yourself, however, the advice is to bring in a respected third party to act as a mediator.

But no matter how "right" you are, the sages add, if you engage in conflict it doesn't make any difference if you are successful; you will eventually lose because those whom you defeat will come back again and again to oppose you.

In other words, conflict, unless you have been attacked and it is for the purpose of defense, will not eliminate opposition arising out of profound differences of opinion, such as often occurs in cases of politics and religion.

Of course, China's Communist regime has made a mockery of this ancient wisdom in recent decades, breaking every guideline ever set down, with all of the disastrous results prophesied by the sages. During the tense days of the student occupation of Tiananmen Square in May and June 1989 many people urged the students to defer to the insurmountable power of *song* and leave the square. But they stayed and government tanks eventually prevailed. Some Chinese predict that the democracy movement itself creates the *song* that will overcome communism in China.

As far as most individual Chinese are concerned the ancient wisdom incorporated in the *song* concept applies across the board to personal affairs, to commercial relations, including consumer reaction to new products, and to affairs between nations.

Most present-day Chinese will normally go to extremes to avoid open conflict with anyone about anything, preferring to settle differences by compromise and, if the problem persists, by bringing in an outside party to make a binding decision.

Foreigners dealing with China often have to restrain their propensity to resort to direct confrontation in order to achieve their goals.

221

损

Sun

(Suun)

"Living with Bad Times"

High achievers like Americans, Europeans, Japanese and Koreans could benefit greatly from one of the oldest lessons of the Chinese way—namely how to accept and live with disappointment and failure without losing one's sense of balance and purpose.

More than most people, the Chinese have been forced time and again to cope with natural and man-made disasters, and very early in their history they developed philosophical and practical guidelines for reacting to changes and events they could not control.

This phase of human life is specifically addressed in the concept of *sun* (suun) or "decline," which refers to the periods of time when things get bad and there is absolutely no way they can be quickly and completely reversed. One stage of decline that all people must go through is aging.

The first philosophical lesson in coping with *sun* is that since these times cannot be avoided, the best recourse is to accept them and change both your expectations and behavior to conform to the existing circumstances.

This reaction, say the sages, requires that people get their emotions under control, reduce the intensity of their feelings about the situation, simplify their lifestyles, and be fully satisfied with life in the slow lane.

Sun cycles include personal relationships, and in this area as well the sages advise that people stay calm, not try to force heavy emotional burdens on others when they are not receptive, and spend the time improving their own personal situation.

The sages add that the simpler your lifestyle the less you have to lose during periods of decline; and the more focused you can be on things that really matter—remaining true to your family and friends, and strengthening your own character.

One of the primary keys to getting through *sun* periods without losing your balance or damaging your character, add the sages, is to continuously reevaluate your own character and behavior and maintain a high level of dignity.

By using periods of decline to clarify your own goals in life, to refine your own character, and to polish your skills in dealing with other people, the sages promise that good fortune will follow bad times.

In business matters, the worst *sun* periods may result in substantial losses of all kinds, but the sages optimistically predict that if you persevere, remain diligent, honest and forthright, and do the best that you can for clients or customers, the cycle will come around, they will remember your efforts on their behalf and will help you recover.

The concept of *sun* has probably been the most efficacious in encouraging the Chinese to develop an abiding sense of dignity as they age—a cultural attitude and behavior that Westerners would do well to emulate.

泰

Tai

(Tie)

"The Ducks Are Lined Up"

Tai (tie) or *prospering*, is one of the most encouraging and optimistic symbols in the Chinese cosmology. It represents a time and an environment when the lines of communication between individuals and the world at large are totally open, and people are receptive to new ideas, new plans.

It is an especially good time for doing things in support of others because whatever acts of goodwill are performed will be returned in the form of good fortune, and new contacts that are made in the process will contribute to success.

Tai does not refer only to a time that is auspicious for an individual. It applies equally to the whole of society, and refers to a time of great advances and renewal in business and politics. It is said to be especially propitious for making new laws and reforming old outmoded institutions.

How long a period of *tai* lasts and how effectively individuals can take advantage of it depends upon the quality of their character and their goals.

China's wise men counsel that it is essential for people wishing to ride the wave of "prospering" to be in harmony with both themselves and the cosmos. If this condition exists, they say, your most innocuous actions will result in extraordinary success.

A period of *tai* does not mean that one doesn't have to work for success or that there are no snags along the way. The sages say it is essential that you challenge yourself by taking on difficult tasks, that you treat people fairly, and that you avoid getting involved with people who are short-sighted, selfish and seeking only to gain some advantage for themselves and their particular group.

It is also vital, they say, that you remain humble and modest in your expectations, and that you show as much concern for the welfare of your co-workers as you do for yourself. As always, the good times are bound to end, and anyone who fails to recognize the beginning of a downturn and keeps barreling ahead will inevitably suffer.

When the first signs of a political or business downturn appear, the Chinese counsel that you slow up and solidify both your political and business relationships. By doing so, they add, you can continue to prosper even during bad times.

Tai also influences one's personal health, and can be a time of eliminating bad habits and developing new ones, which will contribute to your physical as well as your spiritual well-being.

The Chinese are just as diligent about watching for signs heralding the approach of a period of *tai* as they are for signals that a period of prospering is ending. Foreigners wanting to do business with the Chinese can get a very good sense of the mood of their potential partners by learning if they are in or out of a cycle of *tai*.

太极拳

Tai Ji Quan

(Tie Jee Chuu-ahn)

"Using the Great Fist"

First-time visitors to China and to such overseas Chinese areas as Singapore and Taiwan who are out and about in the early morning are invariably exposed to a feature of Chinese life that is both strange and intriguing.

Alongside of streets and byways, in parks, on overhead walkways and on the tops of buildings, they see small to large groups of Chinese men and women of all ages, but especially older Chinese, engaging in a continuous series of slow-motion movements that are akin to a stylized form of dancing.

The "dancers," mostly dressed in loose, light-colored clothing, are silent and composed. There is no music. Some of the performers act in unison, executing the same movements. Others perform solo, oblivious to those around them.

The actors on these impromptu stages are ordinary people performing *tai ji quan* (tie jee chuu-ahn), one of the oldest and often most controversial forms of calisthenics on earth (and better known in the West as *tai chi chuan*, its Cantonese pronunciation).

Some authorities say that *tai ji quan*, which literally means *Great Ultimate Fist*, was originated during the Tang Dynasty well over a thousand years ago. Others say it dates from the later Song Dynasty, and was created by a master named Zhang Shan Feng.

Legend has it that the art is based on the movements of a snake attacked by a large meat-eating bird. The snake bobbed and weaved, avoiding each attack. (When the bird finally tired and became careless, the snake nailed it with a lighting strike—and it was this aspect of the skill that was later developed into a powerful martial art).

Affluent upper-class Chinese were engaging in calisthenics for health purposes as early as 300 B.C. Physical education was taught in schools, and a wide variety of sports, including swimming, a type of soccer, boxing, high-jumping and stone-throwing, were popular both as pastimes and for their health benefits.

In a commentary entitled *On Heaven* written in the 3rd century B.C., Xun Zi noted: "If you take good care of yourself and exercise regularly, Heaven cannot make you ill. If you don't do so, Heaven cannot make you healthy."

One version of present-day *tai ji quan* consists of thirteen movements, eight with the arms and five with the legs. The movements are performed slowly with the body in perfect balance in order to stimulate all of the nerves and muscles. The movements of the arms are circular, with the body gradually turned to eight points on the compass, denoting the cyclical cosmic changes and evolution of nature.

The exercise has traditionally been used as a preventive and remedy for headaches, digestive problems and rheumatism. In the 1970s and 1980s it became popular as a treatment for cancer and other major afflictions, with some documented results that verge on the miraculous.

Tai ji quan was primarily a personal endeavor until the 1980s when the Chinese government gave it semi-official standing by funding research to determine the scientific basis for its benefits. A large-scale *tai ji quan* academy in Beijing sends its graduates all over the country to start up branch schools.

There are no formalities involved in joining a group practicing *tai ji quan*. Anyone, including foreigners, may participate.

224

谈恋爱

Tanlian Ai
(Tahn-lee-enn Aye)

"Love Talk"

One of the most humane and admirable changes to have occurred in China in more than four thousand years of history was initiated by Chinese Communist Party Chairman Mao Zedung—a man who also was to become guilty of inflicting as much if not more suffering, death and destruction upon the Chinese people than any in a long line of cruel despots.

Prior to the victory of the CCP over the Nationalist armies of Chiang Kai-shek in 1949, women in China were generally treated like bonded servants or slaves. They had no choice in the work they did or in marriage, and were totally subject to the will of their fathers, brothers, husbands, fathers-in-law, mothers-in-law and finally their sons.

Marriages were arranged, and with the rare exceptions of a few women at the top of society, brides generally never met their husbands until they were delivered to their homes. There was no escape for the new wives, no matter how mismatched the couples might be or how much the women might suffer at the hands of unsympathetic husbands or cruel mothers-in-law.

The horrible custom of foot-binding was typical of the pain and hardships that Chinese women were forced to endure since ancient times. See **Guo-Jiao**.

Oddly enough, Mao Zedung was one of China's earliest feminists. In the 1920s, long before he rose to the top of the Chinese Communist Party, he came out strongly against arranged marriages and the vestiges of foot-binding that persisted even though it had been outlawed years before by the last Imperial dynasty.

When Mao emerged as the Communist "emperor" of China in 1949 one of the first laws that he had passed was designed to emancipate women and bring them into the mainstream of Chinese life.

Prior to this, relations between Chinese men and women were generally loveless, there was very little personal, intimate conversation—there was virtually no such thing as *tanlian ai* (tahn-lee-enn aye) or *love talk*.

Mao's new law prohibiting arranged marriages did not result in instant emancipation for Chinese women or the rapid development of romantic dialogue between them and boyfriends. There was still too much political chaos and fighting in the country, and such skills do not automatically materialize over a short period of time.

But by the 1960s romance was in the air in China. *Tanlian ai*, a totally new language as far as the Chinese were concerned, became the most interesting subject to most high school and college students.

Then the disruptive Cultural Revolution erupted in 1966 and for the next 10 years personal relationships among the young ranged from difficult to impossible. When this madness ended, the young people of China took up where they had left off.

By the 1980s young people in China were enjoying one of the pleasures of humankind that had been denied their parents and ancestors throughout most of the early history of the country. However, intermediaries or "go-betweens" remain the most prevalent means for young couples to meet and become engaged.

One of the few remaining obstacles to courting and carrying on love affairs in China today is teachers who constantly advise their students to spend their time and energy studying, not engaging in *tanlian ai*.

225

淘气

Taoqi
(Tow-chee)

"Indulging the Young"

In earlier times children in China were a mixed blessing. It was essential that each generational couple produce a son, because only males could carry on the traditional rituals of ancestor worship.

It was also vital to the survival of families that they produce several children, especially males for their labor as well as to carry on the family line, because the infant mortality rate was high—in some periods and areas as much as forty percent.

Having mostly female or all female children was therefore a major threat to the spiritual as well as the economic well-being of a Chinese family—a tragic situation that resulted in the widespread killing of female infants during the periodic famines that struck portions of the country.

As late as the mid-20th century, marriage in China was not associated with love, but with the need to produce children to continue the family. Marriages were arranged, and whether or not any affection developed between couples was coincidental.

In this cultural and economic environment life was certainly prized but it was not sacred in the Western sense. Children were desired and valued for their role in sustaining the family, but love did not play a specific family role in Chinese society.

As in most cultures around the world that were not based on love, there was also an element of extreme callousness and cruelty in Chinese society that often resulted in men, women and children being abused and slaughtered as if they were unfeeling things.

This is not to suggest that the Chinese were not capable of love and that all children were treated as objects. In the traditional Chinese environment children were conditioned physically and emotionally from birth to be docile and obedient. But most parents treated their young children with great kindness, and during their childhood years were especially tolerant of their behavior.

There was a special phrase, *taoqi* (tow-chee), which was used to describe the kind of naughtiness that was allowed to children.

Taoqi did not come into its own, however, until the Chinese Communist Party in 1980 decreed that families that were members of the main Han group of Chinese could have only one child—a draconian measure aimed at capping the burgeoning population.

This decree, combined with other fundamental social and economic changes that brought a degree of personal freedom and affluence never before experienced by the general population, resulted in Chinese families becoming even more indulgent toward their young children.

One of the most frequently heard complaints in China today is that parents are too lenient with their children, that *taoqi* has been broadened to the point that young kids, especially sons, are treated like little "emperors" and allowed to get by with any kind of behavior.

226

天安门广场

Tiananmen Guangchang

(Tee-enn-ahn-mun Gwahng-chahng)

"Tiananmen Square"

Tiananmen Square, in the heart of Beijing, is a holy place in China—not because of any religious connotations but because it has been the site of so much of the country's history.

Red Square in Moscow, St. Peter's Square in Rome, Times Square in New York, and similar places around the world are renowned for their role in history, but none is as charged with historical significance as Beijing's *Tiananmen*, or *Heavenly Gate*, Square, and none are as imposing in size.

When Mao Zedung declared the founding of the People's Republic of China from the top of Tiananmen Gate on October 1, 1949, the square was a dusty unpaved lot with little more to distinguish it than the gate and the walls surrounding the Forbidden Palace.

In the fall of 1958 Mao Zedung set out to change that and make the square a symbol of the power and future of the new Central Kingdom. He had a huge workforce of "volunteers" assembled, and between November 1958 and September 1959 they razed the walls around the Forbidden City, expanded the area of the square to 100 acres, paved it, built the gigantic Great Hall of the People (actually it consists of 17 halls, one for each of the country's 17 provinces), the imposing twin museums of history, and several other structures.

One grand image of Tiananmen Square that was broadcast to the people of the world resulted from mass meetings held there in the 1960s and 1970s, when it was packed with young people who were dressed alike and looked alike and were waving a sea of Little Red Books in adulation of Mao Zedung.

But Tiananmen Square gained a different kind of international fame in late May and early June of 1989 as the place where China's Communist Party government used tanks and other heavy weapons to squash yet another effort by the people to achieve some degree of democratic freedom.

This was far from the first time that Tiananmen Square was turned into a killing field by despotic government leaders determined to stay in power.

Almost exactly 70 years earlier, on May 4, 1919, another auspicious day in the history of modern China, the first large-scale demonstration by Chinese students against an inept, corrupt and oppressive government took place in Tiananmen Square, and was brutally squashed.

Students in other cities around China took up the protest, giving rise to the so-called "May Fourth Movement," in reference to growing resistance against the squabbling Nationalist government forces and warlords and continuing usurpation of China's sovereignty by foreign powers.

Some of this revolutionary activity was inspired by a number of famous foreigners who visited and lectured in China during this period of turmoil. Among them: philosophers John Dewey and Bertrand Russell, Albert Einstein, and Rabindranath Tagore, the great Indian scholar who had recently won the Nobel Prize for poetry.

In 1918, prior to the May 4, 1919 incident, there were an estimated 7,000 offices and branches of foreign firms in China, with huge Japanese, American and European corporations virtually controlling a number of key industrial segments of the economy.

After the first student demonstration in 1919, student uprisings became regular incidents, with larger ones occurring in 1925 (when many were killed by British troops), in 1926 (when dozens were killed by warlords), and again in 1935, 1948, 1972, 1976, and 1978.

The spring of 1976 demonstration, prompted by the death of Premier Zhou Enlai, involved dozens of thousands of students demanding an end to the dictatorship form of government, and laws guaranteeing intellectual and political freedom.

Resistance by students and intellectuals continued to build during the 1980s. The Tiananmen Square Incident of 1989 was presaged by a large-scale student demonstration in Shanghai in December 1986. Students marched to government buildings and handed out slips of paper calling for an end to the abusive, autocratic rule of the CCP and the establishment of a democratic form of government. Despite a ban, wall posters (*zi bao*) once again appeared on walls and buildings in the city.

Beijing University was a cauldron of political activity during the same period, and both discontent and agitation continued to rise throughout 1988 and the winter and spring of 1989.

By early spring, thousands of students gathered regularly in Tiananmen Square to hear the latest news and be a part of the growing mass movement. Posters, forbidden in 1980, began appearing again on Democracy Wall and elsewhere in Beijing.

On April 15, Hu Yaobang, a more moderate leader, died suddenly of a heart attack. The government quickly banned all demonstrations in

Tiananmen Square and set April 24 as the official day for marking Yu's death. But on April 17 huge numbers of students from universities all over Beijing defied the ban and gathered in the square.

This direct defiance of the government began approaching an explosion point. On May 18 a large group of students began a sit-in near the Great Hall of the People, literally throwing the gauntlet in the face of the CCP leaders.

On May 20 the CCP leadership declared martial law and ordered military units stationed in the outskirts of the city to clear the students out of the square. But students and ordinary Beijing citizens prevented the troops from reaching Tiananmen Square by putting up roadblocks and themselves physically barring passage through the streets.

The students repeatedly asked Premier Li Peng to come out and talk to them. He refused. On the 24th, students across the city began boycotting their classes. Some 3,000 students began a lay-in hunger strike in the square, turning it into a tent city.

Squads of students on motorcycles, calling themselves the "Flying Tigers" after the famous squadron of American pilots who helped China battle the Japanese in the late 1930s and early 1940s, began carrying messages throughout the city to keep other student groups informed about what was going on in Tiananmen Square.

The students began demanding that both Premier Li Peng and supreme leader Deng Xiaoping resign. Li invited several student leaders to a meeting, but it went badly for everyone.

Fully realizing the threat to the CCP, Deng and other hardline leaders secretly ordered regional military commanders to send detachments of veteran troops to the city. These troops initiated a blitzkrieg tank attack on the student fortifications on the night of June 3, routing them and sweeping inito Tiananmen Square.

The tanks blocked all exits to the square. It seemed that the demonstration was over. Many of the students began gathering up their things and leaving the square. Then the troops began firing randomly at the huge crowd, killing and wounding hundreds if not thousads. The tanks advanced into the square, crushing the makeshift structures the students had put up, including a huge "Liberty Statue," and running over some of the students.

Thousands of students and citizens began fighting back, attacking the troops with their hands and whatever weapons they could find. Some attacked tanks with hastily prepared Molotov cocktails. Dozens of the troops were beaten and burned to death.

The big difference this time was not only the massive size of the demonstration, and the involvement of thousands of Beijing residents, it was also the presence of dozens of foreign correspondents in Beijing, and massive foreign television coverage that brought the drama and the carnage into the homes of millions of people around the world.

After the battle ended the army removed all evidence of the demonstration from the square (it took days to scrub up all of the blood), and for months thereafter it was off-limits to visitors.

Thousands of the student demonstrators were quickly arrested and imprisoned. It is estimated that hundreds were executed. A few of the student leaders escaped to the U.S. and elsewhere. "Emperor" Deng justified the carnage by labeling the protesters "the dregs of society."

For several days after the uprising, the Public Security Bureau in Beijing received a flood of phone calls, accusing people who had not yet been arrested of having taken part in the rebellion or being in sympathy with the students.

Many of these callers made accusations against people because they were envious of them or had some kind of grudge against them. Most of those who were turned in were totally innocent, yet they were subjected to PSB interrogation, including mental and physical torture, for weeks to months.

See **Minzhu Qiang, Zi Bao**.

铁饭碗

Tie Fan Wan
(Tee-eh Fahn Wahn)

"Breaking the Iron Rice Bowl"

The Chinese Communist Party (CCP) was able to take over China in 1949 because it was supported by a majority of the country's farmers, who made up more than 80 percent of the huge population. Farmers provided a virtually unlimited supply of recruits for the "People's Liberation Army," and the food necessary to sustain the army and the Communist cadre.

Mao Zedung, the most capable and farsighted of the early Communist revolutionaries, won the loyalty and cooperation of a significant percentage of the peasants by giving them permission to drive out or kill the nation's several hundred thousand landlords, and take the land for themselves.

Mao's efforts to win over the non-farm working class were far less successful (over a 25-year period he had over 20 million of them put in prison and several hundred thousand executed). In addition to a mass program to convert the country's millions of urban residents to loyal Party workers through force, he introduced the concept of the *tie fan wan* (tee-eh fahn wahn) or the *iron rice bowl*.

The connotation of the *tie fan wan* was that all non-farm adults who were capable of working would be guaranteed a job, which would ensure that they would always be able to feed themselves and their families—the first concern of the Chinese throughout the history of the country.

But like so many of the CCP's other programs, the iron rice bowl was doomed to failure because the whole Communist system was flawed. But it prevailed until the early part of the 1980s, when market forces began to bring it under extreme pressure.

The first cracks in the *tie fan wan* were large enough to see by the mid-1980s, and by 1995 it was leaking like a sieve. Jobs were no longer guaranteed, and growing numbers of people were being fired by their over-employed and generally inefficient companies.

Tie fan wan remains among China's most important "code words," however, and lifetime employment with cradle-to-grave welfare is not likely to disappear from the country. But the government no longer stands behind it, and for the most part it is up to individual companies and organizations as to whether or not they have an iron rice bowl system.

Tie fan wan is frequently used in China today in reference to people who are fired from their state-run jobs, or quit on their own, start their own companies and within a few years become millionaires.

These brave souls, who elicit envy as well as jealousy, are among the most exciting people in China. All of them are helping to rid the country of the rigidity and irrationalism of the past. Hopefully they will one day be recognized as the true heroes of the 20th century.

228

提法

Tifa

(Tee-fah)

"Speaking in Tongues"

Over the centuries the Chinese developed specific *tifa* (tee-fah) or *ways of saying things* that became institutionalized, ritualized and sanctified. If these things were not said in the precise, ritualized way, they were not culturally or socially correct, and were considered un-Chinese, immoral and sometimes an offense punishable by death.

When the Chinese Communist Party took over China in 1949 it began using its own *tifa*, and quickly created a "second language" made up of a carefully devised Chinese Communist Party jargon that in George Orwell terms would be called "Communist-speak."

Communist-speak became the "official" language of China, while ordinary Chinese was referred to as the "unofficial" language.

Communist *tifa* was designed to change and then control the way people thought, and in the process condition them to conform absolutely to Communist thinking and behavior.

Virtually every aspect of existence in China—economic, political and social—was prescribed in Communist-speak terms that had their own meanings.

One of the most conspicuous and sinister facets of Communist *tifa* terms was their vagueness; the fact that they could be interpreted in a number of different ways, depending on the goals of the speakers.

This vagueness became one of the most common and deadliest techniques the CCP used to entrap people, and either destroy them or make their lives and the lives of their families miserable.

People were forced to hide the truth and tell lies, to deny reality—not only in their own lives but in the actions of the government. They never knew where they stood. There was no way they could discern what might be used against them.

What was politically correct one day to one interrogator could be different the next day or to the next interrogator. The smallest thing could lead to devastating consequences.

An innocuous remark like "I'm not sure" could be enough to destroy people's lives and bring untold suffering to their families for decades afterward. A mother giving gifts to her own children was construed as a plot by her to influence them and turn them away from the correct Communist Party path.

During the first years of the Cultural Revolution (1966–1976), the pressure on young children to criticize their parents was diabolically cruel and effective. Red Guards and Party agents would lead children on, bribe them, and get them to say what they wanted to hear, resulting in their parents' lives and their own lives becoming nightmares.

Children of mothers or fathers accused of being Rightists were made to suffer in a variety of ways, from verbal abuse and beatings to being refused entry into schools. Once accused, people of all ages were treated like dangerous criminals.

Husbands were turned against wives; wives were turned against husbands; and children were turned against their parents. The over-riding concern of everyone was to avoid becoming a suspect, which meant a black mark in their personal file that would never be erased and would have a permanently negative effect on their lives.

Coping with this mad world meant dealing with the irrationalities and insidious traps of Communist-speak, which had its own vocabulary, grammar and style. To be politically correct, adjectives, describing the Party or Mao, for example, had to be used in a precise, set order.

Communist-speak, the new *tifa* of China, is still the official government language. It still requires extraordinary insight into the inner workings of the CCP mind and a profound knowledge of the real meaning of its special code words to interpret it correctly.

See **Youhuan Yishi**.

229

体用

Ti-Yong

(Tee-Yung)

"Chinese Wisdom / Western Technology"

When China's last dynasty started breaking up in the late 1800s—primarily because of increasing political and military pressure from England, Japan, Germany and other foreign countries—many Chinese intellectuals began to fear that the country would not survive.

The disastrous war with Japan in 1894-1895, in which the power of the newly Westernized Japanese army and navy proved to be overwhelming, convinced this handful of Chinese that despite its enormous size, huge population and accumulated stock of cultural wisdom, China was no match for the industrialized nations of the world and, like Japan, would have to adopt some of the ways of the West.

These intellectuals began formulating a philosophical base for this proposed new relationship with the West—a relationship which they labeled *ti-yong* (tee yung). *Ti* was defined as *essence* and *yong* as *practicality*, and together meant *Chinese wisdom combined with Western technology*.

Zhang Zhidong, a veteran Confucian scholar-official who had served as the governor-general of Human and Hubei Provinces, became the most aggressive and forthright of this group. He began urging provincial and national authorities to follow the example set by Japan—to import Western engineers, technicians, teachers and professionals in other fields to come to China and help modernize its economy and military establishment.

Zhang pointed out that this approach would allow China to maintain its culture while taking advantage of the practical knowledge and experience of the West to transform China into a modern power.

After China was forced to sign a humiliating treaty with Japan following the end of the Sino-Japanese war in 1895, many more of China's Confucian scholars began calling for the modernization of the country.

Among this growing group, *ti-yong* became a rationale for breaking with the past and seeking help from abroad. It also became a slogan that appealed to international-minded Chinese who had traveled and studied in Japan and in the West. [Another slogan that was popularized during this period was *Zi Qiang* (jee chee-ahng), or *Strengthen One's Self*—referring to the country as well as individuals.]

By this time, however, the weak and jaded Imperial Court had lost control of events, and in late 1911 collapsed altogether. A new republican form of government under the famed Dr. Sun Yatsen ostensibly took over the affairs of the government in early 1912, but political and social chaos reigned.

For the next four decades China was wracked by bloody battles between regional warlords; between Communist forces led by Mao Zedung, Zhou Enlai and others, and Nationalist forces led by Chiang Kai-shek; and finally by all-out war with Japan.

During this period the concept of *ti-yong* sputtered forward in a disjointed, disorganized manner. The warlords and both the Nationalists and Communists imported Western weapons and military experts. Mining, manufacturing and railway transport came under the domination of foreign interests, and made substantial progress.

The Communist victory in 1949 brought China into the Soviet bloc, and for the next decade the new People's Republic of China depended upon the Soviet Union for a limited amount of technology and technical help, and like the Soviet Union, soon initiated a covert campaign to steal technology from the West.

Following the Chinese Communists' break with the Soviet Union in 1957 and the cracking of its doors to the West in the 1970s, the concept of *ti-yong* came into its own, resulting in a flood of Western technology and Western experts into China.

Ti-yong is no longer used as a slogan but it continues to be one of the key factors in China's foreign policy.

230

同仁

Tong Ren

(Tung Rune)

"Holding People Together"

When America's General Douglas MacArthur was serving as the Supreme Commander of the Allied Powers that occupied Japan following the end of World War II in 1945, he commented that Japanese adults were like 12-year-olds.

A well-known Japanese scholar agreed with MacArthur, saying that the Japanese did indeed have two personalities—one an emotional 12-year-old who had an inferiority complex, and the other a mature philosopher who felt intellectually and spiritually superior to everyone else. He added that it was necessary to appease both of these personalities when dealing with the Japanese.

The Chinese, like the Japanese, also have split personalities, but there is a significant difference between the two faces of the Japanese and the two faces of the Chinese. The Chinese have traditionally felt superior on both their emotional and intellectual sides—with good reason.

Chinese feelings of cultural and spiritual superiority were a natural outgrowth of both the age and the accomplishments of their civilization, particularly their understanding of human nature and their development of social structures that had sustained their civilization for more than four thousand years.

The heart of the Chinese social system was expressed in the term *tong ren* (tung rune), which may be translated as *community* or literally as the *same people*, and implies absolute dedication to a broad range of attitudes and behavior.

In the traditional Chinese community everyone knows his or her place, first within the family and then within society at large, and everyone fulfills his or her obligations to protect and sustain the community.

But the heart of the traditional Chinese community was not just protecting and preserving the community for its own sake, although that was the ultimate outcome. The primary purpose of the *tong ren* was to fulfill the fundamental need that each member had for companionship; for regular intimate, positive, harmonious interaction with family, friends and others.

It is axiomatic that no matter how wealthy or powerful a person may become in a lifetime of success, when all is said and done the thing that means the most is the love, respect and companionship of family and friends.

China's philosophers understood this basic need, and made it the foundation of their society. Rather than seek independence and self-sufficiency, they sought interdependence and mutual benefit.

In the Chinese context, the more people labored on behalf of their families and communities, the purer their character and the more they were to be honored.

The *tong ren* concept in Chinese society has been under direct assault since the opening of the country to capitalism and free enterprise, but enough of it remains to be clearly visible and to play a significant role in the society and economy.

Foreigners seeking to establish joint ventures or other types of close relationships with Chinese businesspeople and government officials should pursue their goals by first establishing a *tong ren* bond with their Chinese counterparts.

This means basing the relationship on common needs and interests, making a special effort to accommodate any selfish or personal agendas within the context of the project, and maintaining an open and sincere community spirit.

头衔

Touxian

(Toe-uu-she-enn)

"The Importance of Titles"

Social systems based on authoritarianism and the division of people into vertically structured classes invariably emphasize rank and the use of titles. Military organizations are, of course, perfect examples of this practice.

Traditional Chinese society fit this pattern precisely. Not only were the people divided into classes. Those in charge, on every level, had titles. In addition, the clothing that people wore was usually enough to distinguish their class and rank.

But in the case of China the use of *touxian* (toe-uu-she-enn) or *titles* went much further than what was generally common for despotic, vertically structured societies—for a reason that appears to be unique in world history.

According to historical records, the Chinese trace their beginnings to 100 families, with 100 family names. Whether or not this is absolutely true, the point is well taken. The small number of founding families multiplied and multiplied, while the family names remained the same throughout the generations.

Until very recent times there were still only about 440 surnames in China to account for several hundred million families. Today there are an estimated 5,662 family names in the country, but the population is now over one billion.

The original 100 family names still account for some 90 percent of China's one billion-plus people. Only 19 surnames account for around 60 percent of the population. Ten percent of the population, over 100 million Chinese, are named Zhang (Chang). There are also millions of Wangs and Lis.

Early in Chinese history kinship, work-related and official government titles became institutionalized as vital parts of the hierarchical and ethical systems, while also serving the purpose of helping to overcome the mass duplication of names.

In a large enterprise or government agency, where there are generally dozens to several hundred Zhangs, having both the name and title is often not enough to successfully identify an individual. The person's department, section, and sometimes their home address as well, are usually necessary.

Generally, it is not advisable for foreigners to use the common kinship titles when addressing Chinese—unless they speak the language and are fully aware of all the subtle nuances that go with the titles. It is easy to make embarrassing mistakes, and in many cases the familiar terms suggest an intimacy that is inappropriate.

The safest, and perfectly acceptable, bet for non-Chinese speakers is to use the English titles Mr., Mrs. and Miss in all social situations. In business, government and professional affairs, however, it pays to learn the titles of the ranking individuals and to use them.

Here are some of the more common professional titles:

Director of a government bureau	*juzhang* (joo-chahng)
Director of a government department	*sizhang* (suh-chahng)
Director of a sub-department	*chuzhang* (choo-chahng)

Section head	*kezhang* (kuh-chahng)
Minister	*buzhang* (boo-chahng)
Vice minister	*fu buzhang* (foo boo-chahng)
Governor	*shengzhang* (shung-chahng)
Mayor	*shizhang* (shur-chahng)
Director (factory manager)	*changzhang* (chang-chahng)
General manager	*zong jingli* (chong jing-lee)
Manager	*jingli* (jing-lee)
Chief engineer	*zong gongchengshi*
	(chong gong-chung-shur)
Engineer	*gongchengshi* (gong-chung-shur)
Shop foreman	*chejian zhuren* (chuh-jee-enn chu-ren)
Department head (university)	*xi shuren* (she shu-ren)
Professor	*jiaoshou* (jee-ow-sho-uo)
Teacher	*laoshi* (lah-oh-she)
Medical doctor	*yisheng* (eee-shung)

232

屯

Tun

(Toon)

"Watch That First Step"

Revenge has traditionally been a common feature in Chinese life, as it always is in societies based on the will and whims of people rather than universal human rights. One of the ways the Chinese sought revenge against those who had wronged or shamed them was to curse them with the oblique expression, "May you live in interesting times."

Of course, by "interesting times" the Chinese meant times of great change, which usually result in chaos, when few if any remain unscathed.

Chinese history had numerous long eras of peace and relative prosperity, but it also had more than its share of interesting times, as is evidenced by the appearance of *tun* (toon) or *difficult beginnings* as the third element in the sixty-four hexagrams of the famous *I Ching* or *Book of Changes*.

Tun recognizes the virtually universal presence of obstacles and confusion at the beginning of any new enterprise, or any change in the fundamental values and behavior of people in a society as well as on an individual basis, and serves as a cautionary warning sign.

The *tun* hexagram reveals a seemingly pessimistic image of mankind and the world at large, emphasizing that in virtually all new enterprises and times of change the beginning stage as well as every stage thereafter is especially subject to serious mistakes that can spell failure.

Chaos suggested by *tun* is not limited to external factors over which the individual may or may not have any control. It also applies to internal factors—to one's own state of mind and activities.

But within the concept of *tun* is the implicit promise that if one weathers the storm of confusion and chaos the turmoil will eventually end, the sun will shine and those who persevered will enjoy good fortune.

Tun related advice begins with the need for the individual to remain calm and centered, and to allow external changes over which he or she has no control to run their course, while concentrating on keeping his or her own thoughts and behavior organized to surmount the problems at hand.

Tun also emphasizes the importance of keeping a low profile during the early stage of new endeavors, and conducting your affairs in such a manner that you attract like-minded people. But warning, at the same time, that to accept outside help too early, when progress is simply impossible, will result in future obligations that will cause problems.

Other *tun* warnings and advice apply to problems encountered once you are beyond the first stage of "difficult beginnings." These include avoiding egotism and vanity, enlisting the aid of wiser people, using strong connections, not overextending yourself, and not losing your perspective—all solid advice that is appropriate at all times for all people.

233

托儿

Tuor

(Tuu-orr)

"Hoodwinking Customers"

In the 1950s and 1960s the Chinese Communist Party initiated nationwide programs designed to put all adult Chinese to work in cooperatives and communes.

As part of these programs, hundreds of thousands of *tuoryuan* (tuu-orr-yuu-enn) or *kindergarten* child-care centers were established throughout the country to house and raise the country's children.

The CCP's attempts to communize the entire country failed miserably, but the various programs did put most women to work and broke up so many families that the child-care centers became a fixture in Chinese life.

These child-care centers, with their hundreds of toddlers regimented like trainees in military boot camps, are now one of the most impressive sights in China. The tableau of two or three hundred two-year-olds participating in simultaneous potty-training regimes is a favorite of foreign photographers.

By the early 1990s Chinese cities were also rife with an age-old confidence game used by unscrupulous shopkeepers and sidewalk salesmen to con naive customers into buying imitation or cheap products for high prices.

In this scam a decoy, who "happens" to be in the shop or walks up to the sidewalk stall, plays the role of a customer who previously bought one of the products concerned, claims enthusiastically that it is genuine, and recommends it as a wonderful bargain.

This personal testimony, more often than not, results in the normally suspicious Chinese customer paying an exorbitant price for something that is a rip-off—usually jewelry or some other kind of accessory or clothing that is represented as being an import from the U.S., Italy, France or elsewhere.

In typical Chinese fashion, this rampant illegal activity is known by the poetic euphemism *tuor* (tuu-orr)—a take-off on the concept of kindergarten that in effect means *lifting up* or *bringing up* the customer.

Most of the victims of the *tuor* scam are unsophisticated Chinese visiting cities from the countryside, or only recently arrived from rural areas to work in factories.

But foreign visitors as well are often targeted by these skilled conmen, in which case the products offered are more likely to be represented as authentic antiques.

In addition to being wary of *tuor* schemes, foreigners in China who are inexperienced or uncomfortable with haggling might want to prepare themselves in advance if they intend to shop in street markets.

Bargaining is also common in many reputable "downtown" gift and jewelry shops, which normally mark their merchandise up to allow for a discount of 10 percent or more. State-run stores generally do not bargain.

外办

Waiban

(Wye-bahn)

"Watching over Foreigners"

One of the most conspicuous and important features of the Chinese Communist Party system during its first decades in power was the degree to which it organized and controlled all political and economic activity in the country. Practically all social interactions were also precisely organized and controlled.

Virtually all non-farm activity took place in what were called *danwei*, which is translated as *work units*. This designation was applied to all companies, schools, hospitals, state-run enterprises, state agencies, research institutes, or whatever.

During the first decades of the Communist regime, all foreigners doing any kind of business with China or teaching in China had to have specific *danwei* as their sponsors, and deal exclusively with their appointed work units.

All *danwei* that had or were likely to have any dealings with foreigners had a department known as the *waiban* (wye-bahn), which translates more or less as *foreign affairs office*, and it was this office that acted as the liaison for all the unit's foreign connections and activities.

Waiban handled *everything* having to do with foreigners, from providing them with the necessary official invitations to visit China (required for obtaining visas), making hotel or housing arrangements for them, providing transportation, interpreters and any personal services they might want while in China (such as tickets to see opera).

The *waiban* were responsible not only for taking care of the professional and private needs of foreign visitors and/or employees, they were also responsible for the *behavior* of their foreign charges while they were in China.

Because of the roles played by the *waiban*, getting on and staying on the "right side" of the "foreign affairs office" staff was vital to foreigners working in or visiting China for business and professional reasons.

Uncooperative or vindictive *waiban* staff members could make life miserable for foreigners assigned to them. And since foreigners could not change to another *danwei* or choose which member of the "foreign affairs office" they dealt with, their only recourse when impasses did occur was to take the problem to a senior manager in the work unit—and if this wasn't done very diplomatically, it could make matters worse.

Both *danwei* and *waiban* are still a conspicuous part of the Chinese system, but dealing with work units is now a lot less restrictive, and foreign businesspeople and other professionals visiting or working in China are no longer strictly tied to the "foreign affairs offices" of the companies or organizations they are involved with.

Generally speaking, the *waiban* provide a valuable service by handling details that would be difficult or impossible for many foreigners to take care of on their own. See **Danwei.**

235

坑命

Wan Ming

(Wahn Meeng)

"Going for Broke"

There are times in life when people, usually individuals but sometimes small groups as well, will set aside all personal concerns for their welfare and sacrifice themselves for someone else or what they perceive as the common good.

The more conspicuous of these spiritual and emotional manifestations occur suddenly, in a split second, such as when people risk their own lives to save other people threatened by some kind of disaster.

History is filled with such spontaneous incidents as well as more deliberate ones, including many involving soldiers who willingly went into battles they knew they could not win or survive.

But this extraordinary spirit is also regularly demonstrated by individuals who deliberately set out to achieve some goal over a long period of time, whether good or bad, without any thought of their own health or other obligations.

In extreme cases, the commitment of such people is an obsession. They have no other thoughts; no other concerns—a state of mind that the Chinese refer to as *wan ming* (wahn meeng), which might be translated as *total dedication*, or *total commitment*.

Mao Zedung, the founder of the People's Republic of China, was a good example of someone who was in a partial state of *wan ming* for all of his adult life. He was obsessed with the idea of transforming China into a perfect Socialist state.

But Mao's obsession was gargantuan in scale and he knew that to achieve his goal he would have to prevail upon practically all of the people of China to go even further than he did—to, in fact, sacrifice their comfort, their families, their health *and* their lives for the realization of a new kind of society.

Wan ming is alive and well in China today, but it is no longer the monopoly of the Chinese Communist Party or any megalomaniacal political potentate such as Mao. It is like some kind of virus that is spreading through the population.

More and more Chinese are becoming obsessed with the goal of achieving social security through financial success—of making as much money as they can as quickly as possible.

These *wan ming*-driven people are motivated by a compelling desire to escape from the insecurity and suffering that has been the lot of most Chinese from time immemorial.

Much of this obsessive commitment to achieve financial security is positive and is contributing enormously to the overall standard of living in China. But many of the people who are out to make it as big as possible are unhampered by any moralistic or ethical concerns.

There is another level of *wan ming* that makes the Chinese people as a whole one of the most formidable groups in the world today. This level is the one that motivates most of them to study harder and work more diligently in pursuing life-long goals than what is characteristic of most other people.

236

晚稀少

Wan-Xi-Shao

(Wahn-She-Shah-oh)

"Feeding Fewer Mouths"

One of the few significant successes of the Communist government of China was to reduce the population growth rate from 5.6 children per woman in 1950 to approximately 1.5 by the early 1990s.

This reduction program was mostly voluntary until 1978 because supreme leader Mao Zedung did not really believe in population control. His famous rejoinder was that "every mouth comes with two hands so why worry!"—meaning, of course, that more mouths meant more workers who could feed themselves.

Other more rational minds prevailed, however, and *wan-xi-shao* (wahn-she-shah-oh) became the official policy of the Chinese government. *Wan* means *late*, *xi* means *thin* and *shao* means *fewer*. In this context, the slogan refers to marrying later than usual, spacing children farther apart, and having fewer children.

In essence, the Chinese government looked upon having children as another form of production, and in the case of China's population, there was overproduction on a prodigious scale.

Realizing there was no way that the living standard of the average Chinese could be raised without a dramatic reduction in the population growth, the government made population control one of the primary features of its famous Five-Year Plans.

Laws were passed prohibiting most women from having more than one child; with severe punishment, ranging from fines to loss of entitlements and other privileges, for anyone who flouted the laws. But there were a number of exceptions to the blanket law of "one couple one child."

The law did not apply to ethnic minorities living in remote, sparsely populated areas; to Han Chinese living in sparsely populated mountainous regions if there had been only one son for three generations in a row; if the first child was born with a handicap; in the case of a second marriage in which the other ex-spouse got custody of the one child; if the couple had adopted a child because one or the other of the parents was believed to be sterile; and so on.

Because this draconian law went against almost everything the Chinese had believed in and practiced for millennia, the government instituted equally drastic methods for enforcing it.

Every woman of childbearing age was closely monitored, whether she was married or not. The law required that individuals wanting to have a child obtain written permission from their place of work and appropriate local authorities.

A record was kept on each woman, showing the dates of her monthly periods. If a woman missed a period, she was called in for an interview and examination to find out if she was pregnant. If she was pregnant and did not have the required permission to have a child she was subject to punishment.

To make sure that local government workers in charge of enforcing the fertility laws were diligent in their efforts, they themselves were subject to criticism and punishment if women they were assigned to monitor became pregnant without authorization.

The effect of China's one-couple one-child policy, which is still in force, goes far beyond capping the population growth and beginning the slow process of cutting the population back to more reasonable and manageable proportions.

It is bringing about a fundamental change in the way the Chinese think and live. It is changing the whole concept of the family and society in general, from revering one's ancestors and male supremacy to women's rights, child-raising, education, inheritance customs, housing, consumption, and more.

In this one area, at least, China is setting an example of dealing with a frightening problem that most of the rest of the world continues to ignore.

See **Jihua Shengyu**.

文化

Wenhua

(Win-wha)

"Country of Cultural Essence"

Westerners mostly think of culture in terms of music, the arts and literature. But culture is much more than that. It is the way people think, talk and behave, the way they work, and the essence of the things they create. It is what makes the lifestyle of one group of people different from that of another group.

The idea that people must be formally educated in the fine arts to be "cultured" and behave "properly" also totally misses the point, as is demonstrated continuously on a daily basis by people in many societies around the world.

Because culture is a set of beliefs, an attitude and a style of behavior, it is a living, changing thing that is absorbed as one grows up, and although it varies from person to person it nevertheless leaves its mark on everyone raised within a group of people.

The culture of China is one of the most enduring and powerful ever to be developed, and since it is the force that motivates and guides the behavior of over one billion people it is obviously one of the most important cultures in the world today.

The Chinese term for culture is *wenhua* (win-wha), which can be translated as *patterns of thought and behavior*—although more orthodox translations generally equate it with art, music, literature, ritual, and being the ideal "gentleman."

As Richard J. Smith notes in his wonderfully perceptive book, *China's Cultural Heritage*, the Chinese view their homeland as a "cultural entity"—not just as a land mass and a political unit—which, of course, is true of virtually all other culturally distinct people.

But the Chinese are far more sensitive about culture than most other people—no doubt because they have been contemplating it for more than four thousand years and have so much of it.

Some of China's literary works have gone so far as to use the term *Chung Hua* or Central Cultural Essence as a more appropriate name for the country itself—a name which infers that China is—or was—a living example of "the right way"—a country that followed the ethics and etiquette as set down by Confucius.

Like most other groups of people who have created unique lifestyles, the Chinese have integrated a vision of the cosmos into their culture, and not surprisingly theirs is one of the most elaborate and comprehensive of any ever conceived.

Also like all people everywhere the Chinese created their own gods, patterning the best of them after superior and idealized human beings, many of whom were first heroes and later became legends.

Historically the Chinese believed that their culture was sacred and should not be revealed to foreigners. They also believed that the most routine kind of statistical information about China should be kept secret. Some of this attitude still endures.

文化大革命
Wenhua Da Ge Ming
(Win-wha Dah Guh Meeng)

"The Chinese Holocaust"

In 1956 the Chinese Communist Party (CCP), following orders from supreme leader Mao Zedung, initiated a free-speech campaign known as "Let a Hundred Flowers Bloom, a Hundred Schools of Thought Contend."

Some were later to say that the program was a sincere effort on the part of Mao to get constructive criticism of the Party in order to improve it; others say it was done as a trap, to reveal people who were against the CCP. It was no doubt some of both.

Whatever the case, the program resulted in an avalanche of criticism of the CCP and its policies that increased in crescendo with every passing day. Shocked at this unexpected outburst of opposition, Mao and his government henchmen inaugurated a counter campaign by labeling whole segments of the population who were among the most vocal of the critics as "Rightists" and therefore enemies of the state.

The careers of all of those who had dared to criticize the CCP and its leaders were ruined.

Wholesale arrests were begun, and within a few months more than 300,000 students, scholars, scientists, writers, economists and other professionals were taken into custody. Dozens of thousands of them were imprisoned for long periods of time. Some were executed. Three student leaders, selected to serve as warning examples, were executed before an assembly of 10,000 other students.

By the early 1960s Mao Zedung and his hardline henchmen were becoming increasingly frustrated at the failure of their efforts to convert China's middle and upper class to communism, to revitalize the country's economy and to catch up with Hong Kong, Japan, Singapore and Taiwan.

Mao blamed most of this failure on the traditional Confucian attitudes and practices that still prevailed in Chinese culture, on the influence of Western thinking and Western-type capitalism that had spread in China over the previous two centuries, and on "enemies" within the Communist leadership, particularly Liu Shaoqi, the president of the PRC and his old friend, whom he felt were not sufficiently dedicated to his brand of communism and had become disloyal to him.

In the summer of 1966, as conditions continued to get worse and those who opposed him got stronger, Mao decided on a course of action that was to unleash a holocaust—a period of turmoil and destruction that was to last for ten years and change China forever.

This new Mao-sponsored program was called the *Wenhua Da Ge Ming* (win-wha dah guh meeng) or *Great Proletariat Cultural Revolution*. Mao's goal was to totally destroy the country's traditional culture and to wipe out every vestige of non-Communist thought, including members of the Communist Party itself, on every level.

Mao chose the students of China as the primary instrument for this revolution. By this time, Mao's old friend General Lin Biao and Mao's wife, Jiang Qing, had turned him into a god-like figure who was literally worshipped by young students.

Knowing that the country's millions of students were frustrated by the lack of educational and economic opportunities, by the repressive nature of their parents and teachers, by their anger at the inefficiency and corruption of the huge bureaucracy, and by sexual repression, Mao turned them loose, ordering them to seek out and destroy everything relating to "Old China."

Quickly dubbed *Hong Weibing* (hong way-e-beeng) or *Red Guards*, the students went wild. All schools were closed. Red Guard brigades sprang up by the hundreds of thousands and began a rampage the likes of which had never been seen before in any country. In an effort to "out-red" the reddest, rival Red Guards became more and more extreme in their behavior.

Each of the brigades throughout the country was given lists bearing the names and addresses of people who were to be "exposed" and persecuted—including some of Mao's oldest and closest friends and associates going back to the days of the Long March. The Red Guards were also given the right to attack anyone else they regarded as an "enemy of the people."

In addition to destroying Buddhist shrines, religious objects, libraries, museums and works of art, Mao's Red Guards attacked teachers, school administrators, scholars, writers, poets, landlords, bureaucrats, businesspeople—virtually anyone who had anything in the way of property or position; often including their own parents. Farmers were programmed to attack landlords, force them to confess their sins and then have them arrested and imprisoned, or to kill them outright.

Traditional burial rituals were prohibited. So-called "Street Committees" forced people to burn their ancestral tables and household altars. Virtually all of the village and neighborhood ancestral halls, where the key life-cycle rituals (birthdays, weddings, funerals) were held, were destroyed.

Victims of the student Red Guards were insulted, humiliated, tortured, forced to write long confessions, to confess their alleged sins at public gatherings, and to give up their homes and their belongings.

Thousands of the most respected professors, writers, scientists and other intellectuals in the country were forced to wear large "dunce caps" and to endure torture and being paraded through the streets while being harangued and denounced as criminals—a process that came to be known as being "hatted."

Hundreds of thousands of people were forcibly taken to primitive labor camps in remote areas of the country where there were no services or facilities. Untold thousands were summarily executed or so badly beaten that they died.

As the onslaught grew, many of the Red Guards and farmers became so frenzied that they began eating the flesh of their victims to demonstrate their total commitment and loyalty to Mao's revolution.

Among the terms used by the Red Guards to label their victims were such things as "cow demons" and "snake spirits"—which, one of the survivors of the horror said later, allowed them to view their victims as monsters and to torture and kill them without any feelings of pity or remorse.

By the spring of 1967 many of the Red Guard brigades had joined forces with groups of workers, and begun to take over factories and local and district government offices.

Chaos continued to spread. There was almost no law enforcement. During the first days and weeks of the Cultural Revolution one of the loudest and most popular cries was "Smash the Police, the Procuracy (Public Prosecutors) and the Judiciary!" and the Red Guards did just that—adding to the lawlessness and destruction that swept the country.

Lawyers and law professors were arrested and sent to labor camps, law libraries were burned, law schools were trashed and closed. Farming and manufacturing were beginning to disintegrate. Finally, authorities on several levels began calling out China's famed People's Liberation Army to stop the rampaging Red Guards and their worker allies.

Thousands of the Red Guards were killed by the army. Other thousands became the victims of other Red Guards, and themselves forced to confess to alleged crimes and become prisoners in the same labor camps already filled with their own victims.

The most destructive period of the Cultural Revolution was over by the early 1970s, but Mao and the other hardliners in the government kept it alive until 1976, the year Mao died. During the course of the turmoil, it is estimated that well over 100 million people were prosecuted and punished.

During the 10-year period, more than 16 million city dwellers and students were dispatched into rural areas, to learn the virtues of hard labor, to rid themselves of any traditional thoughts, and to convert the country's millions of farmers to Maoist communism.

The idea of sending youths from the city into the countryside to learn about peasant life was originated by revolutionary thinker-writer Li Dazhao around 1918, before the CCP was founded. The first group of students to be "sent down" were from Beijing University, and were known as "The Mass Education Speech Corps."

Deng Xiaoping, one of the famed members of the Long March and a veteran Communist who had worked with Mao from the earliest years of the Communist movement in China, was himself purged from the leadership as an enemy of the revolution.

But when Mao's health and strength began to fail and the Cultural Revolution started winding down in 1976, Deng was returned to power and quickly became the supreme leader.

One of the first things that Deng did was begin restoring the country's legal institutions. But virtually all of the changes he introduced were little more than "paper reforms"

The government maintained the right to use administrative procedures to arrest and imprison anyone without any legal justification or procedures. This meant that the Public Security Bureau, down to the local level, could arrest anyone without a warrant, hold them for any length of time, and sentence them to prison terms without any possibility of review.

People arrested were automatically presumed to be guilty, and the role of lawyers was severely limited.

For millions of Chinese who survived the Cultural Revolution, including the student Red Guards, the 10 years that it lasted was a lost decade. Some 16 million teenagers had been relocated from cities to rural farm and labor camps and in effect were prisoners since they could not leave and were under guard. In addition to the educational and economic loss, there was a loss of faith in humanity.

The psychological scars left by the *Wenhua Da Ge Ming* will be with the Chinese for many generations.

稳住阵脚

Wenzhu Zhenjiao
(Wun-chu Chen-jee-ah-oh)

"Holding Your Ground"

In ancient China armies of opposing clans, warlords and other factions used to face each other in battle formations that were only yards apart—usually close enough that they could communicate with each other by shouting.

Leaders of the opposing forces would sometimes meet each other in one-on-one combat in the open space between the armies. But whether the battle involved only the leaders or all of their troops, one of the first rules of combat was *wenzhu zhenjiao* or *hold your ground*.

It was well understood that the first army to break ranks and give ground would almost certainly lose the battle—unless the maneuver had been carefully planned in advance.

This military strategy was eventually incorporated into the thinking and behavior of all Chinese when faced with a challenge, whether social, political, military or business.

In today's China *wenzhu zhenjiao* (wun-chu chen-jee-ah-oh) is something of a catchall phrase that is used to cover any kind of setback or development that may have undesirable repercussions.

If a government ministry suddenly imposes a new tax or announces that such-and-such a product can no longer be made or imported, the first rule is *wenzhu zhenjiao*—which includes the connotation of maintaining your balance so as to prevent the setback from causing irreparable damage.

In the Chinese context "keeping your balance" and "holding your ground" are basically the same thing, with the result that *wenzhu zhenjiao* can be applied to practically any situation that is upsetting.

As the Chinese say, "in any situation the first priority is *wenzhu zhenjiao*" or *keeping your balance.*

The term is often used in the direct sense of "we must (or you should) make the best of the situation," particularly when people are confused by or about something.

Outsiders are most apt to encounter this mentality when they present something that the Chinese do not approve of, do not want, or are not satisfied with and want changes made.

In many instances today Chinese bureaucrats in particular feel obligated to "hold their ground" against foreign interests they believe are trying to take advantage of China, or are not paying as much as they should for the privilege of doing business in China.

On other occasions, the *wenzhu zhenjiao* mode is used by both bureaucrats and businesspeople who are determined to profit personally from new relationships. They simply withhold their approval or cooperation until their minimum "requirements" are met.

It is just as important for foreigners operating in China to develop skill in keeping their balance. The Chinese are masters at discerning weaknesses and are conditioned to take every advantage of them.

Generally speaking, the outsider must keep in mind that fair play is not a part of the Chinese experience, and even when the English term is used it will be interpreted from the Chinese viewpoint.

240

我母亲的家

Wo Muqin De Jia

(Wu Muu-cheen Duh Jee-ah)

"My Mother's House"

Among the remarkable changes that have taken place in Chinese society since the founding of the Communist regime in 1949, none are more fundamental than the position and role of women in the household and workplace.

A significant part of this change can be attributed to Mao Zedung, who began his career as a minor member of the revolutionary movement that brought communism to China, and ended up as the chief theoretician and supreme leader—the Vladimir Lenin of China if you will.

When still in his twenties, Mao recognized that the age-old Chinese custom of denying women social and political rights and generally treating them as property was not only irrational but wasteful.

Mao recognized that even in upper-class Chinese families where women exercised considerable influence within the household and sometimes in public life as well, most of their talents were misused and abused and the overall effect on society was profoundly negative.

The more power Mao achieved, the more determined he became to unshackle the women of China. After he became head of the Communist state in 1949, he initiated legislation that dramatically changed the legal status of women.

But patterns of behavior that are more than 4,000 years old are not that easily changed, and it was to be Mao's subsequent wars against Confucianism and Chinese society as a whole, including his militant campaigns to forcibly convert all Chinese to Communist ideology, that finally shattered the system that had imprisoned Chinese women for so long.

It was Mao's success in breaking up the country's Confucian-oriented family system, in which women were absolutely subservient to men, that finally liberated women. Mao did this by causing hundreds of thousands of men to be exterminated, millions to be imprisoned, and other millions to be separated from their families by forced labor in remote areas of the country.

Mao's Cultural Revolution (1966–1976) resulted in virtually every urban family in the country being broken up, with husbands and wives assigned to work in different areas, young children placed in care centers, and teenage youths sent out into rural areas as workers and political agents.

These revolutionary measures, which began in 1949 and lasted until 1976, resulted in China's urban women having to survive on their own, to learn how to get by without fathers and husbands to run their lives.

For females born after 1950 China was a new world, a world in which most urban homes were mother-centered instead of father-centered; a world in which mothers represented the security figures and "home."

It was this social metamorphosis that gave rise to the new concept of *wo muqin de jia* (wu muu-cheen duh jee-ah)—*my mother's house*, as opposed to the old gender terms such as *niang jia*, used by wives in reference to visiting their mothers' homes. (*Niang jia* means "parents home of a married woman.")

241

五伦

Wu Lun
(Wuu Luun)

"The Five Family Rules"

Rules governing the hierarchical relationships in traditional Chinese families were based on five rules (in Confucian terms, the Five Cardinal Relations), known as *wu lun* (wuu luun). These Cardinal Relations established the order of rank and obligations of the individual members.

The five rules began with the paramount father-son relationship, and then in descending order covered husband-wife, elder brother-younger brother, older friend-younger friend, and ruler-subject.

Properly abiding by these rules was known, again in Confucian terms, as the Constant Virtues, the most important of which was *ren* (rune) or *humanness* because it was only through the humanness of the father or ruler that the despotic nature of the system was mitigated.

Still, the emotional, intellectual and spiritual restraint that had to be exercised by the lower ranking members of a Chinese family resulted in the buildup of tension and, frequently, no-holds-barred infighting.

But since life outside of the family was a dangerous no-man's-land, discontented members generally had no choice but to swallow their frustrations and reach some kind of accommodation.

An extraordinarily high degree of etiquette between people was therefore necessary to fulfill the surface demands of the Constant Virtues and produce anything near the standards of moral behavior advocated by Confucius.

This system of family relationships was so demanding that Confucius gave self-cultivation and the development of extraordinary self-control a high priority. But this cultivation was internalized and did not lead to the development of strong individual personalities by lower ranking family members.

Chinese society was therefore a society of families; not individuals.

A traditional Chinese family has been described as a combination welfare state and police state. It was organized to be as economically self-sufficient as possible and to police its own members, primarily by the threat of shame and expulsion out into the cold, cruel world, and, in earlier times, corporal punishment as well.

While family clans and communities acted as collectives or unions in many respects, each family was still an independent entity responsible for its own survival. Rivalry between families was therefore intense, greatly limiting cooperation.

Anthropologists say that neither Chinese villages nor urban districts were communities in the Western sense of sharing responsibilities, looking out for each other, and cooperating in joint efforts such as street cleaning, staging social events or recreational activities. These functions, and others, when they existed, were generally carried out by voluntary associations involving relatives, birthplace, language, and occupation.

The *wu lun* remain important to most rural families in China but they are no longer the defining principles of the typical urban Chinese family. Still, they continue to set the tone for family life throughout China, and are not likely to disappear any time soon.

242

无妄

Wuwang

(Wuu-wahng)

"Keeping Your Slate Clean"

If the Chinese had been able to follow the path proposed by the cultural code word *wuwang* (wuu-wahng) they might have been able to create a society that was as close as possible to a paradise on earth.

Wuwang means *innocence*, and refers to behavior that is without artifice or selfish motives, is utterly spontaneous and instinctive, and is infused with what Chinese philosophers call the "natural goodness" of man.

Wuwang ranks high among the personal traits traditionally prescribed by Chinese sages as both ideal and essential for coping with the exigencies of life because it requires no special training or experience and meets with the least amount of resistance from others.

While a constant state of *wuwang* would obviously be the ideal, Chinese sages note that there are particular times when a conscious and deliberate use of *wuwang* is the only effective way to contend with certain circumstances.

On these occasions, the sages say, if you are unable to harmonize your actions with the cosmic flow of things by taking a *wuwang* approach you will make one mistake after the other and cannot succeed in your efforts.

Living a *wuwang* directed life, or adjusting your behavior to take advantage of the power of "innocence" on a case-by-case basis, will make your life more exciting, according to the sages.

They say that when people are in a natural state of *wuwang*, or have deliberately assumed an innocent mode, they have no control over external events, cannot predict what will happen, and should be prepared for surprises.

Of course, the inherent promise is that good things will happen because people will generally react in a positive way when they are met by genuine innocence—an optimistic supposition that all too often is wrong.

The corollary of *wuwang* is that it works well, and is recommended, only if the individuals concerned are, in fact, people of high moral standards and integrity and are not "acting innocent" in order to take advantage of others.

Despite the recent general impression of China given by the presence of so much political violence the average Chinese has traditionally been non-violent, kind and generous, and has exhibited far more *wuwang* that one might suppose possible.

The women of China have traditionally been more influenced by the concept of *wuwang* than the male population, and it was primarily the beauty, innocence and goodwill of the women that gave life in China most of the charm that it did have—particularly where foreigners were concerned.

Not surprisingly, Chinese women, especially teenage girls and young women, remain one of the country's most valuable assets, and as they gain more social, economic and political power they will change the essence of Chinese culture for the better.

午休

Wu Xin (Chi Fan, Xiu Di)
(Wuu Sheen)

"A Chinese Nooner"

If anyone involved with China should ever want to do anything that is questionable or against the law, including such things as enter China illegally, escape from China, or launch a war against the country, it should be done between noon and 1 P.M. or maybe as late as 1:30 in the afternoon.

Much of China shuts down at or shortly before noon and does not start up again until at least 1:15 P.M. Government workers in particular are prone to fudge on both sides of this time frame, and like judges in some Western courts, don't like to and often won't start anything new from about 11 A.M. or before 2:30 P.M.

The reason for this phenomenon is that in the early 1950s the Chinese Communist Party made it "legal" for workers in offices and factories to adopt the peasants' age-old practice of taking lengthy noonday lunch-and-sleep periods, virtually shutting down the government and business for up to two hours.

The CCP took this step with very little consideration for the differences involved in rural and urban activities as a means of emphasizing its role as the champion of both peasants and the working class.

Like farmers everywhere, Chinese peasants have traditionally gone to work around dawn, and by noon have already put in from five to seven hours of physically demanding work. Furthermore, until the latter part of the 1980s their diet was often so poor they were exhausted by midday, making a long break necessary.

This traditional noonday rest is known as *wu xin* (wuu sheen) or *eat-rest*, for short. It is also sometimes referred to as *chi fan* and *xiu di*, which mean the same thing. Whatever it is called its rural traditions go back to the dawn of Chinese civilization, and is very close to being sacred.

Over the next two decades China's urban workers came to regard the daily *wu xin* as their natural right, ignoring its frequently adverse effects on production schedules and other business matters.

Beginning in the early 1980s the central government began trying to curtail the custom in all government and commercial offices and to eliminate it entirely in some, but with only limited success. Beijing outlawed the midday nap in 1986 for government workers, causing vociferous protests. And still today many people ignore the law. Many workplaces still have beds for employees to take noonday naps.

Today there is a growing number of Chinese businesspeople, with a bureaucrat thrown in here and there, who mix lunch and work the way most Westerners do, but in proportion to the size of China's industry and the government, the number is still small and the chances of "your" businessperson or lower ranking bureaucrat being one of this special group is smaller still.

When in China it is wise to keep the *wu xin* custom in mind when setting up appointments, and especially when making cold calls. Depending on the company or government office, the actual working period may not be more than three hours in the morning and three hours in the afternoon. In the case of some higher officials, this is sometimes reduced to as little as four or five hours a day.

The further the city or region is away from Beijing and the more industrialized areas of southern and eastern China, the more likely the people are to follow traditional customs in taking long rest-breaks at noon. Many people make a practice of eating their lunch before the official starting time so eating will not interfere with their *xiu di*.

244

下海

Xia Hai

(She-ah Hah-ee)

"Putting Out to Sea"

Despite the cultural and social cohesiveness of the Chinese for more than 40 centuries, particularly the age-old customs and traditions of collective responsibility and mutual help, the Chinese have mostly lived lives filled with fear.

This ever-present fear grew out of the fact that neither their persons nor their property—if they had any—were guaranteed by any philosophy, any law, or even by custom. The only real security they had was invested in personal relationships.

Those relationships that were outside of the family, and over which they had the least control, were arbitrary and therefore difficult to maintain. Sustaining these outside relationships was primarily based on sacrificing one's own interests to serve the larger community and the government.

In addition to being subject to the will of the community and to the aims and whims of government authorities, the Chinese were also historically victimized by famine, floods, war, earthquakes and other phenomena.

The arbitrariness of their existence made the Chinese ultra-conservative in every aspect of their lives, and was responsible for virtually all of the character and cultural traits for which they have been know for centuries.

Now, for the first time in the history of China, there is a rapidly growing new breed of Chinese who have thrown off the chains of conservatism and are taking their lives and their security into their own hands.

This new phenomenon is known in colloquial terms as *xia hai* (she-ah hah-ee), or *putting out to sea*, with the connotation being that these people are embarking on a dangerous voyage from which there may be no rewards and no return.

Xia hai refers specifically to people who give up relatively secure positions with larger, stable companies, or the government, to become private entrepreneurs or join other companies that are still struggling and may not succeed.

Most of those who "put out to sea" are people with specialized education and training who are leaving government-run operations where salaries are low and opportunities for advancement are limited.

These include technicians, engineers and scientists in various fields who are in growing demand by the private sector, and whose leaving puts state-run enterprises, already plagued by bureaucratic inefficiency, in even more precarious positions.

This indicates that as long as the private sector of China's economy continues to grow it will siphon off more and more of the best people from money-losing state enterprises, contributing to their eventual demise.

If this turns out to be the case, it will complete the cycle began by the Communist Party of China when it arbitrarily brought to an end all private enterprise in the country.

245

Xian

(She-enn)

"The Glue That Binds"

Much of the wisdom of China—which was virtually unused over the ages because of government restrictions and interference—is based on cosmological and ontological insights of its great philosophers, and despite its lofty origins it is applicable to every human relationship.

The foundation of Chinese wisdom is the *yin-yang* principle of duality in the cosmos, and the attraction that exists between every atom of matter in the universe. If this magnetic attraction did not exist, all matter would literally come apart and fly off in all directions.

Since every spark of energy, every action, attracts or repels, and harmony in the universe, on both a galactic and personal human level, is achieved only when these forces complement each other, the Chinese say the secret to developing and keeping positive personal relations and achieving goals, whether social, economic or political, is to learn how to recognize and manipulate the *xian* (she-enn) or attraction in all relationships and encounters.

Xian is the essence of what makes a thing or an idea desirable, and becoming able to identify this essence and to use it to obtain what you want is a source of great power over people and events. By the same token, not being able to discern the "attraction" of a person, thing or situation, is a serious disadvantage.

Xian may be used in either a negative or positive way. Which way it is used naturally depends upon the character of the person involved. Obviously, the advice of the sages in how to use this great power is aimed at people with high standards and integrity.

As in all Chinese wisdom, however, the recognition of *xian* and the ability to use it effectively does not always come easy. It requires a significant level of intelligence and insight into human behavior, including the likes, dislikes, strengths and weaknesses of the various people you are involved with.

In business it involves determining what your employees and customers want; in politics it involves knowing what your constituents want—what will excite them and get them to support you.

Some people, of both good and bad character, have so much *xian* that people flock to them, anxious to do their bidding or to help them in any way they can. When these are people of superior character they can achieve wonderful things for themselves, their companies or their countries.

And, of course, the reverse is true. Virtually all of the great villains of history were masters at manipulating and using people because they understood what attracted them.

In the Chinese context, the master of using *xian* who deserves the support he or she gets is the one who remains humble and is dedicated to serving the best interests of the people around him or her and the general public.

乡土情

Xiang Tu Qing

(She-ahng Tuu Cheeng)

"There's No Place Like Home"

There is ongoing evidence that human beings have an inherent kinship with nature—with the land, with trees, with water—that goes well beyond any physical attachment to embrace the spiritual world as well.

All preindustrial people were apparently aware of this relationship, and in many if not all ancient societies it was the central theme in their religious and economic activities. Native Americans, who belong to the same racial and cultural stock as the Chinese, are well-known examples of people whose traditional cultures were based on worshipping nature and its forces.

And, of course, it is common knowledge that people whose ancestors have lived in cities for centuries still feel the spiritual attraction of fields, forests, mountains, rivers and lakes.

In China this spiritual connection with nature has been centered on one's birthplace from time immemorial, and has been a key factor in the survival and strength of Chinese culture down through the ages.

Another primary factor in what the Chinese call *xiang tu qing* (she-ahng tuu cheeng) or *feelings of local affinity*, has been ancestor worship. The Chinese have traditionally believed that the human spirit or soul survives the death of the body, and although disembodied and invisible after death remains in the dimension of the living and must continue to be venerated and placated.

Because the spirits of deceased parents and other relatives remain in the vicinity of their former homes, the feelings the Chinese have for their home villages and towns is greatly intensified, and spans generations.

The traditional attachment of the Chinese to their birthplace and home villages suffered grievously during the revolutionary turmoil from the 1930s to the 1970s because so many of them were uprooted and forced to settle in distant places. The efforts of the Chinese Communist Party to eliminate all of the traditional religious customs and break up families also impacted negatively on *xiang tu qing*. One of supreme leader Mao Zedung's primary goals was to eliminate class identifications based on birthplace.

But *xiang tu qing* continues to play a significant role in all facets of life in China—socially, politically and economically. Attachments to home villages not only serves to keep people separated into definable groups, it also influences their behavior towards others.

People naturally favor those who come from or near their home villages in situations involving employment or marriage. Home village ties, combined with school ties, serve as the primary source for connections when people are seeking work or help of any kind.

"Feelings of local affinity" survive among overseas Chinese for several generations, and have been the traditional source of links between tiny villages and Chinese communities in San Francisco, Los Angeles, New York and other major world cities.

Non-Chinese who come from cities with Chinese communities and are seeking to establish ties in China might explore the possibility of linking up with the hometowns or villages of Chinese residents through some of their own Chinese neighbors.

Xiao

(She-ah-oh)

"Respecting Your Betters"

In feudal China the calendar was based on a sixty-year cycle because, among other things, that figure was considered the ideal span of a lifetime. It was, in fact, so rare for a person to live to be sixty years old that it was an occasion for great rejoicing.

Anyone who reached the age of sixty was believed to have finished their allotted years and figuratively started over again. It was common to give the 60-year-old person a red undergarment, which was symbolic of childhood and a sign that they could once again behave like a child, indulging themselves.

Another tradition was that the 60-year-old could carry a wooden staff, not necessarily to aid in walking but as a symbol of having achieved such a venerable age.

Anyone who reached the age of seventy was permitted to use a staff to aid in walking. It was said that anyone who attained the age of eighty could appear before the emperor with a staff and did not have to bow. A 90-year-old person was regarded with such esteem that he was considered qualified to give advice to the emperor.

These attitudes toward age were a part of the Chinese tradition of *xiao* (she-ah-oh) or *filial piety*—respect for and veneration of parents—that went back to the dawn of China's history and ancestor worship.

The cultural concept of *xiao* was already a key factor in the lives of the Chinese when the great sage Confucius appeared on the scene in 551 B.C. He helped lock it into place for posterity by making it one of his five principles governing interpersonal relationships.

Confucius' goal was to eliminate the supernatural elements that permeated Chinese society at that time and provide an ethical foundation for the structure and behavior of the family—and by extension the entire society.

The key to the position and role of members in the Confucian family was a patriarchy based on *xiao*. Children were to respect, honor and obey their parents without reservations, throughout the lifetimes of the parents. The older the parents, the more they were to be honored and the more obligation there was to obey them.

This system bound the Chinese family together as a single unit, and, as long as there were male heirs, transcended all generational lines. As time passed each family evolved into branches and sub-branches, but the lines remained unbroken.

Xiao thus became the binding force—the glue—that held the Chinese and their culture together for one generation after the other, bringing stability and continuity to the society.

With the weight of Confucius added to the practice of ancestor worship, *xiao* became a mainstay of China's patriarchal family system, and has long since been described as one of the greatest virtues of Chinese culture.

But along with stability the *xiao*-bound patriarchal family also brought extreme conservatism, and an abhorrence to change that was to help keep China marking time for more than two millennia.

Xiao is still an important element in Chinese society, helping to bond families, and contributing significantly to generational success in business.

Foreigners involved with China can often improve their chances of success by doing things that demonstrate their awareness of the role and importance of *xiao*, particularly in situations involving parents who are quite elderly and are in need of something that can be provided readily.

小道消息

Xiaodao Xiaoxi

(She-ah-oh-dah-oh She-ah-oh-she)

"Back-Alley News Network"

During the long ages of the Imperial dynasties, the philosophy of the Imperial Courts was that virtually all government affairs were state secrets, and that generally the only information that should be made public were announcements of warnings or edicts pertaining to the obligations of the people.

The stated reason for this policy was that the less people knew the less likely they would be to cause problems and the easier it would be to control them.

Until the early 1990s, China's Communist government continued this traditional policy of severely limiting the kind and volume of news it made available, or allowed others to make available, to the general public.

Government announcements that were released through controlled publications were generally so brief and obtuse that it was impossible to fully understand their implications.

Foreign news carried by the government-sponsored media was carefully selected to advance the interests and policies of the Chinese Communist Party.

This policy inadvertently gave rise to a number of unofficial "networks" by which news, real and imagined, was spread around the country orally and via underground presses.

China's oral news network, known as *Xiaodao Xiaoxi* (she-ah-oh-dah-oh she-ah-oh-she) or *Alleyway News*, specializes in stories with political themes, especially stories that poke fun at or criticize the country's Communist leaders.

The Chinese learned a long time ago that one of the most effective weapons that can be used against an oppressive mandarin, warlord or Imperial leader is humor, and they have long since been masters at puncturing the arrogance, pride and pretensions of political bigwigs.

Throughout its history the Chinese Communist Party has used secrecy as one of its primary methods of enforcing discipline within its own ranks, and keeping the public under control.

The *Xiaodao Xiaoxi* plays an important role in constantly trying to penetrate this veil of secrecy in an effort to keep the public informed about what is going on behind closed doors in Beijing's government center.

Foreign residents in China must become plugged into the *Alleyway News* channel if they ever hope to have even a partly clear perspective of what is going on in any level of government in the country.

Generally speaking, only those foreigners who have mastered Mandarin, can read Chinese publications—both the official and unofficial—understand the newscasts, have in-depth conversations with well-informed Chinese, and listen in on office and drinking-place gossip can get behind the secrecy barrier.

小过

Xiao Guo
(She-ah-oh Gwoh)

"Paying Attention to Details"

Chinese employers have a significant advantage when it comes to judging the character and ability of other Chinese. Their common cultural heritage attunes them to the same cues and criteria, and takes a great deal of the guesswork out of what in the U.S. and other Western cultures is often a hit-or-miss situation.

Another advantage that Chinese employers have over foreign managers who employ local workers in China, particularly when the Chinese are hired for management positions, is a better understanding of both the needs and aspirations of their employees, and the fact that they are not, and often cannot be, held to foreign standards of productivity, pay and privileges.

Among other things, there is typically an enormous gap between the salaries received by foreigners stationed in China and the compensation normally received by Chinese workers and managers. This disparity generally results in varying degrees of envy and frustration among Chinese who work for the same foreign companies alongside highly paid foreigners.

When the Chinese are older than the foreign employees, and when they consider themselves as well or better educated than the foreigners, they see the disparity in income as both unfair and insulting—a situation that is often exacerbated by the fact that many of them do not directly relate income with performance or responsibility.

This latter factor is one of present-day China's most serious problems. The Communist regime came close to wiping out the traditional devotion of the Chinese to *xiao guo* (she-ah-oh gwoh), which is translated as *conscientiousness*, and figuratively means "concern with small things."

Prior to the imposition of communism the Chinese were famed for their conscientiousness—for their attention to detail in every facet of their lives, and particularly in their work. The whole of Chinese culture emphasized *xiao guo*. One might even say that it was impossible to *be* Chinese without being conscientious.

Not surprisingly, one of the chief characteristics of Chinese style *xiao guo* is its conservatism. Its primary theme is that one should be absolutely meticulous in taking care of the small details of work and life in general, and avoid undertaking anything out of the ordinary.

While the tradition of *xiao guo* has been greatly diminished in China itself, it is alive and well in all Chinese communities overseas, and was a major factor in the rise of Hong Kong as one of the world's great economic dynamos.

In fact, overseas Chinese have gone a long way toward removing much of the overly conservative element that was traditionally inherent in *xiao guo*. The Chinese entrepreneurs of Hong Kong, Singapore and Taiwan in particular have given new meaning to the concept, and little by little are taking this new approach back to their homeland.

小畜

Xiao Xu
(She-ah-oh Shuu)

"The Times Are Not Right"

Despite their cultural diversity, the Chinese share a number of characteristics that makes it possible to generalize about their attitudes and behavior in many common situations, particularly those involving the family and personal relationships.

There are also common patterns of behavior that apply to their reactions to outside influences, and especially in achieving goals when there are substantial obstacles that make success very difficult.

Centuries of experience in living under the foot of an intractable government has conditioned the Chinese to be patient and take a long-term view of everything.

Similar experiences in dealing with the power of nature have predisposed the Chinese to take an incremental approach to achieving their goals, whether great or small, moving forward a little at a time.

An incremental approach has, in fact, long been typical of Chinese behavior in virtually every area of their lives, and is especially conspicuous in international political and economic affairs.

On the few occasions when China's political leaders have attempted to do things rapidly the results have been total disaster—witness practically every program initiated by Mao Zedung during the 1950s and 1960s to convert China to communism, particularly his "Great Leap Forward" which among other things was intended to turn farming villages into sites for metal foundries, and the "Cultural Revolution" in 1966, which was aimed at destroying the very basis of China's traditional culture. The cultural concept that embraces the Chinese affinity for small, slow incremental actions is expressed in the term *xiao xu* (she-ah-oh shuu), which means *restrained*, with the nuance that any goal, no matter how great or difficult, can be achieved if one pursues it in small steps, retreating in the face of resistance and advancing when and where there are few if any barriers.

Even in situations where the Chinese have ample or absolute control they generally prefer to operate in a *xiao xu* mode to avoid making mistakes and to prevent causing the buildup of any kind of resistance. Instances of the use of sudden, aggressive force in China are usually the aberration of a single individual.

The application of *xiao xu*, particularly in business and political affairs involving foreigners, is carefully planned and crafted to give an appearance of friendly harmony and goodwill. The Chinese learned a long time ago that polite, gentle steps will get them a lot further than aggressive action in conducting such matters.

Chinese etiquette and hospitality are major assets that they use with masterful skill in applying *xiao xu* techniques to achieve their goals.

Attempts to persuade or force the Chinese to ignore *xiao xu*, particularly for purposes of international trade, are usually futile, as outsiders regularly discover.

251

下乡

Xia Xiang
(She-ah She-ahng)

"Going Down to the Country"

More than a decade after the Chinese Communist Party took over China in 1949 it had failed in its efforts to eradicate all of the elements of traditionalism, capitalism and other influences that Chairman Mao Zedung regarded as blocking the conversion of China to a Socialist state.

Mao decided that the only way the CCP could purify China of all bourgeois behavior was to force millions of people to leave the cities and go into the countryside, to learn from peasants about the reality of life and the value of socialism.

This program was referred to as *xia xiang* (she-ah she-ahng), *sending down*, or *going down to the country*—a concept that had originated in the late 1800s when the last of China's Imperial dynasties was breaking up.

When China's political thinkers of that time tried to come up with answers to the country's mounting problems they realized that China's urban intellectuals knew practically nothing about the thinking of the huge mass of peasants making up the bulk of the population.

These early political reformers made arrangements for hundreds of educated young people to spend months to years in farm villages, learning about rural life in the country. Their experiences were later incorporated into some of the changes promoted by the reformers.

But the *xia xiang* program initiated by Chairman Mao was on such a vast scale and was so ill-planned and disorganized that it became one of the several "great failures" of the Great Helmsman. It is estimated that between 1968 and 1975 some 10 percent of the urban population of China—more than twelve million people—were forced to move into rural villages, where they did much more harm than good.

In addition to sending intellectuals, landlords, business owners and students out into rural areas, the Communist Party of China also used the *xia xiang* program to get rid of political enemies and anyone else the entrenched leaders thought might be troublemakers.

Mao explained that the aim of the program was to free the targeted segments of the urban population from Western influence and purify them—to make sure they ended up with "dark skins and red hearts"—meaning that they would become suntanned from working in the fields, and that learning about the hardships of rural life would help dedicate them to Communist ideology.

Not surprisingly, however, the peasants deeply resented having to house and feed people from the cities, and they were especially put out by having to listen to the rantings of young politicized city dwellers.

At first the young urbanites were flush with excitement and a strong desire to quickly convert China's millions of peasants to socialism. But they were soon disillusioned with the rigors of life in the countryside, and the intransigence and resentment of the peasants.

Mao and his henchmen allowed the *xia xiang* program to continue for several years after its failure had become obvious. In millions of cases, people "assigned" to farm villages and work projects in remote provinces were kept there, like slave laborers, for as many as 20 years.

Some of those sent out of the urban areas, estimated in the hundreds of thousands, were never able to return because they could not get new residence permits to return to the cities they originally came from.

The term *xia xiang* reminds the older generations of Chinese of this tragic epoch in their lives—not a pleasant rural outing.

252

协

Xie
(She-eh)

"All for One"

It was not Confucianism, Buddhism, Daoism or any combination of these three philosophies that sustained the survival of Chinese culture and the empire of China over the centuries. These great bodies of thought influenced the nature, structure and style of life throughout the huge landmass, but by themselves they were not sufficient to bind together the diverse regions and peoples into a single country.

Distance, forbidding mountain ranges, geographic isolation and different spoken languages would have been more than enough to permanently splinter the empire into a number of kingdoms if it had not been for some other fundamental factor.

The facet of Chinese culture that helped keep the empire together, and today links all Chinese like a common umbilical cord, were the ideograms of "Chinese letters" that were used to transcribe the many languages of China into a single system of communication.

The first of these ideograms were apparently used on bones and tortoise shells for divination purposes between 2000 and 1000 B.C. By 200 B.C. the number of characters had grown into the thousands and been standardized into a full-fledged writing system.

While the pockets of Chinese who broke off from the original stock and settled the far regions to the south, east and west, developed their own distinctive languages that eventually became unintelligible to other groups, they all continued to use the same ideograms to write their languages.

One of the concepts that is dear to the hearts of all Chinese, and is written with the same character in all of the Chinese languages, is *xie* (she-eh) or *unity*.

The ideogram for *xie* represents the coming together and acting together of several people; pooling their numbers to enhance their strength. While all Chinese today share a desire to improve their economic situation, unity, in the sense of close cooperation, applies more to families and close connections than it does to the general population.

The Chinese are, in fact, notorious for being especially difficult to work with in groups, exactly the opposite of the Japanese, because they all have opinions that they are reluctant to give up and therefore do much better operating on their own.

However, *xie* is an essential ingredient in creating and maintaining the "right" atmosphere for doing business in China, and should be emphasized in all relationships. A major part of this challenge is being very knowledgeable about overall Chinese morality, particularly as it applies to families.

Foreign businesspeople first approaching China may be able to speed up the process by building this term into their presentations and thereafter repeating it often.

One suggestion for getting regular mileage out of the power of this concept: have the ideogram imprinted on your name card and/or stationery as part of the design.

253

Xin

(Sheen)

"Putting on a Happy Face"

Face-reading, or more precisely, expression-reading, is one of the first skills developed by human beings. The practice begins in infancy, as soon as a baby can focus its eyes, and continues throughout our lives.

Parents immediately scrutinize the faces of newborn babies, looking for familiar signs, and long before infants can talk they have become programmed to react to the faces around them.

When people have been conditioned from infancy to depend upon expression-reading for much of their communication with others, they subconsciously become ill-at-ease and eventually frustrated if they are unable to do so.

If this situation persists for any length of time, and face-to-face encounters involve matters of some importance, not being able to read faces often contributes to frustration turning into anger.

Westerners are especially dependent upon face-reading for virtually all of their interpersonal relations, and there is nothing at all subtle about most Western facial expressions. We emphasize facial expressions, often giving them precedence over speech.

The situation is quite different in China, where there is a saying to the effect that even though people may be smiling outwardly, inwardly they may be throwing stones—meaning that what you see on a person's face is not necessarily what you get.

Throughout most of China's history maintaining an outwardly neutral or benign expression was not only good manners and part of the overall effort to live in harmony, it was also a defense against upsetting anyone and getting into trouble.

The Chinese were taught to wear blank expressions for the specific purpose of concealing their feelings—to keep them private, to protect themselves, and to avoid burdening other people with their problems.

Centuries of conditioning in masking their personal feelings eventually resulted in the practice becoming one of the most important facets of Chinese character.

Unfortunately, Westerners tend to believe that this still common Chinese behavior is a subterfuge for misleading people. In fact, one of the primary sources of tension and misunderstandings between Chinese and Westerners is their general inability to read each others' faces.

The image that Westerners have traditionally had of the Chinese (and other Asians) as "inscrutable" and untrustworthy resulted almost entirely from the fact that Westerners could not read their faces.

Unaware of the reasons behind the blank faces of the Chinese, Westerners presumed that they were deliberately being dishonest, devious and evasive.

In fact, however, the neutral faces of the Chinese were expressions of *xin* (sheen) or *sincerity*, as dictated by Chinese morality. *Not* revealing one's feelings through facial expressions was a key part of proper etiquette as far as the Chinese were concerned.

Understanding *xin* in its proper cultural context is vital to an understanding and appreciation of Chinese behavior, since its meaning is often quite different from its English equivalent.

The Chinese naturally relate *sincerity* with abiding by all of the rules that control traditional Chinese behavior, including fulfilling all of the expectations that are normal in personal as well as professional relationships.

Fully extrapolated in its Chinese sense, *xin* means to conform to all of the attitudes and behavior that the Chinese believe are correct, whether traditional or modern, including filial piety, respect for hierarchy and age, collective welfare, speaking indirectly, keeping a low profile, behaving in a humble manner, avoiding confrontations, repaying social debts, protecting one's face as well as the face of others, extracting revenge for insults or wrong-doing, etc.

When Westerners are in the process of initiating and nurturing relationships with the Chinese and either side uses the term *xin* or *sincerity*, it is obviously very important that they understand and consider what *xin* means to the Chinese.

See **Kan-Xiang**.

254

洗脑

Xi-Nao

(She-Nah-oh)

"Brain-washing in China"

In the 1930s, when Mao Zedung and other Communist leaders were in the early stages of their revolution to communize China, one of the key programs they initiated was "thought-reform" through imprisonment and hard labor.

The idea of forcing intellectuals to engage in hard manual labor while undergoing intensive re-indoctrination to awaken them to the errors in their thinking and behavior was proposed in the early 1920s by Li Dazhao, the leading Chinese Communist theorist of the times.

Enemies captured in battle as well as others who were regarded as natural enemies of the Communist Revolution (landlords, businessmen, intellectuals) were systematically imprisoned. Part of the rationale for this program was to take advantage of their free or mostly free labor, but the primary purpose was to subject them to *xi-nao* (she-nah-oh) or *brain-washing* and convert them over to communism.

After the Chinese Communist Party took over the country in 1949, Li's thought-reform program was expanded to cover millions of people who were arrested, charged with being "enemies of the people," and sentenced to prison.

All new prisoners were assigned to "study groups" or "introductory teams" that were responsible for applying a variety of brain-washing techniques designed to break down all old beliefs and attitudes and replace them with Communist-Socialist thoughts.

Prison authorities assigned older convicts to oversee the groups and manage the brain-washing of the new inmates.

The third stage of the brain-washing process was known as *fuguan fi-jiao*, or *submitting to teaching*. In addition to confessing to crimes and criticizing themselves, inmates were required to study the rules and regulations of the prisons, to submit totally to the rules and orders of the prison cadre, and to write out in detail how they planned to carry through with reforming themselves.

Another key part of the brain-washing process used on prisoners was called *kaolong zhengfu* or *expose treachery and show allegiance to the government.* This meant that all inmates were expected to provide the names of and information about anyone they believed might be guilty of any anti-Socialist act or even harboring anti-government thoughts.

Each prisoner was expected to be constantly on the alert for any kind of anti-government act or comment by anyone they knew or came into contact with. Chinese authorities had learned ages ago that the best way to control the behavior of large masses of people was to force them to spy on each other.

It was automatically assumed that inmates who did not report any misbehavior or "incorrect" comments by other inmates were themselves guilty of uncooperative, anti-government behavior, and therefore subject to punishment.

Because of this insidious system, inmates routinely turned in false reports on others just to protect themselves. And, ingeniously, there was no punishment for turning in a report that turned out to be false. The idea was to condition everybody to readily spy on everyone else in order to catch those who were guilty of counterrevolutionary thinking or behavior.

Finally, the Public Security Bureau utilized the ultimate weapon in the control of human behavior, collective responsibility—a technique that had been traditional in China for millennia. The whole study group was punished when one member broke a rule or failed to perform as expected.

Collective treatment applied to each prison as well. Every prison in the whole system was evaluated on the behavior and work performance of its inmates, three different levels of supervision and overall treatment of the prisoners.

These levels of treatment were classified as light, heavy and general supervision. The higher the evaluation, the lighter the supervision and the better the living conditions for the prisoners—from food allotments to furloughs and family visits.

Misbehavior by just one individual in a prison was enough to get the evaluation of the whole prison changed from light to heavy or extra-heavy supervision, resulting in a reduction in, or loss of, privileges for all. This resulted in it becoming common for prisoners to beat and kill each other.

In addition to the actual physical punishment meted out to prisoners, the threat of punishment and death was constant. This resulted in all of the now well-known psychological defense mechanisms becoming endemic throughout the huge prison population.

All rationality, all logic was turned upside down. The CCP had mastered the insidious art of orchestrating what writer Bette Bao Lord described as "invisible and silent misery." Because of this draconian system, inmates controlled each other to the point that their behavior became robotic.

Among other things, the mental and physical torture suffered by millions of Chinese, and the constant threat of similar treatment to those not arrested, resulted in the development of a disease known as *houpa* (how-pah) or "delayed fear"—something that remains just below the surface in China today.

See **Gongchanzhuyi, Lao Gai Dui, Lao Jiao, Laodong Jiaoyang**.

性别

Xingbie

(Sheng-bee-eh)

"Not Tonight, Dear!"

Caucasian men resident in Hong Kong from the 1950s through the 1980s, and those who had occasion to regularly visit mainland China during that period, generally rated Chinese women as the "prudes of Asia"—cold, distant and passive when it came to sex—a historical legacy that they still have not fully overcome.

Despite the presence of concubines and courtesans throughout the history of China, and the existence of some of the world's first and most explicit pornographic books, sex as a subject for discussion or learning was practically taboo until the 1980s.

The sexually explicit material that did exist, and access to women for sexual pleasure, was mostly limited to the elite.

For centuries, most young Chinese women went to the marriage bed without any knowledge of the male genitalia or the sex act, and most probably never learned that the act can be pleasurable.

Social psychologists say that the reason Chinese society kept sexual behavior under such strict control was because attraction between the sexes, and behavior based on sexual attraction, was diametrically opposed to every facet of Chinese culture, from the inferior position of women and arranged marriages, to the demands of respect and loyalty between sons and fathers, and the patriarchal society in general.

In fact, the effective functioning of China's traditional society was based to an extraordinary degree on keeping most women absolutely ignorant of sex, preventing them from having affectionate relationships with men, and generally suppressing any kind of sexual activity other than male-initiated intercourse following marriage.

Some Chinese critics say that sexual repression is responsible for the extraordinary amount of spitting, farting and littering that takes place in China, as well as for the Chinese obsession with food.

The Chinese Communist Party, which took over the country in 1949, continued the policy of generally ignoring the sexual needs of the people. Sexual liaisons among unmarried people were prohibited. Husbands and wives were routinely assigned to workplaces that made it impossible for them to live together and often limited their visits to once a year.

Sex education was prohibited in the schools. As far as the government was concerned, *xingbie* (sheng-bee-eh), or *sexuality*, was incompatible with Communist ideology, just as it had historically been incompatible with Confucianism.

It was not until the Communist Party began to grant a modicum of freedom to the people of China in the late 1970s and 1980s that the trauma inflicted upon the population by the suppression of human sexuality began to be addressed publicly, and that young people began to take the situation into their own hands.

Statistics made public during these years revealed that hospitals and clinics throughout the country were swamped by young female patients whose physical and mental ailments could be traced to sexual repression or trauma resulting from their first experiences with sexual intercourse.

By the early 1990s, the position of *xingbie* in China had changed dramatically. Imitating Western films and television shows, young Chinese men and women were dating and engaging in premarital sex very much like they do in the U.S. and Europe. Brothels and call-girl rings were flourishing, despite regular attempts to squash them.

If China continues to develop along the same paths followed by Japan and Korea, both of which had similar Confucian-oriented societies before they embraced modernism, China's sexual pendulum will continue its swing away from repression to the opposite extreme—freedom to indulge and experiment that goes well beyond what is common in the U.S. and other Western countries.

姓名

Xing Ming

(Sheeng Meeng)

"Old Hundred Names"

The Chinese were among the first people to have family names—a custom attributed to the Emperor Fu Xi some 5,000 years ago, who probably came up with the concept as a means of helping to keep track of the growing population.

It appears that Fu started the practice by assigning names to 100 families (hence the now famous "Old Hundred Names"), taking the names from occupations, titles, locations and other common designations. For centuries, "Old Hundred Names" has been synonymous with the "Chinese people."

Wang, for example, means *title*; Wu means *trade*, Tang means *district*, Jiang means *feudal territory*, and so on.

For the first 2,000 or so years of recorded Chinese history the social system was matriarchal. All descent was traced through the mother and it was the mother's name that was passed on from one generation to the next.

However, by 1200 B.C., during the Shang Dynasty, Chinese society had become patriarchal, and since then it has been the father's name that is passed on to children.

While some authorities say there were fewer than 500 family names in China during dynastic times, recent statistics released by the government indicate that there are around 5,700 *xing ming* (sheeng meeng) in the country.

Traditionally all Chinese had three names—the family name, a generational name, which they shared with all other siblings and first cousins, and a given name. It was also common for babies to have "milk names," and for people to assume new names when they became adults.

It is the custom in China to give, and write, the family name first, followed by the generational name and/or the given name (since nowadays not all people have generational names).

In earlier times generational names were selected by the clan associations. Now they are more likely to be chosen by elder members of the extended family. Fathers have traditionally selected the given names, always striving to pick names that will bring good fortune and long life to the children.

It has also become common in recent decades to run generational and *ming zi* or *given names* together as one word when writing them in roman letters, making it appear that people have only a family name and a personal given name.

Because of the scarcity of family names, the commonality of generational names, and the general practice of not using given names, it has long been customary in China for people to be given nicknames, which are usually names that refer to a physical characteristic or distinctive habit, and are noted for their humorous nuances.

It is also becoming more and more common for Chinese involved in international trade or other foreign affairs to adopt Western first names, both for the international flavor and to make it easier for foreigners to pronounce and remember their names.

Chinese women do not take the family names of their husbands when they marry. They keep their own family names.

性骚扰

Xing Saorao
(Sheeng Sah-oh-rah-oh)

"Introducing Sexual Harassment"

In pre-modern China well-to-do men, which mostly meant government officials and landlords, were socially and legally permitted to have a number of wives, concubines and female servants to whom they had sexual access.

Prostitution existed throughout the ages in China, and it was often said that the only recreation engaged in by the millions of men living in rural China was having sex with women—a custom energetically followed by Mao Zedung, the founder of the People's Republic of China, despite his enlightened views about women. After Mao's death his personal physician revealed that Mao was a serial mistress-keeper, regularly romped with two or three girls at a time in his private quarters, and that at the time of his death, September 9, 1976, he had two live-in mistresses.

Many of China's most famous literary works ranged from liberal to pornographic in their treatment of sexual themes. But these too were primarily male-oriented and treated women as playthings for men.

To say that pre-modern Chinese men were male chauvinists begs the point. Women had absolutely no inherent rights to their sexuality—something that has changed dramatically, however, since the 1980s.

One of the signs of change in China is the appearance of more and more female entrepreneurs, many of whom have been successful enough to attract national attention and become celebrities.

But most Chinese women who step outside of the traditional female roles expose themselves to the harsh realities of a society that remains sexist to the core, despite women having made conspicuous advances in sports, entertainment, medicine, politics and other fields.

Some of the abuses of the past, such as buying and selling young women to be used as slaves or concubines, are now rare, although in many rural areas of China girls are still committed to marriages when they are only two or three years old.

Men in power in China, whether government officials or private individuals, and on whatever level, have traditionally used their positions to take sexual advantage of women, and things in New China have not changed that much.

This practice was, in fact, the accepted norm and there was no concept of *xing saorao* (sheeng sah-oh-rah-oh) or *sexual harassment* in the country until the 1990s. Li Quingshan, head of China's Social Psychology Association, says the idea of sexual harassment is still totally alien to most Chinese men.

The extent of sexual abuse in China is revealed by surveys which show that more than nine out of ten women between the ages of 16 and 30 have experienced sexual harassment, and one quarter of these women report that the abuse included forced sexual intercourse.

Not surprisingly, China's move toward a market economy has resulted in sexual abuse of women being "modernized" in keeping with the times. While sex has not yet become the primary theme of most consumer advertising in China, as it has in the U.S. and elsewhere, practically every woman in business is subjected to systematic sexual harassment of one kind or another.

Female entrepreneurs in particular are victimized by the male-dominated business world, where it often appears to be taken for granted that a woman will "grant sexual favors" as part of her dues for doing business. Stories of women having to engage in sex for such simple things as getting orders filled are common.

One businesswoman in Beijing observed that men in positions of power who gladly accept bribes of cash, gifts and sumptuous banquets from men, almost always think in terms of sex when approached by women, and readily admitted that she took advantage of this male penchant.

This woman, whom the newspapers dubbed "The Iron Lady" because her business continued to prosper during bad times, said she first tried offering cash bribes like everyone else. When that failed she began offering "special relaxation programs" to suppliers and clients to relieve them of job stress. Her business boomed.

During the early decades of the Communist regime in China it was official CCP doctrine that premarital sex was degenerate and should be severely punished. Anything referring to the pleasure provided by sexual activity was denigrated as "bourgeois humanism," which, as far as the government was concerned, was beneath true Socialist men and women.

By the 1980s this denial of human sexuality had become one of the more irrational anachronisms of Maoism, and was in the process of being "humanized" by the young people of the country.

But intimate relationships between foreign males and Chinese females are still a sensitive issue throughout most of China, and should be approached with discretion.

信用

Xin Yong

(Sheen Yung)

"Ties Binding Businessmen"

Top-class Chinese businessmen in Hong Kong, and in Taiwan, Malaysia, Singapore and other major overseas Chinese communities, live and operate by a set of rules and relationships that significantly distinguishes them from both their cousins in mainland China and their non-Chinese counterparts.

The extraordinary success of these business tycoons is based to a substantial degree on their being members of specific groups of other ethnic Chinese in their own cities and countries, as well as in other areas.

These group memberships in turn are based on a special kind of relationship that is referred to as *xin yong* (sheen yung), which means something like *social-financial credit*.

Xin yong refers to an individual's trustworthiness, personal reliability and corporate financial stability—the criterion by which overseas Chinese in particular determine the qualifications for a potential business relationship.

Becoming an accepted member of such a group begins with establishing strong personal ties founded on character, reliability as business partners, trust, confidence, discretion, mutual obligations and impeccable credit rating.

These are the famous but still shadowy men making the mega-deals that are modernizing Asia at a fantastic pace—deals involving power, transportation, huge industrial parks, hotels, entertainment facilities, and more. Stories have it that these tycoons regularly agree on multimillion dollar deals without any input from consultants, accountants or lawyers, and with no written record other than possibly a personal note they write to themselves.

Members of this group have not invented anything new, but they are taking the traditional Chinese concept of using personal connections to its ultimate, on a local as well as regional basis. In one sense, they operate in a different dimension than most Western businesspeople. Theirs is much more of a private, personal world—not one that revolves around accountants, bankers, lawyers, consultants and others.

On a personal note, these entrepreneurs generally follow the Chinese philosophy of receding into the background as they become more successful. The Chinese have learned over the ages that it is much easier and generally more effective to exercise power from behind the scenes, staying totally away from the daily hubbub of business.

Because of the size of some of their deals, however, these men have had to come out of the shadows to some extent in order to coordinate their projects with the appropriate governments, but they have not forgotten the age-old Chinese warning "Fear fame as pigs fear getting fat," and they continue to keep low profiles.

Virtually none of the original founders of these great commercial empires had any Western-type training in business management, and the first generation did not expose their sons to such training.

Said one: "We learned from our fathers, primarily around the dinner table. Practically every meal was a seminar at which our fathers lectured us on philosophy, ethics and human relations—not on doing business in the Western sense.

"We were taught to take a human approach to business—not the rational, logical approach that deals with products, productivity, prices and profits.

"Our guidelines were very strict standards of loyalty, trust, sincerity, modesty, and always behaving like ideal Chinese gentleman. We were taught to put ourselves in the other person's place, to avoid confrontation, and to make business decisions based on our intuition, our cultural knowledge, our ability to 'read' people."

It is difficult for Chinese businesspeople to apply the *xin yong* criterion to foreigners because they know foreigners generally do not do business on trust alone; are not intimately affiliated with networks that will help guarantee their reliability and performance; and generally do not have their own financial networks.

But there are growing indications that Western businesspeople are beginning to pick up on the philosophy and principles of *xin yong*. Those who are able to commit themselves to this ancient Chinese practice will certainly find it much easier to do business in Asia.

Xu
(Shuu)

"Winning Through Waiting"

The people of China waited for nearly five thousand years for the few freedoms they now enjoy and for the possibility that they may be granted more freedoms in the near future. This long wait produced a number of distinctive qualities in the Chinese character that set them apart from other people.

Of course, premiere among these character traits is almost infinite patience. Traditionally the Chinese have had to wait for weeks to months to get action from bureaucrat offices; to wait for years for the opportunity to improve their lifestyle; even to wait for generations for significant social or political changes—that could have been made immediately if those in power had the will.

The whole weight of the traditional Chinese system of government and the philosophies that sustained it gave the highest priority to approaching all things slowly and cautiously, and to keeping the lowest possible profile in all activities in order to avoid attracting dangerous attention from gods, enemies and the authorities.

The fifth element in the great *Book of Changes*, which dates back more than three thousand years, details the importance of *xu* (shuu) or *calculated waiting* in the affairs of men—emphasizing that it takes precedence over all but a few of the factors controlling and impacting on human life.

Xu, say the sages with infinite common sense, is the most crucial during times of chaos, when political powers are contending against each other; when immorality, corruption and violence are stalking the land; when new causes and new concepts are being introduced, and when things are out of control.

During such times, the sages warn, anything that an individual wants or tries that is out of the ordinary is likely to result in serious problems, and it is therefore best to practice *xu*.

Such times, the sages add, do not have to be entirely negative because they can be used to test and strengthen one's character and resolve, and that if you show great confidence and steadiness in times of crisis people will seek your advice and assistance, and help you survive.

It is also advised that surviving and not losing ground during chaotic times is greatly enhanced if you maintain a positive, friendly attitude, and seek to develop relationships with other people who are of the same mind.

By maintaining your mental balance through *xu*, continue the sages, you will be in a position to recognize the opportunities that do exist and can safely take advantage of them—often through outside help that comes to you unexpectedly.

Foreigners who persevere in living and working in China, and are successful, are invariably those who develop the mental skills and physical toughness to engage in *xu*.

There is, however, a way that often helps to speed up the "calculated waiting" period that is characteristically built into Chinese behavior.

The first step is to go beyond interfacing with just one individual, identifying and developing a personal relationship with others who have any interest or involvement in the decision/action you are seeking, or who have strong connections with the person you are trying to influence.

The key to influencing the behavior of Chinese is always to create a scenario in which they immediately see a personal advantage to themselves—or a disadvantage if you don't want them to react positively.

260

贾

Ya
(Yah)

"Things Couldn't Be Better"

Some aspects of Chinese culture have a timeless grace that pleasures the soul. But all too often the Chinese scenes of grace that are the most memorable last for very brief periods of time—sometimes just for instants—and more likely than not are separated in an unworldly way from the harsh realities of life.

One such tableau that always comes to my mind are scenes of farmers in distant fields, or workers on distant hills, etched against a background of timelessness that could be anywhere on the Chinese continuum.

Other examples are reflected in some of the architecture, fine arts and handicrafts of China. Temples and pagodas are often imbued with an element of grace that transcends space and time as are many of the lacquerwares and ceramics.

There is also a conspicuous element of *ya* (yah) or *grace* in the appearance and behavior of many older Chinese—their faces chiseled into masks of serenity; their movements as natural as that of flowing water.

These same qualities are often present, but less apt to be identified as such, in Chinese women of all ages, including young, beautiful women who are as modern and stylish as one can be.

China's sages of old put a great deal of emphasis on the importance of *ya* in life, perhaps because it was something that everyone could aspire to because it did not represent any danger to the individual or the state, and because it brought a measure of contentment to lives that were generally mean and drab.

But there were warnings that came with the pursuit of grace. It was noted in blunt terms that grace was an ephemeral quality and even though it brought peace of mind it was not solid enough to build relationships on and was no substitute for knowledge, hard work and diligence.

At the same time, the sages acknowledged that a measure of *ya* was a significant asset in one's earthly endeavors; not only because of its tranquilizing effect on the individual but also because its influence on others was positive, resulting in them paying more attention and respect to the graceful person.

The sages also advised that at its highest level, grace was not put on or ostentatious, but was the essence of natural simplicity in all things—thoughts as well as actions.

Recognizing the graceful aspects of Chinese culture is not an automatic skill. It is something that often eludes Westerners, particularly those who are in a hurry and have their eyes focused on a different dimension.

Westerners who do recognize *ya* and are capable of incorporating a substantial degree of it into their own lives will find themselves much more comfortable in China, and much better received by their Chinese friends and associates.

261

严打

Yanda

(Yen-dah)

"Hitting Criminals Hard"

Criminals, political enemies and people who "embarrass the state" have always been treated harshly in China, with the death penalty being the preferred punishment.

And historically, government authorities, military commanders, warlords and others in positions to condemn and execute people were not content merely to dispatch them in an efficient or painless manner.

Among the more gruesome ways of executing prisoners or victims was by "slicing." Victims were killed by a slow and exceedingly painful process of having their flesh cut off in slices, as a butcher carves meat.

In earlier times there were almost always four motives involved in most executions: eliminating the condemned to get them out of the way and avoid any future problems with them, punishing them for their behavior or attitudes, extracting revenge by making them suffer, and providing shocking examples to deter other people from becoming offenders.

The preferred method of execution in China today is a bullet in the back of the head. But the death penalty, often carried out in public, is still arbitrarily used by the government as a deterrent, to shock other people into obeying laws as well as extra-legal guidelines set down by the authorities.

In present-day China there are some forty-nine kinds of crimes that are subject to the death penalty, ranging from murder, espionage, rape, bribery, corruption, embezzlement and pandering to the destruction of property.

Although China's judicial system is supposed to be independent of the executive branch, political leaders routinely assume the power to order blanket use of the death penalty for relatively minor offenses.

China's Supreme Court (the Supreme People's Court) has vowed to sentence to death anyone guilty of crimes that harm the country's image or jeopardize its economic reforms—generally leaving it up to local courts to decide when either of these two offenses has occurred.

Zhang Xin, legal expert at the Chinese University in Hong Kong, notes: "Law has and always needs to serve political purposes in China."

In some provinces people guilty of economic crimes involving as little as 30,000 yuan ($5,300) face the death penalty. Killing an animal on the endangered species list and selling its fur for profit is punishable by the death penalty.

China's anti-crime campaigns that call for the death penalty in economic corruption and morals cases are known as *yanda* (yen-dah), or *hardhits*—based on the public position of the Supreme People's Court that China "cannot have a soft hand" in dealing with criminals.

One of the practices that is common in China, Japan and other Asian countries is for the authorities to appear to be lax about enforcing laws for several months, and then stage large-scale raids, arresting hundreds to thousands in a single night, and then stage equally conspicuous showcase trials and, in the case of China, public executions.

The *yanda* approach to law enforcement is typically Communist Party Chinese because people never know what is going to be suddenly labeled an offense calling for the death penalty, or when such a campaign is to be initiated.

Foreign businesspeople active in China should at all times be aware of the arbitrary actions of local authorities and courts in deciding on what constitutes an economic crime, and what the punishment will be.

262

宴会

Yanhui

(Yahn-huu-ee)

"A Chinese Style Banquet"

Western visitors to China frequently comment on the fact that, in rural areas in particular, Chinese toddlers that have not yet been toilet-trained are dressed in bottomless outfits that allow them to "go" anywhere, anytime, without soiling their clothing.

Whatever else this custom might do to the personality of the Chinese it apparently does not result in any kind of anal fixations because all Western authorities who have studied China seem to agree that the Chinese are orally fixated.

Descriptions of eating habits as well as sexual activity in China, both old and contemporary, appear to reinforce the idea that the Chinese are more oral than anal.

A Chinese style *yanhui* (yahn-huu-ee) *banquet* is one of the greatest "oral orgies" available to man, designed as it is to please the eye, the mouth and the mind.

The Chinese consider 12 the maximum number of diners that should be seated at a single table—insofar as food, conversation and personal interaction are concerned—and the standard *yanhui* round table seats this number.

It is also generally standard to order one dish per person, which means that a "full table course" will usually consist of one or two cold appetizers, eight or ten middle dishes and one or two "desserts."

Foreigners who are not familiar with Chinese banquets all too often gorge themselves on the appetizers and first two or three middle dishes, and are unable to fully enjoy the rest of the meal.

In many banquet situations, the course has been ordered in advance. If not, the waiter or waitress brings one menu for the host, who orders for the entire group. The challenge to the host is to demonstrate his or her knowledge of the *yin-yang* balance of the dishes, and to order them in the right sequence.

Foreigners who have not had considerable practice in the art of ordering Chinese food for Chinese guests would be better off not making the attempt. Chances are what and how they order will reveal their ignorance and spoil the meal for their guests.

If you find yourself in this position the best idea is to arrive at the restaurant early, or before sitting down, get the chef or head waiter aside, explain how many guests there will be, how much you want to spend per person, and ask their advice on the dishes or the set course.

Another point to keep in mind when hosting or attending a *yanhui*: rice or rice dishes are not served until near the end or at the end of the meal. At really upscale banquets there may be no rice served at all, because rice has the image of being a cheap food that is primarily eaten by lower class people who can't afford anything better.

However, most internationalized Chinese hosts have learned that foreigners generally think of rice as bread and like to eat it with the other dishes, and, if asked, will have plain rice brought at the beginning of the meal.

Learning how to order Chinese food is by itself an interesting lesson in Chinese philosophy. It is also a very effective way to demonstrate your interest in Chinese culture and your respect for Chinese traditions, and will get you a lot of social and business mileage in your dealings with Chinese.

(Peking duck—now "Beijing duck!" in Beijing—and shark's fin soup are always acceptable as main dishes.)

At business and formal social or political banquets, it is very important for the host to personally welcome each guest and to also see them off when the banquet ends. The host generally makes a short welcome speech and calls for a toast, and the chief guest is expected to respond in kind.

If guests are not bilingual the host should make sure that one or more interpreters are available to facilitate mingling and light-hearted conversations. (There is a saying in China, "Before doing business, first laugh together.")

A significant difference between Chinese banquets and similar gatherings in the West is that the Chinese do not drag out the ending of a dinner party. The practice is for everyone to leave immediately after the farewell toast—not break up into small groups and linger for private chats.

A regular evening dinner party in Mandarin (Putongua) is *wan can hui*.

263

夷

Yi

(Eee)

"Dealing with Barbarians"

For more than four thousand years of China's recorded history, the world consisted of the culturally and technologically advanced Chinese living within the confines of the Middle Kingdom and trying to keep hordes of non-Chinese barbarians, mostly on the northern frontiers, on the outside.

One of the earliest ideograms created in the now famous Chinese system of writing was the character *yi* (eee) in reference to these savage outsiders.

Eventually the Chinese began referring to all non-Chinese as *yi* because virtually all the people they came into contact with were primitive and culturally savage by their standards.

When numbers of Europeans began showing up in the Middle Kingdom from the 15th century and on, the Chinese also referred to them as *yi*, unofficially as well as officially.

Yi translates as *barbarian*, a nomenclature that did not sit well with the representatives of foreign countries who began visiting China for diplomatic and trade purposes, because they generally regarded themselves and their cultures as superior to the Chinese.

Despite the cultural sophistication and the advanced technology of some of these first European visitors to China, the majority of the foreigners who came into early contact with China were pirates, sailors and other rough characters with atrocious manners and habits that repelled the Chinese and did nothing to change their image of all foreigners as barbarians.

When the British became active in China in the early 1800s, primarily as opium merchants, they were greatly disturbed at being called *yi* by the Chinese government.

Angered at China's attempts to halt the opium trade, the British attacked and captured Canton in December 1857, took the forts of Dagu outside of Tianjin in May 1858, and began threatening Beijing itself.

The Qing government capitulated and agreed to sign a new treaty, opening more ports to foreign trade, allowing for a British ambassador to be stationed in Beijing, and permitting travel in the country and the preaching of Christianity.

In addition, the "Treaty of Tianjin" stipulated that all interior transit taxes on foreign imports would be dropped, that English would be the official language of communication between Great Britain and China, and that the character for barbarian, *yi* would no longer be used in Chinese documents referring to the British.

Cultural habits molded over a period of forty centuries are not that easy to erase, however, and the "Treaty of Tianjin" did not end the use of *yi* to describe foreigners.

Yi was still in common use in China in the mid–1900s, but it had lost some of its "barbarian" connotation and become little more than a derogatory term for foreigners. Now, foreigners are more apt to use the term than the Chinese—usually as self-deprecating humor.

264

易

Yi

(Eee)

"Here Today Gone Tomorrow"

Western wise men (religious prophets, philosophers, law-makers or whatever) looked at the world and saw that it was filled with forces and events that could not be controlled; that even within the most tranquil-appearing setting, there was constant change and that the natural order of the universe seemed to be chaos.

These wise men were determined to bring order to that tiny portion of the cosmos they inhabited, and began by creating gods to act as their divine messengers so that people would pay attention to what they had to say.

They then set about creating worlds based on moral absolutes. There was the divine and the profane; the good and the evil; and nothing in between. Because they could not reconcile that man can be good one time and bad another, they separated him into flesh and spirit.

Because Westerners could not understand or control the destructive forces of nature, they attributed them to the anger of gods who were displeased with human behavior. Disobeying god-given laws, and in some societies even thinking "immoral" thoughts, became a sin punishable on earth as well as in heaven.

China's wise men took an entirely different approach to dealing with the cosmos. They concluded that *yi* (eee) or *change* was the natural state of the cosmos, that change was therefore inevitable and forever, and that the logical approach for man was to attempt to stay in harmony with the constant changing.

The Chinese did not create absolute laws handed down by gods or based on universal principles of good and bad. They created an earth-bound moral system based on a social hierarchy in which morality was defined by the relationship between people, not adherence to unchanging universal principles.

Yi thus became a fundamental part of Chinese morality. Relationships were circumstantial; morality was therefore circumstantial. Over the millennia the practical side of Chinese nature has resulted in the construction of numerous guidelines for behavior that are based on absolutes, but *yi* remains the starting point of Chinese ethics.

One of the biggest challenges facing Westerners dealing with Chinese is overcoming the obstacles presented by a mutually contradictory approach to agreements. The Chinese way is to structure the relationship on a personal, circumstantial basis, while the Western way is to base the relationship on unchanging principles of fairness and reciprocal benefit.

For Westerners and Chinese to forge durable business and political relations, both sides must make numerous compromises in their attitudes and behavior, and the relationships must be constantly nurtured to keep them on the same or even parallel tracks.

One of the biggest and most common mistakes Westerners make in their dealings with Chinese is to reduce the degree and scope of their relationship-building and nurturing as soon as the agreement or contract is signed.

颐

Yi

(Eee)

"Nourishing Your Spirit"

Centuries of experience, observation and contemplation have gone into the Chinese concept of properly nourishing the spirit and the intellect in order to achieve one's highest personal potential and contribute the most to family, friends, associates and the world at large.

This concept of nurturing the mind is expressed in the word *yi* (eee), which is pronounced the same as the ideogram for *change* (as are more than fifty other characters). But this *yi* literally means *nourishing*, and reflects the holistic view that China's sages recommend for all personal relationships.

The *yi* concept covers the "correct nourishing" of one's self as well as everyone else with whom one has contact or wishes to support. The key word in this endeavor is "correct," since nourishing may be good or bad—and obviously if it is bad the influence is negative.

Given the importance of positive nourishing, the first challenge in nurturing one's self, according to the sages, is to determine if your own attitudes and motives are constructive and worthy, or if you are motivated by narrow-minded, selfish goals that may harm yourself as well as others.

The advice of the sages is to clean up your own character before trying to strengthen your influence over others or manipulate events to your advantage. By the same token, they say you should exercise equal care in choosing the people you support.

As is always the case in Chinese guidelines for behavior, the foundation of *yi* is self-discipline; to be unrelenting in your efforts to avoid exposure to unsettling images or thoughts, to maintain a calm, balanced attitude toward all things, and to speak in moderate terms.

In the Chinese context of *yi* the human failing that is the most destructive to the proper nourishing of the mind and spirit is envy, and unless envy is eliminated misfortune will surely result. The next most dangerous pitfall is relying on inadequate methods or unreliable people in pursuing your goals.

Looking for nourishment in the wrong places and from the wrong things is given as the next most common failing among people, and can only be resolved by self-reflection, a commitment to find the right path and not deviate from it.

Once on the right path, the sages continue, the individual should not depend only on his or her own strength and efforts to achieve worthy goals, and is advised to enlist the aid of others, particularly people in superior positions who have mastered themselves and the practice of *yi*.

The Chinese believe that those who follow the path of *yi* will achieve personal success, and in their senior years will themselves be in a position to nourish others and contribute to their success and happiness.

In interacting with foreigners, the Chinese are constantly trying to "read" their spirits and passing judgment on how and to what degree the foreigners practice *yi*.

Foreigners who do not exhibit any significant cultural and spiritual depth and basically ignore *yi* invariably come up short by Chinese standards.

266

益

Yi

(Eee)

"Your Brother's Keeper"

Throughout the history of China its philosophers have taught that virtue is the foundation for all human affairs, and that virtue—Chinese style, of course—is the single most important quality in all areas and on all levels of human life.

In its traditional Chinese context, virtue consisted of a selfless, overriding devotion to the welfare of others, to the point that one would readily sacrifice his or her life.

It was further taught that the more authority one had over others the greater should be his or her virtue. The emperor, as the supreme being in the land, was expected to be the most virtuous of all—and, in theory at least, his right to rule was based on maintaining an unblemished record of serving his subjects.

One of the keys to the expression of Chinese style virtue is bound up in the concept of *yi* (eee), another of the many *yi* compounds in Chinese, which in this instance means *benefit*.

At its deepest level, *yi* represents an "increase" in all of the elements that make up a healthy, thriving society, and when used for that purpose it is at its most powerful.

Yi is a special kind of energy that is a static force, at rest you might say, that has extraordinary potential for benefitting others, and in the process one's self as well, when it is applied at the right time in the right way.

The "right way and right time" refer to situations when the successful attainment of your own goals can be coordinated with direct, significant benefits to your employees, followers or society as a whole, with these benefits taking precedence over what you yourself gain.

In other words, the true power of *yi* is fully expressed only when it is being used for the benefit of others. This does not mean, however, that the power of *yi* cannot be deliberately used for personal gain when your goals are worthy. The benefit to others simply has to be there and be conspicuously obvious.

The psychology behind *yi* is that the more generous you are and the more you help others the more they will help and support you, and the more loyal they will be in your time of need.

As usual, the Chinese sages recommend that *yi* be used in conjunction with improving one's character, noting that the potential rewards will be greatly enhanced.

The Chinese believe that a person who, through self-reflection and self-discipline, has achieved complete virtue—has eliminated ego, is no longer selfish in any way, and is concerned only about the needs of others—can exercise enormous influence over others without persuasion or pressure.

This is the ultimate manifestation of the energy of *yi*, and represents the philosophical as well as the practical goal of Chinese sages.

Suffice to say that throughout China's history, the people who were most apt to live by the rules of *yi* were the philosophers themselves—not the ruling elite.

Foreigners who become deeply involved with China (and other Confucian-influenced countries of Asia) soon learn that the most admired people in the country are those who exhibit the purest qualities of *yi*.

A word of warning for non-Asians, however. All too often non-Asians mistake the refined manners, humble mien, and gentle appearance of older, senior Chinese businesspeople and political leaders for virtue in the Western sense.

Some of the most amoral and unscrupulous Chinese imaginable are often kind-looking and gentle-behaving grandfatherly types who appear to be the epitome of virtue and integrity to Westerners and others who are not attuned to Chinese ways.

267

Yi

(Eee)

"Doing What Is Right"

Not surprisingly, the ancient Chinese looked upon sheep as the epitome of selfless docility and as symbolic of the character and behavior that was ideal for human beings.

The symbol for sheep thus became the first building block in the ideogram for *yi* (eee) or *righteousness*—which refers not only to basic character but also to the way one should behave. (The other two building block radicals in *yi* are a hand and a spear; the hand representing an individual and the spear apparently representing determination to pierce the heart of the matter.)

Confucius taught that *yi* was one of the virtues that was inherent in human beings but that it was a seed that had to be carefully and continuously cultivated in order for it to manifest itself in one's behavior.

Confucius also taught that righteous behavior was its own reward, that people should be good for the sake of goodness and their own development, not for any benefit here or in the hereafter. He preached that it was only by living a righteous life that people could achieve their full potential as spiritual beings.

Mencius, the noted Confucianist sage who lived from 371 B.C. to 289 B.C., expanded on the horizons of *yi*, saying that it should be the basis for a universal philosophy that would make mankind citizens of the universe.

As typically happens, however, selfishness, avarice and a lust for power got in the way of enlightened philosophy, and the practice of universal righteousness in China was primarily limited to the philosophers themselves and to people who were poor and powerless.

Among the better-to-do Chinese, including the ruling elite, who often saw themselves as champions of *yi*, the practice was generally confined to relatives, close associates and friends.

In present-day China there are at least five kinds of *yi*. There is Confucian and Mencian righteousness, Communist righteousness, Socialist righteousness, capitalist righteousness and the righteousness of ordinary people trying to survive in a society in which policies take precedence over principles.

All of these variations of *yi* are, of course, muted by the ongoing attitudes and activities of the nonbelievers; those who subscribe totally to the virtue of selfishness.

One of the challenges in dealing with individual Chinese today is determining the kind of righteousness that motivates them, and fashioning your response accordingly.

Generally, it is safer and often the most effective, to base your approach on the traditional Confucian and Mencian models of the ideal human being, letting your Chinese counterparts know that you are a firm believer in the guidelines set down by Confucius (Kung Fuzi), and that his ideals are the basis for the relationship you are seeking with them.

印记
Yinji (Zhang)
(Een-jee / Chahng)

"Making Things Official"

Historians tell us that until the end of the Ming Dynasty in 1644 the bureaucracy of Imperial China was the largest, best organized and most efficient civil service in the world.

With a population of more than 120 million (more than all of Europe combined), the country's towns and cities were thriving centers of commerce. Art, literature and music was an integral part of the lives of the middle and upper classes.

The country's infrastructure—its system of canals, barges, boats, roads, inns, government buildings and the like—were unsurpassed anywhere. The size, architecture and luxury of the Imperial palaces in Beijing made most of the rest of the world's famous buildings pale in comparison.

The nation's elite lived in surroundings that were luxurious even by today's standards.

The territory of China was divided into 15 huge provinces that were presided over by a hierarchy of bureaucrats under the control of Beijing, beginning with governors and going all the way down from city mayors and county magistrates, to tax officials, police and mail couriers.

One of the ways this bureaucracy exercised its control, and made itself indispensable, was through the use of *yinji* (een-jee) or inked *seals* required on a wide variety of documents to make them official.

All government offices and officials had official seals or stamps that they used to certify letters, records and documents of whatever kind as a key part of their activities.

For many centuries these seals were made of stone and were called *feng yin* or *stone seals*. But stone was replaced by rubber as soon as this material became available, and now official office seals are called *gong zhang*.

Bureaucracy still rules in China, and *zhang* are still an important part of the business scene—although reforms first initiated in the southeastern provinces have greatly reduced the number of individual seals required on many business documents.

In the early 1980s as many as 100 or more different seals were required on applications for joint ventures, a process that took anywhere from one to two years to complete. One governor, frustrated by the existence of this *yin-ji* overkill, ordered all of the different agencies involved to consolidate in one building and gave them a 3-day deadline for stamping new business applications that already had his approval.

Individual Chinese as well are required to have personal *zhang* for all of the occasions when they must "sign" official documents of any kind. To be official, their name seals must be registered with their local district office.

It would seem that one of the reasons why name seals rather than signatures came into use in China was because of the infinitesimally small number of family names. It is therefore a bit odd that the common term for seals is *zhang*, the most common family name in the country, with an estimated 100 million people named Zhang (Chang).

隐私

Yinsi

(Eeen-suh)

"Doing Without Privacy"

Many foreign visitors to China have described some of their experiences there as like being in a zoo in which they were one of the main attractions. They were referring to the propensity of the Chinese, especially those in outlying areas where foreigners are still rare, to stare unabashedly and sometimes intrusively at foreigners.

This experience, which is still common and may occur anytime the visitor is in public and involve dozens to hundreds of people, can be very upsetting to someone who is not inured to it and does not understand or appreciate the reason for it.

All Han Chinese look very much alike, while foreigners come in all colors, shapes and sizes and are therefore strange, exotic creatures that fascinate those Chinese who are not familiar with such human variety.

Furthermore, Chinese who have not been exposed to Western culture do not regard staring at someone as a rude or aggressive act, even when it is in a setting that the visitor regards as private. To them it is natural to stare at anybody or anything that is different and interesting, and as far as they are concerned the act is perfectly neutral.

The concept of privacy in the Western sense, in public or private, did not develop in China as it did in the West where populations were small, space was not a premium, and large homes with several rooms have been common for many centuries.

And until recent times there was no word for the Western concept of privacy. *Yinsi* (eeen-suh), although translated as *privacy*, basically means *hidden affairs* and has the connotation of something shady or secret.

The Chinese were culturally conditioned for millennia to share the same space and the same things, including belongings that Westerners regard as personal. There is still no word in the Chinese language that accurately expresses the Western concept, and little genuine appreciation of what it means and how important it is to Westerners.

It is because of this fundamental difference in lifestyle that most Chinese today see nothing wrong with staring at people in public, looking into open windows, entering rooms without knocking, reading other people's mail or business documents, poking into unattended purses, or using someone else's personal belongings.

Until recent times there was very little sense of individual ownership in a Chinese family. Generally speaking all possessions belonged to the family as a group. Since members did not "own" individual items of furniture or whatever, just as they did not "own" themselves, there were no restraints about using someone's comb or hairbrush, etc.

A growing number of Chinese families in the more affluent areas of the country are now able to afford multiroom homes and apartments just for themselves, but still today in the rural areas of China the concept of personal privacy and personal time is either very weak or nonexistent.

One aspect of the lack of privacy and private time that occurs regularly in business in China was humorously documented by Bill Purves in his book *Barefoot in the Boardroom* which recounted his "ventures and misadventures" in managing an iron products factory in Guangdong Province.

Purves noted that foremen or others wanting to talk to him—or to talk to people who were talking to him—would just wander into his office, pore themselves a cup of tea, sit around, read whatever documents he might have left on his desk, join in whatever conversation was going on, regardless of the topic, and eventually introduce their own subject when there was a break in the conversation.

He added that when a foreman or someone else, including visitors from the outside, was in a hurry to talk to him, they would customarily break into any conversation going on by beginning to talk in a loud voice when they were still one or two steps away from his door.

Purves said that this lack of any concept of privacy or personal time was very upsetting when he first took over as manager of the factory. But, knowing that he could not change the beliefs and habits of everyone who visited him, he changed his own values and accommodated himself to the Chinese way, eventually arriving at a point where he could function effectively within the system.

Other observers have noted that the Chinese are not passive by nature, as is suggested by their overseas image. Said one: "They are aggressive and regularly intrude on the space and privacy of others, apparently without any thought that they might be unwelcome."

Foreign visitors to China who are curious about how the Chinese handle more intimate relations when sharing rooms have been known to learn firsthand on crowded trains, with special reference to honeymooning couples.

Two other Chinese words that come fairly close to the Western concept of privacy, *sishi* and *sichu*, have strongly negative nuances of loneliness, secrecy and wanting to be alone because of a dislike of people.

Generally speaking the Chinese do not like to be alone and cannot understand why anyone would want to be by themselves. Because of this, they commonly try to fill up every hour of the foreign visitor's or resident's time, often to the point that it becomes a serious intrusion.

About the only way to counter these bothersome but good intentions is to very clearly, and often repeatedly, inform your Chinese hosts or friends that you have some personal business that you must take care of, and be specific about the hours or days that you want to yourself.

Having said all this, most Chinese, especially those in urban areas, do, in fact, have a sense of *personal* privacy and they do not like for it to be invaded. But, generally speaking, this applies only to their own privacy, not that of others.

See **Ai**.

阴／阳

Yin / Yang

(Een/Yahng)

"Dealing with Duality"

It may well be that China's greatest philosophical and scientific achievement was the concept of the bipolarity of the cosmic forces that create and animate all natural phenomena in the universe.

The Chinese learned a long time ago that the workings of nature along with the affairs of human beings are based on the unity of complementary opposites—the positive and negative, the light and dark, hot and cold, male and female, and so.

All of the actions and reactions in nature, the waxing and waning, rising and falling, growing and decaying, all were seen as phenomena of the cosmic process. They named the cold, dark, passive, negative side of this duality *yin* (een), and the hot, light, aggressive, positive side *yang* (yahng).

In this concept, none of the forces of the universe, or actions in the universe, were seen as good or bad within themselves. They became disruptive and destructive, however, if they got out of sync. Therefore the secret to living a "good, moral" life was to keep these forces in balance.

In this *yin-yang* world the ultimate goal was harmony, and in the hierarchical form of society that developed in China, anything that disturbed this harmony was undesirable or bad and things that contributed to harmony were desirable and good—a concept that was totally different from the view of good and evil that developed in the West.

The Chinese approach to explaining the mysteries of life and the universe did not begin or end with a god who created and controlled all things, and in whose name good and evil were defined by his earth-bound human ministers.

Obviously, the difference between behavior designed to maintain harmony, and behavior designed to abide by Christian-oriented morality can be as marked as the difference between day and night.

Among other things, the Christian orientation of Western thinking led to the creation of laws for the protection of individual human rights, whereas in China the primary aim of laws and regulations was to protect and preserve the ruling powers and to force the people to conduct themselves in the harmonious manner prescribed by those powers.

In practical terms, the harmony-oriented system that developed in China meant that people could lie, take "unfair" advantage, abuse others, engage in extramarital sexual behavior and do a variety of other things that Westerners consider immoral, and feel no guilt pangs whatsoever.

Most present-day Chinese still have a *yin-yang* perspective of the universe at large, meaning that maintaining harmony takes precedence in every aspect of their lives, from how they build homes, arrange their furniture, eat, conduct their personal lives and work, to interacting with other people.

_____271_____

用公司包围中央

Yong Gongsi Baowei Zhongyang

(Yung Gung-suh Bah-oh-way Chong-yahng)

"Smothering the Party"

The Communist Party of China (CCP) rode to power on the backs and bodies of the nation's poorest farmers—the so-called peasants who had suffered for generations, first under the heel of the emperors and a succession of warlords, and finally under Chiang Kai-shek and his Nationalist armies and administrators.

The CCP was begun in Beijing and Shanghai by a small core of well-educated intellectuals who were determined to rid China of foreign domination and destroy the elite power structure that had ruled the country from the beginning of its history.

But the Party wasn't strong enough, either philosophically or militarily, to win over the landlords, businesspeople and intellectuals, or to defeat the Nationalist armies of Chiang Kai-shek.

After several years of political and military effort, Mao Zedung, one of the junior leaders of the CCP, ended up in a remote rural area where he practiced and perfected a technique of getting the farmers on his side by encouraging and helping them to destroy the landlord class in their districts, assigning them plots of land that had been confiscated, and implementing a variety of reforms, including prohibiting arranged marriages.

After perfecting the strategy of using peasant-soldiers and creating his own economic base in the rural areas under his control, Mao turned the strategy into a revolutionary slogan which proclaimed that the CCP would use the countryside (farmers) to "surround, smother and take over the cities."

Mao's dream of creating a new Communist China was delayed for nearly two decades by ongoing battles with the Nationalist forces of Chang Kai-shek and the invasion of China by Japan, but in the end his strategy worked.

After achieving power in 1949, Mao and the CCP attempted the impossible. They tried to obliterate from the minds of the Chinese all thoughts of democracy and free enterprise by a combination of genocide and brainwashing that went way beyond the example set by Stalin and the Communist Party of the Soviet Union.

Of course, the effort failed but it left the CCP in absolute power. And in 1965 Lin Biao, the minister of defense and titular head of the People's Liberation Army, grandly announced that the poor third countries of the world would surround and strangle the superpowers and other capitalist countries.

This too failed, and as time went by it became more and more obvious that the people of China still preferred a democracy and a free market to the CCP and socialism, and that the real enemy of the country was the CCP itself.

This led to a take-off on the old Mao slogan of using the countryside (farmers) to crush the cities. The new slogan was *Yong Gongsi Baowei Zhongyang* (yung gung-suh bah-oh-way chong-yahng) or *Use Private Enterprise to Surround the Party Center*—the connotation being, of course, that private enterprise would eventually smother and kill the CCP; a typically Chinese way of turning the tables on an enemy.

The strategy, although neither planned nor coordinated, appears to be working.

272

有创造力的

Youchuangzaoli De
(Yoe-uu-chuu-ahng-zah-oh-lee Duh)

"Creativity in China"

The impulse to innovate and invent seems to be a natural instinct when people are faced with challenges and have the freedom to explore the possibility of doing things differently. This impulse also appears to increase as the level of knowledge rises.

China's long-suffering people have traditionally had more than their share of challenges, and among the upper class the accumulation of knowledge has always had the highest priority.

This combination of challenge and education resulted in a remarkable number of inventions in China between 2000 B.C. and 200 B.C.

Among the things invented by the Chinese during that period: cast iron, the iron plow (in the 6th century B.C.), the seed drill, the suspension bridge, the segmented arch bridge, the trace harness, paddlewheel boats that would travel at more than thirty miles per hour (in the 5th century B.C.), the belt drive, double-acting piston bellows, and steel.

From around 200 B.C., however, China's increasingly feudalistic social, economic and political systems became less and less conducive to innovation or invention, and in many cases prohibited change outright.

The overriding aim of the country's successive Imperial dynasties was to maintain themselves in power by keeping the people poor and powerless. Culture became fixated on the past, learning from it and sustaining it.

All of China's religion-like philosophies, Daoism, Confucianism and Buddhism, were based on a doctrine of conformity to the natural order of things, obedience to a higher social order, and sublimation of the ego and individuality—all of which entailed a high degree of passivity and tolerance.

The characteristics nurtured by these doctrines, combined with a deep reverence for the past, virtually eliminated any creative impulse in the Chinese, precluding all but the most innocuous and incremental innovations or changes.

In this milieu, the idea of allowing inventors to profit from the commercialization of their inventions and for merchants to build large profit-making businesses contradicted the very foundations of the Imperial system.

But despite this compulsion to maintain the status quo and emphasis on the past, the list of inventions remains impressive. Paper was invented by an Imperial Palace eunuch named Chai Lun in the year A.D. 105. He pulped tree bark, then screened a film of it onto a fish net.

The Sung Dynasty, from A.D. 960 to 1279, was distinguished by a second flood of technological and scientific advances, including printing with movable type and rockets.

During this period, China was not only the most populous country in the world, with over fifty cities that had populations in excess of half a million each, it was the richest and most advanced country in the world.

By the early 1600s, political conditions once again virtually stopped all innovation and experimenting in China, beginning a new stagnant period that was to last until after the middle of the 20th century.

The democracy movement that began in China in 1978, with "Big Letter Posters" put up on "Democracy Wall," could be called the first real step of the Chinese people toward the freedom that is necessary to release the genie of their *youchangzaoli de* (yoe-ou-chuu-ahng-zah-oh-lee duh) or *creativity*.

Just as the end of centuries of political repression in Japan in 1945 resulted in an explosion of creativity, the same will surely hold true in China. But there is reason to believe that the Chinese will develop their inherent creative abilities faster than the Japanese, and go farther.

While there were many similarities in traditional Chinese and Japanese culture, the Chinese remained far more independent minded and individualistic than the Japanese, and historically were far more creative.

Because of this factor, the Chinese will not have to go through a long reculturization process to become entrepreneurs and inventors. Virtually every Chinese is already highly motivated to become as independent and as individually rich and powerful as possible.

When the Chinese have the political freedom necessary to give full rein to their talents and ambitions, the results should be awesome.

忧患意识

Youhuan Yishi

(Yoe-ou-huu-enn Eee-she)

"The Disease of Patriotism"

Since ancient times China's intellectuals have played a dual, often contradictory role. On the one hand, they provided the country with an elite class of scholar-administrators who, for the most part, brought order and stability to the world's largest number of people.

On the other hand, the philosophical and moral systems these scholars created and helped to sustain for one millennium after the other kept the overwhelming majority of all Chinese illiterate, ignorant and in virtual bondage down to modern times.

Over the centuries it was bred into China's intellectuals that they were responsible for the security and progress of the country, but in practically every instance in which they and the country were challenged, they failed.

The most recent challenge to face China's intellectuals was the invasion of the alien and inhuman ideology of communism—an event that turned out to be the greatest challenge the intellectuals and China had ever faced—and their failure was in keeping with the scope of the challenge.

Following the end of the holocaust known as the Cultural Revolution, in 1976, China's intellectuals began scourging themselves, asking themselves over and over how the excesses of the Communist Revolution could have happened; how they could have *allowed* them to happen.

This soul-searching brought into question the validity of all the wisdom accumulated by their predecessors; of the very foundations of China's traditional culture; and gave rise to a new malaise known as *youhuan yishi* (yoe-ou-huu-enn eee-she) or *worry mentality*.

Youhuan yishi afflicts virtually all educated Chinese to some degree, but in particular those articulate and active intellectuals who see themselves as the inheritors of the role of the wise men of old—those who have traditionally been responsible for "all things under heaven."

Generally speaking this modern version of *youhuan yishi* is expressed in terms of patriotism—in what each individual can and should do to help repair the damage done to the Chinese psyche, and contribute to making the country strong.

There is no denying the sincerity or the strength of the "worry mentality," but it is being forced to manifest itself in a psychological environment that is filled with risk.

In today's China there is still a political context to every statement, every concept; and caution, often to the extreme, must be exercised to avoid causing the "official shadow" to fall on one.

Hopefully, wiser leaders in China will recognize the opportunity presented by *youhuan yishi* and harness its energy and strength to finally, after more than 5,000 years, let the innate genius of the Chinese flower.

274

友谊

Youyi

(Yoe-ou-ee)

"Here's to Friendship"

In broad terms, most Western societies are based on the concept of equality and laws. In contrast, Chinese society was traditionally based on the concept of inequality and personal relationships, rather than laws.

These fundamental differences made life in China far more uncertain, insecure and demanding than it was for most Westerners.

While Americans and other Westerners could take a wide range of things for granted, and not only expect but demand fair and equal treatment from government offices, private enterprises and individuals alike, the Chinese had no such expectations and could make no such demands.

Social interaction in China was initially determined by one's sex, age, class and rank, and secondarily by personal connections or relationships.

Within this milieu, family and friends were of extreme importance to the Chinese, because without them they had no access to the world at large; no one to support them; no one to lend them a helping hand.

This situation, which continues to exist today in only slightly weakened form, compels the Chinese to pay special attention to making and keeping friends, and adds a special poignancy to their friendships.

Westerners, who are often not used to regarding or conducting their friendships with such effusive enthusiasm, are frequently taken aback by the lengths to which the Chinese go to bind their relationships.

Because of the importance and the intensity of these personal ties, both the concept and practice of *youyi* (yoe-ou-ee), or *friendship*, means more to the Chinese than it does to many Westerners, and Chinese frequently use the term on an entirely different level.

In its Chinese context *youyi* does not mean the same thing as the English translation. It refers to a business relationship in which both parties fully respect the feelings and positions of each other, will do everything humanly possible to fulfill the spirit as well as the letter of all of their commitments to each other, and can be trusted to do the "right thing" no matter what happens.

To the Chinese, *youyi* is not a sentimental or casual thing. It is a life-long clan or blood-brother type of commitment—a relationship that some have referred to as "soul-binding."

Generally speaking, the Chinese prefer that *youyi* come before business. And before friendship, there is the necessary personal relationship that preferably is the result of an introduction from mutual friends.

In Chinese eyes, bestowing the title of "friend" on someone, and especially on a foreigner, is a very significant act that is not done lightly. But once done, whether sincerely or for ulterior motives, it is unashamedly used as a ploy to manipulate foreigners in business and political dealings.

When the "friend" is a foreigner and the bestower is a person of some stature, particularly a high-ranking government official, the act is regarded by the Chinese as a signal honor—for which the recipient is expected to show appropriate appreciation by thereafter demonstrating his or her friendship when called upon to do so.

Foreigners dealing with China should be aware of the more subtle and important meanings attached to friendships, and be prepared to follow through when they accept them.

275

豫

"Staying in Sync"

Staying in Chinese style harmony with the cosmos is a lot more complicated, and requires a lot more knowledge, insight and effort, than what one might think. It is far more than just staying in tune with the seasons, with day and night, and with the established passages of human life.

Staying in sync with the cosmos in the full sense means that you have to be aware of and totally understand the social, economic and political environments in which you live, in all of their nuances and implications.

The obvious point is that if you do not understand the forces that are in play around you there is no way that you can harmonize your attitudes and actions with these forces to the extent that you can succeed in your goals, much less manipulate the forces to your advantage.

This means you must have intimate insight into the psychology of people, their values and aspirations, their fears—what turns them on and off—and conduct yourself accordingly.

Achieving harmony with your environment is a process and a state of mind that the Chinese call *yu* (yuu), which by itself is translated as *harmonize*. It refers not only to the act of harmonizing one's self with the environment, but also to a time when harmonizing is especially powerful.

The effective use of *yu* naturally involves more than dealing with external matters. It also requires comprehensive knowledge of one's self, high personal standards, benevolence, integrity, enthusiasm and diligence in pursuing one's goals.

If all of these elements come together at the same time, *yu* promises to be an extraordinary experience—a time when there is no tension, no doubts; when people will admire you and cooperate with you without holding back.

There are the usual warnings that go with *yu*, however. Like everything else in the Chinese cosmos, *yu* comes and goes, and one must be especially careful of misreading the signs and depending on *yu* to carry them through when the forces are aligned against them and are too powerful to be swayed by their efforts.

In a commercial sense, when *yu* is at a high level is the time to introduce new products, open new markets, and generally grow your business.

The concept of *yu* permeates Chinese attitudes and behavior on a subconscious level, and might be described as "cultural instinct." It is a part of most of the traits that have traditionally been attributed to the Chinese, from bending with the wind and taking the path of least resistance, to taking a long-term view in all matters.

One of the most common *yu* responses that Westerners hear in their dealings with the Chinese is that the timing is not right. When this occurs, attempts to push forward generally result in resistance and may cause all kinds of problems.

276

运

Yun

(Yuun)

"Living with Natural Disasters"

There are two kinds of *yun* (yuun) or *fate* in the world of the Chinese. One has to do with nature, and the other with the rules and expectations of the society in which people live.

In their characteristic way of labeling and numbering things, the Chinese say there are five factors that influence human life—predetermined destiny, destiny that can be changed, the flow of cosmic energy, virtue, and education.

The Chinese have long been famous—or infamous, depending on one's viewpoint—for their stoic acceptance of both the regular ravages of nature and the selfish egotism and occasional savagery of their own kind.

From the Western side of the philosophical fence, such fatalism is generally regarded as a failure in character, and is seen by some as one of the main reasons why China remained time-locked in a feudalistic system of government for so many centuries.

The periodic floods, droughts, earthquakes, and depredations by warlords and kings that have plagued the Chinese from the beginning of their civilization have been looked upon by the Chinese as just plain bad luck—or as some Westerners are prone to say, "God's will."

Also from the beginning, the lives of most Chinese seldom rose above subsistence level, virtually eliminating their ability to resist the forces of nature or their governments.

But even the famed patience and fatalism of the Chinese had its breaking points and at intervals, usually generations apart, groups of them would rise up in rebellion and attempt to improve the quality of their lives.

Much of what is described today as typical Chinese behavior is a holdover from the historical attitude toward *yun*, a Buddhist term that refers to a predestined fate. Until there is a far more dramatic improvement in the options available to the mass of rural Chinese they will not doubt continue to regard fate as a shadow they cannot escape.

Obviously, people who have very little control over their lives must resign themselves to *yun* in order to maintain any degree of emotional stability, and it was this reality that resulted in the Chinese traditionally behaving in a stoic and passive manner.

But there is a macabre kind of silver lining to the Chinese reaction to *yun*—or so say some Western psychotherapists. According to this school of thought, because the Chinese were programmed to automatically accept events they could not control, they seldom suffered the kind of depression that is so common in the West, where people are conditioned to believe they can and should control their own fate.

There is another important aspect to the Chinese distrust in governments and gods. In addition to joining together as families and groups to help each other, those who can afford to do so stash away some gold or other precious thing to be used in dire emergencies.

Others, especially those who leave the homeland, are obsessed with the desire to establish their own businesses and raise themselves beyond the reach of *yun*.

In many respects, the Chinese acceptance of *yun*, previously seen as a weakness, may turn out to be one of their greatest strengths, giving them a significant advantage over other people.

277

Yun
(Yuun)

"Living with Man-Made Fate"

Contemporary social scientists say that the traditional sexual behavior of the Chinese was primarily influenced by the relationship forced upon fathers and sons.

Pre-modern Chinese society demanded that fathers and sons bond for life to the exclusion of all other relationships. Because sexual bonding with wives or women in general would have been in direct competition with the father-son relationship, according to this explanation, such relationships were made taboo.

Extrapolating on this, arranged marriages, the existence of concubines and second wives, treating male and female children differently, the role of the extended family and clan, and other characteristic aspects of Chinese society grew out of the imperative of the father-son relationship.

In order for this kind of artificial system to survive and function effectively for generation after generation it was necessary that powerful sanctions be used to enforce it.

This system, and the political and social sanctions used to make it work, virtually eliminated the concept of individuality and freedom of choice from Chinese society.

In this environment, the upbringing, personal relationships and work activities of the people were preprogrammed down to the smallest details from birth to death, leaving them very little control over their lives.

When these individual social constraints were combined with the requirements of the authoritarian government for public order and the dependence of the people on unpredictable and uncontrollable nature, the result was an apathetic acceptance of *yun* (yuun) or *man-made fate* that became characteristic of Chinese mentality and behavior.

From the beginning of their civilization the Chinese have been forced to accept their fate and attempt to find satisfaction and happiness whenever and wherever they could. Because they had no civil rights under the government, they came to accept the inevitability of external forces controlling their lives.

While stoicism and passivity are still primary traits in the behavior of most Chinese, particularly those tied to the land, there have been dramatic changes since the breakup of the Qing (Ching) Dynasty in 1912 and the loosening of the grip of the Communist regime in the latter part of the 1970s.

For the first time in the history of China, the people are legally and socially free to love and to marry, to directly confront fate in an attempt to avoid many of the things that plagued them in the past and to improve the quality of their lives overall.

This freedom is far from complete, however, and generally speaking much of the lives of most Chinese remain in the hands of both nature and a government that puts its own survival above the needs and aspirations of the people.

278

运气

Yunqi

(Yuun-chee)

"Fate, Luck and Intuition"

Most Chinese believe that luck plays a significant role in the lives of people, and that it is important to do everything possible to ensure good luck (*hao yunqi*) and avoid bad luck (*dao mei*). This includes avoiding unlucky numbers and paying scrupulous attention to the advice of astrologers and geomancers. See **Feng Shui**.

Many Chinese meticulously follow the guidelines of the astrological calendar, scheduling such activities as burials, weddings, starting new businesses, traveling, visiting friends, and so on, to coincide with "good days."

Numbers are of vital importance to the Chinese. Two is associated with "double happiness" and the duality of the cosmos. Three is symbolic of growth. Four, on the other hand, is regarded as very unlucky because the pronunciation of the word is the same as the word for "death." (Some hotels do not have 4th floors.)

The number five is especially significant because it relates directly to fundamental elements in Chinese culture and cosmology: the five elements of nature (metal, earth, wood, fire, water); the five tastes (sweet, sour, salty, bitter, pungent); the five basic colors; the five-generation lineage groups; the ideal family size (three boys and two girls), and so on.

Six is symbolic of good luck, and seven is associated with certainty.

Number eight is even more favored as a lucky omen because it is associated with so many auspicious things in Chinese culture: the Eight Buddhist Emblems; the Eight Treasures; the Eight Immortals (god-like spirits who represent the eight conditions of life—poverty, wealth, aristocracy, peasantry, age, youth, masculinity and femininity); the Eight Diagrams that are the basis for the famed *Book of Changes*, etc.

The number eight is especially important to Cantonese because the word for eight, *baat*, suggests the generation of wealth and prosperity. Nine is associated with longevity.

A combination of eights relating to any event, such as the signing of a contract or the inauguration of a new project or whatever, or to anything, such as an address or license number, is considered especially auspicious. In

Hong Kong automobile plates with auspicious numbers are auctioned off at the beginning of each new year. One year, plate number "8" went for $640,000.

Red, a color that has long been associated with China, is believed to symbolize and attract *yunqi* (yuun-chee) or *good luck*.

Chinese businesspeople tend to believe more in fate, luck and the use of intuition than in what is taught in business schools. Many do little or no market research before going into new businesses or launching new products. They prefer to rely on intuition, their web of connections, and human relations.

Foreign businesspeople dealing with China would be wise to familiarize themselves with China's astrological calendar, and avoid scheduling key events on "bad luck" days.

See **Lishu, Zhanxingxue.**

杂技演员

Zajiyanyuan

(Zah-jee-yahn-yuu-enn)

"A Special Chinese Skill"

Acrobatics had become an established form of entertainment in China by 700 B.C. Ancient records show that the centuries between 206 B.C. and A.D. 220 were a golden age for acrobats.

Skills and acts that flourished during this period included demonstrations of strength, sword-flying, ball-leaping and rope-walking.

During the reign of Sui Dynasty Emperor Yang Di (A.D. 607–617), acrobats from all over China were summoned to the capital each spring to entertain at annual spring festival banquets.

Records indicate that the most elaborate of these shows were held between the years 610 and 616, when over 30,000 acrobats staged simultaneous performances over an area that extended more than eight miles from center stage. These spring festivals lasted for 14 days.

Emperors also generally had court acrobats for their own personal pleasure as well as to entertain guests.

But during the Song Dynasty (A.D. 960–1368) Imperial patronage for *zajiyanyuan* (zah-jee-yahn-yuu-enn) or *acrobatics* gradually disappeared, forcing them to become much more commercial. The popularity of acrobatics remained strong, however, and many of the skills became folk arts that were passed on from one generation to the next.

But as more centuries passed, the once honored practice degenerated to the point that it was more of a side-show that included charlatans and other circus-type entertainers who did such things as swallow iron balls and drink snake venom to attract audiences.

Zhou Enlai, foreign minister of China from 1949 to 1957 and then the premier from 1957 until his death in 1976, rescued acrobatics from the back alleys by ordering the Ministry of Culture to set up a China Acrobatics Troupe.

The new troupe was an instant success, not only in China but on trips abroad as well. This inspired the formation of dozens of new commercial troupes that found ready audiences all over the country.

This revival was to be short-lived, however. During the Cultural Revolution, instigated by Chairman Mao Zedung in 1966, acrobatics was one of the many things that came under attack by Red Guard zealots who were ordered to destroy every vestige of old China.

After the Cultural Revolution ended, Zhou Enlai once again came to the rescue. He ordered the China Acrobatics Troupe to be reinstated, and also instructed the government to assign professional choreographers, stage designers, writers, directors and composers to new acrobatic troupes to upgrade their performances.

Although the content of the shows was thereafter politicized to further the aims of the Communist government, the industry was saved from extinction.

In 1981 the Ministry of Culture cooperated with the various troupes to establish the Association of Chinese Acrobats, and provide additional government resources for the troupes. Subsequently, leading acrobatic troupes began entering international competition, winning gold medals around the world.

Today, *zajiyanyuan* is considered a national treasure.

280

赠品

Zen-Ping

(Zun-Peeng)

"Gift-giving in China"

In Imperial China gifts in money and kind from subordinates and the public made up much of the income of officials, especially lower ranking cadre, and played a key role in building and sustaining the network of connections that were essential in both business and private life.

Gifts were given to pave the way for appointments as government officials and for advancement to higher ranks. Gifts were given when any official approval was required, to smooth over ruffled feelings, when favors were needed, and just to stay on the good side of officials.

Zen-ping (zun-peeng) or *gift-giving* is still an important institutionalized part of life in China, for business as well as personal affairs, and generally exceeds what is customary in Western countries.

The most common gift-giving occasions in China include when you visit relatives or friends during Spring Festival, Mid-Autumn Festival and New Year's, upon returning from a long trip (whether within China or abroad), when going to someone's home for a meal, when visiting someone who is ill or has been injured, to show appreciation for significant favors, and when attending birthday parties and weddings.

The type of gift is generally determined by the occasion. When visiting sick people or going to a private home for lunch or dinner, food items and drinks are appropriate. If the individual concerned reads English, books and magazines are also appreciated.

Money is the traditional gift for weddings (wrapped in red paper or in an envelope made for that purpose), but nowadays it is also common to give something for the house or kitchen. Money gifts are always handed over to a third party designated to receive them. Other gifts are placed on a gift table.

When visiting Chinese families during festivals it is customary to give small money gifts to children (also wrapped in red paper or placed in red envelopes), and personal items or other kinds of gifts for adults. When giving money to children it is customary to include two of whatever coins or bills are in the envelope.

Like everyone else, the Chinese especially appreciate famous regional products as gifts, both domestic and foreign. The Chinese especially appreciate gifts brought from distant places, and have a saying referring to them: *Qian li song e mao—A swan feather brought from 1,000 li away.* (One li is equal to half a kilometer or .311 of a mile.)

On other occasions, the same guidelines followed for gift-giving in the U.S. and elsewhere are appropriate—personal accessories, items of clothing, sporting or recreational items, and so on. Catering to any special interest a person may have is always a good idea.

More traditional Chinese will automatically decline to accept proffered gifts as a matter of politeness and to avoid appearing selfish or greedy. Established protocol calls for you to politely but firmly offer gifts a second and sometimes a third time.

281

长城

Zhang Zheng / Wan Li Zhang Zheng
(Chahng Chung / Wahn Lee Chahng Chung)

"The Great Wall Syndrome"

From the beginning of the first Chinese communities in the Yellow River Valley well before 2000 B.C., the Chinese were regularly threatened by savage nomadic tribesmen who lived in what is now northern China, southern Siberia and Mongolia.

During the Shang Dynasty (1550–1030 B.C.) and the famous Chou Dynasty, 1030–256 B.C., various rulers constructed high walls across many of the valleys and mountain passes most often used by raiders coming down from the north. Altogether, these walls covered a distance of some 31,000 miles.

Shortly after the beginning of the Qin (Chin) Dynasty in 221 B.C., Emperor Qin Shi Huang Di ordered that construction begin on a program to tie a number of these walls together in one long "Great Wall" that could easily be defended against mounted attackers.

The *Zhang Zheng* (chahng chung) or *Great Wall* of China was "completed" over a period of 200 years. At times, as many as 300,000 workers were engaged on the project. Emperor Qin Shi Huang Di assigned so many workers to the wall project, and to other major development programs, that agriculture throughout the country suffered, resulting in several assassination attempts against him.

The Great Wall began on the east coast, just north of what is now the city of Tangshan in Hebei Province, and snaked westward for more than 6,350 kilometers, passing within 80 kilometers of Beijing and reaching into the interior of the western province of Gansu.

The Great Wall averaged eight meters in height and seven meters in width at its base. The wall consisted of rammed earth encased in large stone blocks that had been carved by hand. Sections of the wall had inner as well as outer walls.

At regular intervals along the wall there were signal towers, fortified guard towers and troop garrisons. (The first American astronauts to reach the moon said that the Great Wall was the only man-made thing on earth visible to the naked eye.)

For centuries the *Zhang Zheng* has been held up to foreigners and to Chinese alike as one of the primary symbols of Chinese civilization; as a monument to the perseverance, diligence and ability of the Chinese.

The Great Wall is China's most famous and most visited attraction. Millions of Chinese and foreign visitors troop to repaired sections of the wall each year to marvel at its awesome size and at what it represents in terms of human ingenuity and effort.

But not all Chinese see the Great Wall as a positive symbol. A number of vocal and influential intellectuals regard the wall as symbolic of the things they say are *wrong* with China—excessive conservatism; too much emphasis on past glories; looking inward instead of outward.

These critics of the Great Wall say it is a perfect example of the ancient Chinese practice of trying to ward off foreigners and foreign influence; to keep them out, rather than benefit from dealing with them directly.

Despite this criticism, however, the *Zhang Zheng* remains as one of the greatest accomplishments of the Chinese people, and continues to serve as a very relevant example of what the Chinese are capable of doing.

The Great Wall is the Grand Canyon of China, and the repaired portions of the wall, only an hour's drive from Beijing, are an awesome thing to behold and well worth the visit.

In more literary references to the Great Wall, many writers call it *Wan Li Zhang Zheng*, or *The 10,000 Li Great Wall*. One li equals one-half a kilometer or .311 of a mile.

占星学

Zhanxingxue

(Chahng-sheeng-shuu-eh)

"Depending on the Stars"

For more than 5,000 years a great deal of Chinese civilization was locked into a time warp that changed very little from one millennium to the next.

The primary thrust of the succeeding governments during most of the long ages of China was to maintain the status quo, to keep the huge mass of peasants under control, to keep foreigners at bay, and to preserve the spiritual and philosophical links with the past.

Much of the spiritual life of the early Chinese revolved around *zhanxingxue* (chahng-sheeng-shuu-eh)—*astrology*, or divination—the art of foretelling the future and revealing occult knowledge by means of supernatural powers.

Chinese records indicate that the first lunar calendar was created around 2697 B.C. by an astronomer named Da Nao, a minister in the Court of Emperor Huang Di. Du based his calendar on a 60-year cycle that he derived from relationships between the earth and heavenly bodies and the positive negative elements making up the cosmos.

The 12 earthly "branches" of these relationships were given signs named after animals—dragon, snake, horse, sheep, monkey, cock, dog, pig, rat, ox, tiger and rabbit.

By 1100 B.C. the Da calendar and a horoscope, made up of the 12 symbolic animals and eight symbols representing two each for the year, month, day and hour of people's birth, was being widely used for divination.

Because of the historical uncertainty of life in China, not only from natural disasters but also from the authoritarian nature of the governments and virtually no legal guarantees of any kind, the Chinese were more or less pawns at the mercy of uncontrollable forces.

This imbued the Chinese with the feeling that their survival was based on staying on good terms with supernatural forces, and doing whatever to keep luck on their side.

Zhanxingxue provided the Chinese with an avenue to "communicate" with the occult; to divine the will of saints and gods, and hedge their bets with the cosmic forces of *yin-yang*.

Astrology was used not only by emperors but by common people as well—sometimes to an extreme that literally controlled their lives and had national as well as international repercussions.

Zhanxingxue spread from China throughout East and Southeast Asia, and until recent decades played key roles in major decisions made by leaders in Japan, Korea, Cambodia, Vietnam and elsewhere.

Astrology is still widely practiced in all of these countries, and it is common for businesspeople as well as political leaders to consult astrologers about the timing of decisions and events.

Westerners dealing with the Chinese should not discount the importance of *zhanxingxue* out of hand. To do so can easily have an effect that is the reverse of what is intended.

283

Zhen
(Chun)

"Dealing with Shocking Events"

Just as it is necessary to temper iron to convert it into much harder and durable steel, human beings as well have to be tested and tempered over and over again to bring out the best in them—an axiom that, in fact, applies to everything in nature.

In human affairs, some of this tempering and testing is deliberate, and is specifically designed to create better human beings. But most of it is a natural process that results from the interaction of cosmic forces that are beyond the control of man—things that the Chinese discovered very early and incorporated into their fundamental philosophy.

The Chinese realized that there is a constant building up and releasing of kinetic energy in the cosmos. The discharging of this energy results in *zhen* (chun), or *shocking* events that range from such uncontrollable things as lightening and thunderstorms, volcanic explosions and earthquakes, to the smallest and most unobtrusive events that affect bacteria on a microscopic level.

They were particularly concerned about the *zhen* events in human life that happen randomly and cannot be prevented, and they attempted to channel these energy releases in such a way that they would result in the least amount of harm, and rather than weaken and discourage people, make them stronger and more resilient.

Zhen events and how to react to them are divided into six levels or stages. The worst are shocking events that are so widespread that they upset the whole of society, particularly revolutions and civil wars, during which time there is little or nothing the individual can do. During these periods of general turmoil the Chinese sages say it is best to retreat and keep a low profile, even in the face of criticism.

On the next level *zhen* events have a direct and immediate impact on individuals, requiring that they change their attitudes and behavior in order to survive. The advice of the sages here is to remain "centered" both internally and externally, meaning to keep mentally balanced in order to control your own emotions and behavior.

A third level of *zhen* events is when the whole situation becomes confused and no matter how well you may have prepared there is nothing that can be done except stay low and wait it out.

In the fourth category of shocking events the shock are so extreme that it puts all of one's courage and strength to the test. The only recourse is to persevere and seek to make changes that will make it possible for you to sidestep the shock.

The fifth category of *zhen* occurrences is when you suffer large losses and there is no way to resist the forces at work, such as a major flood. The only recourse here, the sages say, is to remove yourself from the danger and stay out of harm's way. By doing so you can eventually recover what you have lost.

Finally, there are *zhen* events that are very frightening and appear to be extremely dangerous, causing great worry. But these events turn out to be more fireworks than substance, will soon end, and are often followed by good fortune.

The lesson taught by *zhen* is that people must learn to accept unexpected, unpredictable things they cannot change, and to change themselves when it is necessary to stay in harmony with cosmic energy, and thereby prosper.

正义

Zhengyi
(Chung-eee)

"Might Makes Right"

From the beginning of Chinese civilization, *zhengyi* (chung-eee) or *justice* has primarily been a political decision based on existing circumstances and the personalities involved. It had nothing to do with any inherent human rights, fairness or equality.

There have always been two kinds of crime in China, wrong-doing and political opposition. But even in cases of legal misdemeanors and felonies, the nature and degree of the justice meted out was subject to political interpretation based on social class and other personal considerations.

The Chinese also traditionally took a collective approach to law enforcement and justice. In dynastic times families and sometimes the villages of those accused of crimes or being enemies of the state were subject to punishment.

Because surviving members of families were obligated to revenge any of their kinfolk they believed were unjustly punished or killed, rebels, warlords and others made a practice of wiping out whole families in order to prevent any future retribution. The same rationale was used by the Imperial Court and invaders to eliminate family survivors who might lay claim to normally hereditary positions.

After the Communist Party took power in China in 1949 the whole country was organized into hierarchical units designed to make it possible for the Party to control the thoughts and behavior of the population down to single individuals.

In the countryside people were enrolled in cooperatives, communes and collectives. In the cities, the population was divided into District Neighborhoods of 2,000 to 10,000 families, Resident Committees of 100–800 families, Resident Courtyards or Resident Buildings of 15–40 families; and Residency Groups of 8–15 families.

In addition to police being permanently assigned to each of these larger units, each unit also had a Party cadre in charge of the political indoctrination and control of the group.

One of the most invidious methods used by the Communist Party to ensure absolute obedience physically as well as intellectually was to select people in each unit to watch over the coming and going of their neighbors, reporting on their visitors, if they came in late or left early—anything that was different from a very narrow routine.

These watchers, usually elderly women, were assigned to every Resident Building (including hotels where foreign visitors lived or stayed) and Resident Courtyard.

The neighborhood spies, who sometimes operated in groups, had the right to enter people's homes or apartments without notice, whether they were present or not, to search the premises and question the occupants; even to drink their tea—a system that made it virtually impossible for anyone to develop a full sense of independence or self.

Justice in China continues to confuse and shock foreigners. Having an accident in China is generally regarded as a crime. People who injure themselves in industrial accidents are subject to fines—the rationale apparently being that they are guilty of damaging a "natural resource."

American businessman Bill Purves, general manager of a joint-venture factory in Guangdong Province in the late 1980s, likened the Communist control system to being under perpetual "protective custody." He added that it helped reduce his concern about burglaries, but for single bachelors in China interested in fraternizing with local girls it was a serious problem.

China began to make dramatic progress in reforming its justice system in the 1980s, but it is still far from being based on the concept of inherent human rights or universal laws, and is regularly used by the Chinese Communist Party as an instrument to stifle political opposition and maintain the Party in power.

See **Falu, Lao Gai Dui.**

285

针灸

Zhenjiu

(Chun-jee-uu)

"Needling Cosmic Energy"

Well over 2,000 years ago, Chinese doctors determined that the human nervous system is an amazingly complex network that carries "energy" to and from all parts of the body.

They presumed that if this "energy" was weakened or blocked, the body organ "served" by that particular energy line would also weaken, and if the situation was not corrected, the organ would eventually fail altogether.

Eventually, these doctors pinpointed some 365 "nerve points" that apparently had a direct connection with various bodily functions, and devised a method called *zhenjiu* (chun-jee-uu) for "stimulating" one or more of these points when people suffered any kind of illness.

One of the many publications produced during the Warring States period (A.D. 221–A.D. 581), was the classic *Nei Jing*, a detailed work that explained both the theory and the technology of *zhenjiu*.

Zhenjiu, of course, means *acupuncture*—the inserting of needles into the nerve points of the body to stimulate the energy passing through the point by vibrating, twirling or heating the needles. Nowadays, some acupuncturists run low currents of electricity through the needles.

One of the most famous of China's acupuncturists was Dr. Hua Tuo, who lived during the Three Kingdoms period (A.D. 222–A.D. 277). In addition to his skill in *zhenjiu*, he is credited with having developed one of the most important schools of the controlled breathing exercise system know as *qigong*, as well as an oral anesthesia.

Neither Chinese nor Western scientists have been able to prove by modern-day methods that *zhenjiu* works, but there is overwhelming evidence that it "works" at least sometimes in specific cases.

There are numerous contemporary records of Chinese surgeons performing major operations on patients, including brain surgery, using only acupuncture as an anesthesia—apparently without the patients suffering any pain whatsoever, and continuing to talk to surgeons and bystanders during the operations.

Such operations have been both witnessed and filmed by skeptical Western doctors and scientists who later could not explain what they had seen.

Recent test programs in the U.S. indicate that *zhenjiu* works on some people and not on others. I've had one acupuncture treatment for chronic back pains without any recognizable benefit.

Obviously there is some scientific basis for a procedure that has survived for more than two thousand years, and is now gradually spreading to the rest of the world.

真实

Zhenshi

(Chun-she)

"How to Tell the Truth"

One of my earliest and most memorable introductions to how the Chinese view and use truth, which at the time struck me as being both irrational and unconscionable, was being told by a hotel clerk that there were no rooms available when I knew perfectly well the hotel was less than half full.

The more I protested that there *were* vacant rooms and demanded to know why I couldn't have one, the more insistent the clerk became that there were no open rooms.

I finally gave up the battle in disgust, but when I left the hotel I was determined to find out why the clerk had repeatedly lied to me. A short time later, in Hong Kong, I posed the question to a friend of European ancestry who had been born and raised in Beijing in a Chinese household and was both bilingual and bi-cultural.

This friend explained that there could have been several reasons why I had been refused by the hotel clerk. The clerk did not feel that the accommodations were suitable for a foreigner, dealing with a foreigner who could not speak Chinese was too much trouble, the vacant room had not yet been cleaned up, the hotel was not approved by the government for foreign guests, and so on.

When I pursued the subject, wanting to know why the clerk had chosen to lie about the matter rather than make any kind of factual explanation, my friend said it was a matter of face—the clerk did not want to tell me the real reason because either he or I or both of us would lose face, and lying was the simplest and easiest way out.

I learned later that in the Chinese context *zhenshi* (chun-she) or "truth" is generally situational, not a universal principle. Rather than being an absolute that should be or can be applied to any situation, truth in China is often determined by the circumstances of the moment.

In the widest sense, the goal of Chinese truth is to protect the face of the individual concerned, any group that might be involved, or the whole nation. It is often used in a narrow sense to serve the selfish perceptions, needs, or aspirations of individuals.

Chinese tend to be exceptionally sensitive about the face of China, bridling at any criticism or hint of criticism of the country by outsiders, and vindictive in their response. In their compulsive need to preserve and enhance the image of the country they automatically resort to creating whatever truth they believe will achieve the desired result.

Veteran Old China Hands say businesspeople and government bureaucrats characteristically resort to lies as a way of turning down requests, disproving applications, making excuses for their failure to act on something, or simply to avoid talking about something they don't want to discuss.

Foreigners who believe they are being confronted by the Chinese version of truth should not do as I did with the hotel clerk. Confronting the Chinese in the manner that I did makes them more determined to have their way. A far better ploy is to politely and diplomatically take different approaches until you, hopefully, find one that works.

See **Zhongcheng.**

287

哲学家

Zhexuejia

(Chu-shu-eh-jee-ah)

"Land of Philosophers"

Feudalism flowered during China's famous Chou Dynasty (1122–256 B.C.), with emperors, manors, lords, knights and serfs—just as Europe was to have some two thousand years later. One significant difference was that Chinese lords and knights were better known for their prowess with a pen than with a sword.

But it was the gradual corruption and weakening of the Chou emperors and their courts that gave rise to the legendary philosophers Confucius (551–479 B.C.), Mencius (372–289 B.C.), Hsun (300–235 B.C.), and many others.

These philosophers helped give birth to the Han Dynasty (206 B.C.–A.D. 222), the most glorious period in the history of the country up to that time, and the period that was to give its name, Han, to the main group of Chinese people.

From the Han Dynasty on, education in China consisted of studying the philosophy of the earlier sages, primarily in preparation for government service. Government was administered by philosopher-bureaucrats who attempted to translate what they had learned from philosophers into guidelines for day-to-day living.

As the centuries passed, much of the combined philosophies of the past masters seeped into the thinking and behavior of the great mass of Chinese because the culture itself became a living representation of the combined Buddhist, Daoist and Confucianist philosophies—and was to have a fundamental influence on the neighboring countries of Korea and Japan.*

Thus as ordinary men matured they became imbued with generations of accumulated folk wisdom as well as specific teachings of the great sages of

---

*Note: Much of the traditional culture for which Japan is noted was adopted from China, mostly through Korea, from around A.D. 300 to A.D. 700—including Buddhism, Confucianism, court rituals, city planning, the ideogram writing system, most arts and crafts, and tea-drinking.

One thing the Japanese did *not* copy from China were national civil service examinations by which the Chinese qualified and selected scholars for appointment as government officials. From the 12th century to 1868, Japan's shogunate government was administered by the elite warrior class that came to be known as *samurai*. The *samurai* were not professional scholars but were generally well educated—and all wrote poetry. The shogunate *did* adapt one rule that applied to China's scholars, however. It prohibited *samurai* from working or engaging in commercial business.

the past. By the time they reached their forties or fifties, their added years of personal experience gave them the credentials to assume the role of family philosopher.

Because the men of feudal China had virtually absolute power over their families as husbands and fathers, and over their staffs as bureaucrats or employers, their philosophical character was of extreme importance to those around them because it was their character, not laws or principles of human rights, that determined how they treated people.

Despite the philosophical tone of the Chinese environment, however, it was up to inferiors to maintain harmonious and supportive relationships with their superiors by obeying them without question, and catering to their character and whims.

The more successful Chinese men were the more likely they were to take the role of *zhexuejia* (chu-shu-eh-jee-ah) or "philosophy" seriously and to make an effort to pass their philosophical views on to their families, employees and staff (if they happened to be scholar-officials).

In modern times, one of the ongoing effects of the philosophical bent of most Chinese is for those who have accumulated substantial wealth to become philanthropists and to finance large projects of one kind or another for use by the public.

The older and more successful a Chinese, the more likely he or she is to take philosophy seriously. Foreigners dealing with higher level Chinese businesspeople and bureaucrats must deal first with their philosophical natures.

288

Zhi

(Chih)

"Unbounded Ambition"

By the end of the 19th century it was a joke that no matter where you went in the United States you would find a Chinese laundry. By the middle of the 20th century the same could be said of Chinese restaurants.

Now you find Chinese students, scholars, scientists, engineers and other professional people at universities and in corporations in practically every major American city, and their presence is no longer a joke.

Large enclaves of Chinese residents have been present in major cities throughout East and Southeast Asia for much longer periods, and have been directly responsible for much of the economic growth in those countries.

If there is one trait that is most likely to apply to all overseas Chinese it is *zhi* (chih) or *ambition*—an unbounded compulsion to first become educated and then to achieve success in a chosen field. The ideogram for *zhi* consists of the character for "scholar" over the character for "heart," emphasizing in the strongest possible terms the status the Chinese give to the word and the concept.

In earlier decades, success for overseas Chinese invariably included economic independence, because racial prejudice and a variety of cultural factors effectively barred overseas Chinese from integrating in their local communities. Now, overseas Chinese are in the mainstream, or *are* the mainstream, of life wherever they live.

The world was to see just how ambitious and able overseas Chinese are when Hong Kong, Taiwan, and Singapore emerged as first-class economic powers in just one generation of frenzied development between 1950 and 1980—in extraordinary contrast to homeland China which remained mired in political wars during much of this period.

As a frequent visitor to China during and following these decades, I saw over and over again the forces of repression that had traditionally prevented, and continued to prevent, the great mass of homeland Chinese from manifesting their own ambitions and talents.

From the latter part of the 1970s one could literally feel the long repressed intelligence and energy of the Chinese, particularly in urban areas on the eastern seaboard, struggling to break away from the customs and laws of the past. It became more and more obvious that the political, economic and social chains that had held the Chinese back for more than forty centuries were about to break.

The world has already seen what a few million overseas Chinese can do when they are freed from the shackles of political, economic and social bondage. We are beginning to see what a billion-plus Chinese can do when they have the opportunity to give rein to something that has been denied to them for so long.

289

智

Zhi
(Chih)

"Wisdom of the Chinese"

The old saying, "There is nothing new under the sun," might well have been minted in China. With a country and a culture that have existed continuously for some five thousand years, and a passion for accumulating knowledge that was unmatched until contemporary times, there seems to be virtually nothing that educated Chinese of old did not contemplate and write about.

If a roll of mankind's greatest sages were to be called, the Chinese would be at or near the top of the roster. On any list of mankind's greatest technical accomplishments before modern times, the Chinese would outnumber all others.

The ideogram the Chinese created to refer to their huge store of knowledge, which is read as *zhi* (chih) or *wisdom*, consisted of three parts, one meaning "oath," one meaning "mouth," and the third one meaning "sun." The "oath-mouth" characters represent knowledge. The "sun" character suggests radiation of this learning to the world at large.

But for all the wisdom accumulated in China over the millennia, it never went beyond a narrow, primitive view of ordinary man as a pawn to be ruled over by some supreme power, usually under the guise of a divine mandate.

The Confucian-oriented Imperial dynasties that ruled China until 1912 were authoritarian oligarchies whose main goal was to protect and preserve their own power, not to improve the lives of their subjects—and certainly not to guarantee their freedom.

Because of this authoritarian, backward-looking form of government, most of the fabled wisdom of China was wasted on preserving and elaborating on the past rather than enhancing the lifestyles and options of the people.

There is a growing conviction among many Chinese today that virtually all of the historical weaknesses of the country can be traced directly to Confucianism, and that these inherent weaknesses cannot be overcome so long as the legacy of Confucius and his disciples remains as the foundation of Chinese culture.

It is also one of the great frustrations of present-day educated Chinese that their traditions of scholarship and historical accomplishments in practically every field of human endeavor have been subverted to dictatorial political ends.

And though they yearn for the time when the *zhi* of China's suppressed billion-plus people will be free from the irrational aspects of the past, they are faced with the enormous challenge of preserving the positive side of Confucianism, particularly its advocacy of the family unit, self-restraint, education, mutual responsibility, and living in harmony with others and with nature.

Despite the many aberrations of China's traditional culture, other people can still learn a lot about themselves and the world at large from the great store of *zhi* accumulated by the Chinese over the millennia.

290

忠

Zhong
(Chong)

"Bonds That Bind"

If I were asked to distinguish between Western culture and Chinese culture in seven words or less, my response would be: In the West, love; in China, loyalty.

In the Western context of things, love is generally regarded as the ultimate bond between two people. In Western religions, the relationship between man and God is based on love. Western morality begins and ends with love. Much of Western literature is based on love. The role of love, as the ideal oil and glue of Western life, is practically endless.

Love has played no such role in China. None of the key relationships in Chinese life, whether with gods or man, were based on love. The idea of love-based relationships was totally alien to Chinese thinking. Love is blind, unpredictable and undependable, and therefore incompatible with the Chinese concept of the ideal society.

None of the great sages of China preached the precept of love as a guideline for human behavior. Love was recognized as a human emotion, and on a private level there was often love between mothers and their children, but love was not a principle of human behavior.

Generally speaking, love simply was not a topic for consideration or discussion in feudal China, and was treated more or less as one of those aspects of human behavior that must be suppressed for the good of all. When love did occur between men and women it invariably caused trouble and suffering.

It is recorded that affluent men often loved one or more of their concubines, particularly after they reached middle age, but this was an "irrational" act that threatened the peace and sanctity of the family.

It was not love but *zhong* (chong) or *loyalty* that was the linchpin of Chinese society. Loyalty to one's ruler was the first of the five great principles preached by Confucius. Loyalty, infused with respect, was the foundation for all relationships, between inferiors and superiors, sons and fathers, wives and husbands, and friends.

In societies such as China that have traditionally been ruled by authoritarian edicts and personal relationships, rather than laws detailing and guaranteeing the rights of the people, loyalty to one's family, clan and friends is of paramount value because it is the only guarantee that people have.

Westerners dealing with Chinese today invariably discover that they must make a special effort to demonstrate their loyalty, regardless of the circumstances, in order to be accepted into the inner circle of Chinese life and business.

Once a person has developed loyalty bonds with the Chinese, and continuously nurtures them by the "right" kind of behavior, the relationship transcends virtually all other considerations. Debts and obligations are not forgotten. The loyal Chinese businessperson will take a loss rather than harm the relationship.

Of course, there are a growing number of exceptions to this general rule, as more and more "un-Chinese-like" individuals who will break any code appear on the scene. It goes without saying that outsiders wanting to establish business relationships in China should thoroughly investigate and qualify potential partners.

Zhong, connoting patriotism as well as loyalty, is symbolized in Chinese by the character for heart and the one for center. In other words, the *zhong* individual has his or her heart in the right place, whatever the occasion or circumstance.

See **Pidan.**

291

忠诚

Zhongcheng

(Chong-chung)

"Circumstantial Loyalty"

Throughout most of the history of Imperial China, farmers were tied to the land—and often to landlords. Generally, it was government policy that farmers could not move into cities or change occupations. People who lived in towns and cities had more freedom, but basically they also were fixed in locations and occupations from generation to generation.

This virtually static situation helped give rise to the notion that the Chinese in general were characteristically loyal in their personal relationships, in their ties to the land, and to the ruling authorities.

But this picture gives a false image of *zhongcheng* (chong-chung) or *circumstantial loyalty* in China. Despite all of the Confucian indoctrination, loyalty in China has traditionally been both limited and circumstantial, and based more on practical matters than on principles.

The loyalty that the Chinese have long been rightly famous for was family-based, and generally was not voluntarily extended beyond the immediate family, relatives and close friends.

In all other relationships, whatever loyalty that was shown toward other people, organizations, or the government, was determined by economic and social factors, and lasted only as long as those factors were advantageous.

During the heyday of the Communist regime in China from 1949 to 1976, the only kind of loyalty permitted was loyalty to the Communist Party and its political goals.

The CCP designed and implemented programs to destroy all other kinds of loyalty, including separating families. The government controlled all employment, assigning people to jobs and locations on the basis of its political and economic plans.

One of the most ambitious facets of the CCP's economic policies was the so-called "iron rice bowl" concept, which referred to guaranteed lifetime employment.

This program was very popular among workers during the upheavals caused by other CCP efforts to totally communize the country. But it was popular only because there were no other options.

When the CCP's economic policies failed and the country was on the verge of self-destructing, the government began cautiously allowing some private and state-run enterprises to hire their own employees and to fire employees when they saw fit to do so.

In today's China, employee loyalty is purely an economic decision. Non-family workers tend to have no loyalty at all for the organizations employing them and stay on only because they have no viable alternative. When opportunities do arise, they have no qualms about leaving.

Personal loyalty in China has reverted to its traditional form, centered around family, relatives and close friends. In other relationships it is based on the prevailing circumstances.

中孚

Zhong Fu
(Chong Foo)

"Pursuing True Insight"

In the ideal world of traditional China the ultimate goal of humanity was to achieve knowledge of all things, to merge one's self with that knowledge to achieve insight, and use the resulting insight to achieve harmony with the cosmos.

This extraordinary concept is bound up in the term *zhong fu* (chong foo), translated as *insight*, which, it seems to me, is the foundation of all Chinese philosophy and therefore the key to understanding all that is good about Chinese culture and Chinese character.

Zhong fu, which also means *inner truth*, begins with the principle of "know thyself" (a concept that was to appear centuries later in a biblical injunction) because it was recognized that you cannot understand others or the world at large without knowing yourself, and without a principled perspective that makes it possible for you to correctly interpret what you see and hear.

Zhong fu also holds that you must totally open your mind, be totally unprejudiced, before you can know yourself; following which you must merge yourself with other people, literally joining your spirit to theirs, before you can know them.

Once you have centered yourself and developed the ability to understand the inner truth of others, you have achieved *zhong fu* and are capable of complete empathy and understanding of whatever reality you may face, and thereafter are able to act in accord with the cosmos.

Having mastered *zhong fu* you are able to achieve maximum results with the minimum of effort—the same principle that is the foundation of *tai ji quan*, the martial art, which allows one "to use four ounces to deflect one thousand pounds."

The true *zhong fu* master becomes like a magnet, attracting other people who joyfully follow his or her lead, and thus seemingly without effort he or she becomes a leader. Success is virtually guaranteed. But, in a reminder that personal ambition is not consistent with inner truth, if you aspire to achieve higher personal goals and selfishly call upon others to support you, the power of *zhong fu* will not save you from being toppled from your lofty position.

One of the cultural factors that separates Chinese and foreign businesspeople is that the Chinese automatically, both subconsciously and consciously, make a valiant effort to gain insight into the minds and hearts of the outsiders—a process that is primarily subjective, takes a substantial amount of social time and expense, and is unpredictable.

Westerners, on the other hand, and Americans in particular, are culturally conditioned to conduct business on strictly objective terms based on product, price and profitability. They generally find the more personal, emotional approach of the Chinese frustrating and difficult to deal with.

Understanding the Chinese need for *zhong fu* helps to relieve this frustration.

中国

Zhong Guo

(Chong Gwoh)

"The Great Middle Kingdom"

One of China's most important cultural code words, and one that is essential for understanding Chinese values and attitudes, is the name the Chinese gave to their country a long time ago: *Zhong Guo* (chong gwoh), which, in popular English language usage is translated as "Middle Kingdom."

A more accurate translation of *Zhong Guo* is "Middle Country," and to be still more precise, "Central Country," with "central" being the key word.

Whoever it was that first began calling the country *Zhong Guo* was using the word "central" in the sense of "heart," "main," or the place where everything starts, and from where everything is controlled.

The rationale behind this grand name is simple enough. As far as the Chinese of that time were concerned, China was the center of the civilized universe; the sun that radiated light and wisdom to the rest of the known world.

Just as the "United States of America" (at least to most foreigners) has traditionally conjured up images of a huge, beautiful country, freedom, opportunity and extraordinary affluence, to the Chinese *Zhong Guo* traditionally epitomized the best human accomplishments in the arts, crafts, etiquette, food, letters, philosophy, science and wisdom in general.

But the extraordinary civilization that prompted early Chinese scholars and politicians to look upon their country as the sun was, in fact, a fragile creation which stayed in orbit only because it denied its people the right to think and act for themselves.

The remarkable social system developed by the Chinese was based on what Japanese author-economist Shumpei Kumon, director of the Center for Global Communications, International University of Japan, calls a "religious civilization."

Kumon says that all of the world's civilizations can be divided into two major groups: "religious" civilizations and "modern" civilizations, with religious civilizations predominating in the East and Middle East, and modern civilizations predominating in the West.

He defines civilization as a compound of consciously created living patterns that are based on culture and the influence of environments and other factors and cover both the spiritual and physical aspects of life.

Kumon defines culture as the values and rules that determine human attitudes and actions, most of which are learned, applied and transmitted unconsciously by members of individual societies. He further defines "religious" civilizations as "inclusive" and "modern" civilizations as "self-limiting."

Paraphrasing Kumon, inclusive or religious civilizations—of which China was historically the leading example—base their values and beliefs on the past, and attempt to homogenize their societies so the people will think alike and act alike in perfect harmony.

Eventually, religious civilizations come to regard any kind of social change as a deviation from what is moral and right; as a decline and fall from standards established long ago by saints and saviors and made absolute in holy books and scriptures.

In these societies, "reform" means a return to the "true path" of the past.

Traditional China, with its Confucian-Daoist philosophical foundations, was a perfect example of a religious or inclusive civilization that made every effort to prevent fundamental changes by applying numerous social, political and economic sanctions, including philosophical artifices that made change unthinkable.

China's religious civilization has been under attack from without and within since the early 1600s, but such was the power of its inclusivity that its Confucian-Daoist values and traditional patterns of behavior are still today vital forces in Chinese society.

Kumon warns, in fact, that inclusive or religious civilizations such as exist in the Confucian and Islamic worlds, are ultimately more enduring than modern civilizations because the latter inevitably run head-on into inherent limits to growth and lose the ability to sustain themselves.

He maintains that the only viable answer is for modern civilizations themselves to evolve into "inclusive, maintenance-oriented civilizations"— a movement that is already well underway.

Where China is concerned, the important thing is for Westerners to understand the nature of the social, economic and political conflicts that arise from its still mostly religious civilization—whether these conflicts arise from Confucianism *or* its close cousin, communism.

By recognizing the cultural elements in social and business practices—in Western individualism, in Chinese groupism, and so on—it is much more likely that Chinese and Westerners can accommodate each other by taking a middle road.

While most Chinese today recognize that China is no longer the "Middle Kingdom" in the historical sense, and has not been for more than five hundred years, a growing number of them believe it will be again—soon. (It will be interesting to see how long the Communist name for China, *Zhonghua Renmin Gongheguo* or *People's Republic of China*, a contradiction in terms, survives.)

See **Zihao.**

中国人

Zhongguo Ren
(Chong-gwoh Rune)

"People of the Middle Kingdom"

A visit to Hong Kong, Shanghai, Beijing or any of China's other large cities leaves no doubt that China is a crowded country. But even this intimate exposure is not enough for one to fully appreciate that there are over *one billion Chinese* and that they make up approximately one-fourth of all the people on earth.

In addition to the one billion-plus racial and ethnic *Zhongguo Ren* (Chong-gwoh Rune) or "Chinese people," China is also home to fifty-five minority groups of different racial and ethnic backgrounds. There are some fifteen million of the Zhuang, the largest of these minority groups, and some seven million Uygurs, the second largest minority group.

The core Chinese have traditionally referred to themselves as *Han Chinese*, after the Han Dynasty (206 B.C.–A.D.220), the first dynasty of a newly unified China. The two thousand years prior to the Han Dynasty were an age of city states and a number of independent feudal kingdoms.

Over the centuries the Han Chinese came to regard themselves as a superior race—as indeed they were. For some three thousand years, the Chinese were not only the largest group of people on earth, they were also the most technically and culturally advanced people.

But the self-image of the Chinese was not based solely on the possession of material goods or just on cultural sophistication (some thirty million

Chinese still today live in caves—caves outfitted with modern conveniences, but caves nevertheless). It was inherent in being born a Chinese in China.

Roughly, the Chinese thought of themselves in personal, absolute terms, as made up of one huge close-knit family that ideally thought and behaved as a single unit.

Traditional Chinese society, in its purest idealized form, could be likened to the "Borg" race dreamed up by the writers of *Star Trek: The Next Generation*, the science fiction television series. In the fictional world of *ST:TNG* the Borg are intellectually and emotionally one single huge collective. They share one mind and are incapable of thinking or acting individually or independently.

Like the Borg, the morality of the Chinese collective was an integral, inseparable part of the whole social system. Generally speaking, everybody absorbed the same moral codes along with the culture and, ideally, thought the same thoughts and behaved in the prescribed manner.

Despite the philosophical overtones of Chinese culture, individual Chinese were conditioned to think in concrete terms; not in the abstract—because you cannot eat philosophical notions. They also tended to emphasize the particular and the practical, and to have little patience with propositions that were based on "pie in the sky" kind of thinking.

The ethnocentric view that the Chinese had of themselves has dimmed considerably in recent times, particularly after access to television and other forms of mass communication became widespread. But built-in racial and cultural superiority is still a recognizable ingredient in the personality of the average Chinese.

Of course, this is true of most if not all cultures. But in the case of the Chinese it has existed far longer and been such an integral part of their official philosophy and policies that its influence on their thinking and behavior makes dealing with China especially complicated and time-consuming.

The biggest challenge facing Chinese today is modernizing their thinking and behavior without losing the traditional customs and traits that are worthy of being maintained, particularly their family values, their emphasis on education and achievement, and the role of modesty and moderation.

Of course, this process is already well underway and is perceptibly accelerating. But the road to modernization will not be straight or smooth, as is evidenced daily.

Many Chinese intellectuals are convinced that Confucianism is China's greatest handicap, and that the country cannot pull itself out of the morass of the past without first taking direct action to exorcise the spirit and teachings of the long dead sage. But this too is already happening of its own accord.

One of the most conspicuous examples of cultural and social change in China is the People's Liberation Army (PLA). Originally regarded as the standard-bearer for the Communist Party of China, and as the most brilliant jewel in the CCP firmament, the PLA has long since lost its Socialist purity.

Members of the PLA no longer see themselves as defenders of the Communist faith or as protectors of the people. A growing percentage of its members are from poor farm families and the dregs of society who are in it for either political or economic advantages, or both.

The attitude most common in China today is the one expressed by Y. S. Liang, a villager living in Fujian Province, who was quoted by the *China Daily News* as saying, "There are just two important things in life now—making money and having sons."

This attitude regarding male progeny is leading more and more Chinese couples to use ultrasound scans to determine the sex of fetuses, and to resort to abortion when the fetuses are female. In some rural areas, there are as many as one hundred and thirty boys born to every one hundred girls.

In trying to generalize about the Chinese, however, I am reminded of a comment made by journalist-author David Bonavia. He said he found the Chinese "admirable, infuriating, humorous, priggish, modest, overweening, loyal, mercenary, ethereal, sadistic, and tender."

The Chinese are all of the things David Bonavia said they were, and more. They are both intelligent and street-smart, and they have ambitions that they have been waiting for thousands of years to fulfill.

As one acerbic Chinese critic noted, the world at large should not be too anxious for the Chinese to get their act together. For once they do, they will once again be the colossus of the earth.

See **Zihao.**

中国通

Zhongguo Tong

(Chong-gwoh Tung)

"Don't Be an Expert"

One of the most interesting and often invidious aspects of the dual character of the Chinese is their habit of heaping unwarranted praise upon foreigners.

This deeply entrenched custom in complimentary overkill may be nothing more than following traditional etiquette, in which case it can be sincere even though overdone. But all too often it is manipulative in nature, and is deliberately designed to obtain some advantage.

The etiquette aspect of this custom usually revolves around such simple, mundane things as the ability to use chopsticks, knowing and using a few words of Chinese, referring to a historically famous Chinese novelist or poet, and so on.

To foreigners who are not conditioned to the use of frequent, flowery compliments, even this stylized and transparent use of praise can be disarming and misleading, resulting in them becoming much less discerning and more accepting of things they would normally criticize or reject.

The ultimate in the "professional" or manipulative use of compliments by the Chinese is bestowing the title of *Zhongguo tong* (chong-gwoh tung) on someone who does not truly deserve it—a practice that is all too common and has had dire consequences for those untutored in the ways of China.

Zhongguo Tong literally means *China expert*, but it is also commonly translated as *China hand*. The Chinese learned a long time ago that bestowing this title on foreigners, informally and unofficially as well as formally and officially, almost always had a remarkable effect on their attitudes and behavior toward China, making them much less critical and demanding of China, and far more prone to promote Chinese interests.

If nothing else, the Chinese are pragmatic in their politics and use of power, and the liberal "recognition" of foreigners as *Zhongguo Tong* has proven to be one of their least expensive and most effective techniques in extracting cooperation and tribute from outsiders.

In earlier decades, foreign politicians and diplomats were most frequently targeted for the honorary title of *China expert*. With the opening of the country to capital and technical investments from abroad, the practice was extended to foreign businesspeople.

Foreigners in whatever category who are crowned as *Zhongguo Tong* under any circumstances, should be aware that the honor automatically obligates them to "understand" the Chinese viewpoint, and that this understanding incorporates the obligation that they agree with and do what they can to advance that view.

A *China expert* who fails to live up to the expectations that come with the title, by criticizing or not defending China, is regarded as a traitor. The title thus becomes a kind of trap waiting to be sprung, and is very intimidating to both businesspeople and diplomats, since they have a lot to lose if they displease their hosts.

About the only defense if someone tries to brand you as a *Zhongguo Tong* is to politely deny the appellation, as often as circumstances allow, and just as politely continue to insist that you really know nothing about China, and not accept any of the obligations the title entails.

An additional ploy, which takes a page out of the book of Chinese attitudes—and therefore weakens their approach—is to repeatedly say, "Since I am a foreigner, I will never really understand China!"

中堂

Zhongtang
(Chong-tahng)

"The Role of Centerpieces"

In pre-modern China virtually every home had an ancestral altar that served as the family shrine. In the beginning, the primary purpose of the altar was to act as a stand for wooden tablets commemorating deceased grandparents, parents and other members of the family, along with votive offerings such as rice or other foods.

Given the importance of the role of ancestor worship in Chinese life, the family shrine was a key area in the home and therefore a main focus of attention. In traditional homes of the better-to-do this area was at the end of the main hall. In poorer, smaller homes, it was usually tucked into an area in or near the door or the main room.

Eventually, to further distinguish the area of the altar, some painter or art patron placed a large, painted scroll on the wall behind the altar—establishing a custom that gradually spread throughout the country.

These scrolls were first called *tang hua* or *hall pictures*. The paintings depicted gods, auspicious flowers and trees, tigers, red lobsters, mandarin ducks, cats, and so on. A pair of mandarin ducks was symbolic of marital fidelity and happiness; cranes and pine trees of longevity; peonies of wealth. Tigers were protection from evil spirits, etc.

This custom naturally resulted in the development of a huge market for scroll paintings, which in turn required a large number of painters—many of whom became famous masters whose work and names are still known today.

As more time went by it became the custom to flank these hall pictures with long, narrow scrolls featuring calligraphy that expressed some auspicious sentiment—a development that further promoted the art of calligraphy and the appearance of many calligraphy masters.

Thereafter it became common to call the hall pictures *zhongtang* (chong-tahng), literally *center hall*, but translated as *center pictures* or *centerpieces*.

Finally, the hanging of scroll paintings took on an existence of its own, separate from the ancestral altar, and became an institutionalized decoration in all homes that could afford such things.

More affluent people began incorporating special wall scroll nooks and rooms into the architectural designs of their homes, displaying several scrolls at the same time, changing the theme of the scrolls with the seasons and occasions.

Anyone who has ever been in a Chinese restaurant, shop, store or home has likely seen one or more *zhongtang*, and millions of them have been purchased by non-Chinese as exotic interior decorations.

During the Cultural Revolution in China (1966–1976) virtually all of the ancestral altars in the country, along with most of the *zhongtang*, were destroyed. But after the Communist government decreed in 1983 that art should serve the people instead of politics, the custom of displaying wall pictures was resumed and continues today to play its traditional role in Chinese life.

And although ancestral altars themselves have not made a similar comeback, the arrangement of *zhongtang* over mantels or pieces of furniture remains symbolic of the traditional family shrine. In some cases, large mirrors take the place of centerpiece scrolls.

The motifs of present-day *zhongtang* have broadened to include a much larger variety of themes, from famous scenic places to highly abstract paintings. Recognizing the role and importance of centerpieces to the Chinese is a good way to display your knowledge of Chinese culture, and gain points.

297

中文

Zhongwen
(Chong-win)

"The Chinese Language Labyrinth"

It is common to speak of *Zhongwen* (chong-win) or "Chinese" as if it were one language. Actually there are several fully fledged Chinese languages and dozens of Chinese dialects.

Although all *Zhongwen* are related—as French, Italian and Spanish are related—there are several that are mutually unintelligible in their spoken form.

All of China's mainstream languages are also tonal, meaning they have a sing-song pitch that changes the meaning of syllables and words—and makes the language unusually difficult for tone-deaf foreigners to learn.

Cantonese, the language spoken in southeast China, has seven tones. Mandarin, originally spoken only in the Beijing area and northern China and now being promoted as the national language, has four tones. It is generally regarded as the easiest of the Chinese languages to learn.

Fortunately, the core group of Chinese developed a comprehensive system of writing long before the population split up into distinctive regions, and while the core tongue gradually evolved into separate languages, the writing system did not change. All of China's mainstream languages are written with the same ideograms or characters. The words are just pronounced differently.

In the 3rd century B.C., Prime Minister Li Si prevailed upon the reigning emperor to order all of the characters then in use obsolete, and then to reform and standardize those that scholars determined were necessary to keep.

To emphasize the edict, the emperor also ordered that all books written in the old style were to be burned.

After this draconian approach to language reform, the characters remained very much the same down to modern times, but the spoken languages of the huge country grew further and further apart.

The most recent character reform took place in the 1970s, when the number of strokes necessary to write many of the ideograms were reduced and their form simplified.

Some authorities say that originally there were over 230,000 Chinese characters or ideograms, but today the average well-educated person knows only around 5,000 so-called "common characters."

The same authorities add that to read most publications in Chinese today requires a knowledge of between 2,000 and 4,000 characters.

When the Communist regime took over China in 1949 one of their earliest actions was to designate the language of Beijing and the north, known to Westerners as Mandarin, as the "national language" and to name it *Putong Hua* or *common language*.

Since the 1950s, *Putonghua*, or Mandarin, has been taught in all Chinese schools. But most people outside of the northern districts where Mandarin was traditionally spoken, still speak their native tongue as their first language.

Better educated people are gradually becoming bilingual but it is unlikely that Mandarin will become the first language of China any time soon.

Because of the age, depth and scope of Chinese culture, the core languages of China (Mandarin, Cantonese, Hokkien, Shanghaiese, etc.) are far richer in vocabulary—or more complex, depending on the way you look at it—than most other languages. All of China's main languages have an exceptionally large variety of terms to express shades of meaning in virtually every area of the spiritual and physical world, from eating and taste to interpersonal relationships and kinships.

China's languages, in all of their variations, are therefore more deeply infused into the heart and soul of the Chinese than is true of most other languages and other people. Chinese culture and the Chinese languages are so intimately interwoven that they cannot be separated.

Ample experience has shown that the Chinese can learn foreign languages without losing their Chineseness, but there are few if any examples of Chinese being fully Chinese without having been raised on one of the key languages.

Chinese languages are said to have about 400 sounds (English has 44), and most Chinese words consist of one or two syllables, which means that thousands of words sound very much alike or exactly alike, but have different meanings. People's names, however, normally consist of three syllables in order to distinguish them from ordinary words.

Newcomers to China should be aware that the name card of a business-person who speaks only Cantonese may be written in *Putonghua* the national language, and transliterated into the official *pin yin* system of romanizing the sounds.

This means that the person's name in roman letters will be pronounced totally different from what it is in Chinese characters, making it appear that he or she has two names.

The root meaning of *Zhongwen* is *Chinese writing* but it is now collo-quially used in the sense of *Chinese language*. *Hanyu* is the more formal word for Chinese language.

中医

Zhongyi
(Chong-eee)

"Nature's Way to Health"

Just as wild animals that become ill instinctively seek out grass, leaves, roots, bark, nuts, plants, mud and other things that have medicinal value, the Chinese very early developed a wide range of herbal homeopathic medicines that are still used today by millions of people, and are known as *zhongyi* (chong-eee).

In keeping with traditions and practices that were already well established by the year 4000 B.C. the Chinese minutely catalogued and described practically all of the ailments that commonly befall people and created herbal prescriptions for their relief and remedy.

The Chinese classic *Shen Nong's Materia Medica*, compiled some 2,000 years ago, presents detailed descriptions of some 5,700 herbs, classifying them according to their use and efficacy and explaining how to use them.

In addition to herbs, *zhongyi* also makes use of minerals, extracts from roots, berries and trees, animal organs and such things as snakes, sea horses and powdered pearls.

Among the ailments that are said to respond well to *zhongyi* treatment are bronchial asthma, chronic hepatitis, rheumatoid arthritis, hypertension and menopausal symptoms.

Practitioners of *zhongyi* attempt to diagnose the whole person, with all symptoms interpreted according to the ancient Chinese theories of *yin* and *yang*—the positive and negative forces that bring order to the cosmos.

Rather than trying to pinpoint the precise cause of a disease and treating that cause as Western medicine does, *zhongyi* works in a synergistic manner to boost the body's overall defense systems to help it fight off disease.

The *zhongyi* doctor utilizes a diagnostic concept known as *sho* to assess a patient's condition. This process is based on visual and auditory observation, detailed questioning of the patient, and a physical examination.

In *zhongyi* theory there are six stages in all diseases, going from the positive (*yang*) to the negative (*yin*), with the sixth stage of *yin* resulting in death if the disease is not treated.

Unlike Western medicine which tends to look only at the disease and use the same medicine for everyone, *zhongyi* is highly personalized. Professional *zhongyi* doctors design each treatment specifically for the individual concerned.

Zhongyi ingredients and most prescriptions are still prepared by hand, and a typical Chinese *zhongyi* "factory" may look like something out of the Middle Ages. There is, however, a move to automate the process and produce the final product in tablet and powder form.

Chinese herbal doctors now sometimes combine Western medicine and *zhongyi*, depending on the ailment and the stage of the disease. But mixing the two systems and using them at the same time can be dangerous because it is not clearly understood how Western drugs and Chinese herbs interact with each other.

The Chinese government, which has taken dramatic steps to wipe out a number of common diseases that had plagued China for centuries, is backing studies that are designed to merge the best of *zhongyi* and Western medicine and come up with a new system that does not distinguish between the two.

A major advantage of herbal medicines is that they tend to have fewer side effects than manufactured drugs. One of the most common *zhongyi* prescriptions, for the common cold, flu and chronic infections, is made up of such ingredients as ginseng, ginger, jujube and licorice.

Chinese folklore holds that the five most vital organs of the body have a direct relationship to the emotions: the heart and happiness, the lungs and worry, the liver and anger, the kidneys and fear, the spleen and desire. The negative emotions listed have a deleterious effect on the corresponding organs.

主儿

Zhuer

(Chuu-err)

"Have Specialty, Will Travel"

In old China, itinerant priests and scholars were among the most common travelers on the great rivers, canals and walking roads that linked the country's cities.

They, and others with special skills that made it possible for them to exist independently, were a limited but integral and colorful part of the mosaic of Chinese life.

Now there is a new breed of "have specialty, will travel" Chinese who are growing in number and importance and are playing a fundamental role in making communism, Confucianism and many other aspects of traditional Chinese society obsolete.

This new breed of itinerant Chinese are the *zhuer* (chuu-err), or *specialists* who have skills that make it possible for them to get rich quick in China's expanding market.

Some of the *zhuer* have scientific and other technical skills that are much in demand by China's fast-growing high-tech industries. Others have mastered marketing and business administration techniques that make it possible for them to achieve success virtually overnight.

In a growing number of instances, the knowledge and experience of *zhuer* supersede family, personal connections, and political correctness, and bring a rational element into China's business world that helps to alleviate some of the ongoing political and cultural barriers faced by both Chinese and foreign enterprises.

By the mid-1990s, the term *zhuer* had gained widespread usage, especially among younger Chinese, and *zhuer* had become powerful role models for a growing number of people who were determined to break out of the old system of government control, groupism and favoritism, and create their own lives.

Now, more and more foreign firms approaching China are seeking out and linking up with *zhuer* not only because of their skills but also because they are much easier to deal with.

追星族

Zhuixingzu

(Chu-ee-sheeng-zuh)

"Groupies in China"

One of the most amazing experiences of my life in Japan during the 1950s was watching and listening to teenage Japanese boys and girls imitate popular American singers and musicians of that era.

At first their idols were Frank Sinatra, Bing Crosby, Connie Francis, and other "Establishment" balladeers whose songs were slow, serene and clear.

Then along came jazz and rock-and-roll, both of which were so alien to traditional Japanese behavior and the Japanese language that the idea of that kind of music becoming popular in such an environment was beyond belief.

And yet that is exactly what happened. Using their incredible talents for imitating, young Japanese were like sponges, absorbing the lyrics and music of America's jazz and rock-and-roll stars and then playing them back like recording machines.

By the end of the 1960s there was an enormous Japanese sub-culture based entirely on popular American music, and a correspondingly huge market for the records of American and British pop stars, as well as for live performances.

In the 1980s a similar phenomenon began materializing in Guangdong and Fujian, the two provinces in southeast China that are adjacent to Hong Kong and Taiwan and were the first areas in Communist China to undergo rapid economic development following the 1978 opening of China to Western investment and trade.

Although the foreign pop stars young Chinese began imitating were from Hong Kong, Taiwan and Japan—not from the United States or England—the incongruity of the phenomenon was even more pronounced than it had been in Japan, and this time there was real danger involved.

The young Chinese were not only flying in the face of tradition, they were also thumbing their noses at the still all-powerful Chinese Communist Party, which was diametrically opposed to the importing of such "spiritual pollution," and only a few years earlier had executed thousands and imprisoned hundreds of thousands for lesser offenses.

By the early 1990s this "musical rebellion" of the young had spread throughout the industrialized eastern and central regions of China, and given birth to large numbers of *zhuixingzu* (chu-ee-sheeng-zuh), or *rabid fans*, who were virtually obsessed with this new breed of young Chinese singing stars—a phenomenon that soon spread to movie stars and famous sports figures as well.

While China's official news media regularly criticize the *zhuixingzu* groupies, the phenomenon has become so much a part of the overall political, economic and social revolutions transforming the country that it cannot be separated from them.

Some 2,500 years ago Confucius recognized the power that music has over people, and made positive, uplifting music an integral part of his system for teaching etiquette and ethics. There is little doubt about how he would regard much of today's "protest music" and its influence on attitudes and behavior.

字报

Zi Bao
(Jee Bah-oh)

"Voice of the People"

In pre-modern China national and local authorities used *zi bao* (jee bah-oh) or *character notices* (wall posters) to make official public announcements.

There were two kinds of such posters. One was known as *da zi bao* (dah jee bah-oh) or *big character notices*, and the other was called *xiao zi bao* (she-ah-oh jee bah-oh) or *small character notices*, referring to the size and importance of the posters.

It soon became common for ordinary people to also use *zi bao* because they generally had no other way of bringing their problems to the attention of the authorities or the public.

When wronged, or when the political or economic situation became so bad they could no longer stand it, people would—often surreptitiously—attach a "protest poster" to the wall of the local magistrate's compound.

But such an action was fraught with danger. The protester could be arrested, tortured and imprisoned—or executed if the magistrate himself was offended or wasn't suitably bribed, or if he decided that the protester represented a threat to him or to the government.

Despite the dangers of using *zi bao*, however, such posters became one of the most common ways to protest injustices, to incite the population to take some action, to insult, to cast suspicions and to ruin reputations.

This ancient custom was continued into modern times, and has often been the first official indication that something significant is about to happen in China.

In the 1960s, poster campaigns were used as political tools by opposing parties to bring down unpopular mayors and other local officials.

In 1975 the Chinese government took the unprecedented step of guaranteeing the right of its citizens to make use of *zi bao* in the state constitution. This provision was one of the four "Big Freedoms" advanced by Mao Zedung under his policy of allowing "debates, blooming and contending."

In the late 1970s a section of the wall on the north side of Changan Boulevard in central Beijing became the most popular place for posters calling for a more democratic form of government in China. That part of the wall soon became famous as "Democracy Wall."

But the more famous the wall and the more inflammatory the posters, the more edgy China's Communist leaders became. In 1980 they reversed themselves and banned the posting of political signs in public places.

The infamous Tiananmen Square Incident in 1989, during which the Chinese government used the army to forcefully put down a student led protest, grew out of *da zi bao* illegally posted on "Democracy Wall."

Shortly after the uprising, China's supreme leader, Deng Xiaoping, not surprisingly, had the "four freedoms" provision removed from the constitution.

Zi bao were cheap and easy to create, and were often the only way that people had to make their voices heard in a dictatorship that accepted no dissent, no opposition.

In schools and factories, wall posters are known as *qiang bao* (chee-ahng bah-oh), literally *wall posters*.

Beginning in 1991 Chinese youths came up with a modern version of *zi bao* to comment on the infamous Tiananmen crackdown on the 1989 democracy movement which was mostly led by students. Instead of printing their comments on posters and pasting them on public walls, they began imprinting them on T-shirts, referred to as "cultural shirts."

Not surprisingly, the government quickly banned the wearing of such shirts, and then went to the ludicrous extreme of also banning laughter in Tiananmen Square.

In addition to *zi bao* the Chinese have also traditionally specialized in *min yao* (meen yah-oh) or *popular ditties* that use sarcasm and irony to skewer government officials and Party leaders. The ditties depend on clever wording and rhyme to make them quotable and easy to remember.

See **Tiananmen Guangchang.**

Zihao

(Jee-hah-oh)

"The Proud Ones"

To some people one of the most frightening futuristic scenarios is that some time before the middle of the 21st century China will be the most powerful nation on earth.

There is a great deal to support this notion.

By the year 2050 well over half of the earth's non-Chinese population will most likely still be mired in ignorance and poverty, consumed by racial and ethnic strife, and still too weak to play any kind of leadership role in the world.

China, on the other hand, will surely be an economic giant, possibly larger than the United States and Japan combined. This means that around half of all the affluent people on earth will be Chinese.

It is even more certain that China's military strength will increase in tandem with its economic power, which means that the Chinese could, if they desired, field the largest military force in the world, armed with the latest technical wizardry.

But there is more to China than just size and the potential for military power that is of concern to many people. The real danger, they say, comes from the deep, fundamental compulsion in the Chinese psyche to return China to its position as the "Middle Kingdom," and to demonstrate to the rest of the world that the Chinese are a superior people.

Virtually all Chinese feel that China has been repeatedly violated over the past four centuries by all of the major industrial powers, and there is a pent-up desire for revenge.

Individually the Chinese have always been a proud people, and rightly so. But they have been made to feel and act inferior for so long—for millennia by their own government and then by foreign countries as well—that they are obsessed with the desire to achieve both personal and national power.

Today there are growing signs that *zihao* (jee-hah-oh) or *pride* is welling up in individual Chinese like a fever—a pride that is fed by memories of millennia of powerlessness, insults and abuse.

For the first time in the history of their country the Chinese are now beginning to think and behave as individuals, not as spokes in Confucian or Communist wheels. They are developing egos and taking pride in their own abilities and accomplishments, and more and more, their pride in China is coming to the fore.

But educated Chinese have always been aware of the dangers of pride—the sages of the past invariably ranked pride as one of the greatest weaknesses and most dangerous frailties of mankind—and Chinese sociologists and others now regularly warn against allowing *zihao* to run wild.

Whether or not the Chinese become the Romans of the future, and the worst case scenario of an arrogant, authoritarian China predominant in the world becomes reality, will be determined to a great extent by whether or not the Chinese can control the growth of pride as they become stronger.

See **Duji.**

303

自由

Ziyou

(Jee-yoe-ou)

"License to Be Bad"

In English the word "freedom" generally means both the right and opportunity to make personal decisions about one's day-to-day behavior and overall life—a concept that is at the heart of Western democratic societies.

"Liberty" is another key word in the American and Western lexicon, particularly in the sense of being free to say what one chooses, to come and go as one pleases, and to do anything that does not interfere with the rights of others.

When using these two terms we generally take it for granted that they mean the same thing to other people. But often that is not true at all, and especially so in the case of present-day China.

The Chinese word for *freedom* and *liberty* is *ziyou* (jee-yoe-ou). But in its traditional context, particularly in the context used by the Communist government of China, *ziyou* has negative rather than positive meanings.

Although *ziyou* is written with an ideogram that does, in fact, express the concepts of freedom and liberty, Communist politicians and bureaucrats equate these terms with social disruption, immorality, and acting without conscience.

Not all of these negative connotations come from Communist "misuse" of *ziyou*, however. They also derive from the traditional Confucian viewpoint that individualism and independent behavior are anti-social and thus immoral.

In addition to taking a Confucian view of personal liberty, China's political leaders look at the social and economic violence that is endemic in America and other countries of the world as irrefutable evidence that neither democracy nor pure capitalism, both of which are based on personal freedom, are desirable systems.

It is therefore vital that anyone using the English words "freedom," "liberty," "democracy," or "capitalism," or the Chinese word *ziyou*, to government officials in China be aware of the differences in the perceived meanings.

Chinese businessmen, including those who are familiar with the "Western" meanings of these terms, are also still generally Confucian-oriented in their company and personal relationships, and tend to interpret the words in their Chinese nuance.

However, individual Chinese who are not dedicated members of the Communist Party or cogs in state-run businesses, particularly younger people, are fully aware of the Western connotations of *ziyou*, and many of them yearn for it with a burning passion.

It has been members of this growing group of Chinese who have been staging demonstrations for democracy in China since 1919, and achieved world-wide attention in 1989 when they staged the massive Tiananmen Square demonstration in Beijing.

Ask almost any young Chinese what China most needs to fulfill its potential and they will answer with *ziyou*.

304

做朋友

Zuo Pengyou

(T'su-oh Pung-yoe-ou)

"Making Friends the Chinese Way"

In old China social and professional relationships were not based on mutual interests, common humanity or any other objective criteria. People did not make friends simply because they were friendly and liked to spend time with other people.

As a rule, friendships did not develop between people unless there was a personal connection involving family, school or work. And even then these friendships were limited and severely restricted by the etiquette that controlled all personal behavior.

Also as a general rule, people went out of their way to avoid having to deal with those with whom they had no personal connection—which further limited their opportunities for making friends.

This syndrome remains very much a characteristic of Chinese society today. Friendships are basically closed groups. People do not go out and casually make friends in a matter of moments or hours, the way Americans and other Westerners do.

One of the reasons for this aspect of Chinese society is apparently a hold-over from tribal attitudes, when all non-tribal members were automatically people to be wary of and to avoid, with the extended family now playing the role of the tribe.

Another aspect of this friendship syndrome is that traditionally all affairs in China, private and public, were personalized. You had to establish a binding personal relationship with people before you could do business with them, get help from them, or help them.

Thus *zuo pengyou* (t'su-oh pung-yoe-ou) or *making friends* has traditionally been a serious and important business in China.

It is just as important for outsiders to understand what the Chinese mean when they say *zuo pengyou* and when they refer to friends and friendship.

Visitors to China are repeatedly told that the basis for doing business in China is friendship and that they must invest a great deal of time and money in *zuo pengyou*.

Their explanation is that business and other relationships in the United States and other Western countries are based on a foundation of ethics and laws that guarantee a degree of honesty, fairness and security, but that these guarantees have never existed and still don't exist to any significant extent in China.

Therefore, they continue, there can be no trust, no confidence in any relationship that is not based on personal ties that bind the parties together, and provide them with recourse when there are problems.

Chinese businesspeople are invariably adamant about going through the *zuo pengyou* process before they agree to do business with foreigners, but most of the relationships that do develop remain little more than facades unless the parties involved are able to spend a great deal of personal time together.

祖先

Zuxian

(T'sue-she-enn)

"Revering Your Ancestors"

There is archaeological evidence that humans (Peking Man) lived in the area of the Yellow River some 300,000 to 500,000 years ago, but it is not known if these early people were the ancestors of present-day Chinese.

In any event, the Chinese Garden of Eden was apparently within the confines of what is now China or Mongolia, and the people who originated there were members of the so-called Mongoloid race, which is distinguished by yellowish-brown to white pigmentation, coarse straight black hair, dark eyes with pronounced epicanthic folds, and prominent cheekbones.

Others in this group include North and South American Indians, Eskimos, Siberians, Japanese, Koreans, Maylayans and Mongolians.

Between 10,000 B.C. and 2000 B.C. there were numerous agricultural communities in the Yellow River Valley—the period of time in Chinese history that is referred to as the age of the five mythical dynasties.

China's written history begins with the Hsia Dynasty in 2000 B.C., during which the population grew steadily, there were numerous technological developments, and cities appeared.

Zuxian (t'sue-she-enn), or *reverence for ancestors* was already one of the core features of Chinese life when the Hsia Dynasty started. Like most primitive people around the world, the earliest Chinese were animists, believing that natural phenomena as well as animate and inanimate objects possessed an innate spirit or soul.

Chinese believed that the human soul survived death and existed in spirit form in another plane separated from but still connected to the plane of the living. They believed that if they did not continue to honor and revere their grandparents and parents after they died that the spirits of the deceased would be angry and cause trouble for those still living.

Part of the rituals of ancestor worship were also to prevent forebearers from suffering in the afterworld.

By the beginning of the Shang Dynasty (1550-1030 B.C.), Chinese culture was solidly based on ancestor worship, strictly divided social classes, maintaining strict hierarchical order, the classification of people and things, and bureaucratism—all held together by an authoritarian government.

Zuxian continued to be a primary feature of Chinese life down to the take-over of China by Mao Zedung and his Communist Party in 1949. But ancestor worship was incompatible with Mao's brand of communism, and was soon under attack as a detriment to the building of the new People's Republic of China.

Mao's government-sponsored "Great Proletariat Cultural Revolution" (1966-1976), which was aimed at totally destroying traditional Chinese culture, dealt a near fatal blow to ancestor worship.

In addition to Mao's declaration that all "old thinking" and "old ways" were taboo, the Red Guard brigades of the Cultural Revolution targeted all religious symbols, from Buddhist art to temples, and systematically destroyed most of them.

The Cultural Revolutionary forces also broke up families and moved millions of people away from their home areas where their ancestors were buried, further weakening the practice of *zuxian*.

Ancestor worship in China has continued to decrease in inverse proportion to the growth of personal freedom, private enterprise, the consumer market, mobility, and population control.

The conduct of *zuxian* rituals has traditionally been limited to male members of the family. China's policy of allowing the core "Han" population to have only one child per couple, around half of whom are female, is also having a negative impact on *zuxian*, particularly among urban Chinese.

But *zuxian* remains a custom to be reckoned with, socially, economically and politically. Large numbers of people still visit their ancestral villages annually, crowding trains and buses. The livelihood of hundreds of thousands of people remains built around providing goods and services for these masses.

See **Jihua Shengyu.**